South Asian Borderlands

South Asian Borderlands is an interdisciplinary volume exploring a range of historical, anthropological and literary ideas and issues in South Asian borderlands. Going beyond the territorial and geopolitical imaginaries of contemporary borderlands in South Asia, this book engages with questions of sovereignty, control, policing as well as continuing affections across politically divided borderlands. Modern conceptions of nationhood have created categories of legality and illegality among historically, socially, economically and emotionally connected residents of South Asian borderlands. This volume provides unique insights into the interconnected lives and histories of these borderland spaces and communities.

Farhana Ibrahim is professor in the Department of Humanities and Social Sciences at the Indian Institute of Technology, Delhi. She is the author of *Settlers, Saints, and Sovereigns: An Ethnography of State Formation in Western India* (2009) and *From Family to Police Force: Security and Belonging on a South Asian Border* (2021). Her research interests include the study of borders, policing, migration and ethnographic perspectives on the state.

Tanuja Kothiyal is professor of history in the School of Liberal Studies at Ambedkar University, Delhi. She is the author of *Nomadic Narratives: A History of Mobility and Identity in the Great Indian Desert*, published with the Press in 2016. She is interested in studying shifts in regional formations and questions of authority and sovereignty in the borderlands.

South Asian Borderlands

Mobility, History, Affect

Edited by
Farhana Ibrahim and Tanuja Kothiyal

CAMBRIDGE
UNIVERSITY PRESS

CAMBRIDGE
UNIVERSITY PRESS

University Printing House, Cambridge CB2 8BS, United Kingdom

One Liberty Plaza, 20th Floor, New York, NY 10006, USA

477 Williamstown Road, Port Melbourne, vic 3207, Australia

314 to 321, 3rd Floor, Plot No.3, Splendor Forum, Jasola District Centre, New Delhi 110025, India

103 Penang Road, #05–06/07, Visioncrest Commercial, Singapore 238467

Cambridge University Press is part of the University of Cambridge.

It furthers the University's mission by disseminating knowledge in the pursuit of education, learning and research at the highest international levels of excellence.

www.cambridge.org
Information on this title: www.cambridge.org/9781108844512

© Cambridge University Press 2021

First published 2021

Printed in India by Thomson Press India Ltd.

A catalogue record for this publication is available from the British Library

ISBN 978-1-108-84451-2 Hardback

Contents

Figures and Tables

FIGURES

TABLES

Acknowledgements

The pandemic year of 2020 witnessed the closing down of borders: international, regional and local. Lives of millions of people who occupy territorial and affective borderlands were torn apart as they found themselves questioning their locations across the borders of nations, states, cities and villages. This volume, located in the borderlands of the disciplines of history and anthropology, brings together multiple perspectives on borderlands, navigated through history, mobility and longing by people who share them.

This volume grew out of an initial collection of essays on south Asian borderlands, published as a special section of the *Economic and Political Weekly*. We would like to acknowledge the role played by Aniket Alam in getting that early issue off the ground. Thanks also are due to *Economic and Political Weekly* for permission to republish those essays in a new volume. We are grateful to Qudsiya Ahmed who first saw the promise in our collection, for a special curated edition on south Asian borderlands. Her unstinting and generous support for this project deserves a special mention. We also thank Anwesha Rana and Purvi Gadia at Cambridge University Press for their skilful guidance through the finalising of the volume.

Editing a book is hard work, but it is also a great deal of fun especially when you have such a congenial group of authors and fellow-editors to deal with. This collection would not be what it is without our contributing authors, each of whom has added immeasurably to the final product. We acknowledge with thanks their patience and fortitude in the face of the delays that are an inevitable part of collected volumes.

The editors would like to thank their fellow sojourners in the world of borderland studies, many of whom, even if they could not be there as contributors, are present as intellectual interlocutors in the various chapters of this volume: Nosheen Ali, Mona Bhan, Indrani Chatterjee, Jason Cons, Radhika Gupta, Aditi Saraf and Radhika Singha.

In this difficult year that challenged all communications, it was friendships that sustained and motivated us. We would like to thank Aniket Alam, Aparna Balachandran, Mahuya Bandyopadhyay, Sumangala Damodaran, Shohini Ghosh, Aparna Kapadia, Rukmini Sen, Arindam Banerjee, Reetika Khera, Anasuya Mathur, Salil Misra, Angelie Multani, Samira Sheikh, Swati Shresth and Deborah Sutton for their friendship and intellectual camaraderie that has seen us through the conceptualising and finalising of this volume. This year redefined the idea of family, with people being torn apart and brought together. We dedicate this volume to families and kinships, of blood and of affect, to those who are with us and to those who passed on in this year of hardship.

Introduction

Tanuja Kothiyal and Farhana Ibrahim

Borders and borderlands have perhaps never been as prominently in the public consciousness as they are in the contemporary moment. This is equally true of academic, governance and policy discourse. Globally, refugees are pushing across state borders seeking homes away from sites of conflict, religious persecution, genocide and medical or climate disasters. In response, states are tightening controls over their borders, enforcing stricter surveillance and monitoring of visa regimes for incoming migrants, even as they seek to enforce exclusionary regulatory mechanisms over their own citizens as they determine who can stay and who must leave, amending criteria for citizenship and belonging. Migration across state borders is matched by internal mobility within state boundaries as people move constantly in search of jobs, education and marriage. In crossing borders, whatever their scale, migrants create new borderlands in the process. Through resettlement, they once again become enmeshed in borders of other kinds, as fear, rumour or suspicion serve to configure their relationship with their new neighbours. Within India, the casting of the Muslim citizen as the 'outsider' or the 'internal enemy' is spatially instantiated with areas within cities being referred to as 'mini-Pakistans' (Ghassem-Fachandi 2012: 231) and temporally manifested through a citizenship regime that 'oscillates ambivalently between encompassment and closure' (Roy 2010: 7). The passage of the Citizenship Amendment Act (CAA) in late 2019 marks the latest in a series of legislations on India's 'citizenship regime' (Jayal 2013). This is the third amendment to the Citizenship Act, with earlier changes incorporated in 1986 and 2003, each of which was formulated as a response to the crisis of potential Muslim migration into India. By legalising the status of non-Muslim illegal migrants (who qualify to be settled as 'refugees') from Afghanistan, Bangladesh and Pakistan (in effect all the 'Muslim-dominated' states in its neighbourhood), the 2019 Act renders Indian citizenship as an attribute that is increasingly being seen as exclusive of Islam. Similarly placed Muslim migrants are deemed 'infiltrators' by the Act. The passage of this Act created a nationwide emergency of sorts, with massive popular protests driven especially by students, women and young people who poured out onto the streets protesting what they felt was an exclusionary and anti-constitutional move. The Act also serves to render precarious entire generations of Muslim citizens within India who suddenly find their belonging under threat of erasure, potentially turned into 'illegal infiltrators' overnight. This is particularly the case in the borderlands of Bangladesh and India which have witnessed waves of migration across the two Partitions of the twentieth century. The nation-state's external political borders are thus transposed onto internal spatial, sociopolitical and cultural borders within the geographic heart of the nation. The shifting contours of national belonging, that is, who is or is not a citizen, demonstrates that borders are not encountered—either in law or practice—as always-already existing territorial demarcations. Instead, they are materialised through social practices of *bordering* that are not tethered only to a territorial interpretation of the border. In India's north-east, citizenship is a contested—and ever-shifting—resource. Who is or is not a legitimate citizen of India in the state of Assam is not linked to historical mobility but is increasingly tied to religious or linguistic identity.

In India, 'illegality' in terms of border crossing coalesces for the most part into the figure of the Bangladeshi migrant, who is very much the 'iconic illegal migrant', much as the Mexican migrant is in the United States (de Genova 2005). While some of this xenophobia around Muslim migrants is the South Asian configuration of the Global War on Terror as it uses the justification of national security to deny Muslim claims to citizenship and residency rights (or even refugee status as seen in the Rohingya refugee exodus from Myanmar in 2017–18), it also has a very particular historical context in the debates around the question of migration and citizenship from the early years following the Partition (Roy 2010; Jayal 2013; Zamindar 2007). The Muslim is very much on the margins of citizenship as it is envisioned in India—she is marginalised with respect to the benefits and entitlements of citizenship and arguably also with respect to a larger sense of national identity and belonging. But this is a temporally shifting margin. A 'citizen' one day may become an 'illegal infiltrator' another, depending on the way in which the state chooses to read these attributes of belonging. The fuzzy boundaries between the perception of religious and national identity in these cases suggest that the idea of the margin does not only exist as a stable set of relations *within* the nation (for instance, as a socio-religious category alone) but also enables us to ask the question: *Who* is deemed worthy of inclusion as a citizen in the first place? This volume proposes that the margin is best viewed not in terms of exclusion alone but as a set of relations between forms of regulation and jurisdictions across space *and* time. Borders are thus not about territory alone; they allow us to raise questions about internal jurisdictions and about marginality, and also affect and desire, and about how these are manifested across spatial and temporal sites.

Recent collections on borderlands in South Asia have proceeded in dialogue with ethnographic perspectives on the state (Gellner 2013) or through the conceptual lens of marginality (Cons and Sanyal 2013). This volume seeks to build on the critical insights generated by these preceding works by deepening the historical engagement with both borders *and* the borderlands they generate. All the contributors directly tackle the question of how political, geographical or territorial marginality from administrative centres does not preclude these spaces becoming central to an understanding of authority, sovereignty or legitimacy. Nor does the imposition of state authority seek to constitute its outlying areas in any unilateral fashion. The role of borderland populations is crucial in mediating— even directing—the relationship of the so-called centre and its periphery, thus enabling a re-conceptualisation of the relationship of the state and borders in terms of a centre–periphery framework and of marginality as the only conceptual lens through which to view borders and frontiers.

This volume also steps away from the national and transnational contexts within which histories have been imagined and written, thus fragmenting borderlands that existed prior to the nation-state. Regions and nations have been defined by history-writing that anachronistically shape territories to suit imaginaries of the past. Thus, regional and national territories appear compact and secluded, rather than connected by shared histories of contact, social spaces 'for which ceaseless circulation of humans was a *sine qua non*' (Subrahmanyam 2005: 212–13). Vasudha Pande (in this volume) traces how the writing of histories of distinct spaces within the trans-Himalayan region led to the reorientation of the regions themselves. Kothiyal (2016) has argued that the consolidation of Rajputana, a region oriented towards the Indo-Gangetic plains, distinct from its associations with the western Thar, was a result of historiographic impulses that overlooked the migratory histories of the Rajputs. Chapters in this volume attempt to unravel the connected histories of borderlands, untangling them from the given regional and national historiographic contexts.

Methodologically, this volume traverses a liminal space between history and anthropology, thus occupying a kind of borderland itself. This liminality, however, is not merely engendered by the coming together of two disciplines, but by ways in which these disciplinary practices explore multiple space–time dimensions.

While boundaries as products of modern nation-making processes emphasise the present, this engagement with the idea of borderlands shifts the emphasis to space and time as imagined and experienced in the past, both methodologically and experientially. While history allows us glimpses into how spaces were imagined and defined, and how these imaginaries shifted, anthropology allows us to see how these shifts continue to be experienced in the borderlands.

BORDERS, FRONTIERS AND STATES: RETHINKING SOVEREIGNTY, MARGINALITY AND TERRITORIALITY

It is now well accepted in academic discourse that even though borderlands may constitute the physical margins of the Westphalian state, they are at the very core of nationalist discourses about territorial survival and security and are also integral to the ways in which the nation is both imagined and produced (Aggarwal 2004; Bhan 2008). They may constitute the physical 'edge' but they are fairly central to the business of statecraft. This proposition is important to initiate a discussion on the nature of the state and its authority. Modern states have increasingly come to view themselves as territorially circumscribed, absolute sovereign units with monopolistic claims over violence. This view occludes the fact that the territorial sovereignty of states was not given a priori but often wrested from competing claims to sovereignty that were often considered to be equally legitimate. The emergence of kingdoms and empires from competing claims inevitably led to the creation of frontiers or borderlands: zones where the authority of the state was gradually in dispute. States forged multiple relationships with these frontier zones. In classical Indian political discourse, the margins of the states as well as that of settlements were identified as *aranya* or wilderness, which was at once the 'site for and an object for the exploitation and violence of the state' (Singh 2017: 457). While inflicting violence and attempting to draw the margins into a civilisational centre or *ksetra*, the state also remained fascinated with the wilderness, often drawing imperial symbols of power like the lion and elephant from the forests. The wilderness was the site of *brahmcharya* as well as *sanyasa*, the first and the last stages of human life. For kings, while the city and the palace were sites for the experience of kingship, the space from where moral authority could be drawn was the wilderness. It was both the space of exile, as well a space where kingship could be reclaimed through acts of self-realisation as well as self-actualisation. The Arab philosopher Ibn Khaldun also views the wilderness—in his case the desert—as the space for the renewal of moral authority (Dawood 2005 [1969]:

95–107). Thus, the wilderness rather than being an external space is a space of rejuvenation and reassertion, a 'different kind of borderland' (Singh 2017: 457), an idea explored further through Uberoi's (1978) concept of 'frontier logic'.

However, the wilderness was not always an uninhabited territory outside of civilisation. These were the territories where, according to Kautilya, 'those likely to be won over' lived. Kautilya divides 'those likely to be won over' into four categories, that is, the 'angry', the 'greedy', the 'frightened' and the 'haughty' (Rangarajan 1992: 484–5). These could be instigated against their own kings by stoking anger, greed, fear or pride through the use of conciliation (*sama*), gift (*dana*), won over through sedition (*bheda*) and force (*danda*), the last to be used only if all other means failed (Rangarajan 1992: 572). Revisiting the Mauryan Empire, Thapar (2000: 463) views frontiers as buffer zones that were deliberately kept underdeveloped, with the intention to keep them pliant rather than maintaining firm control. These buffer zones often allowed citizens from either side of the borderland to benefit from the presence of multiple jurisdictions. Citing the fifth-century Roman historian Priscus, Lattimore (1962: 481) refers to the eastern frontiers of the Roman Empire where Roman traders continued to serve the Huns rather than return home because of the pitiless taxation in Roman cities.

The frontiers of pre-modern states were thus zones of competing sovereignties and negotiated loyalties that sustained immense possibilities for the emergence of new social and political formations. These were not merely neutral territories but 'political wombs' where 'cohesive, participatory, segmentary communities, endowed with great military potential' existed with tremendous potentialities for supplying new rulers (Gellner 1995: 164). However, did the political turmoil of these frontiers and the frequent shifts of loyalties represent the unstable nature of sovereignty in the frontiers? Wink suggests that pre-modern states were essentially organised around conflicts and that sovereignty was a 'matter of allegiances' (1986: 27). Tracing the lineages of the word *fitna* through the work of the fourteenth-century Arab philosopher Ibn Khaldun, Wink points out that the term could be interpreted as a disruptive force only in the context of the universalist claims of Islam. In the formation of various Muslim states, *fitna* implied nothing more than the use of conflict and conciliation in local disputes to forge alliances. Ernest Gellner's study of the Berbers of the High Atlas Mountains in Morocco views the history of Morocco as that of conflicting and conciliatory relationships between the states of *makhzen* and *siba*, that is, the pale and beyond the pale (Gellner 1969: 2). This idea has been further developed by Scott who views sovereignties of the core as 'explicit' as opposed to the 'ambiguous, plural and shifting' sovereignties of the frontiers (2009: 59–60). These distinctions became explicit as modern states began to centralise and monopolise territorial control, disputing the claims of inhabitants of the frontiers who could in the past have claimed access to multiple sovereignties. In the Thar Desert, as Kothiyal (in this volume) argues, banditry and highway robbery by local chieftains that came to be viewed as a threat to governance was in fact an overt claim to shared sovereignty that was being overridden by the marking of clear jurisdictions, both ideationally as well as cartographically. It is this access to multiple sovereignties that converts frontiers and borderlands into zones of creative possibilities of many kinds. Rather than anarchy and lawlessness of the margin, the frontier signifies liberty and autonomy, for 'by frontier logic the wall is also a corridor and to divide is also to interconnect' (Uberoi 1978: 73).

Given this creative potential at the frontier, and the ability to potentially subvert the centre, it is not surprising then that even modern borders are not immune to a 'territorial anxiety' on the part of their respective nation-states in South Asia. This anxiety transmutes into a 'sensitivity' with regard to its borders where, as Cons (2016: 7) has recently argued in an ethnography of the enclaves (*chhitmahal*) along the Bangladesh–India border, 'the fragility and instability at the heart of national territory' joins forces with bureaucratic regulation and management to produce *Sensitive Space* that is prone to high degrees of surveillance and control precisely because it is also the site where the ideological belief in the coincidence of nationality and territory begins to unravel. Through the last two millennia, South Asian frontiers have shifted several times with the creation as well as disintegration of kingdoms, empires and nation-states. With the emergence of several nation-states in the last century, it has become difficult to imagine frontiers that do not match the current nation-state boundaries. However, most pre-modern states had very little accurate sense of their territories before cartography came to be extensively used to actually draw maps and mark boundaries from the late eighteenth century onwards. In the Mughal Empire, while attempts were made to mark external boundaries through forts and so forth, the strongest fortifications were erected around towns and cities, giving us a sense of where priorities lay in terms of exercising strict surveillance and control. The control of vaguely defined external frontiers was more often than not left to local rulers and chieftains, thus ensuring little change in the conditions of local sovereignty with the expansion or contraction of frontiers (Embree 1977: 273). In the frontier zones, it is these tribesmen that formed the necessary link in governance (Singh 2006 [1998]: 444–9).

These conditions of conflicting as well as coexisting sovereignties continued well into the colonial period in India, with contiguous zones of direct and indirect rule creating borderlands of competing jurisdictions. While normatively the frontiers between different authorities sought to represent a clear demarcation, in practice, the proximity of multiple competing political, social and juridical authorities made borderlands a space differentiated from nearby areas in terms of the rules that were applied or suspended there (Beverley, in this volume). Beverley views the frontier as a critical social and political resource, which allowed states as well as people living on the frontiers to creatively engage with the new legalities as they emerged with the marking of colonial boundaries in the late nineteenth century. In the Hyderabad–Bombay frontier, legal pluralism of the frontiers allowed the manipulation of instruments of governmentality. The frontier was a space of anomaly where sovereignty was fragmented, allowing for simultaneous expression of British territorialised sovereignty against the decentralised patrimonial features of Hyderabad's governance. Fragmentation produced flexibility, permitting the possibility of participation in alternative regimes of criminality, labour and sexuality. Kothiyal (in this volume) argues that in the harsh and inhospitable Thar Desert, which was a borderland between several princely states and British-controlled areas, the rules of hostility were often suspended in order to ensure safe passage for people and commodities, as their flow was controlled and facilitated by local chieftains and rulers. This was predicated upon the capacity of frontier communities to build widespread networks of fidelities based on kinship and affinity, thus providing channels of co-operation that neither the princely states nor the British were capable of accessing. The liminal spaces that these allegiances created could seamlessly become passages as well as fortifications, as the necessity arose.

To counter this fragmentation, in the nineteenth century the colonial state attempted to make frontiers sites where the state sought to unleash its knowledge-making apparatus to map, to know and to tame—the cartographic impulse (Cons 2016) to render the remote outpost at least as legible to the centre as the core (if not more so). The production of annual reports and revenue, cadastral and topographical surveys led to information that could produce a totalising picture that could transform fragments into a meaningful totality, the 'cartographic truths' (Bhattacharya 2018: 82–5). With advances in cartography by the mid-nineteenth century, it became possible to map clearly defined and ordered territories amenable to governance. In doing so, the search for 'natural frontiers' like mountains, rivers, marshes, deserts, and so on, those 'great obstacles of nature' that could serve as frontiers of separation and defence became a primary objective (Embree 1977: 278). However, what were viewed as 'great obstacles of nature' were in a true sense frontiers that were controlled by a range of state and non-state actors facilitating the flow of people and commodities. The marking of boundaries as well as the creation of new circuits of commodity flows led to shifts in the orientation of the regions themselves, as Pande (in this volume) demonstrates in the case of the Kumaun frontier. Pande explores the shifts in borderlands that Kumaun shared with Nepal, Tibet and Tarai, and argues that in the latter half of the nineteenth century, Kumauni borderlands were redefined owing to multiple factors like shifts in administrative and legal regimes, opening of roads and motorised transport, and shifting of travel and trade. Kumauni borderlands transformed from being a space seamlessly connected with Himalayan and trans-Himalayan regions like western Nepal, Tibet, Terai and Kashmir, through flows of people and commodities like iron implements, salt, wool and borax, to distinct regions marked cartographically, administratively as well as historiographically. The marking of India, Nepal and Tibet as distinct national communities based on the core identities of these nations also led to a homogenisation of community identities within groups like Kumauni, Gorkha and Bhotiya among others, which in the past had shared linkages and could have been at some point indistinguishable. However, while mapping of national boundaries might have created national identities, the shared pasts of borderlands are being constantly evoked in multiple ways across the boundaries of nation-states.

Middleton (in this volume) ethnographically examines the shifting contours of 'Gorkha' identity in Darjeeling as it oscillates between the demands of a pan-ethnic identity as 'Gorkhas' and the 'ethnological straightjacket of tribal recognition', as Scheduled Tribes within the constitutional framework of affirmative action policies within the Indian nation-state. In either case, certain forms of identity are lost even as others may be gained, situationally. Not all forms of difference are equally legible by the state and these forms of recognition are also contextually and historically contingent with respect to national histories. Middleton argues that the politics of Gorkha identity in the border region of Darjeeling is premised on a highly ambivalent relationship with the actual border. As they seek to project themselves as autochthonous citizens of India, their family histories of migration between Nepal and Darjeeling are rendered 'unspeakable' even as kinship (or in this case, its negation) becomes 'the topos on which "nationness" is mapped' (Borneman 1992: 19). Legal and social forms of recognition, however, are not always congruent. Middleton writes, '[B]order populations like the Gorkhas may maintain heightened desires for rights, inclusion, and belonging in India, and increased dependency on the state to achieve those aims. Yet the conditions of life at the border often render these groups unable to meet India's norms of recognition.'

Neither the cartographic practices that informed the marking of these borders in the nineteenth and twentieth centuries nor the bureaucratic practices that went into the implementation of borders were in any way uniform, as in the case of the India–Pakistan border in Kutch (Ibrahim, in this volume). While the nineteenth-century delineation of borders was about jurisdiction and governance, the recognition of national boundaries led to a far more explicit and pronounced reiteration of national identities, particularly in the case of Muslims along the Kutch–Sindh border. This reiteration was however not a pre-given but was the product of administrative debate and arrived at over a period of time.

Cartographic anxiety and state control over its margins should not, however, occlude the fact that the relationship between the centre and the frontier is not always a predictable one. Ethnographic perspectives have contributed to rethinking the state as a site of absolute power. Just as the centre is not always all-powerful or all-knowing, so too we cannot assume the intransigence or opposition of those sites that are geographically remote from the centre (Gupta 2013). Geographical remoteness, in fact, does not merely refer to actual physical distance. Harsh and unforgiving geographies of the mountains, deserts and marshes have been treated to be politically, administratively as well as affectively remote from the centre that is often located in the agrarian plains (Kothiyal 2016). In this collection of borderland studies, we also propose a critical reappraisal of the relationship between the geographic periphery and the concept of marginality. From her study of the location of Kashmir in the Mughal Empire, Maurya (in this volume) argues that 'remoteness' was not a permanent or universal category for the empire. Geographically remote regions on the fringes of the empire were ideationally created as 'core' through practices of the empire.

The idea of the 'remote' has already been unmoored from its geographical and spatial connotations, articulated instead as 'a sociological concept of relative association or familiarity' (Harms et al. 2014: 362). The 'remote' thus speaks to a certain 'edginess' that is about a way of being in the world, a strategically deployed positionality that is less about geographical orientations and more about relative interactions. The 'remote' can exist as urban fringe as much as in rugged and physically inaccessible terrain, for instance. The production of 'remoteness' is then a 'process situated in dynamic fields of power' (Harms et al. 2014: 364) rather than any objectively existing spatial reality. Similarly, the 'margin' is not just exclusion, or opposition to the state, it is 'those sites that do not so much lie outside the state but rather, like rivers, run through its body' (Das and Poole 2004: 13). The margin invites us to examine how the state is constantly reinventing its forms of regulation in tandem with other forms of life, rather than to pose the question in terms of state presence or absence, supporting or subverting the state. What constitutes the various forms of state power is itself a question that needs to be answered. Roitman (2004) proposes delinking 'state power' from 'state regulatory authority', arguing that even when the latter is compromised, it may not always lead to the erosion of the former. She demonstrates that even as new forms of authority emerge—whether merchants or renegade militias—that may challenge the state's regulatory authority, they do not always usurp power from the state; in fact, through the defragmentation and capillarisation of authority, they may end up consolidating the power of the state. This allows us to locate competing frames of sovereignty even within the analytical contours of the modern state with its rhetorical claims to absolute power.

MOBILITY AND AFFECT: TOWARDS A DIACHRONIC VIEW OF BORDERLANDS

Just as the concept of the margin—or border—is delinked from space, this volume also proposes a shift in borderland studies away from a perspective that privileges spatial practices of the state and territorial manifestations of borders. When one moves away from spatial determinism, it allows one to de-singularise the border as more than just a line or a fence or a guard that divides (or connects) people and spaces (Reeves 2014). Uberoi reminds us that the frontier is essentially diachronic: '[I]t is the essential nature and diachronic rhythm of the frontier to change in time alternately from a firm dividing line into its opposite, a meeting point, and back again' (Uberoi 1978: 75).

Similarly, a border also manifests differently across different sites and at different points in time. Middleton (in this volume) argues this for the Gorkhas' relationship with India and Nepal, and Ghosh (in this volume) demonstrates the same in the context of the India–Bangladesh border. In these terms, the border is not a coherent whole; Reeves suggests that each iteration of the border should be taken on its own terms—these are all different borders, not versions of the same (Reeves 2014: 245). As Reeves argues, rather than ask only whether a (territorial) border is maintained or subverted, the question should instead focus on how it is materialised through everyday practices and how these practices shift with time. Ethnographies of administration and the bureaucratic apparatus of the state (Gupta 2012; Hull 2012; Mathur 2016; Navaro-Yashin 2012) seek to do precisely this. They critically review the bureaucracy not as a site of Weberian-style rationality alone, but as spaces that are constituted through individual interpretations that may be an effect for instance of class *habitus* (Chatterji 2013), but also through the very material expressions (the paper, file, cadastral survey or map) that they presume to be driven by. The materials of bureaucratic production are not, then, 'neutral purveyors of discourse, but as mediators that shape the significance of the signs inscribed on them and their relations with the objects they refer to' (Hull 2012: 253). A focus on bureaucratic paperwork not only shifts the emphasis of borderland studies away from discourse and into the realm of materiality (Hull 2008) but also points to the malleability of the material effects of the state. Documents are fetishised by both the state and its citizens (Gupta 2012); but as forms of identification or sources of guarantee, they are elastic and porous. Documents are not, in and of themselves, the sign of the state's protection (Poole 2004).

One of the themes that chapters in this volume engage with is a critical interrogation of the notion that borders—and the nationalist imaginings that they are supposed to engender—are consequences of bureaucratic imposition from above. Disaggregating the bureaucratic production of borders and their everyday management, the role of borderland populations in the border question becomes an important focus of attention. Gohain (in this volume) attends to the multi-layered construction of authority in border regions significantly nuancing a position that looks only at the state and its subjects as locked into relations of either submission or antagonism. In doing so, her chapter echoes other contributions to border studies that have addressed modes of allegiance to the state in complicated borders where the state's performance of sovereignty and people's relationship to the state is scripted in a way that cannot be always-already oppositional (Gupta 2013). Gohain draws attention to the 'material production of the border' in Tawang district of Arunachal Pradesh, on India's north-eastern border with China, marking a shift away from overt preoccupations with forms of imagined community alone (Bhan 2008).

Ethnographic perspectives on the state have for long meditated on the difficulties with locating the state as a singular or embodied entity (Abrams 1988). Trouillot (2003) argued that it was 'state effects' that should be the focus of attention. Gohain's argument on the 'integration' of the Tawang border into the Indian state describes a domain of overlapping jurisdictions that nonetheless have shifted over time. Her attentive ethnography describes a triangulation of authority between the 'state' (even as it leaves open the question of 'what' exactly is the state) and the Tawang monastery as it negotiates the shift from Tibetan to Indian jurisdiction but in no simple or linear terms. The chapter provides a nuanced understanding of the state's so-called control over frontier populations, especially in the context of jurisdictions that are shared between political and religious authority (for example, Eaton 1978).

One of the ways in which the premise of borders as being territorial and cultural demarcators has been disrupted is through cultural cross-border flows and movement. Studies of the borderlands of South Asian nation-states suggest that over centuries these regions had been connected through religio-cultural flows as well as trade. Buddhism and Islam created their own circulatory networks that connected South Asia to both West and East Asia. While the spread of Buddhism integrated East and Central Asian networks, Islam brought about its own diaspora. Andre Wink suggests that by the eighth century the area beyond the Indus River, called Al-Hind by the Arabs, was being drawn into the Islamic world through Arab trading circuits emerging around the Indian Ocean, which he calls 'an Arabic-speaking Mediterranean' (Wink 1990: 2). It is through trade as well as through Ghaznavide and Ghuride conquests that in South Asia, settled agrarian riverine societies came into close contact with traders and warriors from West Asia, leading to shifts in both eastern and western frontiers of Al-Hind. In a more contemporary context, the Partitions of 1947 and 1971 configured movements across new state borders in the east and the west. As indicated above, the Partition was not the first catalyst of large-scale mobility in a region that has been constituted through multiple patterns of cross-border and cross-region mobility for centuries, if we take into account patterns of mobility across the Indian Ocean (Amrith 2013; Ho 2006), and the Thar Desert (Kothiyal 2016) or the Rann of Kutch (Ibrahim 2009). Nor did the Partition signal an end to mobility as people continued to cross borders for marriage and kinship obligations (Ghosh, in this volume) or for work (van Schendel 2001).

In Ghosh's chapter, once again the 'border' is no abstraction but realised through very real and material interactions with border guards and paperwork ('forged' documentary papers, mobile SIM cards, and so on) on the India–Bangladesh border. The Bengal borderlands challenge normative assumptions on border crossing across states to highlight how partition in the east led to a recasting of relations *within* rather than across borderlands. In Bengal, it was often not displacement but remaining in place that transformed one into a 'refugee' (Alexander, Chatterji and Jalais 2016). Drawing attention to the gendering of cross-border mobility, a relatively new sub-theme in the border studies literature, although it has been on the agenda for much longer in feminist engagements with law and trafficking (Kempadoo, Sanghera and Pattanaik 2005; Kapur 2003; Andrijasevic 2009), Ghosh turns to the work of kinship, an obligation that emerges as quintessentially women's work as they strive to maintain family obligations across the border. Legality and illegality in terms of the border is recast in this chapter in terms of kin obligations and the family. A biography of family histories in the borderlands becomes in her chapter a biography of the border itself, as it tracks these biographies 'in terms of closures and openings, porosity and impermeability' (Ghosh, in this volume). She suggests that it is not merely about 'the border' oscillating between permeability and its opposite across time; this depends on who is crossing when and where, in which direction and for what purpose (also Beverley, in this volume). Closure and a (negotiated) porosity coexist *within* a single temporal framework. Women are clearly the greater risk-bearing subjects in crossing borders for the affective work of maintaining familial ties, but risk is also mapped onto class and lifestyle. Yet kinship also constitutes a shared universe that enables—indeed encourages—risks to be taken. Kinship is about risk, about building bridges and negotiating emotional chasms, between the natal and the affinal home, for instance. Then again, it is expressed in forms that are locally resonant. The Bengali border guards in Bangladesh may share culturally evocative notions of the 'affective pull of the heart' (*moner taan*) that the more ethnically heterogeneous, non-Bengali speaking Indian border guards do not possess. Ghosh's rich ethnographic vignettes break apart a rigid divide between those who are policing the border and those whom it claims to be policing. Border crossings are about negotiation, risk and the affective life of the family.

However, a focus on cross-border mobility as a means of subverting or evading state control, as Scott (2009) describes it, cannot be reified into a fluidity that is sometimes taken to be an innate characteristic of borderlands. Borderlands are liminal sites only if we assume a centrifugal and singular source of authority that weakens as it emanates away from the centre. While all borders do not support the same kinds of cross-border flows structurally, borderland populations are also invested differently in the desirability of crossing over to the 'other side' (Navaro-Yashin 2012). While the Bengal border's porosity is configured by risk and kinship through a particular kind of gendered border crossing, the western border that divides Kutch from Sindh is a border that seeks to divide the two sides in a far more finite way. Despite historical trade routes and patterns of migration that occurred across the Thar, the contemporary iteration of the border does not sanction legal border crossing in this section. Besides, as Ibrahim suggests (in this volume), residents of the border may see themselves central to its maintenance rather than seeking to subvert it. Similarly, Middleton (in this volume) argues that the affective centrality of the border may wax and wane over time as a community seeks to define itself relative to it. This identification can be at times oriented across the border to highlight trans-border ethnic identity as when the Gorkhas of Darjeeling sought to identify with a pan-Gorkha identity that transcended state boundaries; at other times, their self-identification may be as unequivocally oriented *away* from the border as when they sought to negate cross-border affiliation in order to seek recognition as autochthonous tribal subjects of an Indian state that brought with it certain constitutional guarantees. The border and its place in the imagination of people is thus diachronic rather than set in stone one way or another.

Alam (in this volume) explores this diachrony in the western Himalayas where markets play an important role in the making of borders in colonial western Himalayas and get shaped by the institution of borders. His study of two markets of Lavi and Shimla proposes that these depended on two very different definitions of borders. Alam uses Anderson's (2015 [1983]) conceptualisation of 'imagined communities' to argue that the Himalayan markets were circumscribed by circulatory regimes spanning across Central Asia, north India, China and south of Siberia. In this circulatory regime, thousands of traders, mule handlers and goods, while never coming across each other, journeyed over long routes, supplying networks that fed into other networks. The coming of the British created its own circuit overshadowing the older Asian highland networks, thus shifting the borderlands themselves. In the context of the eastern Himalayas, Indrani Chatterjee (2013) has argued that monastic assemblages anchored the monastic geographic order, bestowing a commonality of ways of life to people living in the greater Brahmaputra and Surma–Barak valleys. The shifts in patterns of monastic governmentality, by new legalities that questioned the frontiers of religion, household and family, created forgetfulness not just towards the ways of life but also towards shared histories of social and economic dependence.

Beyond being spaces for the expression of authority and control, borderlands have also been explored as sites of affect (Navaro-Yashin 2012). In an ethnographic study of the Greek–Cypriot borderlands, Navaro-Yashin asks: How do people who live on borderlands respond to them affectively? What impact do borders have on the subjective lives of people? These effects are often complicated and contradictory in nature. Indian Muslims on the western border have to deal with fear and mistrust of the state and its military and bureaucratic machinery that more often than not equates Islam in India with a 'natural' affective disposition towards Pakistan and therefore constitutive of 'disloyalty' in India. Despite this, border residents in Kutch see themselves as deeply enmeshed with the project of maintaining the inviolability of the Indian border despite their own cross-border kinship and familial networks which become chasms that remain unbridgeable, quite unlike the negotiated porosity in cross-border kin relations described for the Bengal borderlands by Ghosh (in this volume). Maurya (in this volume) traces the affective resonance that borderlands connote for states as well. They conjure up images and fantasies—of the strange, wondrous and remote, sites of the unknown and the unaccountable. They are also zones of multiple imaginations, frontiers between the known and the unknown. Through the liminality of the known and unknown, borderlands were thus imagined as fantasies. Wink suggests that these fantasies were rooted in the shared experiences of travellers. For example, Arab accounts of *ajai'b al-Hind* ran parallel to the medieval European imagination of *mirabilia Indae* that saw India as a land of wonder, dreams and legends (Wink 1990: 4–5). This was particularly true of the geographically inaccessible and, therefore, hostile frontiers that evoked both awe and revulsion. Maurya's chapter exemplifies this duality of sentiment with regard to Kashmir, which emerged both as a sacral as well as a wondrous space through travellers' accounts as well as the genre of the *ajai'b-garaib*, or the fantastic. The emerging Mughal state that conquered Kashmir in 1586 sought to constitute it through narrative and visual representations, practices of governance and tactile experiences as *jannat nazir*, a paradisiacal space. In doing so, the Mughal state, through an itinerary of leisure and pleasure, was able to convert the binary of awe and revulsion of a frontier space into a spatial imaginary of order. Wonder and the sense of spectacle—already acknowledged as paradisiacal in the landscape of Kashmir—thus became harnessed by the Mughal state into its imperial designs for the frontier. By re-embedding the notion of wonder and spectacle from the unknown and unknowable, squarely into the domain of imperial design, it not only harnesses a public sense of wonder and amazement from the 'natural' world into the state's creations, it also reinforces the fact that 'remote' border areas are often at the heart of imperial and state power. The question of Kashmir continues to lie at the heart of the nation-state's claims about territoriality, control and sovereignty.

Finally, Shakya (in this volume) offers a critical reading of the writings of a feminist-Marxist poet Parijat whose work and life crisscrossed the borders between Nepal and India. This chapter continues with the theme of affect and the border when she writes, '[B]orders are deeply subjective, populated not with pragmatic concerns—let alone considerations of political, cultural or geographic constructs—but with the core of the self.' Shakya argues that nation-state borders are fundamentally incompatible with structures of intimacy and suggests that fiction may possibly provide the language of affect that transcends the vocabulary of both social science and the nation, both of which in their own ways serve to reinstitute the violence of geographical and cartographic classification. She asks, '[C]an fiction generate its own anthropology, allowing us to problematise the politics of knowledge in theorising nationalism?'

This volume is a historical and ethnographic exploration of borders and frontiers in South Asia. Taking the contemporary iteration of South Asian borders as a point of departure, each of the nine chapters is an invitation to think beyond the territorial and jurisdictional confines of states, nations and academic disciplines, and to reflect instead on how concepts like mobility, negotiated sovereignty and affect enable us to disrupt the modern idea of sovereignty as absolute and the state as sole arbiter of borders and frontiers. The chapters that constitute this volume offer densely textured and historically grounded readings of particular borders in the region. Attention to historical depth and geographical spread reveals the difficulty of a retrospective reading of borders from present-day naturalisations of territory and identity in nation-states and their borderlands. The chapters in this volume also caution us against the dangers of homogenising a discourse on borders, for each of the borders under discussion here, speak with and against each other in productive ways. In the chapters, borders are territorially defined limits, as border*lands*, but they are also relational entities that reach over and beyond themselves despite mandates to contain, divide and delimit. Borders are, of course, also structural conditions that can be separated from their territorial manifestations (for example, Piliavsky 2013). In this sense, the border is a conceptual tool that opens up discussions on nationality, statehood, jurisdiction, identity and belonging beyond the trope of the nation-state, for too long naturalised as a unit of analysis by academic disciplines. Our attempt in this Introduction has not been to provide any complete or exhaustive literature review on the subject of borders and frontiers but is an invitation to think through some of the diverse borderlands of South Asia across multiple time periods and different state regimes through the key themes identified above: negotiated sovereignty, diachrony, mobility and affect, in order to generate new debates and conceptual articulations across the disciplines.

REFERENCES

Abrams, Philip. 1988. 'Notes on the Difficulty of Studying the State'. *Journal of Historical Sociology* 1 (1): 58–89.

Aggarwal, Ravina. 2004. *Beyond Lines of Control: Performance and Politics on the Disputed Borders of Ladakh*. Durham: Duke University Press.

Alexander, Claire, Joya Chatterji and Annu Jalais. 2016. *The Bengal Diaspora: Rethinking Muslim Migration*. London and New York: Routledge.

Amrith, Sunil S. 2013. *Crossing the Bay of Bengal*. Cambridge: Harvard University Press.

Anderson, Benedict. 2015 (1983). *Imagined Communities: Reflections on the Origin and Spread of Nationalism*. Jaipur: Rawat Publications (Indian Reprint).

Andrijasevic, Rutvica. 2009. 'Sex on the Move: Gender, Subjectivity and Differential Inclusion'. *Subjectivity* 29 (1): 389–406.

Bhan, Mona. 'Border Practices: Labour and Nationalism among Brogpas of Ladakh'. *Contemporary South Asia* 16 (2): 139–57.

Bhattacharya, Neeladri. 2018. *The Great Agrarian Conquest: The Colonial Reshaping of a Rural World*. Ranikhet: Permanent Black.

Borneman, John. 1992. *Belonging in the Two Berlins: Kin, State, Nation*. Cambridge: Cambridge University Press.

Chatterjee, Indrani. 2013. *Forgotten Friends: Monks, Marriages and Memories of Northeast India*. New Delhi: Oxford University Press.

Chatterji, Joya. 2013. 'Secularisation and Partition Emergencies: Deep Diplomacy in South Asia'. *Economic and Political Weekly* 48 (50): 42–50.

Cons, Jason. 2016. *Sensitive Space: Fragmented Territory at the India-Bangladesh Border*. Seattle: University of Washington Press.

Cons, Jason, and Romola Sanyal. 2013. 'Geographies at the Margins: Borders in South Asia–An Introduction'. *Political Geography* 35: 5–13.

Das, Veena, and Deborah Poole. 2004. 'The State and Its Margins'. In *Anthropology in the Margins of the State*, edited by Veena Das and Deborah Poole, 3–33. New Delhi: Oxford University Press.

Dawood, N. J. 2005 (1969). *Ibn Khaldun: The Muqaddimah* (An Introduction to History: The Classic Islamic History of the World). Edited, translated and introduced by Franz Rosenthal. New Jersey: Princeton University Press.

De Genova, Nicholas. 2005. *Working the Boundaries: Race, Space, and 'Illegality' in Mexican Chicago*. Durham: Duke University Press.

Eaton, Richard Maxwell. 1978. *The Sufis of Bijapur 1300–1700: Social Roles of Sufis in Medieval India*. Princeton: Princeton University Press.

Embree, Ainslie T. 1977. 'Frontiers into Boundaries: From the Traditional to the Modern State'. In *Realm and Region in Traditional India*, edited by R. G. Fox and Durham, 255–81. New Delhi: Vikas Publishers.

Gellner, Ernest. 1969. *Saints of the Atlas*. London: ACLS History e-Book.

———. 1995. 'Tribe and State in the Middle East'. In *Anthropology and Politics: Revolutions in the Sacred Grove*, edited by Ernest Gellner, 180–202. Oxford: Blackwell.

Gellner, David N. 2013. 'Introduction: Northern South Asia's Diverse Borders, from Kachchh to Mizoram'. In *Borderland Lives in Northern South Asia*, edited by David N. Gellner, 1–23. Durham: Duke University Press.

Ghassem-Fachandi, Parvis. 2012. *Pogrom in Gujarat: Hindu Nationalism and Anti-Muslim Violence in India*. Princeton: Princeton University Press.

Gupta, Akhil. 2012. *Red Tape: Bureaucracy, Structural Violence, and Poverty in India*. New Delhi: Permanent Black.

Gupta, Radhika. 2013. 'Allegiance and Alienation: Border Dynamics in Kargil'. In *Borderland Lives in Northern South Asia*, edited by David N. Gellner, 47–71. Durham: Duke University Press.

Harms, Erik et al. 2014. 'Remote and Edgy: New Takes on Old Anthropological Themes'. *HAU: Journal of Ethnographic Theory* 4 (1): 361–81.

Ho, Engseng. 2006. *The Graves of Tarim: Genealogy and Mobility across the Indian Ocean*. Berkeley: University of California Press.

Hull, Matthew S. 2008. 'Ruled by Records: The Expropriation of Land and the Misappropriation of Lists in Islamabad'. *American Ethnologist* 35 (4): 501–18.

———. 2012. 'Documents and Bureaucracy'. *Annual Review of Anthropology* 41 (1): 251–67.

Ibrahim, Farhana. 2009. *Settlers, Saints and Sovereigns: An Ethnography of State Formation in Western India*. New Delhi: Routledge.

Jayal, Niraja Gopal. 2013. *Citizenship and Its Discontents: An Indian History*. New Delhi: Permanent Black.

Kapur, Ratna. 2003. 'The "Other" Side of Globalization: The Legal Regulation of Cross-Border Movements'. *Canadian Woman Studies* 22 (3/4): 6.

Kempadoo, K., J. Sanghera and B. Pattanaik. 2005. *Trafficking and Prostitution Reconsidered: New Perspectives on Migration, Sex Work, and Human Rights*. New York: Routledge.

Kothiyal, Tanuja. 2016. *Nomadic Narratives: A History of Mobility and Identity in the Great Indian Desert*. New Delhi: Cambridge University Press.

Lattimore, Owen. 1962. *Studies in Frontier History: Collected Papers 1928–1958*. London: Oxford University Press.

Mathur, Nayanika. 2016. *Paper Tiger: Law, Bureaucracy and the Developmental State in Himalayan India*. New Delhi: Cambridge University Press.

Navaro-Yashin, Yael. 2012. *The Make-Believe Space: Affective Geography in a Postwar Polity*. Durham: Duke University Press.

Piliavsky, Anastasia. 2013. 'Borders without Borderlands: On the Social Reproduction of State Demarcation in Rajasthan'. In *Borderland Lives in Northern South Asia*, edited by David N. Gellner, 24–46. Durham: Duke University Press.

Poole, Deborah. 2004. 'Between Threat and Guarantee: Justice and Community in the Margins of the Peruvian State'. In *Anthropology in the Margins of the State*, edited by Veena Das and Deborah Poole, 35–65. New Delhi: Oxford University Press.

Rangarajan, L.N. 1992. *Kautilya: The Arthashastra*. New Delhi: Penguin.

Reeves, Madeleine. 2014. *Border Work: Spatial Lives of the State in Rural Central Asia*. Ithaca: Cornell University Press.

Roitman, Janet. 2004. 'Productivity in the Margins: The Reconstitution of State Power in the Chad Basin'. In *Anthropology in the Margins of the State*, edited by Veena Das and Deborah Poole, 191–224. New Delhi: Oxford University Press.

Roy, Anupama. 2010. *Mapping Citizenship in India*. New Delhi: Oxford University Press.

Scott, James. 2009. *The Art of Not Being Governed: An Anarchist History of Upland South East Asia*. New Haven: Yale University Press.

Singh, Chetan. 2006 (1998). 'Conformity and Conflict: Tribes and the "Agrarian System" of Mughal India'. In *The Mughal State 1526–1750*, edited by Muzaffar Alam and Sanjay Subrahmanyam, 421–49. New Delhi: Oxford University Press.

Singh, Upinder. 2017. *Political Violence in Ancient India*. Cambridge: Harvard University Press.

Thapar, Romila. 2000. 'The Mauryas Revisited'. In *Cultural Pasts*, edited by Romila Thapar, 462–88. New Delhi: Oxford University Press.

Trouillot, Michel-Rolph. 2003. 'The Anthropology of the State in the Age of Globalization: Close Encounters of the Deceptive Kind'. In *Global Transformations: Anthropology and the Modern World*, edited by Michel-Rolph Trouillot, 79–96. New York: Palgrave Macmillan.

Uberoi, J. P. S. 1978. 'The Structural Concept of Asian Frontier'. In *History and Society: Essays in Honour of Professor Nilanjan Ray*, edited by D. Chattopadhyaya, 67–77. Calcutta: K. P. Bagchi.

van Schendel, Willem. 2001. 'Working through Partition: Making a Living in the Bengal Borderlands'. *International Review of Social History* 46 (3): 393–421.

Wink, Andre. 2008 (1986). *Land and Sovereignty in India: Agrarian Society and Politics under the Eighteenth Century Maratha Svarajya*. Cambridge: Cambridge University Press.

Wink, Andre. 1996 (1990). *Al-Hind: The Making of the Indo-Islamic World*. Vol. I. Brill: Leiden.

Zamindar, Vazira Fazila-Yacoobali. 2007. *The Long Partition and the Making of Modern South Asia: Refugees, Boundaries, Histories*. New York: Columbia University Press.

1

Paradise at the Frontier

Kashmir as a Political Terrain and Literary Landscape in the Mughal Empire

ANUBHUTI MAURYA

For the inhabitants of the Mughal milieu, Kashmir was an evocative word. In the literature of the court—poetry, travel accounts and chronicles—it was described as *Kashmir jannat nazir* (Kashmir that is paradise-like) and *suba i dil pazir* (a province close to the heart). However, there is a duality to Kashmir's landscape. This valley in the western Himalayas nestles behind a high wall of mountains. While the paradisiacal region beckoned emperors and poets, it could only be reached by negotiating difficult roads up high mountains and through narrow passes. The journey to Kashmir, Mughal writings proclaimed in horror, was torturous and perilous. The representations of Kashmir as a difficult to access paradisiacal space made its landscape the focus of the courtly imagination.

The relationship between the Mughal state and Kashmir was framed by its geographical position at the territorial margins of the empire as well as by its topographical characteristics. With its conquest in 1586, Kashmir became the northern political frontier of the Mughal Empire.[1] It became a part of the Mughal court's Central Asian aspirations. Unlike the north-western or southern parts of the empire, Kashmir as a frontier was neither porous nor mobile. Over time, with repeated royal sojourns in the region, it became a destination, a place where journeys came to an end. At the same time, continuing political challenges to Mughal authority from within the region over the sixteenth and seventeenth centuries made Kashmir a site of anxiety for the Mughal Empire. This characteristic of tenuous political control, I would argue, marked it as a borderland, but one that was internal to the empire.

In this chapter, I examine the representations of Kashmir in the textual productions of the Mughal court. Over the sixteenth and seventeenth centuries, a corpus of texts—chronicles, travel accounts, epistles and administrative documents—described and discussed the region. Contiguously, from the late sixteenth century, its landscape became the subject of literary compositions (S. Sharma 2017). The concept of *Kashmir jannat nazir* emerged as a literary imaginary in the poetry of the late sixteenth century and evolved over the seventeenth century. I argue that what appears as a description of an extraordinary landscape was a discourse of political authority about a borderland region of the Mughal Empire. Over the sixteenth and seventeenth centuries, Kashmir moved from being an uncharted borderland to a province cognisable within the imperial ecumene.

In the poetry of the early seventeenth century, court poets eulogised the lush greenery, streams, springs, lakes, abundance of flowers and fruits, the high mountains and the salubrity of Kashmir's climate. By the mid-seventeenth century, the gardens laid out by the Mughal elites—emperors, members of the royal family, and the court—became marvels; a source of wonder. The landscape of the Valley served as the frame for the marvels of the Mughal gardens. These shifts in the literary imaginary of the paradisiacal reflected the changing relationship between the empire and landscape of Kashmir. By the mid-seventeenth century, the literary imaginary had travelled into the imperial chronicles and became a part of the language of Mughal sovereignty.

Historiography on sixteenth and seventeenth century Kashmir has divided the Mughal rule over the Valley into two distinct parts—acts of governance and acts of leisure (Mattoo 1988; Kaw 2001; Bazaz 1967; Parmu 1969; Sufi 1996; Bamzai 1962). The royal journeys into Kashmir and spatial practices of the Mughal elite, such as the construction of gardens, have been looked upon as acts of leisure. Within this perspective, Kashmir is reduced to a site of aesthetic gratification, as a space for the enactment of royal leisure. I argue that in Kashmir aesthetic and literary practices, acts of leisure and pleasure were not discrete from the exercise of imperial authority. These practices were specific to the empire's interaction with Kashmir and constituted a response to it. They informed the performance of governance as well as the rituals of sovereignty.

Further, I argue that *Kashmir jannat nazir* was a political imaginary, constituted by tactile experiences, practices of governance, and narrative and visual representations. It fashioned a relationship between the region and the political world of the Mughal court. It was a discourse of power through which this borderland was made familiar and moulded in line with imperial aesthetics. In the seventeenth century, Kashmir moved from being a borderland to becoming the centre of Mughal articulations of its sovereignty.

KASHMIR AS AN INTERNAL BORDERLAND

Over the first half of the sixteenth century, under Babur and Humayun, Kashmir was the site of expansionary interests and ambitions of the Mughal state. In 1540, while Humayun sought shelter in the Safavid court, Mirza Haider Dughlat, a military commander and a member of the ruling collective in Humayun's court, led a small force to Kashmir. Negotiating the fractures within the ruling elites in the region, Mirza established control over the Valley. He claimed it as a commander of Humayun's army and had the *khutba* (the Friday sermon) read in the name of the Mughal emperor (Elias and Ross 1973: 479–80). Subsequently, Mirza Haider's act of conquest placed Kashmir within the Mughal imagination of the territorial claims of Akbar's empire.

The relationship between the region and the imperial court evolved over the sixteenth century. From about the 1560s, Akbar's emissaries were regularly sent to the court of the Kashmiri Sultans. While the Mughal court recognised the Sultans as rulers of Kashmir, they were seen as subservient to the political claims of Mughal suzerainty. In its territorial imagination, Kashmir was a frontier region of the Mughal Empire and its rulers were guardians of the frontier. In the Mughal chronicles, especially Abul Fazl's *Akbarnama*, the kings of Kashmir were referred to as *marzban*—a word which means rulers but was also used to signify the guardians of the frontiers (Fazl 1872: 405; Habib 1999: 223).[2]

In the second half of the sixteenth century, as a political frontier, Kashmir was entangled with the politics of the Mughal Empire in Kabul and Lahore. Though it did not serve as a base for military expeditions, its political orientation was in alignment with Mughal concerns and ambitions in Central Asia. It formed a part of the Mughal relationship with Central Asian polities such as Balkh, Qandahar, Yarkand and political groups such as the Afghans and the Uzbeks.

There was one more way in which Kashmir appeared as a borderland region in the Mughal territorial imagination. Throughout its history, the politics of Kashmir had played out across its landscape in the form of contests between multiple local actors over control of heights, passes, important forts and its capital city, Srinagar.[3] Its topography was intertwined with its politics. In the sixteenth century, the expansionary Mughal forces had to overcome the combined challenge of the local ruling elites and the Himalayas. In their battles with the Mughal armies, the Kashmiri leadership deployed their ability to control the entry to and passage through the Valley. But in their accounts of the Mughal conquest of Kashmir, courtly texts described it primarily as a victory over the mountainous terrain. By focusing on the landscape, these narratives diminished the nature of the political opposition in the region. Its ability to overcome its topographical challenges territorialised the Mughal's claim over Kashmir. Well into the seventeenth century, the Kashmiri elite continued to oppose Mughal rule. These challenges became local in character, taking the form of incidents and attacks in small pockets in different parts of the Valley.[4] As a result, for the Mughal Empire, Kashmir remained a site of anxiety.

Across the Mughal Empire, there were zones, areas and localities where imperial authority was deeply contested. These could be areas at the territorial margins of the empire, such as Bengal, Sindh, Kutch or Deccan in the sixteenth century.[5] But they were not necessarily always faraway areas. They could also be regions where the Mughal Empire had a strained relationship with the ruling elite, such as the Bundelas or the Afghans (Sharma and Sharma 2000; A. Ahmad 2005; Aquil 2012; Gommans 1995; Kolff 2002). Their history stood at variance with the wider narratives of the universal authority of the Mughal emperor and the seamless functioning of its institutions of governance. The idea of internal borderlands in the Mughal Empire allows us to challenge the idea of uniform imperial control or governance through universal imperial institutions. It allows us to see the evolution of political processes in a region over a longer historical period and to see state structures as locally constituted, through the interaction between the politics of the locality and the empire.

Both the representations of Kashmir as a difficult geography and a paradisiacal valley were the Mughal Empire's response to a borderland region. The former reflected the imperial anxiety about the attenuated nature of its control over the region. In the literary and political imaginary of *Kashmir jannat nazir*, the paradise-like characteristics of the region were defined from within the aesthetics of the Mughal court. The graphic descriptions of the perils of journeys to Kashmir reflected the anxiety of the empire. They also reiterated the empire's abilities to overcome a difficult geography.

Writings of the Mughal court drew their lineage from a number of different textual traditions where Kashmir, poised on networks of trade and as a political frontier, was discussed through the tropes of wonder. Acts of description in the Mughal texts moved away from the sense of wonder and marvel and made the region familiar and knowable. Through these, the region acquired an interiority in the Mughal writings. From being a borderland, Kashmir moved to the centre of how the empire came to represent itself.

TALES OF WONDER

The valley of Kashmir was discussed in a number of Arab and Persianate textual traditions, such as the Arab geographies and *'ajaib* (wonder tales) tales of the ninth and tenth centuries and the literature from the Ghaznavid and the Timurid courts. In these textual traditions, Kashmir was painted as a desirable but insular land, guarded by high mountain walls. Many of these texts circulated in the Mughal court and influenced how, in the mid-sixteenth century, the court perceived the region.

Between the ninth and the fifteenth centuries, Kashmir was discussed in a number of Arab geographies[6] and, contiguously, in *'ajaib* tales[7]. In *'Ajaib i Hind* of Nakhuda Buzurg ibn Shahryar, stories of Kashmir ranged from the conversion of the king to Islam (Shahryar 2000: 2)[8]; the description of a gorge between mountains which held a large cache of diamonds of unparalleled beauty, protected by a ring of fire (Shahryar 2000: 103); to a market place, invisible to the human eye, where *jinnat* (spirits) gathered to buy, sell and to gossip (Shahryar 2000: 2–3).[9] The Arab geographies and the *'ajaib* tales formed different epistemes within the larger body of the literature of routes and realms (Zadeh 2010; Antrim 2012). The *'ajaib* tales were premised upon the distance between Kashmir and the place of telling or reading. At the same time, they marked the region with a series of characteristics and made it cognisable within larger geographies. Al Beruni's *Kitab fi tahqia ma lil-Hind* (Book of Investigations in Hind) and Yazdi's *Zafarnama* were influential texts in the Mughal court. Al Beruni's *Kitab al Hind* was written in the Ghaznavid court in the eleventh century. Al Beruni had travelled to Hindustan with Mahmud's armies. In his larger work on Al-Hind, Al Beruni had significant descriptions of Kashmir. His discussions of Kashmir focussed on two aspects of the region. One, he described the geography of the region, routes and passes, chief modes of transportation, the origin and course of the Rivers Jhelum (Jailam in Sachau translation) and Sindh, the city he called Kashmir (Srinagar) and the surrounding regions (Sachau 2003: 150–2). In his discussion on its topographic features, Al Beruni stressed the insularity of the region.

Two, he wrote of Kashmir as a significant centre of Sanskritic learning, with a strong indigenous and independent tradition. Though it was engaged in debates with other centres and schools of Sanskritic education, Al Beruni suggested that the innovative character of the Kashmiri academy was linked to its geographic insularity (Sachau 2003: 87, 94, 123, 125).

Yazdi's *Zafarnama* was written in the early fifteenth century, as the chronicle of *Sahib i qiran timur*. The *Zafarnama* has a brief discussion on Kashmir. The text described the clime and climate of Kashmir. It talked of the number of inhabited villages, the streams, vegetation, fruits and flowers. It mentioned the city of Srinagar, which, like Baghdad, had a river running through it, surmounted by a number of bridges—both permanent as well as boat bridges. It identified the roads into the Valley; though each, the text informed the readers, was marked by its own set of impossibilities.[10] The *Zafarnama* stressed the difficulty of access to the region hidden behind high mountains.

These textual traditions constituted Kashmir as an insular place. Paradoxically, these discussions in the Arab geographies, 'ajaib tales, Al Beruni's *Kitab al Hind* and in the Persianate traditions of the Timurid court were informed by reports of itinerant travellers and trading caravans. Kashmir appeared in these different textual imaginations because of its presence in overlapping networks of commerce, piety and politics. It was located off the traditional Silk Route and was part of trade networks that spanned from Central Asia to Ladakh, which were spread as far as Bijapur and Golconda in the Deccan. From the late thirteenth century, it was home to a number of Sufi orders, which originated in Central Asia and operated in the regions of the western and central Himalayas. Sufi saints moved between Balkh, Badakhshan, Kashmir, Kishtawar, Ladakh, Yarkand and Tibet and had deep links with Harmin (the cities of Mecca and Medina).

In 1539–40, when Humayun was besieged by Sher Shah, he sought the advice of the Moghul collective. Mirza Haider Dughlat[11] suggested that the conquest of Kashmir was a possibility and that the Valley offered the safest of refuges possible to the emperor on the run (Elias and Ross 1973). Humayun's advisors turned down the Mirza's proposal on the grounds that Kashmir was isolated and difficult to access and that Humayun would be trapped there. These discussions and decisions in the Mughal court in the mid-sixteenth century drew upon the image of intransitivity constituted through the older textual traditions.

In the decade he spent as the ruler of Kashmir, Mirza Haider wrote *Tarikh i rashidi*.[12] While the text dealt only briefly with the Valley, Dughlat's descriptions of Kashmir challenged the older imaginations of the region. Mirza Haider's account of Kashmir looked outward from the region, establishing equivalences, comparisons and contemporaneity with processes and events in other parts of Central and South Asia.

In the late sixteenth century, when Akbar demanded subservience from the Kashmiri rulers, he referred back to the Mirza's conquest of Kashmir on behalf of Humayun, as the basis for the Mughal claim on Kashmir.

These discussions in the Arabic and Persianate traditions influenced the political actions and intellectual engagements with Kashmir in the courts of Akbar.

EARLY DISCUSSIONS ON KASHMIR IN AKBAR'S COURT

In 1586, after a difficult battle, Mughal armies entered Srinagar. Though the establishment of Mughal authority in the region took much longer, imperial chronicles proclaimed the entry into Srinagar as the moment of conquest of Kashmir (Fazl 1998: 774; N. Ahmed 1992 [1936]: 617). Conquest and annexation were acts of territorial expansion but in the case of Kashmir, the land was not merely the site of battle. In the imperial narratives, the very landscape—the mountainous terrain, arduous roads and adverse climate—posed a challenge and had to be conquered.

Early writings on Kashmir in Akbar's court were suggestive of an imperial centre exploring a newly conquered province and slowly establishing authority over it. Imperial chronicles like *Tarikh i alfi* by Mullah Ahmad bin Nasrullah Tattavi, *Akbarnama* and *Ain i Akbari* by Abul Fazl and *Tabaqat i Akbari* by Nizamuddin Ahmad compiled descriptive, factual and statistical accounts of the region. In these chronicles, especially in Abul Fazl's *Akbarnama* and *Ain i Akbari*, discussions on Kashmir contained ethnographic notices, synoptic histories, geographic descriptions, accounts of customs, lore, tales of the marvellous and the fantastic, theistic and philosophical traditions.

These accounts of the newly conquered province were produced through a multi-layered process, which involved observations of and investigations into the region as well as engagement with existing intellectual traditions. In their discussions on Kashmir, the court chroniclers drew from the Arab and Persianate traditions and the writings of the predecessors of Mughal rule, such as Mirza Haider's *Tarikh i rashidi* (Elias and Ross 1973). They drew upon regional intellectual traditions, both textual, such as the *Rajatarangini*, and oral accounts.

In the third *daftar* (section) of the *Ain i Akbari*, in 'An Account of Twelve Provinces' (*Ahwal i dawazdah subah*), Abul Fazl (1872: 562–89) gave a detailed account of the provinces of the empire, as they were getting formed at the time of writing. The discussion on Kashmir in the *Ain i Akbari* can be divided into three distinct parts. There is an ethnographic and geographic description of the region. The second part is in the form of notices, organised in tabular form—listing the revenue figures, dominant castes, cavalry and infantry of each district. The third part gives a brief history of the region.

Abul Fazl's account of Kashmir began with a simple statement of facts about the climate, best routes into the Valley and weather. In the act of noting details about places, Fazl recorded the local lore that laid out, in a way, the geography of sacred sites of the region. The *Ain i Akbari* gave descriptions of the houses, the bazaars, food habits, clothes and fabrics, and means of transportation of the region. Fazl commented on Kashmiri as the dominant language of the region and the continuing use of Sanskrit in literature. He noted that Kashmir had an old tradition of learning. He made disparaging remarks about the music of the region. He commented on the presence of different religious groups. There was a detailed description of the city of Srinagar, its length and breadth, the main industries and manufactures, geographical spread and location, water available in the city, and so on.

In the third part of the discussion on Kashmir, Abul Fazl gave an abridged account of the history of Kashmir. This abridgement, especially of the early history of the region, drew upon the new translation of the *Rajatarangini*. Fazl's account of the history of the region began from the story of the origin of the Valley as a large lake, emergence of the institution of kingship and culminated in conquest by Akbar's army.

In the summary account of Kashmir's history, Abul Fazl recounted incidents from a few specific kings from the *Rajatarangini*. These rulers were set up as exemplars of good and bad kingship. But more importantly, they formed the medium through which Fazl outlined issues of morality and virtue in the exercise of kingship. Fazl's account of the history of Kashmir ended with the conquest of the region by the Mughal armies. The institution of kingship, which in the original narrative had emerged from a quest for peace and justice, culminated in the establishment of Akbar's rule over Kashmir.

The late sixteenth century chronicles of the Mughal court were, in a sense, writing the empire into being. Through the discussions in the court chronicles, Kashmir moved away from the older associations of insularity and the unknown. By creating summary geographic, ethnographic and historical accounts of the region, Abul Fazl and other court chroniclers made Kashmir familiar within the ecumene of the court and the empire.

Dar wasf i Kashmir: *In Praise of Kashmir*

While court chronicles were compiling information on Kashmir, synchronically the region was entering the poetic and literary imagination of the Mughal court. The concept of *Kashmir jannat nazir* first emerged as an imaginary in the literary productions of the court in the late sixteenth century.

Urfi Shirazi's *qasida* (praise poem) *Dar wasf i Kashmir* (In Praise of Kashmir) began with the lines,

> *Har Sokhteh jani ke be Kashmir dar ayad*
> *Gar Murgh kabab ast ke ba-bal wa pur ayad.*[13] (Shirazi n.d.: 31)

In this *qasida*, Urfi described Kashmir as the land of soul alleviating beauty, with the miraculous ability to rejuvenate and revitalise.

In 1589, when Akbar travelled to Kashmir, Faizi, the poet laureate of the court, travelled with him.[14] In his *qasida, Dar tausif i Kashmir wa tahniyat i fateh an wa madah i Akbar padshah*,[15] Faizi described the excellences of the region and applauded its conquest by Akbar's armies. He celebrated Kashmir as a land especially blessed— by both its soul refreshing beauty and its good fortune that it was entering the benevolent embrace of Akbar Padshah (Faizi 1342 hijri shamsi: 42).

In this *qasida*, Faizi described Kashmir as '*ajab karnamah i taqdir*, the wondrous work of destiny (Faizi 1342 hijri shamsi: 42). *Ta'jjub* (wonder) remained an important part of the response to Kashmir, but the nature of wonder had changed. While, in the '*ajaib* traditions of the ninth to eleventh centuries, the anxieties generated by the mountainous insularity of Kashmir were articulated in stories of danger lurking behind the mountain walls. In the poetry of the Mughal court in the late sixteenth century, the *ta'jjub* was expressed at the beauty of the landscape of Kashmir. The poetry of the court wove the high mountains, salubrious climate, springs, streams and lakes, and the verdure of the Valley into a literary imaginary of the paradisiacal beauty of Kashmir.

In the first half of the seventeenth century, Kashmir remained a distinct topic of literary compositions of the court. Most major poets of the court such as Salim Tehrani, Mohammad Jan Qudsi (d. 1646), Talib Amuli (d. 1652), Zafar Khan 'Ahsan' (d. 1670), Mir Ilahi (d. 1653), Tughra Mashhadi (d. 1667–8), and others, had distinctive poems on Kashmir in their oeuvre.[16] These poems still spoke of the region in terms of wonder. But now, they expressed wonder at the gardens and buildings constructed by the Mughal elite. The gardens were described as paradisiacal and the landscape of the Valley appeared as a worthy background to these imperial creations.

Majma' ul afkar was a 'miscellaneous collection of Mughal *Insha'* (Kinra 2015: 186), dated to the early eighteenth century (Shekhar 2009–10: 114–56). It offered models of laments, elegies, letters of congratulation, commiseration to the sick, letters of praise, of constructions by the patron, assemblies held, *bazm wa razm* (battles won), and so on. It also contained copies of special letters, such as letters from Humayun to Bairam Khan, Jahangir to Shah Abbas, and Shahjahan to Mulla Shah.[17] In this collection of *Insha*, there was a discrete section on Kashmir. It included excerpts from Mohammad Salih Kamboh's *Aml i salih*, Tabatabai's *Padshahnama*, a long section from a *risalah* (account) by Maulana Shaida, and a letter from Mulla Tughra to Qazi Zahid. The section from Kamboh was a *safarnama* (travel account) and described Shahjahan's journey into Kashmir. From Tabatabai's *Padshahnama*, *Majma'* excerpted the description of Srinagar. Other sections of the *Majma'* contained a panegyric poem to the beauty of the region and a satire on the dangers of the mountain roads. These selections disaggregated the literary imaginary of *Kashmir jannat nazir* into a number of themes: the journey up to the Valley, the difficulties of the road, the beauty of the region and the wonders of the garden.

The literary imaginary of *Kashmir jannat nazir* emerged in the poetry of the Mughal court over the late sixteenth and early seventeenth centuries. In this period, the poetry and other writings of the Mughal court were concerned with the landscape and natural features of the region. By the mid-seventeenth century, the *jannat naziri* of Kashmir had shifted to the gardens laid out by the Mughal emperors.

The discussions across the different narrative traditions from the court chronicles to the poetry of the court represented multiple imaginations of Kashmir. The textual productions of the late sixteenth and early seventeenth centuries mapped the region as well as produced a vocabulary by which to speak of it, making it legible for the court and within the empire. These texts were a part of the exercise of establishing Mughal authority in the region. At the same time, these texts reflected the anxiety of the empire in establishing authority in this distant province.

ANXIETIES OF THE EMPIRE

In the twelfth regnal year (1617), when he was travelling through Gujarat, Jahangir received two different reports from Kashmir. He noted these in his memoirs. The first reported the birth of two daughters in the house of a silk merchant, born with teeth and joined from the back to the waist. The life of this pair of Siamese twins was brief (Jahangir 1940: 231).

The other report informed the emperor about an outbreak of the plague in Kashmir. The region was ravaged by an epidemic. Jahangir provided details of the affliction. On the first day, a person would experience headache, fever and nosebleed. By the second day, the afflicted person would be dead. If one member of the household fell ill, every other inhabitant of the house would soon follow. Anybody who went near a sick person or a dead body would be infected. The plague was deadly in its potency.

> There was one person who had died, and they laid his body on straw to wash it. By chance a cow ate some of the straw and died. Thereupon, several dogs ate some of the cow's flesh and they all died. Things have gotten so bad that neither will fathers come near their sons for fear of death, nor will sons approach their fathers. (Thackston 1999: 254)

The end of the epidemic came with a mysterious chain of events. One morning, when the plague was at its worst, people in the city and its outskirts woke up to find symbols marking their doors:

'There were three large circles, one on top of the other, two middle sized circles and one small circle. There were also two empty circles' (Thackston 1999: 254). Following this, the part of the city where the plague had originated burnt down to the ground. The fire and the appearance of these symbols marked the diminution in the fierceness of the epidemic.

In his recording of these reports from Kashmir, Jahangir positioned himself in a discursive terrain that was both incredulous as well as scientific (Mottahedeh 1997: 37). Jahangir's record of these curious incidents was marked by a fullness of details and created parallels with his customarily methodical observations of natural and other phenomenon.[18] At the same time, Jahangir described these events as strange or tinged with *ghraib* (horror) (Jahangir 1940: 252). He ended his description of the plague and the fire with the words that the story 'does not agree with the canons of reason, and my intellect cannot accept it' (*ghaitan be qanun khirad rast na-mi ayad wa 'aql i man qabul in ma'ni na-mi kunad*) (Jahangir 1940: 252).

It is striking that the two incidents recorded by Jahangir came to him as hearsay, albeit relayed to the court by the *waqi' nawis* (news writer) from the region. They were heard while the emperor and the court were on a journey through the province of Gujarat. These stories—the birth of Siamese twins and the appearance of strange symbols in times of catastrophe—invoked elements of the fantastic and echoed the genre of *'ajaib wa ghraib* (Zadeh 2010; Bates 2005 and Ghadessi 2011).

Ahmed (2011) has argued that the *'ajaib* and *ghraib* tales were characteristics of borderlands—'areas which were liminal to the geography of large empires but central to their imagination of the self'. The element of the fantastic in these stories represented a distinct episteme, which reinforced the distance of the *suba* (province) of Kashmir from the royal court. It measured the distance not in miles and metres but by marking Kashmir as a faraway place where the inexplicable and unknowable could occur. These stories were in marked contrast to Jahangir's writings on Kashmir. In the *Jahangirnama*, descriptions and discussions of the region were carefully parsed through methods of investigation and observation. Jahangir's knowledge of the region was premised upon actually seeing. These stories, in contrast, were reported. The record of these stories in the *Tuzuk* reflected the tension between the multiple imaginations of Kashmir in the imperial chronicles. While the detailed reports in the imperial chronicles made the region knowable, the distance between the region and the imperial court generated anxieties of control.

Imperial Journeys to Kashmir

By the early seventeenth century, it had become an established practice for emperors, members of the royal family and the court to travel to Kashmir. These royal sojourns to Kashmir were deeply intertwined with the literary imaginary of *Kashmir jannat nazir*. Akbar visited Kashmir three times (1589, 1593 and 1597). As emperor, Jahangir journeyed to Kashmir five times (1619, 1622, 1624, 1625 and 1627) and Shahjahan an equal number of times, if not more. On their sojourns in the Valley, emperors visited spectacles, experienced the novelties of the region and undertook hunting expeditions. They travelled through the Valley mostly by water, sitting in specially designed boats and made camp in gardens.

On his three trips to Kashmir, Akbar surveyed the region and identified certain sites as important. Akbar made camp and spent time in the environs of Dal Lake, Shihabuddinpur, Achhwal, Virnag, Wular Lake and Pampore. In Jahangir's reign, the imperial camp undertook longer and more extensive journeys and investigated local lore and natural phenomenon. Jahangir ordered the exploration of the deep caves at Burzahom (Chadurah 1991: 12–13) and an examination of the medicinal properties of saffron (Thackston 1999: 433). In Shahjahan's reign, imperial cavalcades followed the timetable that had been established in the previous decades. Shahjahan's first trip to Kashmir as emperor began from Agra in February 1634. He travelled across the plains of north India to Lahore. The ascent began from Lahore. The route into the Valley was chosen to ensure arrival in the Valley in time to see the spring and the blossoming of flowers. The emperor returned to Hindustan after all the offerings of the region—from the spring blossoming of flowers to the autumnal maturing of the saffron fields—had been sampled. At the same time, the return journey had to be made before the travellers were overtaken by the cold and snow of winters.

In Akbar's reign, the imperial cavalcades toured the region, surveying the sights. In Jahangir's reign, construction was carried out at a number of these sites. For instance, Jahangir parcelled out the lands on the banks of the Dal Lake amongst members of the royal family and the nobility. A series of gardens were built along the shores of the lake.

By the mid-seventeenth century, Kashmir had become a spectacle. In the accounts of these journeys, Kashmir was no longer marked by its insularity. On the contrary, the act of visiting and looking was central to the imperial relationship with *Kashmir jannat nazir*. For instance, when Shahjahan travelled to Kashmir in the eighteenth regnal year (1645–6), he insisted that Nusrat Jung, who was about to begin his assignment in Deccan, accompany him to the Valley. Lahori wrote that,

> Because Nusrat Jung had never visited Kashmir, order was given that
> he should ride with the king and should be in attendance. It was said
> that he should view the verdant valley, the blossoming trees and after
> taking pleasure in the valley and enjoying its delights, he was to return
> to Deccan. (Lahori 1867: 218)

This imperial directive prescribed Nusrat Jung's enjoyment of Kashmir. At the same time, by riding along the emperor on his maiden visit to the region, his enjoyment also became an object of viewing. His enjoyment had to be visible to the emperor.

In 1639–40, on a visit to the Valley, Shahjahan invited the *ilchis* (emissaries) from the courts of Rum and Bukhara to visit Kashmir (Lahori 1867: 197). These emissaries became the audience for an enactment of Mughal grandeur. In the gardens on the shore of Dal Lake, lamps were lit behind cascades of water, bringing two idioms of beauty—water and light—to create a celebratory spectacle. Lahori described it thus:

> On the eve of 24th [Rabi' ul awwal], in front of the imperial harem,
> order was given to decorate the gardens of Farah and Faiz Bakhsh, the
> most wondrous sites in this city. From the parterres to the beginning
> of the wall to the banks, in each of the two gardens, on both sides of
> Shah Nahar and on all sides of the tanks, lamps were placed. After that,
> at small intervals, tied to the wood were colourful lanterns. Behind
> the screens/sheets of cascading water, in holders of marble, lamps were
> arranged, creating wonder.

> The emperor arrived from the north, distributing gold coins, serving the poor ... And till one *pahar* of the evening was spent in pleasure giving and spreading in the garden, after which a return was made to the imperial palace. (Lahori 1867: 199–200)

As emperors travelled across Kashmir, they altered its landscape. In 1620, on the road back to Lahore, Jahangir was struck by the beauty of a spring and a waterfall near the village of Bahramgala (Thackston 1999: 349). He ordered the construction of a viewing platform, a seat to watch the spectacle. An inscription on the stone noted the date of his passage. Ebba Koch has discussed Jahangir's practices of claiming nature as his own by making a permanent imprint on it with artistic means, with 'architectural features, sculptures and inscriptions' (Koch 2009: 161–2). By taking over natural phenomenon, Jahangir, she says, accentuated them with 'dynastic imprints' (Koch 2009: 168). In later periods, when Shahjahan visited the Valley, the imperial chronicles discussed the seat built by Jahangir to view the waterfall. Bahramgala was distinguished by the royal intervention at the site.

The emperors gave new names to places as they travelled through the Valley. New names drew from an event or a specific person linked to the Mughal presence in the region. Inch was renamed Islamabad. Shahjahan on his visit to Inch had ordered the destruction of a *ziarat* (pilgrimage) there. Islam Khan Mir Bakhshi held the area in *tuyul* (Lahori 1867: 47–8). The name Islamabad memorialised both the person and the incident. Machhi Bhawan was given in *jagir* (revenue-fee) to Yaminuddaulah Asaf Khan. He had carried out extensive construction in the area, building tanks, canals and gardens. Shahjahan renamed the place Asafabad (Lahori 1867: 50). Shahjahan modified the garden laid out by Jahangir at Virnag. He raised pavilions, which overlooked the garden and the canals in which the waters from the spring of Virnag flowed. He gave this garden the name of Shahabad (Lahori 1867: 52–3).

The practice of renaming marked the land with imperial presence, interventions and personnel. It created new political and cultural associations between Kashmir and the Mughal Empire. Names such as Islamabad and Shahabad resonated with other places in the empire. The similarity of names did not indicate a similarity of characteristics between these places. The meaning and relevance of these names could only be located within the histories of the Mughal Empire. At the same time, sites in Kashmir continued to carry new names and old. Locally, the story of Mughal refashioning became joined to older associations with these sites.

Royal journeys to Kashmir dismantled earlier notions of insularity of the region. Accounts of these journeys reflect the reconstitution of the sense of wonder associated with Kashmir. Kashmir became the setting for imperial creations. By the mid-seventeenth century, these sites of imperial action were viewed as the spaces of paradisiacal beauty.

MUGHAL GARDENS OF KASHMIR

Discussions on the Mughal gardens of Kashmir have focussed on themes of aesthetic and visual practices of the Mughal court. These gardens have been viewed as spaces distant and discrete from governance. However, I would argue that these gardens represented spatial practices by which the authority of the Mughal state was territorialised in the landscape of Kashmir. The metaphor of paradise on earth invoked the philosophical ideal of a benevolent Mughal *badshahi* (kingship). The gardens became the space where this ideal was articulated in land. The lay out, deployment of water ways, choice of trees and plants, use of symmetry and wilderness within these gardens constituted a specific aesthetic vocabulary. High mountains served as the background to these gardens, waters from springs, streams and rivers were directed into channels running through them, gushing out in fountains and pooling in tanks. Flowers such as *laleh* (tulips) and *nargis* (daffodils) and trees such as chinar (plane), aspen, poplars, apple and cherry populated these gardens.

The patronage and commission of these constructions reflected the contestations within the spheres of Mughal authority. They also represented the interventions by the Mughal state in public spaces, popular memory and local politics. These gardens were employed within imperial frameworks of governance, habitation and leisure. In time, the gardens came to take on the sense of a settlement, with names such as Zafarabad and Saifabad.

Bagh i Faiz Bakhsh and Farah Bakhsh, known as Shalimar Bagh, were the most celebrated of the Mughal gardens. The area of Shalimar, on the bank of Dal Lake, had been a site of pilgrimage, with a natural spring (Fazl 1998: 366). Raja Pravar Sen, remembered as the founder of the city of Srinagar, had first laid out a garden at this site. Though the garden laid out by Pravar Sen had long since disappeared, the village that came up at the site retained the name Shalimar (Kuihami n.d.: 286).

While distributing the land around the Dal Lake amongst the nobles of the court, Jahangir gave this piece of land to Shahjahan, with the directive to construct a garden at this site. Shahjahan named the garden Bagh i Faiz Bakhsh. The garden was built on the principals of 'mountain garden', with terraced gardens, organised in three distinct parts. The highest part of the garden was the *zenana* garden, which offered open spaces as well as privacy to the women of the palace

(Villiers-Stuart 1913; Ruggles 2008). The second zone was the courtly domain. A third, and public, section was laid out later (Ruggles 2008: 216). In the 1630s, Shahjahan added another garden to the existing one and named it Farah Bakhsh. This formed the third part, the public part of the garden.

> The best of the gardens is Farah Bakhsh, which was constructed at the command of the emperor. The flowered earth of this garden is modelled on the evergreen paradise; waters of Shah Nahr flowing through the gardens remind one of the waters of Salsabil and Kausar; the fruits of the garden are the most delicious in the world; the buildings of palaces are like the faultless paradise. The architect of this marvel is the emperor, *Sahib i Qiran Sani.* (Lahori 1867: 24)

Lahori's description exalted this garden to an approximation of paradise. *Sahib i Qiran Sani*, Shahjahan, (the second lord of conjunction) designed this garden. The greenery of the garden, the blossoming of flowers and the buildings in it were reminiscent of the imagery of paradise. Shah Nahr, the canal that channelled the water from the old spring, was compared with Salsabil and Kausar, the spring and canal through which waters flowed through paradise.

Although under Shahjahan's directive, this part of Dal's shore was refashioned into a new space, the older name of Shalimar persisted and became the popular name for these gardens. Shalimar Bagh drew a line of continuity between the king who founded the city of Srinagar and the Mughal emperor who fashioned it into paradise-like gardens.

In time, the word Shalimar itself became a synonym for the grand Mughal gardens. When Shahjahan laid out gardens in Lahore, he called them Bagh i Faiz Bakhsh and Farah Bakhsh. They came to be popularly known as Shalimar Bagh. Similarly, Shalimar Bagh came up in Delhi, with the construction of Shahjahanabad. Repeated appearance of Shalimar in the name of Mughal gardens across north India invoked the gardens of Kashmir as the imagery of paradise.

The names given to places in Kashmir referred to events and people linked to the Mughal presence in the region. The changed appellations inserted the Mughal presence into the everyday imagination of these places as well as infused them with the histories of localities. When names such as Shalimar and Sahibabad travelled to other parts of the empire, they specifically invoked the *jannat naziri* of Kashmir. This imaginary, by the mid-seventeenth century, had become a part of the imperial vocabulary of self-representation.

The Mughal gardens of Kashmir moulded nature into carefully crafted spaces. In the construction of these gardens, local geographies were significantly altered. Springs were harnessed, canals were dug and small rivers were diverted.

These gardens were also spaces of horticultural experimentation. Varieties of plants were transplanted and fruits such as cherries, guavas and apples were brought from other parts of the empire. Underlying the descriptions of the fruits of Kashmir were careful records of their size and quality, comparing them to the produce of other provinces. New horticultural techniques such as grafting were introduced.

Patronage of construction—of buildings and gardens—was a sphere of competing authorities. In his perambulations from Agra to Lahore and then to Kashmir, Shahjahan modified or reconstructed a number of buildings and gardens laid out by Jahangir. His reconstructions at Virnag were just one example. Lahori explained it by noting that Jahangir's constructions were not to the taste of Shahjahan (Lahori 1867: 11–12). In the complicated politics of lineage and inheritance and the desire to mark legacy, divergent aesthetics were sites of contestation.

When Asaf Khan constructed Nishat Bagh, adjoining Faiz and Farah Bakhsh, it competed with Shahjahan's gardens in beauty. The story is that Shahjahan coveted Asaf Khan's garden. But Asaf Khan steadfastly failed to offer it to him. A peevish emperor ordered the shutting off of the water supply to the garden (Villiers-Stuart 1913: 167–8). The conflict in this matter was on issues of ownership—not only of land but also of a wondrous creation.

Zafar Khan 'Ahsan' in his first term as governor in Kashmir reconstructed the *ziarat* at Zadibal. Zadibal was the *dargah* (resting place) of the Nurbakhshi saint Mir Shams Iraqi and a site of veneration for the Shias of the Valley. He laid out a garden at the site and gave it the name of Hasanabad. These constructions by Zafar Khan marked an intervention in the local politics of the region and his garden came to carry political and religious valence. In 1635, when riots broke out in Srinagar as a result of sectarian conflicts, Hasanabad was ransacked (Mattoo 1988: 150–1).

Jahanara Begum owned three gardens in Kashmir: The garden of Jawahir Khan Khwaja Sara on the island in Dal Lake, Bagh i Nur Afshan laid out by Nur Jahan on the banks of Jhelum, and the garden at Safapur which had originally been laid out by Mirza Haider Dughlat (Lahori 1867: 195). Jahanara laid out a garden in her *jagir* at Achhwal and renamed it Sahibabad, based on her title of Begum Sahiba. Jahanara's use of her title in the act of renaming the garden was a political gesture. When Jahanara Begum laid out gardens in Chandni Chowk in Shahjahanabad, she gave them also the name of Sahibabad. The name inscribed her presence in a very public and urban space of the main street of the capital of the empire. The nomenclature of her gardens in Chandni Chowk invoked the gardens in Kashmir. Like she had inscribed her claim on the garden at Achhwal, her garden in Chandni Chowk marked the land with her claim of authority.

The aesthetic practice of laying out gardens in Kashmir was informed by the literary imaginary of *Kashmir jannat nazir*. In time, in the poetry of the court, the Mughal gardens became the sites of paradisiacal beauty. By laying out gardens, the Mughal elite moulded the land of Kashmir and inscribed Mughal authority into the landscape. They inserted Mughal rule in the local memories and histories of places. I would argue that the laying out of gardens was not just a mark of imperial control. The gardens were a part of the spatial practice of the Mughal Empire, by which imperial authority was territorialised in the distant province of Kashmir.

CONCLUSION

From the earliest discussions on the region, there has been a sense of exceptionalism associated with the geography of Kashmir. The narrative traditions from Kashmir of the early medieval and the medieval invested sacrality in the landscape. It would seem that the idea of a sacred land segued into the metaphor of Kashmir as paradise in the Mughal traditions in the early modern period (Zutshi 2014).

I have argued that the invocation of the imagery of paradise in the discussions on Kashmir was not simply a descriptive device, nor was it a continuation of the older imagination of Kashmir as a sacred land. In the sixteenth century, Kashmir served as a political frontier for the Mughal Empire. Over the sixteenth and early parts of the seventeenth centuries, the region was also a borderland internal to the empire. The challenges to the Mughal authority and the difficult geography of the region made it a site of anxiety for the Mughal state. The act of description in the poetry and other literature from the Mughal court made this borderland knowable and brought it within the ambit of imperial ecumene. Kashmir moved from being a borderland in the territorial as well as narrative imagination to the centre of Mughal representation of its kingship.

Kashmir jannat nazir was a distinct literary and political imaginary, which emerged in the late sixteenth century in the Mughal court and evolved over the seventeenth century. It was a discourse of authority, which informed institutions of governance and the spatial practices of the empire. In turn, these practices territorialised the Mughal Empire in the region.

Kashmir remains an evocative word for us today—as the site of competing nationalisms, political contestations, deep suffering and fear. Ironically, this Kashmir sits alongside a strong visual memory of a heavenly land.[19] I would argue that while the landscape of the Valley has appeared in different discursive traditions, our imagination today draws its lineage from the very specific Mughal imaginary of *Kashmir jannat nazir*.

NOTES

1   I use the word in the sense deployed by Powers and Standen (1999).

2   Dehkhoda Dictionary gives this as the meaning: *Nigāhbān ya māmūr i marz; sarhaddār*, https://www.vajehyab.com/?q=%D9%85%D8%B1%D8%B2%D8%A 8%D8%A7%D9%86, accessed on 17 March 2020.

3   See, for example, Stein (1989 [1900]: 304–7, 360).

4   *Baharistan i shahi* has a description of a number of small-scale, mostly local, rebellions against early Mughal presence in Kashmir. See, for instance, Pandit (1991: 263).

5   See discussions in Kothiyal (2016); M. Ahmed (2016); Eaton and Wagoner (2014) and Chatterjee (2009).

6   Kashmir is mentioned in a number of Arab geographies. Among some of these are authors such as Al Baladhuri (d. 892), *Futuh al-buldan;* Ibn Khurdadhbih (d. 912), *Kitab al masalik wa'l mamalik;* Gardizi, *Zayn-ul Akhbar;* Al-Mas'udi (d. 956), *Muruj al dhahab* and Al-Idrisi (d. 1156), *Kitab nuzhat al-mushtaq fi khtiraq al-afaq.* See the discussion in S. M. Ahmad (1989) and Ahmad and Bano (1984).

7   See discussion on the body of literature classified as *'ajaib* in M. Ahmed (2016); Behl (2006) and Zadeh (2010).

8   This story qualifies as an *'ajaib* because this particular text is dated to the tenth century, which predates the first Muslim ruler of Kashmir by a few centuries.

9   Interestingly, this story is retold by a much later author, Al Qalqashi (d. 1418). There are modifications in the names of the principal actors and the region is identified as Alor or Alwar in the later story. A story that was initially narrated as an *'ajaib* became a credible tale in a later context. For Al Qalqashi's narration, see Zaki ed. (2009: 51–2).

10 As quoted in Elias and Ross (1973: 432).

11 Mirza Haider Dughlat was a Moghul noble man in the service of Sultan Said Khan of Kashghar. In 1533, he led the Kashghari armies in a successful campaign in Kashmir. However, upon the plea of his armies, he returned to Kashghar. Upon the death of Sultan Said Khan, Mirza Haider lost favour at the court. He turned to Kabul and joined his cousin Babur. On Babur's death, he joined the service of Mirza Kamran. When Humayun was looking for allies, Mirza Haider joined him. In 1540, he conquered Kashmir again and ruled as its proxy ruler. In 1546, he read the *khutba* and minted coins in Humayun's name. He died in 1551 in Kashmir.

12 Anooshahr (2014) and Faruqui (2012) discuss the *Tarikh i rashidi* within the larger context of Mughal political identities.

13 'Every burnt soul that has come to Kashmīr [is revived]/ Even a chicken made into a kebab becomes whole.'
14 For a longer discussion on Faizi, see Alam and Subrahmanyam (2012) and Kinra (2015).
15 The title of this *qasida* can be translated as *Description of Kashmir, Congratulations on Its Victory and Praise of the Emperor Akbar*.
16 See the discussion in Tikku (1971: 83–157).
17 *Majma' ul Afkar*, Khudabakhsh Oriental Library, ms. HL 840. See Shekhar (2009–10: 114–56).
18 See Koch (2009) and Lefebvre (2007) for discussions on Jahangir's notions of rationality.
19 See Kabir (2009) for a discussion on the contrasting yet contiguous political and popular discourses which constitute Kashmir as the 'Territory of Desire'.

REFERENCES

Fazl, Abul. *Akbarnama*. Vol. III. Persian typescript by W. M. Thackston, manuscript papers of W. M. Thackston.
———. 1872. *Ain i Akbari*. Vol. II. Edited by H. Blochmann. Calcutta: Asiatic Society of Bengal.
Ahmad, Amir. 2005. 'The Bundela Revolts during the Mughal Period: A Dynastic Affair'. *Proceedings of the Indian History Congress* 66: 438–45.
Ahmad, S. Maqbul. 1989. *Arabic Classical Accounts of India and China*. Shimla: Indian Institute of Advanced Studies.
Ahmad, S. Maqbul, and Raja Bano. 1984. *Historical Geography of Kashmir*. New Delhi: Ariana Publishing House.
———. 2011. 'Adam's Mirror: The Frontier in the Imperial Imagination'. *Economic and Political Weekly* 46 (13): 60–5.
———. 2016. *A Book of Conquest: The Chachnama and Muslim Origins in South Asia*. Cambridge, Massachusetts: Harvard University Press.
Ahmed, Nizamuddin. 1992 (1936). *The Tabaqat i Akbari, A History of India from the Early Musalman Invasions to the Thirty Eighth Year of the Reign of Akbar*. Translated by Brajendranath De. Delhi: Low Price Publication.
Alam, Muzaffar, and Sanjay Subrahmanyam. 2012. *Writing the Mughal World*. Ranikhet: Permanent Black.
Anooshahr, Ali. 2014. 'Mughals, Mongols and Mongrels: The Challenge of Aristocracy and the Rise of the Mughal State in the Tarikh i Rashidi'. *Journal of Early Modern History* 18 (6): 559–77.

Antrim, Zayde. 2012. *Routes and Realms: The Power of Place in the Early Islamic World.* New York: Oxford University Press.

Aquil, Raziuddin. 2012. *Sufism, Culture and Politics: Afghans and Islam in Medieval North India.* New Delhi: Oxford University Press.

Bamzai, P. N. K. 1962. *A History of Kashmir: Political, Social and Cultural, from the Earliest Times to the Present Day.* Delhi: Metropolitan Book Co.

Bates, Alan. 2005. 'Good, Common, Regular and Orderly: Early Modern Classifications of Monstrous Births'. *Social History of Medicine* 18 (2): 141–58.

Bazaz, P. N. 1967. *Kashmir in Crucible.* Delhi: Pamposh Publications.

Behl, Aditya. 2006. 'The Magic Doe: Desire and Narrative in a Hindavi Sufi Romance, circa 1503'. In *India's Islamic Traditions*, edited by R. M. Eaton, 711–1750. Delhi: Oxford University Press.

Chadurah, Haider Malik. 1991. *History of Kashmir.* Edited and translated by Razia Bano. Delhi: Bhavna Prakashan.

Chatterjee, Kumkum. 2009. The *Cultures of History in Early Modern India: Persianisation and Mughal Culture in Bengal.* New Delhi: Oxford University Press.

Faizi. 1342 (Hijri Shamsi). *Diwan i Faizi.* Lahore: Idarah Tahqiqat Pakistan, Danishgah i Punjab.

Eaton, Richard, and Philip Wagoner. 2014. Power, *Memory and Architecture: Contested Sites on India's Deccan Plateau, 1300–1600.* New Delhi: Oxford University Press.

Elias, N., and E. Denison Ross, trans. 1973. *Tarikh- i Rashidi of Mirza Muhammad Haidar Dughlat: A History of the Moghuls of Central Asia.* Patna: Academia Asiatica.

Faruqui, Munis. 2012. *The Princes of the Mughal Empire, 1504–1719.* New York: Cambridge University Press.

Ghadessi, Touba. 2011. 'Inventoried Monsters'. *Journal of the History of Collections* 23 (2): 267–81.

Gommans, Jos J. L. 1995. *The Rise of the Indo — Afghan Empire: c. 1710–1780.* Leiden: E. J. Brill.

Jahangir Gurgani, Nuruddin Mohammad. 1349/1940. *Jahangirnama.* Edited by Mohammad Hashim. Tehran: Intesharat Bunyad Farhang i Iran.

Habib, Irfan. 1999. *The Agrarian System of the Mughal Empire.* New Delhi: Oxford University Press.

ibn Shahryar al Ram Hurmuzi, Nakhuda Buzurg. 2000. *Ajaib i-Hind.* Translated from Arabic to Persian by Mohammad Malik Zadeh. Tehran.

Kabir, Ananya Jahanara. 2009. *Territory of Desire: Representing the Valley of Kashmir.* Ranikhet: Permanent Black.

Kaw, M. A. 2001. *The Agrarian System of Kashmir, 1586–1819 AD.* Srinagar: Aiman Publishers.

Kinra, Rajeev. 2015. *Writing Self, Writing Empire: Chander Bhan Brahman and the Cultural World of the Indo-Persian State Secretary*. Oakland: University of California Press.

Koch, Ebba. 2009. 'Jahangir as Francis Bacon's Ideal of the King as an Observer and Investigator of Nature'. *Journal of Royal Asiatic Society* 19 (3): 293–338.

Kolff, Dirk H. A. 2002. *Naukar, Rajput and Sepoy: The Ethnohistory of Military Labour Market of Hindostan, 1450–1850*. Delhi: Cambridge University Press.

Kothiyal, Tanuja. 2016. *Nomadic Narratives: A History of Mobility and Identity in the Great Indian Desert*. Delhi: Cambridge University Press.

Kuihami, Pir Hasan. n.d. *Tarikh i Hasan*. Vol. I. Srinagar: Research & Publication Division, J&K Archives.

Lahori, Abdal Hamid. 1867. *Badshahnama*. Vol. II. Edited by Maulavi Kabiruddin Ahmad and Maulavi Abul Rahim. Calcutta: Asiatic Society of Bengal.

Mattoo, A. M. 1988. *Kashmir under the Mughals 1586–1752*. Srinagar: Golden Horde Enterprises.

Mottahedeh, Roy P. 1997. 'Ajaib in The Thousand and One Nights'. In *The Thousand and One Nights in Arabic Literature*, edited by Richard G. Hovannisian and George Sabagh, 29–39. Cambridge: Cambridge University Press.

Pandit, K. N. 1991. *Bahāristān i Shahi*. Calcutta: Firma KLM.

Parmu, R. K. 1969. *History of Muslim Rule in Kashmir*. Delhi: People's Publishing House.

Powers, Daniel, and Naomi Standen, eds. 1999. *Frontiers in Question: Eurasian Borderlands, 700–1700*. New York: Palgrave Macmillan.

Ruggles, D. Fairchild. 2008. *Islamic Gardens and Landscapes*. Philadelphia: University of Pennsylvania Press.

Sachau, Edward C. 2003. *Al Beruni's India*. New Delhi: Indialog Publications Pvt Ltd.

Sharma, Namrita, and Namrata Sharma. 2000. 'Geographical Determinism and the Emergence of Medieval Bundelkhand'. *Proceedings of the Indian History Congress* 61 (1): 553–65.

Sharma, Sunil. 2017. *Mughal Arcadia: Persian Literature in an Indian Court*. Cambridge, Massachusetts: Harvard University Press.

Shekhar, Chander. 2009–10. 'Hadis i Kashmir dar Nuskheh e Khatti Majma' ul Afkar'. *Qand i Parsi: The Quarterly Journal of Persian Culture, Language and Literature* nos. 47–8: 116–56.

Shirazi, Urfi. n.d. *Kulliyat Urfi Shirazi*. Edited by Jawahari. Kitabkhana e Shinasi.

Stein, M. A. trans. 1989 (1900). *Kalhana's Rajatarangini*. Vol. II. Delhi: Munshiram Manoharlal Publishers Pvt. Ltd.

Sufi, G. M. D. 1996. *Kashir, Being a History of Kashmir from the Earliest Times to Our Own*. New Delhi: Capital Publishing House.

Thackston, Wheeler M. ed. 1999. *Jahangirnama: Memoirs of Jahangir, Emperor of India*. New York: Oxford University Press.

Tikku, G. L. 1971. *Persian Poetry in Kashmir 1339–1846: An Introduction*. Los Angeles: University of California Press.

Villiers-Stuart, Constance. 1913. *The Gardens of the Great Mughals*. London: A&C Black.

Zadeh, Travis. 2010. 'The Wiles of Creation: Philosophy, Fiction and the 'Aja'ib Tradition'. *Middle Eastern Literatures* 13 (1): 21–48.

Zaki, M. ed. 2009. *Arab Accounts of India (During the Fourteenth Century)*. Delhi.

Zutshi, Chitralekha. 2014. *Kashmir's Contested Pasts: Narratives, Sacred Geographies and the Historical Imagination*. Delhi: Oxford University Press.

2

Borders in the Age of Empire and Nation-States

The Honeycomb of Borderlands—Kumaun, Western Tibet and Far Western Nepal

VASUDHA PANDE

The map, a totalizing stage on which elements of diverse origin are brought together to form the tableau of a 'state' of geographical knowledge, pushes away into its prehistory or into its posterity, as if into the wings, the operations of which it is the result or the necessary condition. It remains alone on the stage. The tour describers have disappeared.

—Michele de Certeau, *The Practice of Everyday Life* (1984), 122

Borderlands are not fixed, but contingent, the product of historical circumstances. Modern cartography and state systems constructed 'frontiers' and modified exchange and interaction through new governmentalities. Imperial polities and nation-states that replaced them continued to function through such borders, affecting deeply the lives of those at these outposts. I propose to study the impact of such boundaries on communities inhabiting the highlands of South Asia.

This chapter argues that the intrusions of the British imperium into the central Himalayas (Uttarakhand and Far Western Nepal) and the trans-Himalayas (western Tibet) eroded the practice of altitudinal zonation or 'verticality' (Rhoades and Thompson 1975: 535–51), which linked variegated bio-geographies of the trans-Himalayas, upper Himalayas, middle Himalayas and the Bhabhar-Tarai in seasonal rhythms for optimal use of natural resources. The dreaded Tarai, in the south, functioned as the natural boundary (with *awl* fevers and foul vapours). The British transformed the Tarai landscape through rail and road networks which also helped them acquire formal control over the Kumaun Division and informal control over Nepal and Tibet. This reconfiguration modified the northward orientation of the central Himalayas, altered trade flows and affected agro-pastoral regimes, eventually leading to extensive out-migration (towards the south).

Figure 2.1 Himalayan and Trans-Himalayan Mountains
Source: Map from Burrard and Hayden (1933).

An interesting aspect of the mapping of this mountainous terrain was the recognition of the sacred geographies. The connection of the trans-Himalayas, western Nepal and Kumaun through the Kailash Manasarovar circuit, though well known, was now reworked through rail, road, bridle path and other networks. The Gosains of the earlier circuit were replaced by new ascetic groups from the plains. Sacred geographies obscured earlier interconnections and pilgrimage networks overwhelmed and rendered redundant earlier memories and linkages. As the terrain was mapped, this interconnected system became a honeycomb of the borderlands of British India, Tibet and Nepal.

With the advent of nationalism, these borderlands were yoked to different nation-states and brought into the ambit of overarching spatial narratives organised around homogeneous empty time (Anderson 1983: 22–4; P. Chatterjee

2003: 33–58). These histories were not designed for transnational networks and delegitimated connects across borders. This chapter then uses specific and connected histories across the honeycomb of borderlands to decentre and interrogate nationalist histories to help recover shared pasts that have been overlaid with new geographies and new ways of knowing.

The last two decades have witnessed a phenomenal increase in borderlands studies (Hodge 2019: 1–4).[1] The growing interest in this area is to a large extent because of the growing disquiet with nationalist narratives (Matynia 2011: 75–81) which display a cavalier attitude towards regional cum local affiliations. (Beurskens and Miggelbrink 2017: 749–56; Brunet-Jailly 2010: 1–16). This chapter proposes to contextualise the nineteenth-century demarcation of borders, after the Treaty of Sugauli (agreed to in December 1815, ratified in March 1816) and the resultant honeycomb of borderlands in the Himalayas (Kumaun and Far Western Nepal) and trans-Himalayas (western Tibet). It will detail the interactions in the borderlands that emerged with the marking of borders by the East India Company's state (later the British Empire) in the central Himalayas. The Treaty of Sugauli, between the Gorkhas and the East India Company, brought to an abrupt end the Gorkha imperium consisting of a string of 60 principalities stretching from the Tista in the east to the Sutlej in the west (Regmi 1999: x). The treaty created an independent kingdom of Nepal, which lost its territories between Kali and Sutlej (the western divisions of Kangra, Garhwal and Kumaun) and its far western Tarai to the East India Company's state. The Kali River marked the boundary between western Nepal and eastern Kumaun (Aitchison 1892: 173–5). The far western Tarai or plains was controlled by the British until 1860, when it was restored to the Rana rulers of Nepal. On the northern fringe of British India (Kumaun) lay western Tibet or the trans-Himalayas.

These regions—Kumaun, western Tibet and Far Western Nepal—shared a long history of exchange and interaction from the prehistoric period through the Tibetan Empire (seventh–ninth centuries) to the Gorkha Empire (seventeenth–early nineteenth centuries) (V. Pande 2015: 48–53). The interlinkage was based upon an agro-pastoral system, which involved an annual movement of different groups through distinct ecological niches of the trans-Himalayas, upper Himalayas, middle mountains, Bhabhar and Tarai, with the Tarai forming the natural frontier. This sharing of different habitats over the seasons meant fluid boundaries. Given the nature of the terrain, it required controlling the passes into the trans-Himalayas and the passes into the middle mountains. To maintain these networks, trading and pastoralist communities followed a well-regulated framework of customary and ritual practices to demarcate and mark boundaries. These were zealously implemented and no infringements were permitted. Later, even after the conquest of Kumaun, the British desire to map the region was resisted and many surreptitious journeys and considerable British strategy was devoted to making maps of this region (Pathak 2008: 55–75; Sherring 1906: 263–4).

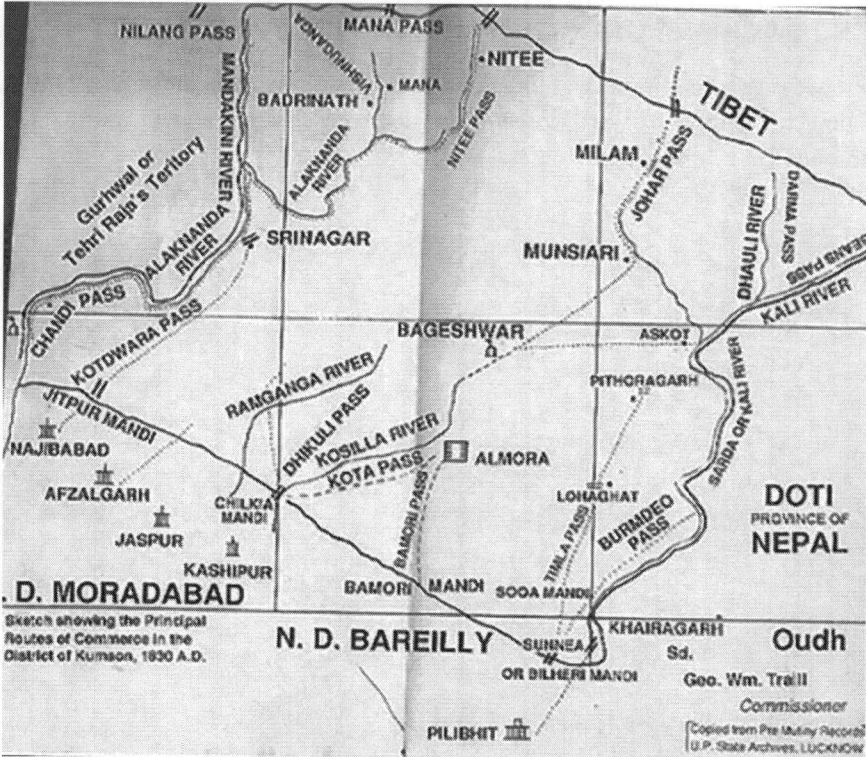

Figure 2.2 Passes of Kumaun
Source: Whalley (1991 [1870]).

In the nineteenth century, all the borderlands under scrutiny were rendered peripheral within their respective states—the Kumaun region was far from the imperial centre at Kolkata (later at Delhi). By peripheral I mean that they were not considered the core regions of those states but were on the margins. As the Kingdom of Nepal, with its capital at Kathmandu, found its feet, Far Western Nepal lost its importance as the epicentre of Khasa culture and the Gorkha state (whose official language was Khasakura) to become an outpost. Western Tibet was also a border province of Tibet, ruled from the capital Lhasa. This chapter is designed to problematise and trace the cross-cutting histories and the impact of new governmentalities of the contiguous regions of Tarai, Kumaun, western Tibet and far western region of Nepal in a single narrative (not premised on nationalist histories or imperial narratives but on interactions and flows of resources).

THE BACKGROUND: GORKHA EMPIRE 1768–1815

From the sixteenth to the eighteenth centuries, the many kingdoms of the central Himalayas and Tibet were closely connected to each other and to north India through a network of trade routes.

Figure 2.3 Trade Routes in the Himalayas
Source: Zurick David and Jalsun Pacheco, illustrated atlas of the Himalayas, map no. 54, http://himalaya.socanth.cam.ac.uk/collections/maps/iah/54-traderoute_color. pdf, accessed on 19 October 2019.
Note: Map not to scale and does not represent authentic international boundaries.

During this period, central Himalayan polities were affected by two major developments—an increase in population subsequent to the introduction of maize, and piecemeal colonisation of the Tarai (Regmi 1999: 72; Whelpton 2005a: 16) The region was divided into a large number of kingdoms, broadly known as the Baisi (22) organised around the Karnali River and the Chaubainsi (24) organised around the Gandaki River. The ascendance of the youngest and smallest member of the Chaubainsi Kingdoms, the Gorkha to overlordship is an inspiring story, fuelled by vision, innovation and enterprise.

Prithvinarayan Shah's success in subjugating Kathmandu was significant (*Regmi Research Series*, 1973, vol. 5: 21–7); after securing his capital he decided to pay attention to trade with Tibet and his concern was the control of the passes with Tibet and a desire to control silver and silver coinage of Tibet (*Regmi Research Series*, 1973, vol. 5: 101–3; Burghart 1984: 101–25). Attempts to wrest greater control over the northern trans-Himalayan trade floundered and a joint force of the Tibetans and the Chinese defeated the Gorkhas (Bahadur Shah) in 1791. Tibet was subsequently closed to outsiders in 1792. Obstructed in the north, the Gorkha state found expansion southwards hampered by other contenders primarily the East India Company (Stiller 1973: 248). The movement westwards, however, continued and the empire eventually stretched from the Tista in the east to the Sutlej in the west. The highland trade network shared by Saukas and Huniyas, Gosains and Naths and other peripatetic groups was affected by increasing monetisation and intervention by an emergent Gorkha elite and also by the East India Company (Whelpton 2005b).

The British were also keen to establish their presence in this trade. Obstructed by the Gorkhali State, they tried to get information by sending their men through Kumaun, where they were arrested by Gorkha administrators (*Regmi Research Series*, 1973, vol. 5: 148–59 and 167–71). The war of 1815 then was significant for control of flows and resources within the Himalayas and the trans-Himalayas and for marking British territorial control on the Anglo-Gorkha Frontier in the Tarai.

THE KUMAUN–RAMPUR AND MORADABAD BORDERLANDS WITHIN BRITISH INDIA

With the takeover of Kumaun, the first issue for the British was access from the south. At the base of the central Himalayan region lay a strip of land called Bhabhar, known for its porous soil where most of the streams and watercourses disappeared into the gravel. Not uniform in breadth, it varied from 0.5 kilometres to 6 kilometres respectively. Below the Bhabhar was the Tarai, a long and narrow strip of low-lying plain, the zone of seepage where the water resurfaced and where the fine sand, silt and clay were deposited by the emerging streams. The level and fertile soil with a high water-table rendered it into a wet and swampy country known for its malarial and *awl* fevers, habitable primarily in the winter. Traditionally, the Kumaun rulers considered both Bhabhar and Tarai integral parts of their kingdom. More significantly, the Tarai formed the upper limit of the Ganga plain, which was increasingly controlled by Rohilla Afghans since the mid-seventeenth century (Gommans 1995: 115; Husain 1994: 71). From this period until 1815, control of the Kumaun Tarai was hotly contested and the north–south connection between the Bhotia traders and the Banjaras suffered disruption until 1815 when British control led to closure of multiple claimants.

In the initial phase of British rule, the Bhabhar and Tarai were not part of Kumaun Division. The upper Bhabhar was under the control of Kumaun, but Bhabhar proper and Tarai were not. The first commissioner of Kumaun, Mr. Traill, found that in Kota and Chakhata Bhabhar of Kumaun, in eight years (1817–23) only 50 villages had been reclaimed by the British administration because of insecurity created by 'bandits'. He argued for a clear demarcation of boundaries. The grazing tax and forest produce tax were farmed out in three leases and cultivation was encouraged. In 1826, a joint report with administrators from neighbouring divisions was adopted, which sorted out boundary disputes. (Atkinson 1981 [1882], vol. III, part I: 58). In 1838, the transfer of magisterial jurisdiction to the plains districts under British control created fresh problems. Kumaun authorities, now attributed the 'falling off of cultivation in the older clearings and of the new ground in the Bhabar' to such administrative issues (Whalley 1991: 71–2). The lieutenant governor was persuaded and the Bhabhar tracts were transferred to Kumaun in 1842, but the 'Tarai was destined to follow a much more tortuous course' (Tolia 1996: 62).

The Tarai (contiguous with Kumaun) presented a different picture. Both cultivation and trade were deeply affected by the uncertain conditions of the eighteenth century. The leaders of the dacoits or marauding groups, the Heris and Mewatis, collected *chowkidari* (watchman) duties on merchandise in transit and a major problem was the theft of cattle. The Gorkha state tried to curb them but eventually not only accepted the status quo but also granted them *jagir*s (revenue free grants of land). Initially, the East India Company government also recognised their *jagir*s. In 1817, Ain Khan Heri was in charge of the traffic passing to and from Bhamauri, Kota and Dhikuli passes with Rudrapur, Chilkia and Kashipur, and Ami Khan Mewati was in charge of trade passing by the Kali Kumaun and Chaubainsi passes with Barmdeo, Bilheri and Pilibhit (Atkinson 1981 [1882], vol. III, part II: 514–16) For a while, military posts were set up and managed by the Kumaun Provincial Battalion. The Heris and Mewatis were encouraged to take to agriculture, but when *dakaiti*s (robberies) continued new measures were enforced.

In 1823, the boundary between Tarai and hill provinces was defined and the Tarai was attached to Rohilkhand Division. In 1832, Mr. Boulderson's Settlement

Report of the Pergunnahs of Gadarpur and Rudrapur noted not only a breakdown of the revenue arrangements but also the complete collapse of the police system. The problem of policing generated a lot of discussion.[2]

Mr. Halhed was deputed as joint magistrate of Moradabad to bring the Heris and the Mewatis under control. *Jagir*s granted to the Heris and the Mewatis were abolished, as was the *chowkidari* system (Atkinson 1981 [1882], vol. III, part II: 514–16). Gradually the entire Tarai, with the exception of the settled portion of Nanakmatta, became an estate under the direct management of the government, to which Kashipur was added in 1870. In 1891, Bhabhar Estate and Tarai Estate were brought together under the deputy commissioner of Nainital. Their amalgamation was proposed in 1894 and ratified in 1895. The pacification and inclusion of the Tarai gave the Kumaun Division a secure southern boundary.

During the nineteenth century, not only were the southern borders of Kumaun restored but British control also facilitated the growth of internal networks. Initially, the British found themselves handicapped not only by the nature of the terrain in the upper Himalayas but also by the very limited nature of the roads in the middle mountains. Through the nineteenth century, the British government worked hard to link Kumaun through roads and railways to the rest of north India. The Gorkhas in their quarter of a century of rule had focussed on the Doti, Baitadi, Almora, Srinagar to Kangra route (*Regmi Research Series*, 1978, vol. 10: 103) which lay on an east–west axis and these were also not of high quality. Constrained by this, Traill noted, '[T]he roads of communication throughout the province consist merely of narrow footpaths, which are only partially practicable for laden cattle, while rocky precipices frequently present themselves, which are scarcely permissible for cattle in any state' (Traill 1828: 137–234). British military activity in the region led to the development of roads on the eastern front, through the foothill passes of Bamouri and Birmdeo (on the Nepal side). One road linked Bamouri with Almora via Bhimtal and Peura, and the other road connected Birmdeo with Pithoragarh via Lohaghat. Almora was also connected with Lohaghat. The fording of rivers by building three bridges began around 1830 and by 1840, six more suspension bridges were constructed over the Ramganga near Rameshwar, Kosilla near Hawalbagh over the Bulleea River, over Saryu, Senril on the Almora–Lohaghat road and over Ramganga on the Pithoragarh road (Tolia 1994: 91). The commercial road in the early years of the nineteenth century was along the Dhikuli pass from Chilkia Mandi to Tibet. Bishop Heber in his journey to Almora in the second decade of the nineteenth century travelled from Rudrapur to Bamouri via Tanda and returned to Meerut via Dhikuli and

Chilkia. He found that Chilkia was the principal mart of trade both into Kumaun and through that country into Tibet (Heber 1873: 212–23)

Gradually as the company consolidated its dominion, and as the threat from Nepal receded, the focus shifted from eastern Kumaun (contiguous with Nepal) towards Nainital. The discovery of Nainital and its development led to the construction of a new route (Pilgrim 1990 [1844]). In 1845, the government assigned the building of a road from Nainital to Khairna and sanctioned money for the establishment of a *mandi* or mart at Kaladhungi.[3] By 1848, a new line from Kaladhungi for passage to Almora and Nainital was sanctioned.[4] In 1855, a new road was built which aligned Kaladhungi to Nainital.[5]

From this period until 1875, Kaladhungi was important because it was on the route from Moradabad to Nainital. By 1873, there were cart roads from Ramnagar to Ranikhet and Almora and from Haldwani to Nainital. Second-class roads were developed from Baramdeo, Haldwani and Ramnagar to Lohaghat, Pithoragarh, Almora, Berinag, Bageshwar and Garhwal, and these bridle roads could be used by mules and horses. Roads also connected Pindari, Milam, Askot, Darma and Byans, the inaccessible upper Himalayas to the rest of the region (Beckett 1874: Appendix 38D). Road construction increased during the commissionership of Ramsay from 1856 to 1884. The growing importance of the forest department also necessitated the building of roads to facilitate the commercialisation of the forests of the hills.

By the early 1880s, communications had improved, with 470 miles of imperial road and 375 miles of road in the Bhotia region of Milam Marchula, Kapkot, Pindar, Munsyari, Thal, Askot, Tejam, Darma, Byans, Chaudans, Berinag and Chaukori (Atkinson 1981 [1882], vol. III, part II: 414–15). The late nineteenth century witnessed a spurt in the construction of roads, not only by the Public Works Department but also by the district boards of Almora and Nainital and also by the Forest Department. The formation of the Nainital district in 1891 probably catalysed the construction of roads (Bengal Secretariat Book Depot: 11). The arrival of the railway line up to Kathgodam on 29 October 1884 linked the region to the rest of north India. In 1907, a railway line to Ramnagar from Moradabad accelerated the process of integration (Sankrityayana 2015: 191). The railway line led to the increasing importance of Haldwani, established in 1834 as a mart.

Gradually, Kumaun was accessible to travellers who were neither adventurers nor explorers. S. Pathak notes that the post-Mutiny period saw a phenomenal increase in the number of tourists to the region (Pathak 1987: 247–52).

The establishment of Nainital in 1846, and the development of a cantonment in Ranikhet in 1869, probably aided this change. By 1901, a visit to the hills was a pleasant affair and the author of *Almoriana* said, '[C]ome to Almora, then, O reader in search of summer residence' (V 1991 [1901]: 5).

The improvement of roads led to the increasing use of ponies and pack animals. Enterprising hillmen with some capital used their mules for carrying surplus produce of the village to local marts and bringing back salt, *gur* (jaggery), cloth, bangles, pins, torches, and so on in exchange (Pant 1935: 112). Part of the grain trade continued in the hands of the Banjaras who had been carrying on business in the region from an early period. The itinerant tradesmen were usually Muslims and Kumbers from the neighbouring plains districts. They kept packs of ponies, mules and asses which brought bales of cloth and grain from Bhabhar and took back bags of turmeric, chillies and potatoes (Matiyani 1990: 204).

The early decades of the twentieth century even saw the development of wheeled traffic in areas where there were fairly serviceable roads. Cart roads between Almora, Ranikhet, Baijnath, Ramnagar and Kathgodam allowed for the use of small bullock carts.[6] By the second decade of the twentieth century, vehicular traffic had started plying along the major routes. In 1919, the price of vehicular traffic was prohibitive (*Shakti*, 4 February 1919). In 1920, Munshi H. P. Tamata started the Hill Motor Transport Company. The lorries ran from Haldwani and Kathgodam to Almora and Ranikhet. Later on, other companies also came up. All companies faced a shortage of drivers and in 1921 H. P. Tamata opened a Hill Motor Training School. By 1930, the major routes were well supplied.

It is found that the British dominion was successful in connecting Kumaun with the plains and the Indian subcontinent, yet Kumaun remained peripheral in many ways.

KUMAUN (INDIA) AND ACROSS THE KALI RIVER–FAR WEST REGION (NEPAL) BORDERLANDS

The Anglo-Gorkha war of 1815 changed many linkages. The British acquired Kumaun and thereby access to Tibet from Kumaun. They also controlled the Kumaun Tarai along with the Kumaun hills. The Gorkhas on the other hand lost not only Kumaun and Kangra but also the far western Tarai. The far western Nepali hill trade and the Tibet–Nepal trade was now inhibited by the problem of access to the plains since the far western Tarai was not under the control of Nepal.

This had an adverse effect on the trade of Darma, Byans and Jumla, which lost all their trade outlets in the Nepal Tarai (Pandey 1997: 455–8).

The nineteenth century was therefore a period of retrogression for the far western region of Nepal. The restructuring of the Nepal kingdom reduced the far western region to an outpost located on the western border (Ojha 1992: 84–102). A government concerned about safety and security placed restrictions on trade, and Indians and Europeans were not granted easy access. In pursuance of this policy, trade routes were closed and the few that remained open were regularly policed (Stiller 1976: 123). An order after Sagauli categorically stated, 'Close all tracks in the area and render them unusable by planting bamboo, cane and thorny bushes as before' (*Regmi Research Series*, 1981, vol. 13: 99). H. A. Oldfield, an English observer, states, 'The Nipalese are averse to the clearing of these forests as they look upon the malarious jungle at the foot of the hills as the safest and surest barrier' (Oldfield 1974 [1880]: 47). The government believed that the forests provided security and did not encourage the building of roads and bridges for the facilitation of trade.

The arterial route between Kathmandu and Baitadi, critical for the expanding Gorkha Empire, now lost its importance and Dotee became a provincial centre. The connection between Dotee and Kathmandu was well established, but provincial centres were not linked to each other. L. F. Stiller finds 'the tedious pace of growth' (Stiller 1976: 134) disturbing. The process of monetisation which had begun in the eighteenth century was now obstructed and, as B. Bishop notes, 'in the central and western hills there was no development of inter-regional trade of the type that could have led to the growth of a system of hat bazars because high rents denied the farmer the agricultural surplus necessary for such trade and government fiscal policies drained off what little cash he had without recirculating it' (Bishop 1970: 11).

In spite of these obstacles, the trade of western Nepal with India and Tibet continued. The Gorkhas and the post-1815 Nepal state may have wanted to close Nepal to the East India Company but they were keen to continue and promote trade with the trans-Himalayas. The Nepal government was clearly aware of the importance of this trade for its own economic well-being. In the mid-nineteenth century, a road was built on the western Himalayas to facilitate the trade (Hodgson 1874: 97). Given the importance of this trade for the Baisi region, local administrators also supported traders and helped the traders of Darma, Byans and Jumla to find new outlets for the import and export of their goods with Tibet.

In the west two important trade points developed, the mart near Jhulaghat in the middle mountains, which connected Kumaun to western Nepal across the Kali from November to June, and at Birmadeo in the Tarai, which connected western Nepal to Tanakpur in India (Batten 1851). In the initial years the far western Tarai was under the control of Awadh, but it was returned to Nepal in 1858. The restoration of the far western Tarai to Nepal marked a new era and a change of policy vis-à-vis British India. The British encouraged the Ranas to open Nepal to informal control. Landlocked Nepal was gradually integrated with the empire without acquiring formal control.

The process of the demarcation of the new borders was completed by 1860, and the western Tarai became a part of the Nepal Kingdom now called Naya Mulk. Jang Bahadur ordered local administrators to reopen existing irrigation channels and to build new ones. The *Muluki-Ain* of 1856 encouraged agricultural enterprise and had a provision which provided any peasant who brought land under the plough a tax exemption for five years and any one bringing virgin land under cultivation would be able to retain one-tenth of that land under *birta* (rent free). Tarai cultivation remained precarious because of the nature of the terrain, which often debilitated the farmer with malaria. A single epidemic could easily lead to the contraction of agriculture. In spite of this, because of the fertility of the soil and support for irrigation by the Rana state, cultivators were willing to shift from the northern hills to the Tarai region (*Regmi Research Series*, 1982, vol. 14: 181–4). Trade was carried on at the marts of Tulsipur, Bairampur and Nanpari in India. Jang Bahadur persuaded Indian merchants to cross the frontier and start trading at Gola Mandi. Regmi suggests that the success of Nepalganj may also be attributed to the coming of railways to the Indian side of the border (*Regmi Research Series*, 1983, vol. 15: 72–5). Eventually, some Indian traders took up residence at Nepalganj and, gradually, the Nepalganj forests were cleared under the supervision of the government and the town of Nepalganj developed on the south-western border of India and Nepal. By the early years of the twentieth century, other market towns—Birgunj, Golaghat, Nepalganj—had also come up in the Tarai with the active support of the Nepali state (*Regmi Research Series*, 1986, vol. 18: 76).

As regards the trade with Tibet, it is found that the boundaries between Nepal and India were porous and a shared sense of identity and history on both sides of the Kali helped. E. T. Atkinson noted that 'the Byans (Upper Himalayas) people can easily evade any order that they think vexatious by migrating to Nepal, and they have no respect for law, except so far as it makes itself felt by them' (Atkinson

1981 [1882], vol. III, part I: 83–151). It is apparent that by the second half of the nineteenth century, Nepal's trade with Tibet was being rerouted through Jhulaghat and Birmdeo in Kumaun. The Nepal government levied taxes on its side of the Kali in Jhulaghat and Birmdeo. The trade of Darma (Kumaun) increased elevenfold (between 1841 and 1900) whereas the trade of neighbouring and prosperous Johar (further west) increased only two and a quarter times (Atkinson 1981 [1882], vol. III, part II: 538). As a consequence, the 'Bhotias' dominated the trade in Shor or Pithoragarh.

The increase in trade probably facilitated the development of the Jauljibi fair, which was held at the confluence of the Kali and the Gori Rivers; it was instituted by the Rajbar of Askot in India in 1914. The importance of Jauljibi was that it lay at the junction of four important routes leading from Nepal, Askot, Johar and Darma, respectively. S. D. Pant noted that

> the celebration of the fair coincides with the opening of the pass and the bridge to Nepal. During the rains the river Kali sweeps away its bridge and it becomes very formidable. But during November a temporary bridge, which lasts until July, is constructed by some of the villagers from Dotee who are exempted from the import and export duties levied by the Nepal government. (Pant 1935: 198)

He reported that the trade in Nepali ghee, grains and fruit formed an important aspect of the transactions. In the first few decades of the twentieth century, ponies from Tibet, Bhot and Jumla were important merchandise.

Prithvi Narayan Shah was aware of 'several dozen types of cloth' of cotton goods produced in the Kathmandu valley and the scope for expansion (Stiller 1976: 124). He elaborates on this in *Dibya Updesh* where he recommends homespun cloth and refuses entry to Indian and East India Company merchants (Stiller 1989: 69–70). In keeping with this policy, the Gorkhas were wary of transactions with the East India Company and the government charged high customs duties on goods coming into Nepal until the 1840s (Oldfield 1974 [1880]: 301). Brian Hodgson, the resident, resented this, but until Bhim Sen Thapa was in charge, he could not intervene. But during the second half of the nineteenth century, under the Rana dispensation, Nepal emerged as an importer of cotton products, raw cotton, yarn (European and Indian) and cotton-piece goods, both European and Indian (Michael 2014: 535–58).

Gradually, over the second half of the nineteenth century, the commodity composition of Nepal's trade with British India underwent a major transformation. Western Nepal witnessed a decline of its iron and copper manufacturers during this period and it gradually started importing metal goods. By the last years of the nineteenth century, its imports of iron and other metal products far exceeded its dwindling exports. Towards the end of the nineteenth century, Nepal was importing iron, copper, other metals, sugar refined and unrefined, petroleum, provisions, woollen-piece goods and even salt. Its exports consisted of timber, livestock, turmeric, fibrous products, rice, pulse, wheat, spring crops, hides and skins, sheep and goats, ghee, wax, and so on.[7] The reports from 1908–18 also indicate an export surplus with British India. An increase in import of sambhar salt also indicates an integration with the Southern imperial economy; between 1833 and 1898 the quantity of salt imported increased 42 times.[8] The change in the commodity composition of trade indicates that Nepal was integrated into the imperial economic system.

This change was also accompanied by an increasing problem of agriculture in the middle Himalayan region of Far Western Nepal. This meant that agricultural productivity did not increase and the petty peasant was under a dual system of control—of state and *jagirdar* where slavery was also recognised. Migration from the hill region in search of employment started during the nineteenth century (Regmi 1978: 134). Migration during the slack season was not a permanent affair, it was linked to the agrarian cycle, and the migrant tended to return home for the labour-intensive season (Dahal, Rai and Manzardo 1977: 1). Shrestha studied the northern region of Jumla and noted that 'expanded seasonal and long-term migrations and extended extra-regional trading became increasingly indispensable components of the subsistence system for a majority of the local population' (Shrestha 1993: 98).

British administrators of Kumaun noted the migration to British territories. As early as 1821, an official noted that Shor (Pithoragarh) on the eastern border of Kumaun 'formed till a late period a part of the principality of Dotee, on the western border of Kumaun.... Within the last three years a considerable influx of cultivators from adjoining Gorkha province of Dotee has taken place in Shor ...'.[9] By the early years of the twentieth century, Shor was the most densely populated pargana of Kumaun, with a density of 540 persons per square mile (Pant 1935: 76). By the early twentieth century, the drain of manpower from the hills of Nepal ceased to be primarily a seasonal phenomenon (Kansakar 1984: 49–69). 'Dotiyal' became the new term for migrants from Dotee to Kumaun in the colonial period, which is still in use (Bill 2003: 55; Bruslé 2008). A factor responsible for increasing migration from western Nepal to Kumaun was the underdevelopment of the far western Tarai, which was yet to be reclaimed. The actual development of the Tarai would have to wait for the malaria eradication programme of the World Health Organisation, which arrived in 1965.

Another fallout of British control was the recruitment of 'Gurkhas' into the British Army. Initially, it was a covert arrangement because the Nepal government did not approve clandestine operations for recruitment and took punitive measures. This did not result in compliance. The British then encouraged migration and 'Gurkha' establishments came up in Dharamshala, Darjeeling, Shillong and Dehradun. The Rana regime, which came to power in 1846, realised the futility of the embargo. It even established an office in Baitadi Jhulaghat to recruit soldiers for the British Army (*Regmi Research Series*, 1981, vol. 13: 61). By 1904, three 'Gurkha' battalions of 1816 had swelled into 16 and by 1908, the 'Gurkha' Brigade had reached its permanent establishment of 20 battalions organised in ten rifle regiments. It is estimated that 200,000 Nepalese participated in the First World War with casualties amounting to 20,000 (Kansakar 1984: 52). The emergence of 'Gurkhas' as a 'race' with exceptional martial qualities is also a product of a new dispensation (Caplan 2006: 225–45). The internal differentiation between the various cultural groups of Nepal that is Magar, Gurung, Limbu and Rai were brought under a single ethnonym of 'Gurkha'.

KUMAUN–WESTERN TIBET BORDERLANDS

Regular trade between Kumaun and western Tibet may be traced back to the ninth century. The routes were difficult and Kumauni folklore is replete with adventures on these journeys. Early travellers to Kumaun and Garhwal also noted the innovative nature of the communication system in the hills. For example, Hardwicke who travelled to Srinagar in 1796 found that the Nayar River was crossed by canoes made from the bark of trees (Hardwicke 1801: 309–47). Other visitors like Colebrooke and Moorcroft were appalled by the difficulty encountered in negotiating the route (Colebrooke 1812: 429–45; Moorcroft 1816: 375–535).

This trade was linked to the exigencies of nomadism in the upper Himalayas and was in the hands of the 'Bhotias' (a term applied to traders of the upper Himalayas who conducted trade with the trans-Himalayan regions) who combined the role of shepherds with merchants. Tibet was accessible through the mountain passes, which were open for about six months of the year. Trade was carried on by migration from one set of summer dwellings situated in high cold valleys towards the Tibetan frontier. These summer habitations at Milam, Martoli, Burfu, Go,

Garbyang, Kuti and Nabi served as bases for the Tibetan trade and as depots and stores for the exports to Tibet (Pant 1935: 48–60). The summer residences were close to the *bugyal/payar* (meadows) where the 'Bhotias' would take their flock for summer pasturing. Usually, two trips to Tibet were undertaken during the summer and the raw wool from Tibet was spun and woven by the women while residing in the summer camps. By late September and early October, the shift to the winter residences in the warmer localities such as Tejam, Dharchula, Sobla, Thal, Galanti, Nigalpani and Askot would begin. The major transactions were carried on at the various fairs.

The 'Bhotia' traders were not a homogeneous undifferentiated community. The difference between the Johari and those of Darma and Byans can be traced back to the seventeenth century when the Joharis were able to extract special concessions from Tibetan authorities.[10] This obviously gave them an edge over the other 'Bhotias'. The difficulties faced by this trade necessitated the elaboration of a rigorous system to regulate trade practices. New entrants to the trade were discouraged by the practice of *mitra*s or designated partner, which sanctioned trade and was initiated by a religious ceremony. Even the amount of exchange was controlled and decided beforehand to prevent an increase in the supply of particular goods. Traders were restricted to trade with their partners, and traders of a certain region were required to trade with a particular region in Tibet. This also prevented a glut in the market and provided a system of monitoring and regulating the volume of trade along the passes. The difficulties of the terrain were overcome with the use of sheep and goats as carriers. Sheep could carry up to 15 to 28 seers and goats from 8 to 10 seers. The routes traversed took many days and in the most difficult part yaks were often used, and sometimes hybrid yaks known as jibus were also used. The exchange was carried out by barter and the exchange rate varied from three to four of wheat or rice for one of salt (Traill 1992: 133–4).

European interest in the trans-Himalayas dates to the early years of the seventeenth century, when the first reconnaissance mission was sent in 1603. This was followed by an expedition headed by Antonio de Andrade and Manuel Marques in 1624. Andrade got as far as Deotal at the head of the Mana valley and then beyond to an awful descent into a desolate country of ravines and canyons, part of the ancient kingdom of Guge (Mckay 2015: 375–6; Wessels 1924: 78–80). The capital of Guge was Tsaparang, which along with the nearby monastery of Toling was the political and religious centre of western Tibet. Ippolito Desideri decided to travel to this region in 1712 (Allen 1982: 33–41). With the help of a Portuguese patron he was able to organise his expedition and approached Tibet via the Kashmir route. From Srinagar in Kashmir to Leh, and then beyond to Tibet, he was able to travel across the Kailash Manasarovar and beyond to Lhasa which he reached in 1716. The East India Company's interest in the Himalayan and trans-Himalayan trade was part of its search for new commodities for exchange between Asia and Europe. With the acquisition of Bengal, the English realised the significance of commercial intercourse between Bengal and Tibet and were keen to expand their network and to participate in this trade. Warren Hastings sent George Bogle to Tibet in 1774, by way of Bhutan. The British traders were interested in the Tibetan trade because they hoped to enter the Central Asian and Chinese trade via Tibet. They felt that Tibet could be accessed through Kumaun in spite of the closure of Nepal to British trade (*Regmi Research Series*, 1973, vol. 5: 148–59 and 167–71).

John Pemble suggests that the East India Company's interest in Tibet and the trans-Himalayan trade was determined by various factors—Tibet was known as a source of precious metals, which would help to rectify the drain of silver from Britain to India, Tibet could provide a market for English cloth and woollens, and Tibet would grant the British access to shawls, a commodity which could replace Indian cotton goods (Pemble 1971: 54–86). By 1815, however, it appears that the calculation may have changed because the flow of treasure from Britain was not required as the investment came from the revenues of Bengal. Eagerness to open new markets for English woollens also was not easy to implement and though interest in shawl wool did persist, it was constrained by considerations of good relations with the Sikhs.

The takeover of Kumaun by the East India Company affected the Indo-Tibetan trade, which was in flux during the turbulent period of the eighteenth century. Increasing monetisation created a problem for the 'Bhotia' traders who needed to invest large amounts of capital in non-barter trade. 'Bhotia' traders had suffered from heavy exactions by the Gorkha government when the revenues of Bhot were farmed out to local moneylenders and financiers.[11]

Many 'Bhotias' were thus indebted to the Sahukars of Almora. The trend towards monetisation was clearly evident in the Bhabhar (south) trade circuit. By the 1930s, the Bhabhar trade was conducted in cash (Pant 1935: 166–71). Like the Gorkhas before them, the British also resented the monopoly of the 'Bhotias' over the Indo-Tibetan trade. The Gorkhas had encouraged the residents of Nagpur, Dasauli and other parganas to enter the trade but they made little impact (Atkinson 1981 [1882], vol. III, part I: 140). In 1815, Dr. Rutherford who was in charge of the Company's investment in Moradabad proposed a deputation to Tibet with a view to open up the trade between the company and the natives of that country. He noticed that the Almora merchants who came to Kashipur for the purchase of English cloth and manufactures went back to Almora and sold them to the 'Bhotias'. From there, the 'Bhotia' traders carried it to Gartok and other places in Tibet, 'thus four sets of profits were made on the goods and this so enhanced the price' (Atkinson 1981 [1882], vol. III, part I: 138). Yet attempts at direct intercourse of the company with Tibet were soon abandoned.

By the middle of the nineteenth century, interest in borax from Tibet had fallen because of the discovery of mines in Tuscany and manufacture from boric acid. Though the trade in borax continued, it was no longer a commodity in great demand. The British were primarily interested in the wool trade. The Sikh interest in wool, with the campaign of Zorawar Singh and his entry into Tibet, brought tensions with the Sikhs to the fore. An aspect of the Anglo-Sikh war of the 1840s was the desire to break the monopoly of Ladakh and Kashmir merchants over the wool trade (Dutta 1970: 16–28; Brown 1992: 146–72). After the Treaty of Amritsar in 1846, the British border was extended and gradually Tibetan trade was integrated into the British imperial system. British presence at the borders gradually led to the restructuring of the wool trade.

By the 1870s, there was an increase in the imports of raw wool and a consequent decline in the imports of manufactured woollen goods (Atkinson 1981 [1882], vol. III, part I: 139). This was linked to the development of the woollen mills at Kanpur (Pant 1935: 62). The growing demand for raw wool led to an increase in the import of raw wool from Tibet and the upper Himalayas of Kumaun. By the 1890s, the amount of wool brought down to Tanakpur, in the east, had increased, and the 'Bhotias' were being paid advances by the Kanpur mills for the supply of this commodity. The demand for raw wool generated through the advances given by the Kanpur mills also led to the diversification of wool from Kulu to Almora. Over the nineteenth century, local handloom industry declined and raw wool was diverted to Kanpur and by the twentieth century, this had restructured the wool trade and brought the Kumaun and Tibet economies into the ambit of the British Empire (Brown 1994: 215–58; Pant 1935: 166–71).

British state policy continued attempts to break the monopoly of 'Bhotia' trade. For example, the Association of Chambers of Commerce in Britain welcomed the 1886 Convention because it opened up Tibet to British trade (Brown 1992: 146–72). Yet the difficulty of penetrating Tibetan commerce remained and British pressure was mounted on Tibet by the expedition of Colonel Younghusband, which yielded three trade agencies in Tibet, Yatung, Gyantse and Gartok in 1904

(McKay 1997: xxvi). The assault on monopolistic trade eventually led to the Treaty of Lhasa in 1904, which 'introduced free trade and changed the old order of things' (McKay 1997: xxvi). Thakur Jai Chand was the appointed agent and the district commissioner of Almora made the first official visit in 1905.

Over the nineteenth century, the 'Bhotias' faced not only a major decline in trade in borax but also as a result of better linkages with the south, the 'Bhotia' trader suffered a decline in (barter trade) the demand for salt. Sambhar salt from the plains was cheaper than Tibetan salt and made inroads into Kumaun. The rising prices of grain, and frequent grain shortages in the last years of the nineteenth century and the early years of the twentieth century, probably facilitated the shift to plains salt in the monetised regions of Kumaun. By the 1930s, trade in salt and borax had diminished enormously owing to Italian borax and salt from the plains (Pant 1935: 120).

The commodity structure of Indo-Tibetan export–import trade by the last years of the nineteenth century indicates a transformation.[12] Earlier, grain was one of the major commodities for export from Kumaun to Tibet. The decline in grain exports around the 1890s can be linked to the increase in agricultural prices and to grain shortages. This can also be linked to the increase in export of European cloth to Tibet over the nineteenth century.

The close and intimate relationship between the Himalayas and the trans-Himalayas was eroded, and the monopolistic structure which regulated the trade declined. Imperial markets penetrated not only the Kumaun Himalayas but also the western Tibet highlands. Local industries based upon wool production declined because of an increase in the exports of raw wool, and the local industries of Kashipur and Jaspur which had provided locally manufactured cotton cloth were overtaken by European cloth and Indian yarn.[13]

The Kumaun intelligentsia reported this in the *Almora Akhbar* (21 August 1900) and attributed the impoverishment of Kumaun to the decline of trade in borax and salt and local wool industry. The system of free trade through the agency system did not simplify the trade situation, and 'Bhotia' complaints against the system multiplied. In 1905, Sherring's visit to Tibet and his negotiations with the Jongpons did not result in any major benefits for the 'Bhotias' or other traders, and the British agent remained ineffective (Sherring 1906: 157). In 1919, the 'Bhotias' complained that they were being denied access to a mart beyond Gartok, and the *Shakti* of 1925 also noted that the new trade policy was creating a fresh set of problems for the 'Bhotia' traders.

The Johari group was the most articulate of the 'Bhotia' groups. Its visibility was also an aspect of its linkage with the intelligentsia of the Kumaun region. In 1920, the Johar branch of the Kumaun Parishad was inaugurated. The Johar traders functioned as a group and established the Johar Himalaya Company with an initial capital of Rs 20,000. It had five directors and was engaged in the wool trade. It advertised regularly in the local newspaper and booked orders by value payable post (V.P.P.) (*Shakti*, 25 February 1921). The innovativeness of the Johar traders helped them to adapt to the changing demands of trade caused by the integration of Kumaun with the British economic system.

The 'Bhotias' found themselves under pressure because of the demands of the colonial regime. They had to pay a large number of taxes to the government—land tax, a tax on livestock, a tax on trade, toll tax, income tax, along with taxes to the Nepal and Tibet governments (*Shakti*, 24 February 1925). They were also required to pay a pasturage fee for transit through areas declared reserved forests. In the region of Kali Kumaun, on the Tanakpur route where the 'Bhotias' had established a wool and borax depot, the forest guards made life particularly difficult for the 'Bhotias' (*Shakti*, 8 December 1923). By the 1930s, the 'Bhotias' were no longer in control either of trade routes or trade. In the south, they were supplanted by new trading groups (Pant 1935: 222) and the Kumaun villager was becoming accustomed to the commercial Muslim traveller and to the itinerant middleman invariably from the poor soil *patti*s (strip of land) of Tikhun and Phaldakot.

Indo-Tibetan trade therefore appears to have been subjected to three phases of change: the first from 1815 to 1850, with some changes as a sequel to the Anglo–Sikh war and the extension of the British boundary up to Tibet, the second from 1850 to 1890 which resulted in the integration of the trans-Himalayan economy with the British imperial system and from 1890 to 1930 when a major restructuring of the Indo-Tibetan trade occurred. Towards the early years of the twentieth century the 'Bhotias' faced a new situation. The relationship between the trans-Himalayas and the Himalayas was eroded by the advent of new modes of transport and communication. The commodity composition of trade was modified, and the 'Bhotias' lost their monopoly. The colonisation of the Kumaun economy changed the structure of its trade; the trans-Himalayas lost its significance and Kumaun looked southwards, beyond the Tarai. A significant aspect of the mapping of the Indo-Tibetan trade from Kumaun was the emergence of the term 'Bhotia' which has been consistently marked with single inverted commas, because it was contested by the people for whom the term was used (Figure 2.4).

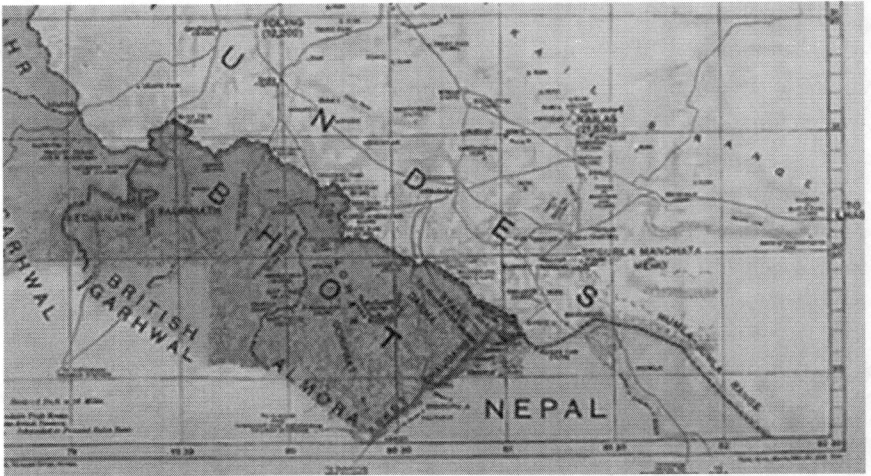

Figure 2.4 Map Showing a Clear Demarcation between Bhot (British) and Hundesh (Tibet)
Source: Sherring (1906).

CHANGING CONFIGURATIONS: NATIONALIST NARRATIVES AND DIVERGENT HISTORIOGRAPHIES

To the imperial order, the Himalayas and the trans-Himalayas held out the promise of trade with China and Central Asia, but it took almost a century to establish control. An infrastructure of roads and communications was required along with knowledge about the region. Over the nineteenth century, the British marked their dominion through a network of roads and also through a massive cartographic exercise (Burrard and Hayden 1933). Gradually, the Tibetan blockade crumbled, and the British were able to enter the trans-Himalayan trade and break into the various trade circuits that spanned the Himalayas and trans-Himalayas (van Spengen 1995: 18–63). In the process, they affected and transformed an intricate patchwork of agro-pastoral regimes that knit together a variety of ecological niches vertically and laterally, with the Tarai as the natural boundary (V. Pande 2018a: 19–58).

British demarcation produced extensive dis-articulation and reconfiguration of borders in the Asian highlands. British concern with land revenue meant the encouragement of agricultural extension and support for the peasant economy at the cost of pastoral nomadism (Dangwal 2009: 84–101). Scientific forestry rendered the forest a state preserve and as peasant control over forest and commons declined (Guha 1985: 1939–41, 1943, 1945–7, 1949, 1951–2), increasing monetisation and shortage of food grains in the region led to an out-migration of male labour from both Kumaun and Nepal (Bora 1996: 13–19). The integration of Kumaun with north India also brought Far Western Nepal and western Tibet into the informal ambit of the empire and produced extensive dis-articulation, within a framework that had been functional for a millennium.

The shared history of this honeycomb of borderlands was now delegitimised and each region was drawn into a contemporary state-oriented narrative. Kumaun wrote its history as part of an emergent Indian nation, Far Western Nepal was now part of the 'unification' and western Tibet enveloped in mystery became part of the 'Forbidden Land'.

In the context of the contiguous region of Far Western Nepal and the region of Kumaun (not the Division), similarities can be illustrated by pre-Gurkha histories and by historical documents of the Gorkha period, yet, the historiographical traditions of Kumaun and western Nepal about Gorkha rule are so utterly different. This divergence can be linked to the fact that after 1815, the two contiguous territories divided by the Kali River became part of two different national traditions—the region of Far Western Nepal was incorporated into the Kingdom of Nepal and Kumaun became a division of the Indian portion of the British Empire. The period of Gorkha rule was therefore contextualised differently in the histories of the nation-states of Nepal and India.

The historiography of Gorkha rule in Kumaun is dominated by colonial writing. Atkinson, who compiled and edited the *Gazetteer* of the Kumaun Division created an image of the Gorkhas as barbaric and savage, with a non-functional administration (Atkinson 1981 [1882], vol. II, part II: 618–34). In his writing on the Gorkha period, he cited the early British visitors to Gorkha Kumaun: F. V. Raper and J. B. Fraser. Citing F. V. Raper, Atkinson noted that 'the people are most vehement in their complaints against the Gorkhalis, of whom they stand in the utmost dread' (Atkinson 1981 [1882], vol. II, part II: 621). He also referred to J. B. Fraser, who travelled in the region around 1814, stating that the

> Gorkhalis ... ruled with a rod of iron and that the country had fallen
> into a lamentable decline. Its villages became deserted, its agriculture
> ruined, and its population decreased beyond computation. It is said
> that two lakhs of people were sold as slaves, while few families of
> consequence, remained in the country.... [The Gorkhas] despised the
> people they had conquered, so that at some distance from the seat of

> government executions went on, insults and scenes of rapine were
> continually acted and the hatred of the people to their tyrants was
> fixed and exasperated ... the country was subdued and crushed, not
> reconciled or accustomed to the yoke. (Atkinson 1981 [1882], vol. II,
> part II: 621–2)

These references were probably chosen by Atkinson in his review of the history
of the region to represent the colonial perspective. It is interesting to find that
Atkinson's quotation from Raper is incorrect—Raper's actual statement was
that 'all classes of people complain much of the peculation of the chiefs, and of
the injustice with the want of method that attends most of their proceedings'
(Raper 1810: 414–563). Atkinson's deliberate exaggeration was motivated by his
desire to contrast Gorkha rule with British rule in Kumaun. This juxtaposition
was illustrated by the Gorkha endorsement of slavery and its abolition by the
British. Gorkha rule was therefore depicted as savage, tyrannical and highly
oppressive, whereas British rule was civilised, enlightened, benevolent and
mild. By his castigation of the Gorkhas, Atkinson was justifying British rule
in Kumaun.

Subsequent authors, even avowed nationalists, accepted his assumptions
without question. B. D. Pande, who wrote the first nationalist history of
Kumaun in Hindi in the 1930s, noted that under Gorkha rule the people of
Kumaun were tortured, compelled to pay heavy taxes and made victims of a
number of atrocities. He cited a number of stories regarding Gorkha atrocities
and was surprised to find that the people of Kumaun did not register their
opposition to Gorkha rule. B. D. Pande (1990 [1937]: 383–405) appears to
take off from where Atkinson had begun. Shekhar Pathak, in his history of
resistance of the Kumaun peasantry to the forced labour levied by British rule,
written in the 1980s, also argued that the Gorkha interregnum was oppressive
and violent. He said that the Gorkhas refined feudal forms of oppression and
established new modes of surplus mobilisation. They imported into Kumaun a
militarist feudal system, based upon slavery, forced labour and revenue taxation
(Pathak 1987: 35–9).

Dabral's study of Gorkha rule, which is much more thorough, and which
was based upon Gorkha records, was also unable to move out of the groove of
the colonial mindset when he chose to view Gorkhas as foreign oppressors. He
noted that under the military rule of the Gorkhas, scholars and artists lost their
employment and many Brahmans were compelled to leave their homeland. He
added that during the 12 years of rule in Garhwal, the Gorkhas kept a large

number of Garhwali women as concubines and had children by them, but no Gorkhali ever settled on a permanent basis in any village of Garhwal (Dabral 2030/1973: 120). This statement is incorrect and it is surprising that someone like Dabral, in spite of available documentary evidence to the contrary, was unable to articulate a different perspective on Gorkha rule. Gorkha rule in Kumaun has to be located in the specific historical perspective of the eighteenth century and in the context of a mountain economy. Kumaun was only one province in the large Gorkha Empire, and it has to be located within that frame rather than taken out of context and located as a Gorkha interregnum in Kumauni history (V. Pande 2014: 106–42).

The historiography of Gorkha rule in western Nepal, on the other hand, is entirely different. Gorkha rule was regarded by writers like Surya Bikram Gyawali (who wrote in the period from 1918 to 1956) as the 'unification' era which created a modern Nepali *jati*. Gyawali's biographies (1933a, 1933b) of the ancestors of Prithvi Narayan Shah—Drabya Shah and Ram Shah—developed the argument for the 'unification' of Nepal under Prithvi Narayan Shah (Gyawali 1976 [1935]). His biography of the 'unifier' king of Nepal glorified his campaigns and conquests. He later on published another biography of the Gorkhali commander Amar Singh Thapa who was central to the expansion of the Gorkha Empire in Garhwal and Kumaun (Gyawali 1943; see also for Amar Singh Thapa, Stiller 1973: 215–47). Amar Singh Thapa was also responsible for the further conquest westwards towards the cis-Sutlej states, and the history of Gorkha expansion from 1791 to 1813 was written as a history of the campaigns of Amar Singh Thapa. Gyawali (2018) also wrote a history of the battle of Nalapani in which the hero Balabhadra defeated a section of the British Army. These histories of the *bir* or heroes of the Gorkha period constructed by intellectuals like Gyawali and Babu Ram Acharya provided the staple for the histories of Nepal written during the period of Panchayat Raj. The Gorkha period was thus contextualised as the glorious period of the 'unification' of the Nepali *jati*, which laid the basis for the formation of the Nepali nation, the foundational history of Nepal (Onta 1996: 37–76). Onta says that construction tends to be mythologised. He argues for a more historical approach and a critical reading of Bir history, 'by the state as the dominant mode of national history of Nepal. During the Panchayat era, it was disseminated through the gradually nationalised education system and became, along with the Nepali language, Hinduism and the monarchy one of the essential features of the national culture of Nepal'.

Kumar Pradhan cites an interesting metaphor:

> Subanandadas views the subjugation of different states (part of
> unification) as different items in the king's sumptuous supper. The items
> are described as the Sinki (dried radish) of Nepal fried in the butter of
> Magrat with condiments like asafoetida and cumin of Palpa, seasoned
> with the pungency of Rising, served with the rice of Tanahu and lentil
> of Bhirkot. This is echoed in an old folk rhyme in which the defeated
> states are referred to metonymically by their respective principal
> products. It describes him (Gorkha) as the wise who pulverized maize
> (Dolakha), held dried fish (terai or Mankwanpur) in the fist, pressed
> sinki (the Nepal Valley), broke the lump of salt (Kaskiand Parbat
> through which salt came from Tibet), mowed down kodo, black millet
> (Western Nepal, especially from Dailekh to Kumaun), prepared curd
> (Dang) and set free (for grazing) his sheep (Kuti and Jerung from
> where sheep were imported; the passes which we surrendered to Tibet)
> for the great festival of *dasai*. (Pradhan 1991: 155–6)

For the people of Kumaun and the far west of Nepal, who were located at the
margins of their respective nation-states this process delegitimised their specific
historical linkages. The break-up of the 'verticality' of connected bio-regimes led
to the articulation of distinct and new identities. An important aspect of British
rule was its legitimation of the Brahmanical perspective as the Hindu world view.
Atkinson's foundational history provided a palimpsest and evolutionary view of
Himalayan history—Doms as aboriginal dwellers, succeeded by Aryan Khasas,
Aryan Khasas defeated by Brahmans and Kshatriyas from the plains, with the
British at the top, dominating the upper castes, the most evolved group of all (V.
Pande 1996: 106–20). As a consequence, in both Nepali and Kumauni history,
Khasa became a category with which none could identify and was relegated to the
hoary past, with no takers amongst the nineteenth- and twentieth-century elite.
Dor Bahadur Bista in his first anthropological piece on the people of Nepal in
1973 did not mention the Khasas, though Khasakura is the other name for Nepali.
Many years later, he included the Khasa in a revised edition of his work, with
an apology (Bista 2052/1995: 65–72). In Nepal, the Khasa Brahmin became the
Jaisi and the Khasa Kshatriya adopted the term Chettri (Sharma 1977: 277–99;
Furer-Haimendorf 1966: 11–160). In Kumaun and Garhwal, the Khasa Brahmins
became *chotti dhoti* (short cloth)[14] Brahmins and the Khasa Kshatriyas chose to
identify with the Rajputs (V. Pande 2013: 38–56).

The historiography of western Tibet, contiguous with the central Himalayas,
was also deeply affected by imperial intrusions and nationalist ideas. The surreptitious

journeys of Moorcroft and the pundits became legendary; Sven Hedin (1913, 1910, 1909) gave western Tibet global recognition. Burrard and the Survey of India (Burrard and Hayden 1933, part 1, Frontispiece, Himalayan and Trans-Himalayan Systems, and part 2: 109–15) completed the cartographic exercise and established Tibet as the roof of the world. The discovery and mapping of the trans-Himalayas makes a fascinating story of adventure and discovery and is well documented by Charles Allen (1982: 75–97, 120–44, 190–212) and Alex McKay (2015, 56–7).

Disaggregated by British boundaries, this marking of dominion also generated a new knowledge that emphasised racial difference. Tibetan culture was marked as Mongoloid, the other of the Indo-Aryan. Central Himalayan cultures were recognised primarily as Indo-Aryan with the Tibeto-Burman traditions confined to the northern fringe. This perspective which placed the Tibeto-Burman culture in the north, chose to ignore the foragers, the Rajis and Rauttes, who lived in the middle Himalayas and spoke a Tibeto-Burman language (Bandhu 2017: 81–113; Bhatt and Pathak 2014). This understanding of 'difference' submerged earlier notions of identity premised upon an internal articulation dependent upon fine distinctions such as language, valley inhabited, form of agriculture practiced, myth of origin, ritual practices and other such coordinates (van Driem 2001, 333–462).

The new geography also generated a new way of 'knowing'. The vital link between Tibet, Kumaun and western Nepal was no longer shared history, but a sacred geography, that of Kailash Manasarovar. Now the sacred traditions could be appropriated for different religious traditions and bounded communities. Over the centuries, it was the *sanyasi*s (ascetics) (Pasupata Lakulisa, the Nath Panthi *jogi*s, Bairagis, Dasnam *sanyasi*s, Nirankaris and Nanakpanthis), who had connected the Himalayas to north India. The ascetics were traders (of high-value goods) and provided security as militia to the small principalities (Baisi, Chaubainsi, Thakurais) of the highlands. Culturally, the ascetics were an integral part of hill society, and according to traditional lore, they were the only groups who were feared by the trans-Himalayan bandits (Thulgharia 1938: 16f). Kumauni and Garhwali folklore is replete with stories about individuals who crossed the passes donning saffron robes (even Moorcroft had done that) and disguising themselves as ascetics (Konrad 1985: xii).

In this context, again, Atkinson's foundational history provides the cue. Atkinson's main informant was a Kumauni pundit by the name of Rudra Dutt Pant. He provided Atkinson with a Sanskrit manuscript called the *Manaskhand*, eventually published in 1989 (G. D. Pande 1989). In the *Gazetteer* (1882), Atkinson provides the historiography of this text through a study of the geography of the

Vedas, where he finds few scattered references to the Himalayan mountains. Then, in the *Itihas* period, he finds the mountains are prominent, and throughout the *Mahabharata*, the Himalayas is considered holy, worthy of pilgrimage and the well-loved home of the gods (Atkinson 1981 [1882], vol. II: 281–8). According to Atkinson, by the Puranic period, 'the North' is fully sanctified, probably because of the Himalayas. But Atkinson provides an important insight into the cosmogony of the Puranas and the significance of the Himalayas, when he locates Meru in the trans-Himalayas. He says,

> Meru in its widest sense embraces the elevated tableland of western Tibet between Kailas on the east and the Muztagh range on the west and between the Himavat on the south and the Kuenluen range on the North. It lies between them like the pericarp of a lotus and the countries of Bharata, Ketumala, Bhadraswa, and Uttara Kuru lie beyond them like the leaves of a lotus. In the valleys of these mountains are the favourite resorts of the Siddhas and Charanas and along their slopes are agreeable forests and pleasant cities peopled by celestial spirits, whilst the Gandharvas, Yakshas, Rakshasas Daityas, and Danavas pursue their pastimes in the vales. (Atkinson 1981 [1882], vol. II: 290)

The *Manaskhand* probably originated as an attempt by the Dasnami *sanyasi*s to establish monopolistic control over this route, rich in minerals, crystal, precious stones and gold. Gorkha and British rule systematically reduced their role by denying *jagir*s and *gunth* (revenue-free lands to temples and monastic institutions). Though local *jogi*s (yogis) (Naths and Bairagis) and *sanyasi*s lost their dominance in colonial Kumaun and were gradually relegated to a low-caste status, the pan-Indian connection brought a new wave of ascetic explorers to the Himalayas.

Alex McKay in his book *Kailas Histories* argues that Kailash, as we know it today is a modern phenomenon constructed primarily by European administrators and cartographers of the nineteenth century. McKay says that Sherring, in particular (Sherring 1906: 30–55), created the understanding of Kailash as the supreme pilgrimage for Hindus and Buddhists. This understanding resonated with the modern Indian intelligentsia who also made Kailash the focal point in the trans-Himalayas, which meant that the long historical connection with the Kumaun region was obscured. By the closing years of the nineteenth century, Vivekananda and Sister Nivedita had popularised the idea of the 'Holy Himalaya' (Oakley 1905: 128–61). By the early decades of the twentieth century, because of railway and road connections, *sanyasi*s from Maharashtra (Swami Hamsa), Andhra Pradesh (Swami Pranavananda), Karnataka (Narayan Swami), Punjab (Ram Teertha), Bengal (Ramakrishna Mission), Kerala (Tapovan Maharaj),

Bihar (Rahul Sankrityayana) and other regions of India were on the Kailash Manaskhand trail, mapping it in detail and advising pilgrims how to negotiate the terrain and the journey. The relationship between the central Himalayas (Kumaun and Garhwal) and western Tibet was now reordered in terms of sacred geography, which completely obscured the shared histories of the two regions. Bhagwan Sri Hamsa's description of his journey to Kailash, in 1908, through the Kumaun route was translated from Marathi and published by the name *The Holy Mountain* in 1934. It has a lengthy introduction by W. B. Yeats (Hamsa 1934: 11–47) and describes a stay at Mayawati, established by the Ramakrishna Mission. Another ascetic, Narayan Swami, on a journey to Kailash Manasarovar, was so enchanted by a place near Dharchula that in 1936, he established an ashram here, which would later become the launching point for the Kailash Manasarovar Yatra. The best known of the ascetics was Swami Pranavananda who first visited western Tibet and Kailash Manasarovar in 1928. He went in 1935 from Mukhuva Gangotri. In 1936–7, he made the journey again through the Lipu Lekh pass. Two years later, after the publication of his first book, he visited Kailash through the Untadhura, Jayanti and Kingri Bingri passes. Pranavananda not only made many visits to the trans-Himalayas but also stayed there many months at a time and on occasion spent an entire year (including winter) in the monastery at Thugholho. Pranavananda endeared himself to the Tibetans by carrying and providing medicines and was fondly referred to as Gyagar Lama Guru, Thugu Rinpoche and Gyagar Amji. Swami Pranavananda's close survey questioned many of Sven Hedin's pronouncements. In particular, he questioned Sven Hedin about the source of the rivers from the Kailash region. What is interesting is that Swami Pranavananda does not refer to the *Manaskhand* (text), though he refers to two versions of Kangri Karchhak—or Tibetan Puranas on Kailash (Swami Pranavananda 1950 [1939]: 9).

The only travellers to interrogate this narrative of sacred geography were Rahul Sankrityayana (1953: 68–70) and Giuseppe Tucci (1962: 51–80; 1973; 1967: 19–63; 1956: 92–130) but their understanding could not displace the dominant view. The trans-Himalayan connection, though alive, was now read through a new lens, which understood the connection with the trans-Himalayas in terms of the pilgrim land of Kailash Manasarovar. For British travellers and Indian pilgrims, the journey to western Tibet became an achievement in itself (V. Pande 2019). McKay says that this perspective 'removed the site from its Indo-Tibetan cultural context and transformed it into a globalized mountain for a globalizing world' (Mckay 2015: 425).

In the nineteenth and early twentieth century, as Tibet experienced modern imperialist pressure because of the Great Game, Tibetan nationalism was stimulated in the early twentieth century by British imperial interests and by Chinese attempts to impose more direct control (Warren 2003: 197–218). Tibet managed to achieve de facto independence under British patronage and Chinese impotence, but failed to achieve international recognition as a nation-state. After the takeover of Tibet by the Chinese, Tibetan culture was subjected to extreme assimilationist pressure during the Cultural Revolution. Nevertheless, despite every effort at its eradication, Tibetan nationalism survived and grew under Chinese rule. In the period of liberalised Chinese policies in Tibet after 1980, Tibetan culture and nationalism revived and though Tibetans sought and gained international support for their cause, yet it continued to be an integral part of the Chinese nation (Smith, Jr. 1996: 1–19; Goldstein 1991: 560–610, 2007: 1–16; Palace 2005: 141–2).

Dominant narratives about Tibet remained located in Lhasa and the focus remained on Tibetan Buddhism. Tibet emerged from the Shangri La as an extraordinary cultural formation nurtured in rugged isolation, shorn of its long historical connections with the entire gamut of Himalayan cultures (from East to West). In this representation, the western Tibet borderland was reduced to a region best known for the Kailash Manasarovar dyad, a place for pilgrimage. This process obscured the long historical linkage, dating to prehistory and the period of the Tibetan Empire (Sankrityayana 2015). Recent research on Bon has helped bring western Tibet into the field of vision, but histories of Tibet continue to refer to western Tibet in the medieval period, but by the modern period it is another border outpost (van Schaik 2011: 180–237).

Imperial and nationalist histories created new geographies of knowledge and neologisms that persist even today (I. Chatterjee 2016: 9–40); these narratives obscured earlier connections and linkages. Through a study of the contiguous regions of three states, India, Nepal and Tibet (China), this chapter has tried to grapple with and decentre nation-state-oriented perspectives by interrogating, excavating and retrieving histories that still resonate and matter as shared concerns of the peoples of their respective borderlands.

NOTES

1. See https://biglobalization.org/outputs/publications-0, accessed on 20 October 2019.
2. See Settlement Report of Pergunnahs Gudderpore and Rooderpore, Commissioner Records, District Archives, Nainital, 29 May 1832 and Whalley (1991: 149).

3. Pre-Mutiny Records, Revenue Letters Issued, vol. 31, UP State Archives, Lucknow, March 1845.

4. Pre-Mutiny Records, Revenue Letters Issued, UP State Archives, Lucknow, 17 November 1848.

5. Pre-Mutiny Records, Revenue Letters Issued, vol. 22, UP State Archives, Lucknow, April 1855.

6. Vernacular Newspaper Reports, 9 June 1890, 'Report on Native Newspapers, N. W. Provinces and Oudh 1890–1937', selection of Vernacular Native Newspapers, National Archives of India, New Delhi, p. 213.

7. Compiled from Administration Reports of the North Western Provinces, 1897, 1898, 1899:

   'Report on the Administration of the Northwest Provinces and Oudh, 1897–1898', North Western Provinces Government, Allahabad.

   'Report on the Administration of the Northwest Provinces and Oudh, 1898–1899', North Western Provinces Government, Allahabad.

   'Report on the Administration of the Northwest Provinces and Oudh, 1899–1900', North Western Provinces Government, Allahabad.

8. 'Report on the Administration of the Northwest Provinces and Oudh, 1899–1900', North Western Provinces Government, Allahabad.

9. Pre-Mutiny Records, Revenue Letters Issued, vol. 17, UP State Archives, Lucknow.

10. Pre-Mutiny Records, Revenue Letters Issued, vol. 7, UP State Archives, Lucknow, 1821.

11. Private papers of Mrs. Jugal Rais, miscellaneous, Almora.

12. Compiled from Administration Reports of the North Western Provinces, 1897, 1898, 1899:

   'Report on the Administration of the Northwest Provinces and Oudh, 1897–1898', North Western Provinces Government, Allahabad.

   'Report on the Administration of the Northwest Provinces and Oudh, 1898–1899', North Western Provinces Government, Allahabad.

   'Report on the Administration of the Northwest Provinces and Oudh, 1899–1900', North Western Provinces Government, Allahabad.

13. 'Report on the Administration of the Northwest Provinces and Oudh, 1899–1900', North Western Provinces Government, Allahabad, pp. 136–52.

14. See https://www.kafaltree.com/type-of-kumaoni-brahmins/, accessed on 1 October 2019.

REFERENCES

Aitchison, C. U. 1892. *A Collection of Treaties Engagements and Sanads Relating to India and Neighbouring Countries*. Calcutta: Superintendent Government Printing.

Allen, Charles. 1982. *A Mountain in Tibet*. London: Andre Deutsch.

Anderson, Benedict. 1983. *Imagined Communities: Reflections on the Origin and Spread of Nationalism*. London and New York: Verso.

Atkinson, E. T. 1981 (1882). *The Himalayan Gazetteer*, 6 vols. Delhi: Cosmo.

Bandhu, C. M. 2017. 'Raute and Raji: Two Endangered Tribes of Central Himalayas'. In *Cradle of Culture*, edited by B. K. Joshi and M. P. Joshi, 81–98. Almora: Almora Book Depot.

Batten, J. H. 1851. *Official Reports on the Province of Kumaon*. Agra: Orphan Press.

Beckett, J. O. B. 1874. 'Report on the Revision of Settlement in the Kumaun District, 1863–1873'. Allahabad: N. W. Provinces Government Press.

Bengal Secretariat Book Depot. 1914. *Almora District Gazetteer Supplementary Notes and Statistics*. Vol. 35. Calcutta: Bengal Secretariat Book Depot.

Beurskens, Kristine, and Judith Miggelbrink. 2017. 'Special Section Introduction—Sovereignty Contested: Theory and Practice in Borderlands'. *Geopolitics* 22 (4): 749–56.

Bhatt, Uma, and Shekhar Pathak, eds. 2014. *The Languages of Uttarakhand: People's Linguistic Survey of India Volume 30, Part 2*. New Delhi: Orient Black Swan.

Bill, Aitken. 2003. *Footloose in the Himalaya*. Ranikhet: Permanent Black.

Bishop, B. 1970. *A Cultural and Ecological Analyses of the Karnali Zone*. Delhi: USAID.

———. 2052/1995. *Sabaii Jat ko Phulwari Bista*. Kathmandu: Sajha Prakashan.

Bora, R. S. 1996. *Himalayan Migration: A Study of the Hill Region of U.P.* New Delhi: Sage Publication.

Brown, C. W. 1992. 'What We Call "Bhotias" Are in Reality Not "Bhotias"'. In *Himalaya Past and Present*, vol. II, edited by M. P. Joshi, A. C. Fanger and C. W. Brown, 147–72. Almora: Almora Book Depot.

———. 1994. 'Salt, Barley, Pashmina and Tincal-Contexts of Being Bhotiya in Traill's Kumaon'. In *Himalaya Past and Present*, vol. III, edited by M. P. Joshi, A. C. Fanger and C. W. Brown, 215–58. Almora: Almora Book Depot.

Brunet-Jailly, Emmanuel. 2010. 'The State of Borders and Borderlands Studies 2009: A Historical View and a View from the Journal of Borderlands Studies'. *Eurasian Border Review* 1 (1): 1–15.

Bruslé, Tristan. 2008. 'Choosing a Destination and Work: Migration Strategies of Nepalese Workers in Uttarakhand and Northern India'. *Mountain Research and Development* 28 (3): 240–7.

Burghart, Richard. 1984. 'The Formation of the Concept of Nation-State in Nepal'. *Journal of Asian Studies* 44 (1): 101–25.

Burrard, S. G., and H. H. Hayden. 1933. *A Sketch of Geography and Geology of the Himalaya Mountains and Tibet*. Delhi: Manager of Publications.

Caplan, Lionel. 2006. 'Martial Gurkhas: The Persistence of a British Military Discourse on Race'. In *War and Society in Colonial India*, edited by Kaushik Roy, second edition. Delhi: Oxford University Press.

Chatterjee, Indrani. 2016. 'Adivasis, Tribes and Other Neologisms for Erasing Pre-Colonial Pasts: An Example from Northeast India.' *Indian Economic and Social History Review* 55 (1): 9–40.

Chatterjee, Partha. 2003. 'The Nation in Heterogeneous Time'. In *Nationalism and Its Futures*, edited by Umut Özkirimli, 33–58. New York: Palgrave and Macmillan.

Colebrooke, H. T. 1812. 'On the Source of the Ganges'. *Asiatic Researches* 11: 429–45.

Dabral, Shiva Prasad. 2030/1973. *Uttarakhanda ka Rajnaitik Tatha Sanskritik Itihasa*. Dogadda: Veergatha Prakashan.

Dahal, Dilli Ram, Navin Kumar Rai and Andrew Manzardo. 1977. *Land and Migration in Far Western Nepal*. Kathmandu T. U.: Institute of Nepal and Asian Studies.

Dangwal, Dhiren. 2009. 'The Lost Mobility: Pastoralism and Modernity in Uttarakhand Himalaya (India)'. *Nomadic Peoples* 13 (2): 84–101.

Dutta, K. K. 1970. 'Significance of Shawl Wool Trade in Himalayan Politics'. *Bengal Past and Present* 89 (1): 16–28.

Furer-Haimendorf, C. von. 1966. 'Chetri Caste of Nepal'. In *Caste and Kin in Nepal India and Ceylon*, edited by C. von Furer Haimendorf, 11–160. Bombay: Asia Publishing House.

Goldstein, Melvyn C. 1991. *A History of Modern Tibet The Demise of the Lamaist State 1913–1951*. Vol. 1. Berkeley: University of California Press.

———. 2007. *A History of Modern Tibet The Calm before the Storm 1951–1955*. Vol. 2. Berkeley: University of California Press.

Gommans, Jos J. L. 1995. *The Rise of the Indo–Afghan Empire c. 1710–1780*. Leiden: Brill.

Guha, Ramachandra. 1985. 'Scientific Forestry and Social Change in Uttarakhand'. *Economic and Political Weekly* 20 (45/47): 1939–41+1943+1945–7+1949+1951–2.

Gyawali, Surya Bikram. 1933a. *Drabya Shah ko Jivani:Gorkha Vijay ko Itihas*. Darjeeling: Nepali Sahitya Sammelan.

———. 1933b. *Ram Shah ko Jivan-Charitra*. Darjeeling: Nepali Sahitya Sammelan.

———. 1943. *Amar Singh Thapa*. Darjeeling: Nepali Sahitya Sammelan.

————. 1976 (1935). *Prithvi Narayan Shah*. Darjeeling: Nepali Sahitya Sammelan.

————. 2018 Vikram Samvat. *Bir Balabhadra*. Kathmandu: Ratna Pustak Bhandar.

Hamsa, Bhagwan Sri. 1934. *The Holy Mountain*. London: Faber & Faber.

Hardwicke, Captain T. 1801. 'Narrative of a Journey to Srinagar'. *Asiatic Researches* 6: 309–47.

Heber, Reginald. 1873. *Narrative of a Journey through the Upper Provinces of India 1824–25*. London: John Murray.

Hedin, Sven. 1909. *Trans-Himalayas, Adventures and Discoveries in Tibet*. Vol. I. New York: Macmillan and Company.

————. 1910. *Trans-Himalayas, Adventures and Discoveries in Tibet*. Vol. II. London: Macmillan and Company.

————. 1913. *Trans-Himalayas, Adventures and Discoveries in Tibet*. Vol. III. London: Macmillan and Company.

Hodgson, B. H. 1874. *Essays on the Languages, Literature and Religion of Nepal and Tibet*. Trubner: London.

Husain, Iqbal. 1994. *The Ruhela Chieftaincies: The Rise and Fall of Ruhela Power in North India in the Eighteenth Century*. Delhi: Oxford University Press.

Kansakar, V. B. S. 1984. 'Indo–Nepal Migration: Problems and Prospects'. *Contribution to Nepalese Studies* 11 (2): 49–69.

Konrad, Meissner. 1985. *Malushahi and Rajula: A Ballad from Kumaun India as Sung by Gopi Das*. Vol. 1. Weisbaden: Otto Harassowitz.

Matiyani, S. 1990. *Gopuli Gafuran*. Allahabad: Vibha Prakashan.

Matynia, Elzbieta. 2011. 'The Promise of Borderlands'. *International Journal of Politics, Culture, and Society* 24 (1/2): 75–81.

McKay, Alex. 2015. *Kailas Histories: Renunciate Traditions and the Construction of Himalayan Sacred Geography*. Leiden: Brill.

————. 1997. *Tibet and the British Raj, the Frontier Cadre, 1904–1947*. Surrey: Curzon.

Michael, Bernardo A. 2014. 'Writing a World History of the Anglo-Gorkha Borderlands in the Early Nineteenth Century'. *Journal of World History* 25 (4): 535–58.

Moorcroft, W. 1816. 'A Journey to Mansarover in Huindes'. *Asiatic Researches* 12: 375–535.

Oakley, E. S. 1905. *Holy Himalaya*. London: Oliphant Anderson and Ferrier.

Ojha, D. P. 1992. *Doti Kshetra ko Itihasa and Sanskriti*. Kathmandu: Sagarmatha Press.

Oldfield, H. A. 1974 (1880). *Sketches from Nipal Historical and Descriptive*, 2 vols. London: Allen and Company.

Onta, Pratyush. 1996. 'Creating a Brave Nepali Nation in British India: The Rhetoric of Jati Improvement and Writing of Bir History'. *Studies in Nepali History and Society* 1 (1): 37–76.

Palace, Wendy. 2005. *The British Empire and Tibet 1900–1922*. London and New York: Routledge Curzon.

Pande, B. D. 1990 (1937). *Kumaun Ka Itihas*. Almora: Almora Book Depot.

Pande, G. D., ed. 1989. *Manaskhand*. Varanasi: Sri Nityanand Smarak Samiti.

Pande, Vasudha. 1996. 'Law, Women and Family in Colonial Kumaun'. *India International Centre Quarterly* 23 (3–4): 106–20.

———. 2013. 'Stratification in Kumaun 1815–1930'. NMML Occasional Paper New Series, History and Society No. 37, Nehru Memorial Museum and Library, Delhi.

———. 2014. 'Divergent Historiographical Traditions: A Comparative Study of Gorkha Rule in Kumaun and Far Western in Nepal'. In *Before Emergence of Nation States*, edited by M. P. Joshi, S. Thapa, J. Pant and R. Shah, 106–42. Almora.

———. 2015. 'Making Kumaun Modern: Family and Custom c. 1815–1930'. NMML Occasional Paper New Series, History and Society No. 66, Nehru Memorial Museum and Library, Delhi.

———. 2018a. 'Anthropogenic Landscapes of the Central Himalayas'. In *At Nature's Edge*, edited by G. Cederlof and M. Rangarajan, 19–58. Delhi: Oxford University Press.

———. 2018b. 'The Making of a "Kumauni" Artifact: The Epic Malushahi'. *Himalaya, the Journal of the Association for Nepal and Himalayan Studies* 38 (1): 145–59.

———. 2019. 'Changing Imaginaries of Geographies and Journeys in Kumaun and Tibet.' *Sudasein-Chronik: South Asia Chronicle* 9: 59–82.

Pandey, R. N. 1997. *The Making of Modern Nepal*. Delhi: Nirala Publications.

Pant, S. D. 1935. *Social Economy of the Himalyans*. London: Allen & Unwin.

Pathak, Shekhar. 1987. *Uttarakhand Mein Coolie Begar Pratha*. Delhi: Radhakrishna Publications.

———. 2008. *Asia ki Peeth Par*. Nainital: Pahar.

Pemble, John. 1971. *The Invasion of Nepal, John Company at War*. Oxford: Clarendon.

Pilgrim. 1990 (1884). *Wanderings in the Himmala*. Nainital: Gyanodaya Prakashan.

Pradhan, Kumar. 1991. *The Gorkha Conquests*. Delhi: Oxford University Press.

Raper, F. V. 1810. 'Narrative of a Survey for the Purpose of Discovering the Source of the Ganges.' *Asiatic Researches* 11: 446–564.

Regmi, M. C. 1978. *Thatched Huts and Stucco Palaces: Peasants and Landlords in 19th Century Nepal*. Delhi: Vikas Publishing House.

————. 1999. *Imperial Gorkha: An Account of Gorkhali Rule in Kumaun 1791–1815*. Delhi: Adroit.

Regmi Research Series. 1973. Vol. 5. *Digital Himalaya*. http://www.digitalhimalaya. com/collections/journals/regmi/. Accessed on 4 October 2009.

————. 1978. Vol. 10. *Digital Himalaya*. http://www.digitalhimalaya.com/ collections/journals/regmi/. Accessed on 4 October 2009.

————. 1981. Vol. 13. *Digital Himalaya*. http://www.digitalhimalaya.com/ collections/journals/regmi/. Accessed on 4 October 2009.

————. 1982. Vol. 14. *Digital Himalaya*. http://www.digitalhimalaya.com/ collections/journals/regmi/. Accessed on 4 October 2009.

————. 1983. Vol. 15. *Digital Himalaya*. http://www.digitalhimalaya.com/ collections/journals/regmi/. Accessed on 4 October 2009.

————. 1986. Vol. 18. *Digital Himalaya*. http://www.digitalhimalaya.com/ collections/journals/regmi/. Accessed on 4 October 2009.

Rhoades, R. E., and S. I. Thompson. 1975. 'Adaptive Strategies in Alpine Environments: Beyond Ecological Particularism'. *American Ethnologist* 2 (3): 535–51.

Sankrityayana, Rahul. 1953. *Himalaya Parichay*, Part I. Allahabad: Law Journal Press.

————. 2015 Vikram Samvat. *Kumaun*. Varanasi: Gyanmandal.

Sharma, P. R. 1977. 'Caste, Social Mobility and Sanskritisation'. *Kailash* 5 (4): 277–99.

Sherring, C. A. 1906. *Western Tibet and the British Borderland: The Sacred Country of Hindus and Buddhists*. London: Edward Arnold.

Shrestha, B. K. 1993. *A Himalayan Enclave in Transition*. Kathmandu: International Centre for Integrated Mountain Development.

Smith, Warren W. Jr. 1996. *Tibetan Nation: A History of Tibetan Nationalism and Sino-Tibetan Relations*. Colorado and Oxford: Westview Press.

Stiller, L. F. 1973. *The Rise of the House of Gorkha*. Kathmandu: Ratna Pustak Bhandar.

————. 1976. *The Silent Cry*. Kathmandu: Ratna Pustak Bhandar.

————. 1989. *Prithvinarayan Shah in the Light of the Dibya Updesh*. Kathmandu: Himalayan Book Centre.

Swami Pranavananda, F. R. G. S. 1949. *History of Kailas Manasarovar with Maps*. Calcutta: Sri Narayan Swami Ashram, Soosa S.P. League.

————. 1950 (1939). *Explorations in Tibet*. Calcutta: University of Calcutta.

Thulgharia, Shah Badri. 1938. *Kurmanchal Kanti*.

Tolia, R. S. 1994. *British Kumaun Garhwal*. Almora: Almora Book Depot.

————. 1996. *British Kumaun–Garhwal: An Administrative History of a Non-Regulation Province*. Vol. 2. Almora: Almora Book Depot.

Traill, G. W. 1828. 'Statistical Sketch of Kumaun'. *Asiatic Researches* 14: 137–234.

Tucci, Giuseppe. 1956. *Preliminary Report on Two Scientific Expeditions in Nepal.* Rome: ISMEO.

———. 1962. *Nepal: The Discovery of the Malla.* New York: Dutton and Company.

———. 1967. *Tibet: Land of the Snows.* Translated by J. E. Stapleton. London: Driver Elek Books.

———. 1973. *The Ancient Civilisation of the Trans-Himalaya.* London: Barry & Jenkins.

V. 1991 (1901). *Almoriana: Travel Account of Kumaun Himalayan Ranges/Leaves from a Hill Journal.* Nainital: Gyanodaya Prakashan.

van Driem, George. 2001. *Languages of the Himalayas: An Ethnolinguistic Handbook of the Greater Himalayan Region.* Leiden: Brill.

van Schaik, Sam. 2011. *Tibet: A History.* London and New York: Yale University Press.

van Spengen, Wim. 1995. 'The Geo-History of Long-Distance Trade in Tibet 1850–1950'. *The Tibet Journal* 20 (2): 18–63.

Wessels, C. 1924. *Early Jesuit Travellers in Central Asia.* The Hague: Martinis Nijhoff.

Whelpton, John. 2005a. *A History of Nepal.* Cambridge: Cambridge University Press.

———. 2005b. 'A Reading Guide to Nepalese History'. *Himalaya, the Journal of the Association for Nepal and Himalayan Studies* 25 (1): 9–18.

Whalley, Peter. 1991. *The Law of the Extra-Regulation Tracts.* Varanasi: Vishwavidyalaya Prakashan.

———. 1991 (1870). *British Kumaon.* Introduction by R. S. Tolia. Varanasi: Vishvavidyalya Publication.

3

Borders, Difference, Recognition
On the Cause(s) of Gorkhaland[*]

TOWNSEND MIDDLETON

There was a report of new dissatisfaction in the hills, gathering insurgency, men and guns. It was the Indian-Nepalis, this time, fed up with being treated like a minority in a place they were the majority. They wanted their own country, or at least their own state in which to manage their own affairs. Here, where India blurred into Sikkim, and the army did pull-ups and push-ups, maintaining their tanks with khaki paint in case the Chinese grew hungry for more territory than Tibet, it had always been a messy map ... despite, ah, despite the mist charging down like a dragon, dissolving, undoing, making ridiculous the drawing of borders.

—Desai (2005: 9)

In the summer of 2017, the Gorkhaland movement returned in force. Touched off by suggestions that Bengali would be made compulsory in schools across Darjeeling, this latest agitation plunged the hills into a turmoil not experienced since the violent days of the first Gorkhaland movement in the 1980s. Yet, after months of strikes, internet blackout, state violence and death, the 2017 agitation, like the first in the 1980s and the second three decades later, failed to deliver a separate state of Gorkhaland within India—and with it, the autonomy, belonging and recognition that the Gorkhas of Darjeeling desire.

Unfolding in a corner of India that many know only as an idyllic vacation spot, the Gorkhaland movement has miffed many across the subcontinent. People have wrongfully assumed that it is secessionist (it is not), that foreign hands are at work (of which there is no evidence), that it will eventually fade away (history suggests otherwise). The misunderstandings of the Gorkhaland movement are legion and part of the problem. In this chapter, I want to step back to examine the cause(s) of Gorkhaland—and, in particular, the ways that the interplays of borders, difference and recognition galvanise this and other ethno-political movements in the Darjeeling Hills. As I attempt to show, to respond to the historic question 'why Gorkhaland?' in these terms opens a wider questioning of what identities count in the border zones of South Asia? What do not? And what are the politics of such reckonings? I draw on a decade and a half of study of Darjeeling's political culture to shed some light on these questions.

STIRRINGS AT THE BORDER

With four sovereign countries in the immediate vicinity (Bangladesh, Bhutan, China and Nepal), Darjeeling stands at a particular nexus of South Asia (Figure 3.1).

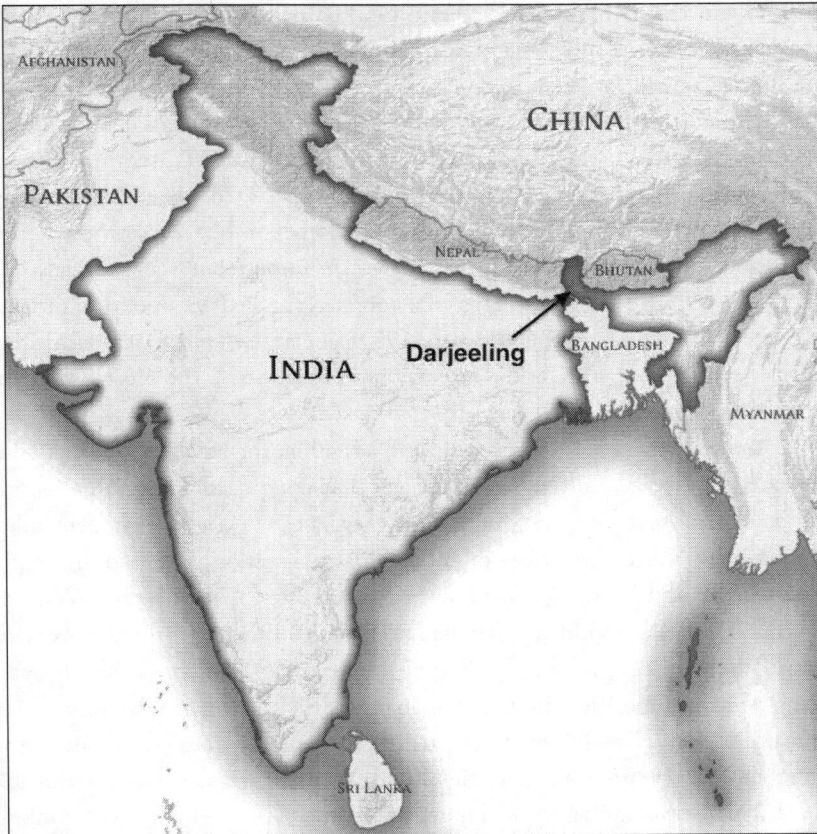

Figure 3.1 Darjeeling in the Context of South Asia
Source: Map adapted from http://commons.wikimedia.org/wiki/File.
Note: Map not to scale and does not represent authentic international boundaries.

Given its strategic location, Darjeeling remains a sensitive borderland where *the army does indeed do push-up and pull-ups, maintaining their tanks in khaki paint.* Yet it is also a highly romanticised, former colonial hill station and, today, a major tourist destination—the 'queen of the hills', as it were. The people of Darjeeling have suffered a less idyllic fate.

Demographically, Darjeeling is dominated by Nepali-Indian communities, who collectively identify as 'Gorkhas'. Nepali-Indian communities today extend throughout northern and northeastern India.[1] Yet how the appellation 'Gorkha' came to be the namesake of Darjeeling's Gorkhaland movement is a more local story—one that cannot be told without due attention to the border. Ever since the nineteenth century, when many (though not all) of the ethnic groups who comprise the Darjeeling's conglomerate Gorkha community migrated to India from Nepal, Sikkim, Bhutan and surrounding areas, this population's place in India has remained in constant doubt. They have been deemed 'foreigners', 'hill tribes' and 'outsiders'—at once geographically, racially and nationally different from the Indo-Aryan majority of plains. Subsequent forms of discrimination and marginalisation have imparted to the Gorkhas deep-seated anxieties over being-in and being-of the Indian nation-state—a phenomenon I have elsewhere termed *anxious belongings* (Middleton 2013a: 608–21). Throughout the twentieth and twenty-first centuries, these anxieties of belonging, coupled with political interests and processes of ethno-genesis (Roosens 1989), generated a range of identification forms. The conglomerate Gorkha identity has proven to be the most formidable among these. But there have been others as well.

In the wake of the 1980s Gorkhaland agitation, for instance, the individual ethnicities (Tamangs, Gurungs, and so on) that comprised the greater Gorkha conglomerate began pursuing alternative avenues to rights by demanding recognition as Scheduled Tribes of India. This designation promised affirmative action benefits and a formal, if symbolic, inclusion into the nation-state. With the terms of identification suddenly switched from 'Gorkha' to 'tribal', these movements strained the populace, at once pulling at the seams of Gorkha solidarity while forcing aspiring minorities into the ethnological straightjacket of tribal recognition. Difficulties notwithstanding, these tribal movements gathered momentum throughout the 1990s, peaking in the 2000s. Yet their efficacy was questionable. With tribal identity failing to yield much in the way of socio-material or symbolic purchase in India, the terms of identity soon switched back to that of the 'Gorkhas' and the 'one and only solution' to their long-standing crisis of identity: Gorkhaland. Figure 3.2 chronicles this shifting array of ethno-political forms.

1986–8	The Gorkhaland National Liberation Front (GNLF) agitates for a separate state of Gorkhaland.
1988	The establishment of the Darjeeling Gorkha Hill Council (DGHC) affords Darjeeling limited autonomy within West Bengal.
1990–present	Ethnicities within the Gorkha conglomerate mobilise for Scheduled Tribe (ST) status.
2005–07	The Gorkhaland National Liberation Front (GNLF) attempts to make Darjeeling an autonomous Sixth Schedule 'Tribal Area'.
2007–11	The Gorkha Janmukti Morcha launches a second Gorkhaland Agitation.
2011–12	The Gorkhaland Territorial Authority (GTA) is established, again providing limited autonomy within West Bengal.
2013	The second Gorkhaland Agitation flares again, on the announcement of a new state of Telangana.
2017	The threat of compulsory Bengali in Darjeeling schools brings protests and, in response, state violence, triggering a third Gorkhaland Agitation.

Figure 3.2 A History of Movements

Source: Timeline compiled by Townsend Middleton.

Throughout this turbulent history, the Gorkhas' cross-border associations with Nepal have been ambivalent. On the one hand, their shared Nepali origins, culture and language have done much to unify these groups. This heritage is necessarily called upon to fulfil the requisites of recognition—tribal and otherwise. On the other hand, these populations have distanced themselves from Nepal by claiming a definitive break with their erstwhile homeland. Far from being secessionist, the Gorkhas of Darjeeling have been steadfast in their claims of being an integral part of India (even while indexing their Nepali heritage to constitute themselves as recognisable communities). The border, in this sense, has proven generative of both ethnicity and paradox. Politically, the resulting identities (Gorkha, tribal and otherwise) have seldom been successful in bringing rights, autonomy and belonging to these marginalised border communities. They instead have been largely stymied by particular paradigms of recognition in India, which continue to dictate the terms by which populations may stake an ethnic claim in the nation-state (cf. Povinelli 2002).

These failures of identity have imparted difficult lessons of the Indian government's power to determine what counts as a politically acceptable identity. Through its programmes of positive discrimination and ethnically attuned governance, India's multicultural state demands particular types of sociocultural forms and content. Given anthropology's chequered past in India, these forms are unmistakably ethnological in their makeup (Dudley-Jenkins 2003; Middleton 2011: 249–66; Middleton 2015). For border communities in particular, satisfying these criteria of recognition and national inclusion can be exceptionally difficult. Groups like the Gorkhas therein find themselves in a double bind. Relegated to the margins, they maintain heightened desires for integration into the national 'mainstream'. Yet *precisely because of* their bordered existence—itself involving transnational migration and significant degrees of sociocultural hybridity—these groups have found it virtually impossible to achieve compliance with the ethno-logics of the multicultural state.

The border is thus a site of both vulnerability and paradox—and a zone in which national ideologies of difference may be powerfully reinscribed. Out of necessity, border communities are often especially reliant on the *state* as a means to symbolic and material inclusion into the *nation*. They are consequently especially susceptible to the paradigms of inclusion and exclusion through which the state determines what kinds of difference may be admitted into the space of the nation, and what kinds may not. Yet borders are also generative of particular kinds of identity, particular formations of difference. In these capacities, borders both mark and make difference. Crucially though—and as the ethno-political history of Darjeeling illustrates—not all of these forms of difference are legible in the eyes of the state (cf. Scott 1998).

To flesh out these paradoxes, I turn now to the (unspeakable) legacy of borders in Darjeeling.

UNSPEAKABLE HISTORIES

Finally, the day had come when I would meet Mr. K. P. Prasad (a pseudonym), one of Darjeeling's premier local historians. Rumour had it that Mr. Prasad held caches of archives, shedding light on the scantily documented history of Darjeeling. I was hoping he would share his knowledge—and perhaps his sources—with me, so I gladly took my seat in his living room among several mutual friends. Over tea, I introduced my work. Mr. Prasad listened intently, until I mentioned my interest in the Gorkhas' history of migration. Suddenly, he diverted the conversation to a different topic. Confused by his non sequitur, I asked again if we might talk about the history of migration that brought many of the Gorkhas to Darjeeling. Again, he ignored me—this time turning to my friend, Prakash, with an unrelated question. Thinking my use of the English term 'migration' might be the problem, I tried the Nepali *basāi sarāi*. Again nothing. Finally I tried the English once more, at which point he turned to me, looked me dead in the eye and said sternly, 'We don't say that word here.'

'What, "migration"?'

'Yes, we don't say that word in Darjeeling.'

Taken aback, I kept quiet, sipping my tea as Mr. Prasad again initiated a new topic of discussion. This was not the first time I had encountered the unwillingness to speak of the Gorkhas' transnational past. Indeed, Mr. Prasad was at the fore of a historical revisionist movement to overwrite the Gorkhas' problematic history of migration with narratives of autochthony. These 'sons of the soil' historiographies were cropping up in the autonomy and recognition movements I had been researching. Autochthony and indigeneity, so the logic went, would be conduits to autonomy and recognition. But while some ethnic groups within the Gorkha conglomerate do indeed have long-standing, perhaps 'ancient', histories in the region, many of these newly emergent autochthony narratives flew in the face of family histories across the hills, where migration (especially from Nepal) was a commonly accepted (if selectively unspoken) aspect of their heritage. For example, my village neighbours, despite speaking freely with me about their ancestors from Nepal, refused to put anything in writing, saying this would be 'proof' that would enable the Indian government 'to send them back to Nepal'. I explained that this was legally impossible—that their ancestors had migrated to India long before the nation-state had come into existence (1947)—but their anxiety would not be quelled. What was it then about this history that made it so problematic and, at times, unspeakable?

For the British, Darjeeling was to be the consummate hill station (cf. Kennedy 1996)—a 'sanatorium' far removed from the plains below. Acquired from Sikkim in 1835, Darjeeling was radically transformed in the nineteenth century. Clearing the rugged landscape, building roads, and peopling the region's budding tea industry required far more labour than the local Bhutia and Lepcha populations could provide. So colonial administrators turned to neighbouring Sikkim, Bhutan and Nepal, where thousands from the 'most vigorous and enterprising of the Nepal races' proved willing to cross the border for work in colonial India.[2] The British had found an ideal and decidedly ethno-logical labour pool, with one problem.

British India's sovereign neighbours (most notably, Nepal) often disapproved of these outward migrations.

The British therefore encouraged the ingress of labour from Nepal (and Sikkim and Bhutan), but washed their hands of its dubious legality by relying on informal labour recruiters known as *sardar*s to move bodies across borders. 'Going to Mugalan', as India was then called in Nepal (Hutt 1998: 195–214), promised a life beyond the feudal toil of Nepal. The Nepali settlers soon became Darjeeling's demographic majority (Chatterjee 2001: 65–80; Hutt 1997: 109–13; Sinha and Subba 2003: 14–17). But while the British offered food, clothes, shelter and wage labour, they did not provide legal recognition as British subjects.[3] These populations thus found themselves in an extended state of liminality.

Life at the border was consequently beset with precarity from the start. These *border affects* manifested in periodic bouts of flight and fright among Darjeeling's labour force, typically associated with the threat of extradition back to Nepal. The British wished to calm their labour force but, for diplomatic reasons, could not guarantee protection as British subjects. And so, the local populations remained on edge. These *border affects* continue to haunt the Gorkhas of Darjeeling to this day, imbuing life and politics with marked anxieties over being-in and being-of India.

Despite being the banner of ethnic sub-nationalism, the Gorkha identity has not always existed. When groups like the Tamangs, Gurungs and Newars (who now comprise the Gorkha community) migrated to Darjeeling, they came with relatively discrete sociocultural and linguistic systems. They were, as modern academics would have it, distinct culture-bearing ethnic groups. Once settled in Darjeeling, these ethnicities began to mix and amalgamate in unprecedented ways. With Nepali emerging as the lingua franca and inter-ethnic mixture intensifying, ethnicities like the Gurungs and Tamangs began to 'lose' (*harāunu*)—as they now say—much of their linguistic and sociocultural distinctiveness. Where former practices were 'lost', however, new forms of ethnic consciousness, solidarity and practice came into existence. In time, these processes of ethno-genesis forever reworked the social and political landscape of Darjeeling.

ENTANGLED FORMATIONS

In the history of Darjeeling, identity and the state have proven to be entangled formations. It is well known that the British colonial government periodically instituted special arrangements—exceptions to the standard rules of law—for aboriginal, frontier and/or 'backward' people and places. The creation of *Scheduled*

Districts in 1874, *Backward Tracts* in 1919 and *Excluded and Partially Excluded Areas* in 1935 are examples of these ethnically attuned forms of governance. Border regions like Darjeeling often fell under this ambit of exceptionalism. Beginning with the carte-blanche authority vested to Superintendent A. Campbell to develop Darjeeling into a proper sanatorium in the 1840s and extending through the most recent administrative arrangements, the 'state of exception' has been the rule in the hills (Agamben 2005; Schmitt 1985). In theory, these exceptional forms of governance were implemented in response to local ethno-political configurations. In practice, they also produced them.

In 1874, Darjeeling was declared a Scheduled District, exempting it from standard governmental procedures. With tea flourishing in the hills, ample labour to bring it to market, and Darjeeling coming into its own as a hill station, the British were content with this exceptional status. It seemed only right that this 'queen of the hills' was kept above the fray of the 'real' India in the plains below. In 1917, the Scheduled Districts Act of 1874 came under review as part of the Montagu–Chelmsford Reforms. In question were the extant laws of the districts, as well as the character of the natives. Not coincidently, this was when the first articulations of a conglomerate Nepali-Indian identity appeared in the archives.

In 1917, the Hillmen's Association (comprised of ethnic elites from Darjeeling's Nepali, Bhutia and Lepcha communities) sent a memorandum to the British Indian government, arguing that Darjeeling should remain excluded from standard governance. The Hillmen appealed to the shared geographic, racial, historical, religious and linguistic traits of the hill people, arguing, 'No real affinity exists between the peoples of this Himalayan and sub-Himalayan region and those of the plains of Bengal. The evolution of our political life should be towards a distinct local government of our own.'[4] Using environmental determinism to define their 'natural' place within India's geography, the border figured prominently in their claims: 'Our people are the natural guardians of the frontier. We would welcome the privilege of keeping ourselves ever-ready to fulfill this function.'[5] With the Hillmen, the Planters Association and the European Association of Darjeeling lobbied to sustain the status quo of exceptionalism—while stopping short of advocating for native self-rule, as had been proposed by the Hillmen.

The question of autonomy arose again in the late 1920s when Darjeeling's status again came under review—this time by the Simon Commission. In question, again, was the ethno-political character of the native population—in particular their 'backwardness' and alterity vis-à-vis the Indians of the plains and their capacities of democratic citizenship.[6] After much debate, Darjeeling was made a 'Partially Excluded Area', extending its exceptional status.

In its early articulations, the Nepali-Indian identity remained an overtly political construction. It was what Bakhtin (1981: 359) would call an intentional hybridity—a conscious cobbling together of communities into a 'political interest group'(Cohen 1974).More organic processes of hybridity were underway, however, imbuing this conglomerate community with increasing sociocultural and affective cohesion. Therefore, as organisations like the Hill People's Social Union (est. 1934) and the All India Gorkha League (est. in Darjeeling in 1940) advanced the cause of Nepali-Indian rights and autonomy in the decades to come, their identification claims increasingly reflected a pan-ethnic community, bound together by shared cultural traits and affective senses of belonging, on the one hand, and enduring, shared forms of marginalisation and discrimination, on the other. Gorkha identity politics gained steam accordingly.

AGITATIONS AT THE BORDER

The post-colonial era brought little change for the Gorkhas of Darjeeling. They remained at the lowest levels of Darjeeling's political economy. They continued to suffer geo-racial and nationalist discrimination and they continued to be marginalised from India's sociopolitical and economic mainstream. As per the political rhetoric of the times, the Gorkhas did not just have an identity; they had an 'identity crisis'.

That crisis came to a head in the 1980s when the Gorkha National Liberation Front (GNLF) launched a violent agitation for a separate state of Gorkhaland. 'Consider our situation', GNLF founder Subash Ghisingh pleaded (*Frontline*, 1986; see also Lama [1996: 50–4]):

> Morarji Desai [India's Prime Minister] described us as foreigners and said were welcome to go back to Nepal.... Such irresponsible talk is possible because we do not have a home. Hence our demand for Gorkhaland. We Indian-Nepalis who have nothing to do with Nepal are constantly confused with 'Nepalis', that is, citizens of Nepal, a foreign country. But if there is Gorkhaland, then our identity as Indians belonging to an Indian state will be clear.

With Ghisingh at the helm, the movement distanced itself from the border. The GNLF did not advocate a transnational identity nor an Indo-Nepali 'ethnoscape' (Appadurai 1996). Neither did it imagine Nepal as a homeland. Instead, the Gorkhas had 'nothing to do with Nepal'. Yes, they were of Nepali heritage, but socially, politically and in their hearts, they were unquestionably Indian. They lived at, but definitely not across, India's border with Nepal. The GNLF coupled spatial reckonings of national inclusion with temporal ones. Ghisingh was firm that since the Gorkhas were settled in Darjeeling long before independence (1947), they were an undeniable part of the nation-state (Ghisingh quoted in Lama 1996: 61, 115).

Yet if Ghisingh countered accusations of Gorkhas being 'foreigners', he also cultivated the ambiguities associated with the border. As a political object, the border became a double-edge sword that could be wielded to stunning affects. Take the question of citizenship: The Indian Constitution states unequivocally that all those residing in India at the time of independence were legal citizens. This would include the majority of Darjeeling's population. Yet Ghisingh threw the Gorkhas' citizenship into question by pointing to Clause 7 of the Indo-Nepali Treaty of 1950, which granted 'reciprocal' rights to Nepalis domiciled in India and vice versa. Never mind that the clause made no mention of citizenship. According to Ghisingh, it 'labeled the whole settled ethnic race of the Gorkhas as foreigners, immigrants or reciprocal peoples'.[7] The Gorkhas therefore were not 'bona fide citizens of India'.[8] These plays upon uncertainty became the stuff of a viral politics of anxiety, itself a galvanising force of the GNLF's sub-nationalist movement.

For three years (1986–8), Darjeeling convulsed in sub-nationalist agitation. The enemy was primarily the state of West Bengal—then ruled by the communist CPI (Marxist) party, which resisted the ethnic division of its territory. Region-wide *bandh*s (strikes) paralysed the hills. GNLF guerrillas launched brazen attacks on the Centre's and West Bengal's military and paramilitary forces, who responded by razing homes and villages. Today, people's memories are punctuated with tales of kidnapping, decapitated heads appearing in the bazaar, disappeared loved ones and countless other atrocities. The suffering was to little avail. The Gorkhaland movement failed to deliver a separate state. In 1988, a conciliatory reward was granted in the form of the Darjeeling Gorkha Hill Council (DGHC). Extending the ambit of exceptionalism, the DGHC was deemed a semi-autonomous administration, but it remained within West Bengal. Ghisingh assumed the helm, but the lustre of the DGHC proved short-lived. The people's desires for rights, recognition and a secure sense of identity remained unrequited.

The Gorkhaland movement did not solve the identity crisis, as was promised. Rather, through its failure, it only exacerbated the Gorkhas' anxieties over being-in and being-of India. The desires that remained soon triggered new ethno-political mobilisations—these of a decidedly more legal bent.

TRIBAL BECOMINGS

In the 1990s and 2000s, new political forays redrew the lines of ethnic identification in Darjeeling. Seeking alternative routes to rights and recognition, individual communities like the Tamangs, Gurungs and Limbus who comprised the Gorkha conglomerate began mobilising for recognition as Scheduled Tribes (ST) of India. ST status promised affirmative action advantages including employment quotas in governmental posts, lower standards of admission to education, eligibility for special tribal development packages and hosts of other entitlements (GoI 2007). Perhaps equally important for the aspiring tribes of Darjeeling was the symbolic inclusion this designation afforded. They would be Scheduled Tribes *of India.*

Not coincidentally, this was when affirmative action was thrust to the fore of national attention by the controversies surrounding the possible implementation of the Mandal Commission's recommendations to raise quotas for Scheduled Castes (SC), Scheduled Tribes (ST) and Other Backward Classes (OBC) in government posts and public universities from 27 per cent to 49.5 per cent. While the violent protests and self-immolations of 1990 informed the nation of the quandaries of positive discrimination, they also alerted minorities to the advantages of SC, ST and OBC status. In Darjeeling, four communities—the Bhutia, Lepcha, Sherpa and Yolmo—had enjoyed ST status since 1950. Now, others believed they were due. The Tamangs and Limbus pioneered these tribal politics, with the Gurungs and Rais following their lead. By the middle years of the 2000s, the quest for tribal recognition had become a pan-ethnic phenomenon, as virtually every non-ST constituent group of the greater Gorkha community had filed for ST status (Middleton 2011, 2015; Shneiderman 2009, 2015; Shneiderman and Turin 2006: 54–8).

These claims of tribal identity marked an abrupt shift in the identification practices and politics of the hills. The quest for tribal recognition necessitated an undoing of the Gorkhas on a number of registers. Politically, the go-it-alone tactics of aspiring STs atomised the Gorkha conglomerate and refigured the unit of ethno-political mobilisation. Socially, the exigencies of ST recognition amplified inter-ethnic competition and distinction. Analytically too, there were tensions. For while the Gorkha identity was predicated on a pan-ethnic hybridity, ST recognition called for this hybridity's undoing—and with it, a possible dissolution of the Gorkha identity.

Consider the formal and informal criteria of tribal recognition in twenty-first century India. Officially, the criteria of ST recognition are as follows: (*a*) Indication of primitive traits, (*b*) distinctive culture, (*c*) geographical isolation, (*d*) shyness of contact with the community at large and (*e*) backwardness (est. 1965; GoI 2005a). But as Darjeeling's aspiring tribes would learn, unofficial paradigms of differentiation also affect ST recognition. The Indian government professes the secular logic that 'religion is no bar to being a tribal' (GoI 2005a). But, as I have shown elsewhere (Middleton 2015), state ethnographers and administrators frequently evoke a radical alterity between tribes and Hindu castes in their adjudications. The evocation of this binary functions then as means of morally regulating (Corrigan and Sayer 1985: 4) the kinds of community deemed eligible for governmental care and national inclusion.

For aspiring tribes like the Gurungs, satisfying these official and unofficial criteria seemed especially impossible. The inter-ethnic mixing that followed the Gurungs' migration to Darjeeling only redoubled generations of syncretisation— or more specifically Hinduisation—within the Hindu kingdom of Nepal. Long before they settled in Darjeeling, the Gurungs thus had a unique, syncretic character. Unlike in Nepal, however, their admixture in India resulted in the Gurungs 'losing' their territorial distinction, language and much of their discrete sociocultural traditions. Paradoxically, these were precisely the ethnological contents they needed to show to become Scheduled Tribes of India. How then did they do this?

They turned to ethnology. Study teams combed the native and academic ethnologies of Nepal looking for representations of the proper Gurung tribal subject. Ethnographic delegations travelled to the Gurung interiors of Nepal to capture the 'authentic', 'original' and 'pure' culture of their ancestors. Brought back to Darjeeling, these findings served a dual purpose: they became the scaffolding of cultural revitalisation *and* the content of their 'tribal' submissions to the Indian government.

Unfortunately, when the Gurungs' application finally reached New Delhi in 2005, the Register General of India (RGI)—Social Sciences Wing rejected their file. The RGI raised 14 points of contention, among them outstanding questions of: the origin and dubious autochthony of the group; evidence of religious, economic and cultural change since the days they were 'nomadic pastoralists, hunters, and shifting cultivators'; their lack of isolation in Darjeeling; the presence of modern amenities such as radios, televisions and cinemas; and the opinion that, because of their 'gradual assimilation into the Great Tradition' of Hinduism, it would be 'a retrograde step' to recognise them as STs (GoI 2005b).

To the Gurungs' relief, the RGI rejection was not a final ruling. They were given another chance to address their ethnological shortcomings. Working with the anthropologists of West Bengal, the Gurungs worked to clarify the RGI's misunderstandings and hopefully re-advance their application. Ethnic elites meanwhile called on their personal contacts in government and sent numerous delegations to Kolkata and Delhi to lobby their cause. This required navigating sociopolitical arenas where, as border communities, the Gurungs had little experience. Thanks to these efforts, the Gurungs' quest for ST status seemed back on track by 2006–7. Boosting hopes were new political developments, which heralded the dawn of a tribal era—not just for the Gurungs but perhaps for all of Darjeeling. It is to this other front of tribal becoming that I now turn.

A TRIBAL AREA?

In 2005, Subash Ghisingh, West Bengal and the Centre signed a Memorandum of Settlement (MoS) declaring their intention to make Darjeeling a 'tribal area' as per the Sixth Schedule of the Indian Constitution. Originally designed for northeast India, the Sixth Schedule incorporates existing tribal political institutions into autonomous District Councils with powers to regulate forest and property rights, social customs and local administrative structures (for instance, the appointment of headmen and chiefs) (see Indian Constitution, Articles 244(2) and 275(1)). Certainly, this was no Gorkhaland, but it promised increased autonomy and recognition nonetheless. How exactly this Sixth Schedule would take form in Darjeeling was unclear, however. To date, the region was only 32 per cent ST—far short of the tribal majority thought necessary. Due to their histories of migration and hybridity, there were no extant tribal political institutions to build upon. And, despite the various movements afoot for ST recognition, tribal identification remained, for many, an alien concept. Twenty years earlier, even Ghisingh himself had rejected the idea, claiming, 'We are not tribals. Such a status is bestowed upon people who are uncivilized, very backward, whose men go around naked and whose women go bare breasted. But we are advanced people. We are civilized' (*Frontline*, 1986; see also Lama [1996: 50–4]).

To bolster the case for Sixth Schedule status, Ghisingh and his administration's Department of Information and Cultural Affairs (DICA) organised massive spectacles of tribal identity. Throughout 2006 and 2007, DICA engineered flamboyant public rituals, broadcasting shamanic, 'nature-worshipping' chants through the streets at mind-numbing decibels. Parades of tribes snaked through town, demonstrating the Gorkhas' new-found tribal identity. Attendance was requested. Dress codes were enforced. Aspiring STs like the Gurungs proved

willing participants, since they believed the Sixth Schedule and Ghisingh could
provide the push they needed to secure ST status. There thus emerged a palpable
synergy between these respective tribal movements. With multicultural governance
providing the carrots and GNLF cadres wielding the stick, tribal identification
became the order of the day.

That synergy produced increasingly bizarre events. During the holiday season
of 2006, DICA did away with all Hindu icons—a major intervention considering
the entire season is structured around holidays of Hindu origin. As but one
example, for Durga Puja (the crown jewel of the holiday season), DICA removed
the idol of Durga that typically presides over the merrymaking and worship, only
to supplant the Hindu goddess with *shilā* (enormous stone) plucked from the bed
of a nearby river by a *jhankri* (local shaman). For days, shamans adorned in full
ritual attire hovered around the rock shaking in trance, as bureaucrats monitored
the proceedings. Musical troops were brought to the stage to sing specially
arranged devotional songs. Processions came and went, bringing thousands to pay
their homage to the rock—the centrepiece of a bizarre, ostensibly tribal ritual.

Philosopher Charles Taylor reminds us that the politics of recognition may
do their most insidious work through processes of misrecognition. According
to Taylor, 'People can suffer real damage, real distortion, if the people or society
around them mirror back to them a demeaning or contemptible picture of
themselves' (Taylor 1992: 5). Certainly, this is true in Darjeeling. For generations,
the Gorkhas have been called 'foreigners', 'outsiders', 'martial races', 'chinkies' and
various other specious monikers of national exclusion. Misrecognition has attended
and defined their questionable place in India. Yet in light of the replacement of
Durga with the rock, I think we might take Taylor's insight a step further. The
question here becomes not merely how the politics of recognition may engender
misrecognition but also misidentification. That is, to what extent do classificatory
systems push people to self-identify as something they are not?

In fact, opponents of the Sixth Schedule seized on this very point. Tribal
identity, they argued, was an absurdity that flew in the face of current sociocultural
practice. Equally, it was an affront to the Gorkhas and the cause of Gorkhaland,
for which so many had lived and died. There were sociopolitical concerns as well.
Since rights and representation in the coming 'tribal area' would be unequally
distributed between ST and non-ST communities, aspiring tribes believed they
would be 'left out' of the benefits of Sixth Schedule status. Seeing a divide-and-
rule strategy in the offing, these 'left-out' (read 'non-ST') communities sent a
memorandum to the Indian government framing their concerns as follows:[9]

> We would like to ask you why many different tribes within the Gorkha community are being discriminately denied the facilities and provisions given to a part of the same community who are so far constitutionally Scheduled Tribes, though they have the same historical, cultural, geographical and economical background and are in the same stage of social and economical development.... Then why should the State government and our government at the Centre adopt this partial and unjust pick-and-choose system, which will definitely give rise to discontent and chaos in this region?

With arguments like these, the Sixth Schedule appeared less a beacon of rights, recognition and autonomy, and more a hollow promise, riddled with seeds of communal disharmony. Throughout 2007, support for the bill rapidly declined, before an unexpected turn of events powerfully reset the table of ethno-politics in the hills.

GORKHALAND RETURNS

On 23 September 2007, a young police constable of Darjeeling named Prashant Tamang won *Indian Idol 3*. With a Gorkha taking top honours at the massively popular television show, Darjeeling and the Nepali-speaking world writ large were ecstatic. The euphoria was short-lived. Several days after Prashant's victory, a Delhi radio-DJ made racial slurs against the Gorkha-turned-Indian Idol. Striking a nerve during an otherwise joyous occasion, the discriminatory remarks prompted outrage across the hills, and eventually a communal riot in Siliguri, wherein more than 800 Gorkhas found themselves pinned under a barrage of debris from Bengali counter protestors. After hours of being held hostage by the Bengali mob, the army eventually freed the Gorkhas. But the damage was done—the swift turn of events, an all-too-familiar reminder of the Gorkhas' precarious place in India.

Soon thereafter, on 7 October 2017, 'Jai Gorkha! Jai Gorkhaland!' reverberated through the Darjeeling streets as 20,000-strong chanted a new liberation front, the Gorkha Janmukti Morcha, into existence. Lauding Gorkhaland as the destiny of the Gorkhas, the Morcha looked suspiciously like the GNLF of old. The resemblance was not coincidental. Morcha founder, Bimal Gurung, had served as a GNLF henchman until just weeks prior. Likewise, most of the party's leadership and constituents had defected from the GNLF. The Morcha went straight to work reinstating the Gorkha identity. Doing so, they championed an identity that mapped closer to the sociocultural and affective realities of the hills than did the tribal ploys of Ghisingh and the GNLF. Where the GNLF brought rocks, the Morcha told the people to celebrate as they always had. Where the GNLF struggled for the Sixth Schedule, the Morcha promised Gorkhaland. So sure was Bimal Gurung himself that *this* Gorkhaland movement would be successful, he promised to commit suicide were a separate state not achieved by 10 March 2010.

Galvanised by this firebrand rhetoric, public support quickly shifted to the Morcha. In February 2008, Ghisingh resigned amid massive Morcha-led protests and inter-party violence. He was quickly chased from the hills. The Morcha suddenly had a monopolistic grip on power and the public imagination. Gorkhaland 2.0 proceeded accordingly. The Morcha framed their agitation as a non-violent, 'Gandhian' affair, but their muscular practices said otherwise. Similar to the 1980s GNLF, the Morcha stoked anxieties over belonging in India while unsettling life with protests, hunger strikes, *bandh*s, inter-party violence and sporadic outbursts of violence against the state of West Bengal. Agitation thus re-emerged as both a phenomenological condition and a political project.

From 2008 onwards, Morcha cadres carried on their agitation for a separate state. Meanwhile, Morcha leaders began negotiations with West Bengal and the Centre to resolve the crisis. Yet as news leaked from these tripartite meetings, the focus seemed to be not a separate state of Gorkhaland, but rather the creation of an 'interim set-up' with dubious autonomy. For the public, this sounded suspiciously like the DGHC administration, which summarily failed to satisfy their desires for autonomy and recognition following the 1980s agitation. As this new agitation wore on, the Morcha's doublespeak became increasingly apparent. Gradually, people grew wary of the party and its promises. Coming as no surprise to anyone, 10 March 2010—the day Gurung was to deliver Gorkhaland or martyr himself—came and went with little ado.

Faltering on their promises of Gorkhaland, the Morcha began 2011 with what they called the 'Long March'. This event would see thousands of Gorkha protestors march to the future borders of Gorkhaland to stake a symbolic and physical claim upon the nation-state. Fittingly, the Long March was stopped short, as it left the geopolitical confines of the hills, by the West Bengal police.

Prevented from advancing into the plains of the Dooars, Bimal Gurung and his 1000-person entourage immediately set up camp in protest. During the two-week standoff that ensued, Morcha agitators, state police and central paramilitary forces flooded to the scene. Tensions reached their breaking point on the morning of 8 February when police and paramilitary personnel resorted to *lathi* (stick/club) charges and tear gas to disperse the now 3000-strong camp-in. The protestors initially scattered, but then reassembled for a vengeful clash with the state.

The ensuing violence left two dead and hundreds injured (*The Telegraph*, 2011a; *The Telegraph*, 2011b).

The events triggered a volley of after-effects in the hills. Angry mobs took to the streets chanting 'Gorkhaland', torching government offices, police outposts and whatever symbols of West Bengal lay in their path. Exacerbating the alarm, the Morcha called an indefinite strike, crippling the hills until further notice. With the Central Reserve Police Force (CRPF) called in to pre-empt further unrest, Darjeeling entered into a familiar state of emergency. The Long March was pregnant with symbolism from start to finish. The ends were all-too-familiar. Yet again the Gorkhas had attempted to claim their place in India. Yet again, they had been relegated to their particular corner of the nation.

CRISES RECONSIDERED

By 2011, the optimism that marked the heady days of the tribal turn in the mid-2000s and the second Gorkhaland movement had given way to the sobering inefficacies of these identities. The Sixth Schedule was off the table. Likewise, Gorkhaland. In July of 2011, tripartite negotiations resolved on the establishment of the Gorkhaland Territorial Authority (GTA), a local administrative set-up with limited autonomy that remained within West Bengal. Not surprisingly, the GTA met with a lukewarm reception on the streets. If the GTA failed to deliver autonomy, the quests for ST recognition similarly suffered setbacks. During this period, multiple communities received rejections of their ST bids. To date (2019), none of Darjeeling's outstanding aspiring tribes has gained recognition. Whether Gorkha or tribal, the story thus remained troublingly the same—ethno-political mobilisations full of hope, met with denial and, in the end, disappointment.

The pattern has only perpetuated. In 2013, Darjeeling again erupted in the name of Gorkhaland, when the Centre announced the creation of a new state of Telangana. Having pegged the cause of Gorkhaland to that of Telangana, the Morcha recommenced their agitation, as violent protests and self-immolations rocked the hills throughout the summer months of 2013. The agitations of 2017, the most severe in decades, ratcheted up the intensity considerably. An unexpected 105 days of crippling strikes, food shortages, bombs going off in the streets, police raids and deaths on both sides marked this latest agitation for Gorkhaland. However, when the dust settled and life began its tentative creep back to some semblance of 'normal', there was little to show for the people's efforts and suffering. Instead, the Morcha had split along factional lines, causing tensions between the parties moderate and more radical wings—and no shortage of concern amongst the populace, as to where these tensions might go. Late in September 2017, West Bengal Chief Minister Mamata Banerjee got in on the act, appointing moderate Morcha leader Binoy Tamang as chairman of a newly constituted GTA. The party's firebrand founder Bimal Gurung, meanwhile, was out of power and on the lam. With warrants issued for his arrest, the one-time saviour of the Gorkhas became instead the subject of a massive manhunt—a telling end to a period of considerable unrest.

And still, after all these agitations, after all these movements, the desires of the people of Darjeeling for autonomy, recognition and belonging remained unrequited. Surveying these shifting forms and terms of ethno-politics over the years, it is not so much identity's manifestations that beg consideration. More provocatively, it is its failures.

Pick up any piece of Gorkhaland propaganda, attend any political rally, and you will hear powerful cries of identity unrequited, of identity denied, of identity in crisis. The affective intensities and underlying histories animating these claims are undeniable. They must be understood and honoured. But with regard to claims of an 'identity crisis', a more nuanced reading is in order. The Gorkhas and its sub-communities like the Gurungs, Magars, and so on do not *lack* identity. Generations of ethno-genesis—entangled as it has been in state formation and the conditions of life at India's borders—have imparted strong senses of group membership, solidarity and shared histories to the people of the hills (Roosens 1989). The recurrent ethno-political mobilisations discussed above make this abundantly clear. Per these terms, these border groups 'have' identities. What they *lack* is that sacred stuff of recognition to affirm their being-in and being-of India—and, in more Hegelian terms, their being-in-and-of-themselves (Hegel 1977: 11). The crisis, in short, is not one of identity, but rather its rightful recognition.

The terms shifted accordingly, we may arrive at new readings of the 'crises' at hand. The failures of these mobilisations are neither the fault of the Gorkhas nor their variously construed identities (whether Gorkha or tribal). To be borne by other shoulders, the failures are rather best understood as the by-products of a pernicious politics of recognition that continues to deny people—and their difference—meaningful inclusion in the nation-state. That these denials have fed back into internal and external forms of agitation only corroborates the power of the Indian state to affect, regulate or otherwise dismiss those forms of difference that amass *at* and *within* its borders.

These interplays of borders, difference and recognition involve a paradox that cannot go unsaid. Border populations like the Gorkhas may maintain heightened desires for rights, inclusion and belonging in India, and increased dependency on the state to achieve those aims. Yet the conditions of life at the border often render these groups unable to meet India's norms of recognition. Contra the poetics of author Kiran Desai, for the Gorkhas of Darjeeling, there would be no *mist charging down like a dragon, dissolving, undoing, making ridiculous the drawing of borders* (Desai 2005: 9). No, for a people relegated to a literal and figurative corner of the national geography, the border remains a 'thing' that must be lived at and lived with. As an integral dimension of both life and politics, it is equally as generative as it is problematic. Herein lies the perennial paradox—and dare we say, crisis—of difference and its recognition at the borders of India and beyond.

NOTES

* An earlier version of this chapter appeared in *Political Geography* in 2013, with some of the content going on to inform my 2015 book (Middleton 2015). Excerpts reprinted from Townsend Middleton, 'States of Difference: Refiguring Ethnicity and Its "Crisis" at India's Borders', *Political Geography* 35 (2013): 14–24, with permission from Elsevier. The materials and framings of that original essay have since been updated and adapted for this volume.

1. Outside of Darjeeling, some of these groups identify as 'Gorkha', a term with a wider history on both sides of the Indo-Nepali border. See Hutt (1997); Subba and Sinha (2003) and Subba (2009). My concerns, however, are with the Gorkha identity in Darjeeling, specifically.

2. WBSA, 1888, West Bengal State Archives, File (India, General, Colonial Emigration, B1-4, July, 1888).

3. WBSA, 1868, West Bengal State Archives, File (India, Foreign, August 1868, 219–20 and 404–5, Political A); WBSA, 1869, West Bengal State Archives, File (India, Foreign, February 1869, 9, Political A); WBSA, 1878, West Bengal State Archives, File (India, Foreign, March 1878, 1–8, Political A).

4. WBSA, 1921, West Bengal State Archives, File (Bengal, Appointment, December 1930, 12–19).

5. WBSA, 1921, West Bengal State Archives, File (Bengal, Appointment, December 1930, 12–19).

6. WBSA, 1930, West Bengal State Archives, File (Bengal, Public, January 1921, 13/22).

7. 'Memorandum to Prime Minister of India' in Lama (1996: 41).
8. 'The Historic Speech' in Lama (1996: 25).
9. BGJMS, 2006, Bharatiya Gorkha Janajati Manyata Samity Office Files (Darjeeling), Memo No./DJ/12/06.

REFERENCES

Agamben, Georgio. 2005. *State of Exception*. Chicago: University of Chicago Press.

Appadurai, Arjun. 1996. *Modernity at Large: Cultural Dimensions of Globalization*. Minneapolis: University of Minnesota Press.

Bakhtin, M. M. 1981. *The Dialogic Imagination: Four Essays*. Austin: University of Texas Press.

BGJMS. 2006. Bharatiya Gorkha Janajati Manyata Samity Office Files (Darjeeling), Memo No./DJ/12/06.

Chatterjee, Piya. 2001. *A Time for Tea: Women, Labor, and Post/Colonial Politics on an Indian Plantation*. Durham: Duke University.

Cohen, Abner. 1974. 'Lessons of Ethnicity'. In *Urban Ethnicity*, edited by A. Cohen, ix–xxiv. London: Tavistock Publications.

Corrigan, Philip, and Derek Sayer. 1985. *The Great Arch: State Formation, Cultural Revolution, and the Rise of Capitalism*. Oxford: Blackwell Press.

Desai, Kiran. 2005. *The Inheritance of Loss*. Jackson, TN: Atlantic Monthly Press.

Dudley-Jenkins, Laura. 2003. *Identity and Identification in India*. New York: Routledge.

Frontline. 1986. '"Nothing Short of a Separate State": Ghisingh Interviewed by M. S. Prabhakara'. 9–22 August, Madras.

GOI. 2005a. *National Commission for Scheduled Tribes: A Handbook, 2005*. New Delhi: Government of India.

———. 2005b. Government of India, Ministry of Tribal Affairs, Letter No. 12026/5/2005.

———. 2007. *Annual Report 2006/7*. New Delhi: Government of India, Ministry of Tribal Affairs.

Hegel, Georg W. F. 1977. *Phenomenology of Spirit*. Translated by A. V. Miller. Oxford: Oxford University Press.

Hutt, Michael. 1997. 'Being Nepali without Nepal'. In *Nationalism and Ethnicity in a Hindu Kingdom*, edited by David N. Gellner and John Whelpton, 101–33. Amsterdam: Harwood Academic Publishers.

———. 1998. 'Going to Mugalan: Nepali Literary Representations of Migration to India and Bhutan'. *South Asia Research* 18 (2): 195–214.

Kennedy, Dane. 1996. *The Magic Mountains: Hill-Stations and the British Raj.* Berkeley: University of California Press.

Lama, Mahendra P., ed. 1996. *Gorkhaland Movement: Quest for an Identity.* Darjeeling: DGHC.

Middleton, Townsend. 2011. 'Across the Interface of State Ethnography: Rethinking Ethnology and Its Subjects in Multicultural India'. *American Ethnologist* 38 (2): 249–66.

———. 2013a. 'Anxious Belongings: Anxiety and the Politics of Belonging in Subnationalist Darjeeling'. *American Anthropologist* 115 (4): 608–21.

———. 2013b. 'States of Difference: Refiguring Ethnicity and Its "Crisis" at India's Borders'. *Political Geography* 35: 14–24.

———. 2015. *The Demands of Recognition: State Anthropology and Ethnopolitics in Darjeeling.* Stanford, CA: Stanford University Press.

Povinelli, Elizabeth. 2002. *The Cunning of Recognition: Indigenous Alterities and the Making of Australian Multiculturalism.* Durham: Duke University Press.

Roosens, E. G. 1989. *Creating Ethnicity: The Process of Ethnogenesis.* London: Sage.

Schmitt, Carl. 1985. *Political Theology: Four Chapters on the Concept of Sovereignty.* Translated by G. D. Schwab. Boston: MIT Press.

Scott, James C. 1998. *Seeing Like a State: How Certain Schemes to Improve the Human Condition Have Failed.* New Haven: Yale University Press.

Shneiderman, Sara. 2009. 'Ethnic (P)reservations'. In *Ethnic Activism and Civil Society in South Asia*, edited by D. Gellner, 115–42. Delhi: Sage.

———. 2015. *Rituals of Ethnicity: Thangmi Identities between Nepal and India.* Philadelphia: University of Pennsylvania Press.

Shneiderman, Sara, and Mark Turin. 2006. 'Seeking the Tribe: Ethno-Politics in Darjeeling and Sikkim'. *Himal Southasian* 19 (2): 54–8.

Sinha, A. C., and Tanka Subba, eds. 2003. *The Nepalis in Northeast India.* New Delhi: Indus.

Subba, Tanka. 1989. *Dynamics of a Hill Society: The Nepalis in Darjeeling and Sikkim Himalayas.* Delhi: Mittal Publishers.

———. 2009. 'The Last Word So Far…'. In *Indian Nepalis: Issues and Perspectives*, edited by T. B. Subba, A. C. Sinha, G. S. Nepal and D. R. Nepal, 383–93. New Delhi: Concept Publishing.

Taylor, Charles. 1992. *Multiculturalism and the Politics of Recognition.* Princeton: Princeton University Press.

The Telegraph. 2011a. 'Khukuri Slash Reopens Gash: Cop Shots Kill 2, Hills on Fire'. 2 September, Kolkata.

————. 2011b. 'On Street with Renewed State Cry'. 2 October, Kolkata.

WBSA. 1868. West Bengal State Archives. File (India, Foreign, August 1868, 219–20 and 404–5, Political A).

————. 1869. West Bengal State Archives. File (India, Foreign, February 1869, 9, Political A).

————. 1878. West Bengal State Archives. File (India, Foreign, March 1878, 1–8, Political A).

————. 1888. West Bengal State Archives. File (India, General, Colonial Emigration, B1-4, July, 1888).

————. 1921. West Bengal State Archives. File (Bengal, Appointment, December 1930, 12–19).

————. 1930. West Bengal State Archives. File (Bengal, Public, January 1921, 13/22).

4

Embattled Frontiers and Emerging Spaces

Transformation of the Tawang Border*

SWARGAJYOTI GOHAIN

In 1964, in the aftermath of the India–China war of 1962, the Indian government sanctioned the construction of the Nehru Gonpa (Tib. *dgon pa*), a monastery to commemorate the visit of India's first prime minister, Jawaharlal Nehru, to Tawang, a far-flung border in northeast India. Locals narrate how stones and bricks from an older *kakaling*, a square arch that serves as an entrance gate to the area, were used to lay the foundation of the new monastery. The Nehru Gonpa, originally built as a *kakaling*, was later rebuilt as a monastery and the charge of its maintenance given over to the Tawang Monastery, which controls the other monasteries in the area. Nehru Gonpa or Nehru Dolma Lakhang now stands in Tawang's Nehru Market area as a symbol of the new relations between the Indian state and Tibetan Buddhist institutions that were being forged in that early post-colonial period in India's north-east frontier.

The year 1962 was a watershed moment in the post-colonial history of Tawang. Having more or less continued until the early 1950s, the policy of loose administration in frontier areas begun by the British colonial government, the Indian government rethought its administrative strategies from a strict security perspective as boundary disputes with China intensified. This meant establishing political offices and agents in untouched frontier regions, including the first paramilitary post in Tawang in 1951. Tawang was of particular strategic importance as it was coveted by the Chinese state as an extension of Tibet, since it had been under Tibetan rule for more than three centuries. When border tensions blew up into a full-scale Sino-Indian war, offices, residences and monasteries were temporarily evacuated as Chinese troops overran Tawang for two months from October to December 1962.

The war hastened the process of state consolidation in Tawang. As the Indian government set up military bases and administrative quarters in Tawang, cooperatives, retail stores and other civic infrastructure also followed in a state-enabled urbanisation process in order to cater to the needs of the military population and the new administrative, business and professional classes, who started trickling in from the early 1970s onwards. How did the people of Tawang respond to the new government and to the politico-economic and demographic changes it initiated?

This chapter looks at the changing dynamics between the Tawang Monastery, local lay population and the state in this changing context, and focuses on how the Tawang Monastery negotiated with the local administration through the medium of official correspondence. This, in turn, contributed to Tawang's 'integration'. Watson (2000) uses integration instead of assimilation to speak of nationalist co-option because unlike assimilation which brinks on denial of distinct cultural identities, integration accepts difference of the 'parts' but as subsumed to the national 'whole'.[1] I use integration to refer to the inclusion of Tawang into the political and economic institutions of India, and eventual cultural integration.

While scholars have written about the role and agency of the state in fashioning border subjects (for example, Aggarwal 2004, van Schendel 2005), I argue that Tawang's incorporation into Indian political networks owed not only to an assertive state but also to the recognition given to the Indian administration by the local elite, that is, high ranking monks, as well as by the lay population.

Historicising the concept of 'recognition', Charles Taylor (1994: 25–73) writes that individual or group identity rests on recognition and is always formed in dialogical relations with others. Ideally, equal recognition means that all individuals and groups are entitled to a uniform set of rights and immunities in the public sphere in modern democratic states. However, in most societies, some individuals or groups with historical disadvantages are denied proper recognition or are misrecognised; hence, Taylor argues that equal recognition should coexist with the politics of difference, so that historically marginalised communities are ensured protection by the state.

I apply recognition in the reverse—in the sense of communities recognising the state as a legitimate presence in their political lives. As sociologist Pierre Bourdieu writes, power of reification does not stem from the personal authority of the person naming it—of the Indian state, in this case—but also from the recognition granted to it by the members of the group (Bourdieu 1991: 223). The state too needs to earn recognition from communities over which it extends its jurisdiction, and it attempts to do so through both iterative (restating its goals) or performative (active staging of its presence by propagating cultural symbols, development goods, and so on) means.

I look at one means which enabled the recognition of the Indian state among the communities of newly merged Tawang. During the period of political transition, highly placed monk officials as well as village leaders in Tawang wrote petitions to the local administration with a variety of requests. The image of an Indian sovereign power acting through the local Tawang administration became entrenched in the minds of Tawang's public as the volume of official correspondence and government circulars grew.

State presence in Tawang was of course not simply enforced through official documents and bureaucratic outreach. Overt state-building measures, such as militarisation, or more covert means, such as the introduction of mainstream education and development programmes, in the post-war period helped the state to penetrate border regions (Gohain 2013).[2] But in this chapter, I highlight two aspects of the material basis of state formation in Tawang. First, very material concerns forged, or forced, alliances between an expanding state apparatus, on the one hand, and a border population driven by instrumental concerns to recognise the former, on the other; second, the participation of the border populations in material technologies of governance, that is, official documents and bureaucratic correspondence, facilitated local recognition of the new administration. This chapter is based on documents retrieved from the deputy commissioner's office in Tawang and, in particular, on the archive of petitions for government grants addressed to the local administration.[3]

FROM MONASTERY SPACE TO ADMINISTRATIVE BASE

Tawang is a town in the district of Tawang in Arunachal Pradesh in northeast India, traditionally inhabited by the Monpa communities, who follow the Tibetan Buddhist faith.[4] Located on the borders between Indian, Tibetan and Bhutanese territories, Tawang is famous for the Tawang Monastery, which was established by Mera Lama, at the initiative of the Fifth Dalai Lama, in 1680 as a Gelugpa outpost in the seventeenth-century sectarian wars between Tibet and Bhutan (Aris 1979). By a decree of the Dalai Lama's office, and with an administration linked to the Tibetan government (Tib. *bodgzhung*), Tawang Monastery was authorised to collect taxes from Monpa villages in and around Tawang. Tawang and its adjacent district West Kameng, together known as Monyul, were divided into administrative centres or *dzong*s (Tib. *rdzong*, meaning fort or district), which were in charge of jurisdiction and tax collection. The present town of Tawang is at a distance of 1 kilometre from the monastery. Monyul had three major dzongs, from south to north—Talung Dzong, Dirang Dzong and Tawang Dzong or Gyanghar Dzong, where grains collected as taxes would be stored, and carried by compulsory or corvée labour, *u-la* (Tib. *u lag*), from villages in relay form until they finally reached Tsona in Tibet, which served as the administrative headquarters of Monyul. Tawang Monastery deputed senior monks as *dzongpon*s (officers) to the dzongs to oversee the collection of agricultural levies and to settle local disputes (Sarkar 1996: 14–15). While people in other parts of what is now Arunachal Pradesh also paid taxes to some Tibetan private families (Grothmann 2012; Huber 2011), it was only in Monyul that the Tibetan state established systematic control mainly through the Tawang Monastery.

British officer Capt. F. M. Bailey—who, along with Capt. H. Morsehead, was deputed to map the boundary between Tibet and India in 1913—gives an account of the relation between Monyul and Tibet (Bailey and Morsehead 1916; cf. Anonymous n.d.; Sarkar 1996).

> Mönyul is the comparatively low-lying district of Tibet which is governed by the lamas of Tawang….The district is governed by a council of six named *Trukdri*. They are the *Kenpo*, or Abbot of Tawang Gompa, another lama in a high position, two monks known as *Nyetsangs* … and two Tsöna [district in Tibet] Dzongpöns. In this way, the Tsöna Dzongpöns have a hand in the Government of Mönyul. In the summer when the Dzongpöns are at Tsöna they keep agents at Tawang to act for them but from November to April they themselves live at Tawang and send their agents to live in the cold climate of Tsöna. Under the Trukdri are the two Dzongs, Dirang and Taklung, each of which is held by two monks sent from Tawang who act together. The Dzongpöns of Taklung live at Amratala on the Assam border in grass huts during the trading season. (Bailey and Morsehead 1916: 41–2)

Tawang Monastery was the spiritual centre for all adjoining areas of Tawang, in relation to which the local people had specified roles. Monasteries, although traditionally located at the outskirts of settlements, were never self-enclosed units; monasteries and villages were bound together in organic ties (Goldstein 1989; Sarkar 1996). Shyo basti (Tib. *zhol*—lower part or that which is below in location), a village located just below Tawang Monastery, and existing until today, was established during the construction of the monastery as part of a monastic tradition whereby a group of people settled down near the monastery premises to work for its maintenance. The monastery, in turn, looked after the needs and problems of the people from Shyo basti, as the two were engaged in what may be termed patron–client relations. Other villagers also actively participated in construction and maintenance of the monastery, and in providing food supplies and supplying labour for various services, including porterage or *u-la*.

The affairs of Tawang Monastery were then, and still are, managed by a governing council known as Lhangye Khang, headed by the abbot. The office of *lopon* (high-level monastic degree) is next in hierarchy to the abbot, and manages the monastery affairs in the latter's absence. Indeed, when I interviewed Tawang Monastery's Lopon Acharya Ngawang Norbu in May 2013, my intermediary Gelong Sangey Leta introduced him as the 'second abbot'. *Changzey* (secretary), secretary to the abbot, *dratsangbuk* (administrative manager), who looks after the properties of the monastery, and the *nyertsang* (revenue manager), who is responsible for collecting the contribution from villagers and issuing provisions to monks according to their entitlement, are other important office-bearers in the monastery administration.[5]

Tawang Monastery has 13 subsidiary monasteries as well as two nunneries in the Tawang region[6]—Nehru Gonpa was later added to the list of the original 12 branches. According to Lama Thupten Phuntsok, who founded the Manjushree orphanage in Tawang, and was awarded the Padma Shri in 2007, when Mera Lama founded the Tawang Monastery, these *gonpa*s (monastery) were constructed in the villages at the request of the villagers for the purpose of spreading religion. In other cases, *gonpa*s which had been built to consecrate a spot where a great lama had sat in meditation, and which did not have any caretaker, were entrusted to the Tawang Monastery by the villagers for better administration. The abbot of Tawang Monastery deputes monks for a period of three years to each of these branches. The monks on deputation have to take care of the affairs of the monastery, and in turn the monastery supplies their provisions. Traditionally, villagers too contributed certain amount of food grains and other articles to the monks (Sarkar 1996: 14).

In those pre-independence days, it was compulsory for each family in the surrounding villages of Tawang having three sons and more to send their second or middle son, *bu sum barma* (Tib. *Bugsum barpa*) to become a monk, the breach of which resulted in community fines. In the traditional system, each family had to contribute food grains to the Tawang Monastery twice a year, once in summer and once in autumn (Anonymous n.d.). Those who paid taxes in the form of grains were *khreipa*s (Tib. *khralpa*) (tax payer). At the time of the monastery's founder Mera Lama, each tax-paying family's landed property was measured in terms of *khrei kang*, a local unit of land measurement, and each householder had to pay for one *khrei kang* a given amount of wheat, millet or barley, which could vary according to the year or area. When the landed property of a householder is divided among his heirs, the *khrei* (tax) was also proportionately shared by them. Families also had to provide firewood to the monastery in rotation and to cultivate land belonging to the monastery, retaining a particular percentage of the produce (Anonymous n.d.: 23; Sarkar 1996: 17).

This system continued until the early decades of the twentieth century. When Chinese Manchu General Chao Ehr-feng conducted some exploratory forays in the south of Tibet towards the North East frontier areas in 1910–11, the British were alerted to the vulnerability of this frontier and as a result, officers F. M. Bailey and H. T. Morsehead were deputed to map the boundary between Tibet and British India in 1913. In 1914, the British and Tibetan representatives met at the Simla Convention to delineate the Indo-Tibetan boundary, known as the McMahon Line, which included Tawang within India. However, as the Chinese representative refused to sign the boundary agreement, the British were reluctant to actively engage in boundary demarcation. Tibetan representatives of the Tawang Monastery sent from Tibet continued to freely collect taxes from the Monpas.

For several years, Tawang had no dealings with the Indian government except for encountering the odd expedition of British officers now and then—Captain Nevill in 1914, Ludlow and Sherriff in 1934–5 and 1938 and Frank Kingdon-Ward in the 1930s, to mention some (Arpi 2013)—and Tawang remained a de facto part of Tibet. In February 1951, almost four years after India's independence, and in the event of an impending Tibetan defeat to Chinese forces,[7] a paramilitary expedition to Tawang led by Major Bob Khating of the Indian Frontier Administration Services put an end to Tibetan tax collection and established the first Indian administrative post in the region.

In October 1962, Chinese troops attacked several posts on the western and eastern sector of the Sino-Indian border (Lamb 1966).[8] After the war ended, the Indian government sealed all border passages between Tawang and Tibet. Tawang was co-opted into the North East Frontier Agency (NEFA), a frontier tract that was initially composed of five divisions: Kameng, Subansiri, Siang, Lohit and Tirap, with each division being governed by the office of the political officer, later renamed as deputy commissioner. Tawang was made a subdivision of the Kameng Frontier Division, and the highest political post in Tawang was that of the additional political officer, later termed the additional deputy commissioner. NEFA was administrated by the Ministry of External Affairs with the governor of Assam acting as the agent to the president of India. In 1972, NEFA became a union territory and was given the name Arunachal Pradesh. In 1987, Arunachal Pradesh was conferred full statehood. At present, it has 16 districts. Tawang became an independent district with its own deputy commissioner on 16 October 1984.[9]

In the years following the India–China war, Tawang underwent a significant makeover. The rise of new administrative quarters and the movement and settlement of Indian army troops and their occupation of local residential, forest and grazing lands for use as housing and cantonment areas and firing ranges reinvented Tawang as a military base. Whereas earlier, the Tawang Monastery and its networks constituted the dominant spaces of Tawang, defining duties, roles, tenancy and tax, with the co-option of the monastery into Indian politico-economic circuits, the old networks were replaced by new ones. In the present time, the abbot of Tawang Monastery, who holds the highest office, and used to be previously appointed from Tibet, is now appointed by the Dalai Lama from Dharamsala, in direct consultation with the Government of India (Anonymous n.d.).

During this phase of political transition, the monastery administration negotiated with the Indian administration for material assistance. Previously used to acquiring religious and commercial supplies mainly through taxes and partly from Tibet's treasuries, the Tawang Monastery now had to rely on grants from the Indian administration in order to meet basic maintenance needs of its inmates and for conducting rituals. In 1996, Sarkar writes about the changed economic situation of the monastery, 'With the establishment of the [Indian] administration, these dzongs had ceased to function and the loss of the tax is made up nowadays from other sources and internal adjustments' (1996: 15).

In this respect, the writing of petitions constituted an important means of gaining access to the state. It was not as if official correspondence came into existence through the dealings with the Indian state. Writing, and not orality, characterised earlier official interactions between the Tibetan government and Tawang. As Lopon Acharya told me,

> Till 1951, the Tibetan Dzongpon ... used to be based at Gyanghar. All orders sent from Tibet would come in two copies, one to Tawang Monastery and the other to the Dzongpon at Gyanghar. Tawang Monastery had many branches upto Udalguri in Assam.... Copies of all the orders that came from Tibet to Tawang Monastery would be sent to these branches. The lama in charge of the branches would communicate this order to all those in the *gonpa* working under him. Copies of orders would also be sent to the villages by the officers at Gyanghar Dzong. All such circulars would be sent from Tawang monastery. (Interview, 27 May 2013)

In the post-colonial Indian state, however, petition writing in the language of modern bureaucracy was a 'technology of governmentality' (A. Gupta 2012) through which the communication and interaction between populations and the state were regulated by standardised rules—the monastery elite as well as local populations discovered that they could now take recourse to writing in the official language of English and adopt the bureaucratic format of government forms and applications in order to reach out to the state. As *mangmas* (village councils) and village headmen discovered that they could directly communicate with state offices, they also drafted appeals to the Tawang administration to provide them infrastructural support for local cultural institutions.

It was not writing per se that was at issue, but official documentation—the legacy of British colonial rule. Scholars have pointed out how bureaucratic documents have a 'generative capacity'—where statistics, data and reports make things come into being (A. Gupta 2012; Hull 2012; Mathur 2012). But documents are central also to how the state comes to be imagined and encountered by subject populations, and how state presence is materialised through such documents (Sharma and Gupta 2006). As people participate in this culture of official documentation—file culture, paperwork, proforma filling, and so on, they allow themselves to be part of a shared identity that is created, coordinated and controlled by the exchange, routing and circulation of documents (Hull 2012). Thus, in engaging with the document culture of the Indian state, the people of Tawang produced themselves as its subjects.

Writing petitions for grants had another material outcome—petitions were oriented towards material objectives of securing financial aid not simply for monastic sustenance but also for new cultural projects, such as the building of monastery schools or cultural committees. The Indian state responded by giving due consideration to these applications and supplications for grants. This was not simply a way of carrying out patrimonial responsibilities towards its marginal frontier inhabitants but also because Indian administrators understood that promoting local cultural institutions was key to holding onto a still slippery border.

CUSTOM, CONFLICT AND CHANGE

At the turn of the century, weighed down by the pressures to keep up with the changing times, the Tawang Monastery underwent major renovations, and also a rehauling of its system of functioning in 2003. The 'Approach Paper for the Workshop on Traditional System and Functioning of Tawang Monastery' brought out by Tawang Monastery during this time focused on the challenges that the monastery had been facing since the shift in its political control from Tibetan to Indian hands. The 'Approach Paper' discusses among other things such as greater disciplining of the monk population, the need to open new channels of communication with the district administration. This included proposals to have a member of the monastery regularly attending meetings convened by the district administration, seeking financial help from the Government of India for constructing a museum and for preserving the monastery's antique treasures. There were also proposals to improve the link between the monastery and laity by involving villagers in the functioning of the monastery, such as appointing and training persons from villages as caretakers of some branches of the Tawang Monastery.

Neither the problems addressed nor the solutions sought in the 'Approach Paper' were new; they had their inception in the period of Tawang's political transition in the 1950s. With the loss of Tibetan networks, former equations between the monastery and laity also shifted. Tawang Monastery lost its authority over former tax-paying subjects who, freed from previous compulsory levies, became lax in discharging traditional duties and services to the monastery.

While doing my doctoral fieldwork (conducted in different phases from 2008 to 2013), elderly Monpa villagers told me that the local population was glad when Indian forces got rid of the Tibetan tax officials in 1951. The Tibetan tax-collector retains the image of a cruel master in Tawang's collective memory. Older people in their 80s recalled the dread that these Tibetan agents would arouse in them when they arrived for collection. Punishments would range from beatings, starvation and jailing for even the most trivial follies, such as failure to feed the horses on time.

A locally published biography of Pema Gombu, an influential man from one of the aristocratic clans of Lhou administrative subdivision and former headman of Lhou village in Tawang, presents a description of how the people of Tawang supported Major Bob Khating's expedition to Tawang.[10] Pema Gombu, who was 89 years old when I interviewed him, and has since passed away, told me that he had guided the Indian forces through Tawang when they arrived. A common local narrative is that the Monpas had requested the Indian state to occupy their areas since they wanted to be free of Tibetan rule. While I am not completely sure whether the discursive element of 'request', whereby the Monpas' wishes are seen as being taken into account, is a later addition to local legend mediated by official representations, it does hint at the fissures that existed between the local lay people and an extractive monastic system.

As the Sino-Indian war raged in the mountainous terrain of Tawang in the cold winter months of 1962, an incident took place which revealed the extent to which the breach between the monastery and the laity had widened. On 24 October 1962, taking advantage of the wartime disorder, some local villagers looted Tawang Monastery of many valuable items, including sacred gifts to deities containing priceless gems, silk robes, gold and diamonds. As the government had evacuated the monastery, looters grabbed the opportunity to pilfer even the personal property of many monks. Many of these villagers, when confronted later, refused to return the items they had robbed.[11] The incident weakened the monastery's position in local society, spiritually and financially, while exposing the declining hold of the monastery on the local people.

A government official touring Tawang in 1972 notes the changing relations between monasteries and the lay public:

> It was pointed out by the Rinpoche [abbot] that the gompa [monastery] is finding difficulties in maintaining the day to day activities of the monastery because of lacking interest on the part of the villagers in the Tawang area. In the past [there was] material assistance by way of food grains, firewood etc to maintain the livelihood of the inmates of the monastery. With the advent of our administration and the expansion of schools, agriculture, and other obligations such as provision of porters for carrying loads, provision of laborers for construction of roads, buildings, and various other government purposes, the religious life of the people are gradually disturbed and traditional pattern of activities seriously eroded. This is a very serious problem for the people of Tawang region, and I thought it worth bringing to the notice of the Administration and the members of Pradesh Council/Zilla Parishad.[12]

With the coming of the Indian administration, ideas of democratic citizenship rather than that of a theocratic order came to define social roles and membership. Previous hierarchies loosened as lay people observed high-ranking monks whom they held in awe, submitting to the local administration. As more and more non-Buddhist people moved into the area to fulfil functions of security, government, trade and education, local Monpas began interacting on a much wider cultural canvas than ever before, and the overarching influence of the local Buddhist institutions began to slowly unravel.

During Tibetan rule, law and order situations in the jurisdiction of the Tawang Monastery rested on the high-ranking lamas, and disputes in Tawang were either settled by Tibetan *dzongpon*s or, if the disagreements were big, taken to the courts of Lhasa. In cases of failure to perform duties or deliver taxes, errant villagers were disciplined through pretty straightforward measures of caning or imprisonment. With the declining influence of the Tawang Monastery in the politico-economic domain, civil disobedience also mounted and monastery authorities turned to the new sovereign power amidst them for resolving these problems. They appealed to the Indian state to bring to account villagers who were not fulfilling their duties as monastery subjects.

In a letter to the additional deputy commissioner of Tawang, the monastery authorities protested that the people of Kharteng village had violated their traditional duties to the monastery by not carrying the grains to Kharteng *gonpa*—affiliated to the Tawang Monastery—as was expected of them, and were instead, diverting them to another village. The Tawang district administration responded by holding a meeting with the villagers of Kharteng and reminded them of their traditional duties. The monastery also turned to the Indian administration to settle or negotiate private disputes, and to enforce discipline among monks by sending the Central Reserve Police Forces (CRPF) to the monastery.[13]

Conversely, villagers too turned to the state as a medium through which to negotiate with the monastery. Official correspondence addressed to the additional deputy commissioner in 1973–4 shows how in the changed social context, villages (Kharman, Gispu, Mago-Thingbu) tried to bargain for greater leeway in discharging traditional services by offering to pay cash in lieu of construction labour in the monastery.[14]

Besides calling upon the state to adjudicate conflicts, monastery authorities also requested the state's financial aid to carry out cultural activities of the monastery. For example, during the earlier Tibetan regime, public funds and levies were used to meet expenses for the celebration of the annual monastic festival Torgya. Expenses for the Dungyur festival, performed every third year, were met by taxes levied from the Talung Dzong area, while the first two days of celebration of the Monlam Chenmoh ceremony performed in the monastery in the first Monpa lunar month Dawa Dangpo was funded by taxes from Dirang (Sarkar 1996: 15). When this source was extinguished as a result of political change, the Tawang Monastery applied to the local administration. In 1974, the monastery not only asked for extra security forces and continuous electricity supply from the administration but also costumes for *cham* (Tib. *Cham*—religious ceremonial dances held in the monastery).

The original cham dress (dress for lama dance) was provided to Tawang gomba by Tibet govt. [*sic*] when this region was under Tibetan region ... after that few items had been replaced by our admin. [*sic*] In general, the dance dresses now used by the lamas during the Tarja [Torgya] are really tattered and miserable and require replacement to keep the prestige of the gomba and admin. [*sic*] because this gomba is now more or less maintained by this administration.[15]

Deprived of earlier sources of sustenance, high-ranking monks had to rely on the new government for maintaining their previous lifestyles. An official letter shows how the abbot of the Tawang Monastery, Rigya Rinpoche, sought government funds for the transport for his pilgrimage as well as a private house that he could use for meditation retreat.

... at present, I am staying in the monastery itself. But sometime I have to stay away from population for meditation.... I decided to construct a house of my own which can be used for meditation mandir cum residence.... I will be grateful if administration can help me in this respect.[16]

The monastery administration was not the only entity which used formal grant applications to generate funding. Rural people were also quick to recognise this new and democratic source of income, as a letter from a village council attests. With the establishment of village councils and Panchayati Raj institutions in 1965, prominent villagers and headmen could directly negotiate with state authorities in their capacity of resource persons to get grants for renovating village or local *gonpa*s. Becoming aware of the state's interest in keeping alive cultural institutions, many of these men asked for and were granted funds for community activities.

Most of the requests from lay people were for financial help to either revive dying customs or renovate decaying cultural structures. One of the first proposals of this kind, submitted under the category of cultural grant in the year 1975–6, was for supporting the *choekor* (Tib. *Chosskor*—cycle of teachings, texts) festival—where lamas and lay representatives from every village carried sacred Buddhist scriptures from the Tawang Monastery in procession around all the villages to ensure good fortune and plentiful crops. Each village receives the procession participants with food and drinks in temporary shelters, and the money to buy the food rations and construct the shelters was sought from the local administration. There were also several petitions for grants to rebuild village *gonpa*s, and in 1978, the local administration sanctioned a total of 93,938 rupees for renovating 10 *gonpa*s that came under Lumla, an administrative section in Tawang district, in response to such a request.

As these relations between monastery, state and laity began to evolve, civil society organisations arose in order to mediate the relations between the state and monastery, and formed the basis of an emergent public sphere (Habermas 1991).[17] In Tawang, the monastery was initially an all-enveloping entity, functioning within the theocratic organisation of the Tibetan state. Public and private interests fused in the operation of monasteries under the religious government of Tibet. The Tawang Monastery claimed absolute rights over its subjects and there was no civil society force to question these claims. But with the dilution of the monastery's powers, and its absorption by the new democratic administration, the situation was reversed, as the monastery was now placed on the side of civil society, in the state–civil society divide, requiring its own mediating organisations.

A new civil body, the Tawang Monpa Cultural Society was inaugurated on 27 July 1974 and was attended by 50 prominent Monpa elders representing different subdivisions of Tawang, the abbot of the Tawang Monastery, lamas, Panchayat members and *gaonbura*s (village headmen). It was agreed that Tawang Monpa Cultural Society would jointly decide with the monastery authority regarding any disciplinary action to be taken against monastery employees. While the pattern of monastic discipline would follow custom, if the need for change arose, the matter would be discussed by senior monks, Panchayat members and *gaonbura*s. This civil society organisation worked initially as the public relations unit of the monastery,[18] but gradually widened its locus to other activities.

The various forms of collaboration between monastery, civil society and state were especially visible in the building and functioning of the Tawang Monastery School, which came into being in the year 1977–8 with grants from the Arunachal Pradesh government. When a political officer in charge of Tawang observed that people now preferred to send their children to the newly set up government schools instead of to the monastery, he conferred with the abbot of Tawang Monastery to discuss solutions. Both parties recognised that the monastery would have to reform its traditional curriculum if it were to attract students by invigorating it with modern subjects. In 1980–1, the monastery administration sought and was given government funds to construct a school and hostel for students.[19]

BARTERING BORDER LOYALTIES

The post-colonial transformations of Tawang call to mind Peter Sahlins' (1991) classic study on the formation of the France–Spain border in the Cerdanya, a border region on the Pyrenees ranges. Sahlins shunts between perspectives of the state/centre and the local Catalan rural society to show how the border was not only the result of state manoeuvres but was also actively shaped by the local elites and rural peasants, who alternated at different moments between a Catalan identity and a French-national identity in order to support their own interests. The construction of a national identity among the border people was thus not a simple imposition from the centre, or a top-down Frenchification process, but rather, a dialogical process, where local inhabitants actively participated in the fashioning of their identity as Frenchmen as opposed to Spaniards.

The integration of Tawang into the Indian state too cannot be entirely captured through relations of dominance and resistance between the centre and the periphery. The reorientation of Tawang from Tibetan to Indian government was not a completely state-directed process. Deliberate calculations were involved in the responses of the local elite and lay people; they were not passive receivers of policy but sought to gain certain leverage in the form of material aid from the new administration in exchange for recognising Indian sovereignty.

The state acknowledged these appeals for material assistance as a tactical measure. Michael de Certeau (1984) opposes 'tactics' and 'strategies'—whereas strategies are the forthright, forceful and well-formed ways of rule used by the strong to have their way, tactics are the 'weapons of the weak' (Scott 1985), a kind of dissimulation where the dominated momentarily inhabit the spaces of the dominant in a fragmentary merging in order to win temporary gains. Here I extend de Certeau's conceptualisation to understand tactics as not just 'weapons of the weak', but as tools utilised by the dominant as well to manufacture hegemonic consensus. In managing subject populations, states frequently combine strategies with tactical means for building consensus.

I have discussed elsewhere how state *strategies* for incorporating the Tawang border have included physical settlement of military personnel and construction of cantonments as well as symbolic forms of occupation such as renaming areas that have Tibetan names with Hindi names. Hindi names, mostly given by the military, co-opt Tawang as part of a Hindi-Indian cultural universe (Gohain 2013; Gohain and Grothmann 2015).

State *tactics* in Tawang, on the other hand, have consisted, for example, of the embracing of symbols and institutions of Tibetan Buddhism; the state seeks to manoeuvre eventual integration through such temporary habitations of the others' spaces. Thus, the Tawang War Memorial, which is dedicated to the 2,420 Indian servicemen who lost their lives in the 1962 Sino-Indian war, is a large white Buddhist *stupa*, complete with prayer wheels adorned with the Pali script.

The concession made to local culture in the architecture is a way to garner local sympathy for the national military through an appropriation of Tibetan Buddhist cultural symbols. In following tactics, the state does not blatantly advertise dominant cultural symbols in the public sphere; its approach to secure hegemonic consent is subtler.

In other border areas, the state has at times attempted soft cultural imperialism to propagate national or dominant symbols. Aggarwal (2004: 223–4) describes how the Sindhu Darshan Festival was inaugurated in Ladakh in 1997 at the specially constructed Sindhu Ghat on the banks of the Indus River. Since its inauguration, there has been a *yatra* or pilgrimage every year in June to this place, and activities during the festival include, apart from worship of the River Indus, reviving patriotism through flag hoisting, chanting of hymns to 'Mother India', and so on.

I have not observed festivals of such a kind or scale in Tawang in the course of my fieldwork. But a trend of state patronage of local Buddhist institutions and cultural programmes is increasingly visible. Since 2012, the Department of Tourism of the Arunachal Pradesh government, with aid from the central government and local support, has been organising the Tawang Festival and Buddha Mahotsava in Tawang and West Kameng districts. One may perceive the Indian state's promotion of activities and organisations that seek to preserve Tibetan Buddhist culture in Tawang as a tactical move to earn loyalty in a disputed border region. It is in keeping with some nationalist narratives, which see Buddhism as an indigenous offshoot of Hinduism, even though many scholars (for example, Omvedt 2003) disagree with this thesis. This view of Buddhism has been deployed in mobilising nationalist pride among marginal communities of India. The mushrooming of Vivekananda Kendra schools in Arunachal Pradesh which adopt a 'culture-based' curriculum emphasising a blending of Buddhist cultural preservation, nationalism and patriotism is just one instance of this attempt to seamlessly assimilate Hinduism, Buddhism and nationalism.[20]

In 2009, the Department of Karmik and Adhyatmik Affairs (DoKAA) (Tib. *chos-rig*) was created by the Arunachal Pradesh state government to look after the religious and cultural affairs of the communities of Tawang and West Kameng, and its objectives included among other things the maintenance and construction of monasteries, renovation of (Buddhist) pilgrimage sites, support of the traditional Bhoti language and Sowa Rigpa medicine system, and so on.[21] The first chairman of DoKAA, the monk and former minister, the 13th Tsona Gontse Rimpoche, was very active in the matter of Buddhist cultural preservation and also founded the movement for a Mon Autonomous Region in 2003, before meeting an untimely death in 2014. The current chairman of DoKAA continues activities to preserve and restore Buddhist sites and monuments in Tawang and West Kameng with the active support of the state government.

The current state sponsorship of Tibetan Buddhist cultural preservation is not simply a design for cultural domination. The revival of the Tibetan Buddhist cultural toolkit is also not a show of cultural resistance by the marginalised. Rather, these are the result of collaboration between the Indian administration and the local political and religious elite. The willingness of the state to entertain pleas for grants-in-aid in the immediate post-independence period was a similar tactic. Alert to that fact that 'the loyalty of the border peoples has always to be earned' (Nanda 1982: 8),[22] the state dispensed with cultural grants in return for loyalty. Then, as now, the state did not invent the idea of bartering aid in return for loyalty, but developed it as a tactical response to local appeals.

In the period after the Sino-Indian war, the Indian state was able to assert its presence in Tawang through the recognition given to it by the border people. The monastery elite and local people not only recognised the new sovereign power amidst them but also submitted to it in order to secure certain material benefits. The state fashioned new spaces that symbolically asserted a symbiosis between itself and the Tawang frontier, and the Nehru Gonpa—with which I began this chapter—was such a kind of space. While the interior of the monastery is like that of any other, with Buddhist statues, the Dalai Lama's portrait, and mandalas, the entrance has the portrait of Jawaharlal Nehru and his daughter, former prime minister Indira Gandhi, on its walls; and three marble busts of Nehru, Indira Gandhi, and her son and political successor Rajiv Gandhi are installed on the left side of the courtyard. The Nehru Gonpa remains symbolic of the emerging relations of recognition between the border people and the Indian state in Tawang.

NOTES

* I carried out the research for this chapter in Tawang in May 2013. This was my return field visit to Tawang after earlier extended stays in 2008, 2009 and 2010. An earlier draft was presented at the Asian Borderlands Research Network conference, 8–10 December 2014, Hong Kong. I am grateful to the Institute of Economic Growth, Delhi, Indian Institute of Technology, Kanpur, and North East India Studies Program, Jawaharlal Nehru University, Delhi, for supporting different stages of the writing and revision of this chapter. I am grateful to Kerstin Grothmann, Humboldt University, Germany, for her valuable comments on the first draft.

1. In India's case, while integration, with a multicultural spirit, views India as a 'composite culture' where diversity is not annihilated, but unified through fusion, it is impaired by the clause of allegiance to a national concept which is primarily defined by the majority culture. Integration, although more nuanced than assimilation, also eventually makes demands for subordinate existence on minority cultures, and assumes that the latter would place their commitment to the national goal over and above their ethnic and religious allegiances.

2. I have dealt with state and military practices in the Tawang frontier in my book manuscript, currently in press (Amsterdam University Press).

3. The archive consisted of several faded-blue government files languishing in unsystematic piles on the floor against the walls of a small dust-filled room in the deputy commissioner's office in Tawang. I am grateful to Deputy Commissioner Mr. Abhishek Deb for gracefully granting permission to access these files. Many government files were either destroyed in the 1962 war or moved to safer central locations, but those that were allowed to remain included correspondence, mostly relating to petitions for grants between monks, lay persons and the local administration from 1960 to 1989.

4. The Monpas are not a homogenous group but consist of different communities which are split in terms of language, custom and traditions. On the basis of language alone, four main (oral) language groups can be identified: Tawang Monpa, Dirang Monpa, Brokeh and Lish. Different Monpa communities follow different sects of Tibetan Buddhism, although the Gelug sect is predominant. There are also some Monpa groups who follow the pre-Buddhist Bon traditions.

5. Sonam Tsering, my friend from Tawang, who was the social cultural officer (SCO) at the Tawang deputy commissioner's office in 2007 when I visited, handed over the 'Approach Paper for the Workshop on Traditional System and Functioning of Tawang Monastery'. He told me that it was brought out a few years ago when the Tawang Monastery was undergoing renovation (2003). However, there is no date on the 'Approach Paper', and although presumably it was published in 2003–4, I have listed it as n.d. (no date). My account of the Tawang Monastery's administrative set-up and present challenges are based on the 'Approach Paper' (n.d.), interviews with Lopon Acharya (27 May 2013) and Sarkar (1996).

6. Sakti, Mormang, Manjing and Khartung in the Lumla sub-division of Tawang, Urgyelling, Changbu, Shormang, Khromten, Ariadung, Brakar and Kimnash in the Tawang area and Namchu in Dirang were the 12 monasteries affiliated to the Tawang Monastery. See Sarkar (1996); interviews with Lopon Acharya Ngawang Norbu, second abbot of Tawang Monastery, 27 May 2013 and Lama Thuptan

Tashi, Tawang Monastery, 22 May 2013. According to Lama Thupten Phunsok, however, the Tawang Monastery has 16 gonpas under its charge, including the nunneries (interview, 20 April 2010).

7. On 25 October 1950, the Chinese announced its intention to militarily occupy Tibet: 'People's Army units have been ordered to advance into Tibet to free three million Tibetans from the imperialist oppression and to consolidate national defense on the western borders of China' (Bhargava 1964: 23).

8. On the eastern sector, which included the entire state of Arunachal Pradesh, the boundary dispute between India and China was concerned with the alignment of the McMahon Line. While the Indian government stuck to the colonially demarcated boundary, the Chinese government claimed almost 33,000 square miles south of the McMahon Line. There has been much debate in scholarly circles regarding the causes leading to the India–China war; while some attribute the war to Chinese expansionist and irredentist aims, others cite the aggressive attitude of Indian nationalist leaders. For more on this debate, see, for instance, the writings of Maxwell (1999); K. Gupta (1974); Murty (1971) and Dutta (2008).

9. From the website of the Tawang deputy commissioner's office: http://tawang.nic. in/page14.html.

10. A Brief Biography of Shri. Pema Gombu (n.d.) Tawang, Arunachal Pradesh, a copy of which I acquired from Pema Gombu's son, Urgen Tsering, chairman of Lhou Secondary School, Tawang.

11. 'Tawang Monastery, Kameng Frontier Division', External Affairs, Commissioner, NEFA, No. PCT 73/63, 1962, Arunachal Pradesh State Archives.

12. 'An Extract Copy of Tour Notes of Shri U. Chakma, IFAS, Security Commissioner, Tezpur, Arunachal Pradesh for the Period from 14 October 1972 to 22 October 1972.'

13. Ibid., note 9.

14. File no. 46, 1972. BDL no. 3, Development Branch, 1970–9, 44–78.

15. 'Dress for Tarjacham', Miscellanous File (B), BDL no 2, 47–65, 1970–9.

16. Extract of the letter from Rigya Rinpoche, Tawang Monastery abbot to Chief Secretary, Arunachal Pradesh, Shillong, dated 24 October 1973.

17. Public sphere, as defined by Jürgen Habermas (1991), is collective public opinion formed through rational and critical debate between civil society members, which then exerts an influence on the workings of the state.

18. One letter from the chairman of the Tawang Cultural Society to All India Radio requesting the latter to broadcast the minutes of a meeting between civil society representatives and administration shows the public relations role played by

this organisation. 'Minutes of the Meeting Held in the Library Hall of Tawang Monastery on 31st July, 1974.'

19. Annexure III to Order no. SO-13/76/PI, 24 November 1980, contains the following announcement:

> Know all men by these presents that we Tawang Monastery School Committee, Tawang (society registered under Societies Registration Act, 1960), and having its office at Tawang in the state of Arunachal Pradesh [herein after called the obligors] are held and firmly bond to the President of India [herein after called the government] in the sum of Rs. 65,100/- only, well and truly to be paid to the government on demand and without a demur for which payment we formally find ourselves and successors and assigns by these presents.
>
> Signed this eighth day of January nineteen eighty one, whereas on the obligor's request, the government has as per AP govt. order no. SO-13/76/PI dated 24.11.80, ... agreed to make in favour of the obligors a grant of 65,100/- ...
>
> Signed by
> ChanzoTashi
> Secretary
> Tawang gompa monastery school committee
>
> A similar bond was presented on 28 January 1980, where the Tawang Gonpa Monastery School Committee acknowledges the receipt of Rs 92,425.

20. Interview with the principal, Vivekananda Kendra School, Kitpi, Tawang, 20 May 2013.

21. See http://www.karmikadhyatmik.in/about-us-2/, accessed on 9 September 2016.

22. Neeru Nanda joined as the first woman additional deputy commissioner of Tawang in 1974 and wrote this book based on her experiences in Tawang. She was a much-beloved administrator and even today, people speak of her with great adoration.

REFERENCES

Aggarwal, Ravina. 2004. *Beyond Lines of Control: Performance and Politics on the Disputed Borders of Ladakh*. Durham: Duke University Press.

Anonymous. n.d. 'Approach Paper for the Workshop on Traditional System and Functioning of Tawang Monastery'. Centre for Buddhist Cultural Studies, Tawang Monastery, Tawang, Arunachal Pradesh, India.

Aris, Michael. 1979. 'Notes on the History of the Monyul Corridor'. In *Tibetan Studies in Honor of Hugh Richardson: Proceedings of the International Seminar on Tibetan Studies*, edited by M. Aris and Aung San Suu Kyi, 9–20. Warminster, UK: Aris and Phillips.

Arpi, Claude. 2013. *1962 and the McMahon Line Saga*. Atlanta, G.A.: Lancer.

Bailey, F. M., and H. T. Morsehead. 1916. 'Report on an Exploration of the Northeast Frontier, Foreign and Political'. Secret E, nos 76–83, October 1916. National Archives, Delhi.

Bhargava, G. S. 1964. *The Battle of NEFA: The Undeclared War*. New Delhi: Allied Publishers.

Bourdieu, Pierre. 1991. 'Identity and Representation: Elements for a Critical Reflection on the Idea of the Region'. In *Language and Symbolic Power*, edited by John Thompson, 220–8. Cambridge, MA: Harvard University Press.

de Certeau, Michel. 1984. *The Practice of Everyday Life*. Berkeley: University of California Press.

Dutta, Sujit. 2008. 'Revisiting China's Territorial Claims on Arunachal'. *Strategic Analysis* 32 (4): 549–81.

Gohain, Swargajyoti. 2013. 'Imagined Places: Politics and Narratives in a Disputed Indo-Tibetan Borderland'. Unpublished PhD dissertation, Emory University, Atlanta, Georgia, USA. (A revised version of this will be published as a book by Amsterdam University Press, 2020.)

Gohain, Swargajyoti, and Kerstin Grothmann. 2015. 'Renaming as Integration'. *IIAS Newsletter* 71: 32–4.

Goldstein, Melvyn C. 1989. *A History of Modern Tibet, 1913–1951*. Berkeley: University of California Press.

Grothmann, Kerstin. 2012. 'Migration Narratives, Official Classifications, and Local Identities: The Memba of the Hidden Land of Pachakshiri'. In *Origins and Migrations in the Extended Eastern Himalaya*, edited by T. Huber and S. Blackburn, 125–52. Leiden: Brill.

Gupta, Akhil. 2012. *Red Tape: Bureaucracy, Structural Violence, and Poverty in India*. Durham: Duke University Press.

Gupta, Karunakar. 1974. *The Hidden History of the Sino-Indian Frontier*. Calcutta: Minerva Associate Publications.

Habermas, Jurgen. 1991. *The Structural Transformation of the Public Sphere*. Massachusetts: MIT Press.

Huber, Toni. 2011. 'Pushing South: Tibetan Economic and Political Activities in the Far Eastern Himalaya, ca. 1900–1950'. In *Buddhist Himalaya: Studies in Religion,*

History and Culture, edited by A. McKay and A. Balicki-Denjongpa, 259–76. Gangtok, Sikkim: Namgyal Institute of Tibetology.

Hull, Mathew. 2012. 'Documents and Bureaucracy'. *Annual Review of Anthropology* 41: 251–67.

Kameng District Brochure. 1972. Miscellanous File (A), BDL no. 1, 1–40, 1970–9. Deputy Commissioner's Office, Tawang.

Lamb, Alastair. 1966. *The McMahon Line*. London: Routledge and Kegan Paul.

Mathur, Nayanika. 2012. 'Transparent-Making Documents and the Crisis of Implementation: A Rural Employment Law and Development Bureaucracy in India'. *PoLAR: Political and Legal Anthropology Review* 35 (2): 167–85.

Maxwell, Neville. 1970. 'China and India: The Un-Negotiated Dispute'. *The China Quarterly* 43: 47–80.

Murty, T. S. 1971. 'Tawang and "The Un-Negotiated Dispute"'. *The China Quarterly* 46: 357–62.

Nanda, Neeru. 1982. *Tawang: The Land of Mon*. Delhi: Vikas.

Maxwell, Neville. 1999. 'Sino-Indian Border Dispute Reconsidered'. *Economic and Political Weekly* 34 (14): 905–18.

Omvedt, Gail. 2003. *Buddhism in India: Challenging Brahminism and Caste*. New Delhi: Sage.

Sahlins, Peter. 1991. *Boundaries: The Making of France and Spain in the Pyrenees*. Berkeley: University of California Press.

Sarkar, Niranjan. 1996. *Tawang Monastery*. Itanagar, India: Directorate of Research, Government of Arunachal Pradesh.

Scott, James. 1985. *Weapons of the Weak: Everyday Forms of Peasant Resistance*. New Haven: Yale University Press.

Sharma, Aradhana, and Akhil Gupta. 2006. *The Anthropology of the State: A Reader*. Malden, MA: Blackwell.

Taylor, Charles. 1994. *Multiculturalism*. Edited by Amy Gutmann. Princeton: Princeton University Press.

van Schendel, Willem. 2005. *The Bengal Borderland*. London: Anthem Press.

Watson, C. W. 2000. *Multiculturalism*. Buckingham, London: Open University Press.

5

Relative Intimacies
Belonging and Difference in Transnational Families across the Bengal Borderland*

SAHANA GHOSH

'I married into India out of greed for the *melas* (fairs) and now I am stuck …
no *jawa-asha* [coming and going] for me,' declared Shefali Barman, with a deep
sigh.[1] A 26-year-old widow in Putimari, a border village in the Coochbehar
district, eastern India, she was bemoaning her inability to cross the border to
attend a nephew's rice-eating ceremony, where all her natal family would be
gathered, in the nearby Bangladeshi border village of Boraibari.[2] The circuitous
route Shefali usually took between Putimari (India—hereafter, Ind) and Boraibari
(Bangladesh—hereafter, BD), across an unfenced portion of the border, had
become closed at the time due to a newly stationed Indian Border Security Force
(BSF) patrol there. She hastened to explain her reason for entering into a marriage
across an international border, lest it be thought flippant.

> In my childhood, our father or older brothers would take my sisters
> and me to the Rash Mela in Coochbehar and smaller *melas* during
> Durga Puja and Rathjatra in Dinhata.[3] You see, it was no fun being
> Hindu in Bangladesh—but each time we would come here [West
> Bengal, India], we would see that so many women, so many families,
> Hindu and Muslim, who would come to these *melas*, travelling to them
> from different places and enjoying them till late at night.… The *border*
> was open in those years [late 1980s to early 1990s], and the distance
> between Boraibari and Dinhata was not very much. *Jawa-asha* was
> very easy, and when it was necessary we occasionally stayed a night or
> two at relatives' homes. Then we would return to Bangladesh with toys,
> new dresses, and sweets.

With two paternal aunts married in the same area of the Coochbehar district, Shefali had also grown up as a witness to the ease of their *jawa-asha* across this international border. Having thus travelled these cross-border routes herself, she had been agreeable to the proposal of marriage when it was broached, with the reassurance that it was close enough within the borderland for her to visit frequently. Shefali's deep disappointment with her present immobility is thus made sharper in contrast to the memories of these cross-border journeys of her childhood and expectations based on those experiences.

JAWA-ASHAR MAJHE: IN BETWEEN COMINGS AND GOINGS ACROSS THE BENGAL BORDER

Stories like Shefali's, of divided families and arrested routes, have become recognisable to us in the context of the subcontinent's partitioned borders through film, literature and scholarship; especially a recent series of excellent work on Partition's legacies (Kaul 2011; Butalia 2015). However, what distinctly sets apart stories like hers is that rather than rupture, they are about the continued making and maintenance of heteronormative kinship ties across transnational family networks and over changing practices of border control. Villages such as Putimari and Boraibari across the region in northern Bengal were all part of the Coochbehar princely state, typically knit together by a dense web of kinship relations and a great deal of historical mobility. Practically every family in this agrarian region, that has come to be reconstituted as borderlands in/of India and Bangladesh, with a Muslim majority demographic, has kin relations who are now on the other side of the border (Chatterji 2007).[4] The formation of the border between India and then-Pakistan, now-Bangladesh, meant that, *within* the borderlands, relations were recast. Even today there are cross-border marriages, although their number has greatly decreased since the steady militarised control of the border on the Indian side from the mid-1990s onwards. In conversations, officers and constables in the Indian BSF, tasked with preventing all cross-border movements, recognised with sympathy the existence and emotional power of cross-border family ties. However, as they encountered these particular kinds of border crossers, and considered differentiating them from others who were transporting petty goods across the border (for example, cumin from India to Bangladesh) or crossing the border in search of work (for example, labourers from Bangladesh into India), I found them puzzling over certain questions.[5] Why do border crossings for kinship persist despite the risks and impediments to safe and fearless border crossing in the borderlands? While one can understand their existence for the Partition generation, how do we understand cross-border marriages in a context where the border has been in visible existence with its growing security apparatus for several decades? In taking these questions seriously as an empirical invitation during my fieldwork, related questions arose. What normative and gendered ideas about kin obligations and morality prevail upon individuals and families as they decide whether or not to continue investment in relations across borders? How do these sit within the larger political economy of the border itself?

Running over 4,096 kilometres, the India–Bangladesh border has 16 official land ports through which the cross-border movement of goods is facilitated, though not all of these accommodate the movement of people, which is tied to the possession of passports and appropriate visas.[6] With accessible measures such as the India–Bangladesh passport, which could be procured at the district level in India, being phased out,[7] residents of agrarian borderlands such as these could hardly afford the cost and hassle of fulfilling these bureaucratic-legal standards in either country.[8] Left to their own paths, 'illegal' border crossings are thus undertaken for a variety of reasons in everyday life: to visit family, for religious and medical purposes, to transport goods and trade or in search of work. This breadth is completely flattened in a global understanding of 'illegal' border crossings as synonymous with labour migrants, gendered and embodied as threatening to national security. In India this figure is rendered in terms of a regionally particular figure of the Bangladeshi Muslim male.

Questions of violence, marginality and belonging have been at the heart of the empirically rich, flourishing scholarship on borders and borderlands in South Asia (van Schendel 2005; Gellner 2013; Cons and Sanyal 2013; Banerjee 2010; Ibrahim 2009; Hussain 2013). These have been explored in the contestations of national sovereign power (Shneiderman 2013; Aggarwal and Bhan 2009; Jones 2011; Cons 2014), cross-border economic networks or enterprises (Harris 2013; Sur 2013), cultural and religious connections and belonging (Ibrahim 2011; Jalais 2013; Bal 2007). Although central to the earlier feminist scholarship on gender, community and violence in Partition and its aftermath (for example, Butalia 2000; Bhasin and Menon 2000; Das 2007), scholars working on contemporary borders and borderlands, taken up by their political-economic formations, have largely overlooked the everyday life of the family and kinship, in its peculiarly short-distance transnational form in the borderlands.[9] Shefali's aborted journey and personal history of border crossings demand that attention be paid to these two aspects together: the trials of transnational kinship across changing practices of border control.

This chapter presents familial spatial practices serving kinship along and across the border in north Bengal, looking not only at moments of historical crisis at and since 1947 but also at ordinary times and the connections between them. It aims to connect the discussions of a 'long Partition' (Zamindar 2007) to the lively scholarship on the contemporary life and politics of the India–Bangladesh borderlands, deepening both in turn. In doing so, it seeks to make three contributions. First, it shows that such histories of family networks across the borderlands complicates our understanding of how the partition of the subcontinent remains a lived reality for those who, marginal to metropolitan Bengali identity, were most affected not by displacement, but by remaining in place in areas which have come to be produced as borderlands in subsequent decades. Second, in tracing these family histories and networks of kin over generations, from the 1950s to present times, it suggests that a particular biography of the border itself emerges, one which destabilises the linear account of the Bengal border from porosity towards closure. And finally, it argues that the transnational family straddling the borderlands, despite its sticky affective life, has become a site on which national differences and stereotypes take root, are cultivated and deployed.

Intimacy as an analytic can guide us in tracking these three productions and formations. Feminist and queer studies of power have turned to intimacy as both a subject of analysis as well as an analytical rubric. I draw on feminist scholarship at the intersections of history, anthropology and post-colonial feminist theory that uses intimacy to interrogate colonialism, globalisation and capitalism, arguing powerfully that intimacy does not merely reside in the private sphere but is infused with worldliness (Stoler 2010; Wilson 2012; Ahmed 2013). In particular I am interested in marshalling intimacy to think about spatial concepts such as distance and scale as well as relations of power in the context of mobility and bordering. To that end I use the phrase 'relative intimacies'—deploying on the multiple meanings of the word relative—to examine how these relational forms of power are learned, inhabited and managed.

I draw on 24 months of ethnographic research conducted in the Indian and Bangladeshi borderlands in northern Bengal between 2012 and 2015 with residents and BSFs. As I travelled back and forth across the India–Bangladesh border through the northern land port of Changrabandha/Burimari, my own movement facilitated the exchange of photographs, gifts and messages between relatives. My entries and exits into India and Bangladesh and each of these homes were not clandestine and instead of eliding those differences of power, I used them generatively in both my research and writing. Family charts grew denser with details of little-known offshoots in between my own comings and goings with 11 sets of transnational families whose histories and experiences I was tracing. They had varying degrees and forms of contact, and I draw on that range in this chapter to show the intertwining of mobility and immobility between unequal sovereign powers and the difficult nature of cross-border kinship ties, often involving prickly decisions, in moral and material terms. The ethnographic focus will be on journeys—imagined, completed, aborted and refused—and their narrative representations.

PULLED BY HEARTSTRINGS: AMBIVALENCES OF KINSHIP, ASYMMETRIES OF BORDER CONTROL

It was the morning after Shahida Bibi's youngest brother's wedding in Madhupur (BD), and at the groom's house an enormous vat of steaming *khichudi* (a dish made of rice and lentils) was at hand to feed all the relatives in the winter cold. 'I never imagined that you would see me here, in my father's house,' said Shahida Bibi to me, as we devoured the spicy *khichudi*, washed down with sweet milky tea. 'I was sure I would not come,' she says, listing all the work and responsibilities she had in Kathalbari (Ind) and referring to the physically arduous walk across the dry sand banks of the River Jay that is a characteristic of the landscape in the winter months. 'Then I came—*shudhumatro moner taaney* [pulled only by the strings of my heart].'

By this point, I had known Shahida Bibi for a few years. In the border villages of Kathalbari (Ind), she had been introduced to me as a local leader and organiser of the government-aided women's self-help groups. In her late 50s, she is an activist for women's and child rights, and had been a community worker for numerous non-governmental organisation (NGO) projects. She was clearly embarrassed that she had been 'caught' in the position of what the Government of India would classify her: an 'illegal' border crosser. This embarrassment tempered her delight at being able to share the joy and pride of her father's home and local influence with someone 'from India'. It was important to her that I understood what had driven her to take such a risk, and that it *was* in fact a substantial risk to her. 'I am always worried before I come. You know people like us have nothing to do with the BSF. I start trembling just at the thought of being stopped and questioned by them.' Ashadul Hossain, her elder son, who lives in Madhupur (BD) with his wife and children, interjected, exasperatedly.

I am always telling her there is nothing to be scared of. She just has to be normal and cross the BSF checkpoint and the river. Once on this side, I go to pick her up from the [unfenced] *border* myself. Once when I was bringing her from the *border* on my *bike*, the BGB [Border Guards Bangladesh] saw and stopped us. I told them the truth and they let us go. It was no problem! We are respected in society, people know us, there is nothing to worry about.

Half a year later, Shahida Bibi was back in Madhupur (BD) and once again deliberating on the chance of 'the BSF on duty to be good'. This time she was on a brief visit to see her newborn granddaughter. 'I have to do my duty, don't I?' she said, rocking the week-old baby in the cradle of her arms. It was a Friday and her son Ashadul, employed in the district government's agriculture department, was at home from work, busy with prayers and meetings at their neighbourhood mosque. We chatted in the kitchen of his house as Shahida Bibi finished preparing the lunchtime meal we would eat together once he returned. In addition to lentils, greens and *aloo bhorta* (spiced mashed potatoes), there was a fish preparation with vegetables, an egg curry, as well as a mutton curry made in my honour. When I remarked on this elaborate menu, where meat and fish were clear signs of wealth and material abundance in rural north Bengal, she pointed out that to her great surprise she found her son's family here in 'Bangladesh' ate very well, often better than she did in 'India'.[10] 'Just imagine, as a mother I am not able to live out my elder son's salaried success and status,' she said woefully, staring into the bubbling mutton gravy, shaking her head in regret.

Ashadul seemed embarrassed that he, the son, had made his mother cross the border rather than doing it himself. He related that he used to go to his parents' house in Kathalbari (Ind) two or three times a year 'earlier'. 'Don't you understand, I am not a boy any more. I am a responsible grown person, also [looking down at his tucked in shirt and jeans] I don't look like a village labourer any more, it is hard to sneak past the BSF.' Indicating that this is a contentious matter between them, his mother whispered out of his earshot, '[H]is sense of pride and dignity is very important now, more than the *moner taan*, affective pull for his parents. He has become obstinate against coming these days.'

Such a call to duty, entangled with deep affective attachments, with women largely bearing the burden of these duties towards both natal and affinal families, to one's son, father and brother is the driving force of Shahida Bibi's decisions to undertake 'illegal' travels across the border over the years. The anthropological literature on kinship has explored its inherent ambivalences (for example, Peletz 1995), the politics of normative demands of kinship (for example, Carsten 1995), often serving as sources of anxiety in the face of inability to fulfil those demands. For numerous borderland residents, like Shahida Bibi and Shefali Barman, kinship obligations were not a moral compulsion that they related to as an undesirable burden. Duty and affective attachment were the two arcs along which kinship as a moral force animated their lives. Their great desire to be a part of family rituals and occasions, to perform kin roles of a daughter, brother and sister, underscored an understanding of kinship as a form of relatedness that could not be taken for granted but had to be constantly performed in order for its promised moral fulfilments, of which reciprocity was a key part, to accrue. Shahida Bibi wanted to perform her roles as much as she wanted reciprocal kin roles to be performed towards her, imagined most poignantly at times of birth and death.

The ambivalences of kinship are also manifest in terms of emotional well-being and the realisation of life-course specific expectations. Transnational separation had the potential to threaten the social reproduction of gender and kinship roles (Charsley 2005). For Shahida Bibi, being denied the fruits of her son's success was particularly upsetting; after all, the ideal life-course of a mother's journey culminates in being taken care of by her son (elder son in particular) and partaking of that kin exchange testifies to the moral uprightness of his character and upbringing to his mother's credit. His relative success as a *Bangladeshi* in contrast to the rest of the family's material conditions in India stood out in sharp relief in Shahida Bibi's descriptions even within intimate networks as it grated against the structural inequalities of border control between the two nation-states.

Shefali's comments, with which I began, disarmingly straightforward, remind us that marriages mean movement, and once formed, marital alliances and kinship ties require movement for their upkeep. What these statements do not reveal is the gendered nature of these movements: marriage is always migration for women, a necessary corrective to dominant paradigms in migration studies.[11] And in the case of this borderland, if the marrying woman finds herself on a different side of the border from her family, it also creates a particular kind of gendered border crosser, with its own politics of suspicion and sympathy in relation to border control practices, as the comparison forced between Shahida Bibi and her son makes painfully clear. Such a border crosser is distinct from those crossing for economic reasons—a distance doubly asserted by Shahida Bibi and her son—and that distinction is vital to the real and perceived social acceptability of her movements, but nevertheless enmeshed in the larger border economy of everyday mobility. As the BSF officers and troops acknowledged the moral rightness of transnational relative intimacies and harboured sympathies for the tribulations of those separated by the legal regime of this border's control, residents mirrored this in their expectations of allowances from those law enforcers. It was such individual recognitions and sympathies that Shahida Bibi counted on, for the BSF to 'be good' as she anticipated to 'manage' her future visits.

Unlike Toba Tek Singh's[12] incomprehension and epistemological denial of the border, the artifice of statist divisions, it becomes clear that the lived experiences of kin relations in this borderland take that artifice of state making into account, embodying its inhumanity, staging a critique of its values in complicated ways. 'If they can make arrangements for the enclave-dwellers, why not for us?' questioned Shefali, about the Indian state, amid the travel and citizenship arrangements being made for the enclave-exchange process between India and Bangladesh in this same region, ongoing at that time.[13] On one occasion, with the border 'closed' near where she lived, Shefali Barman had planned to travel to a cousin's village further east from where they would pass through a gate on the border fence to an acquaintance's house that was located in between the Indian border fence and the actual border. I accompanied her on this journey to meet this cousin at the checkpoint by the fence gate. At the checkpoint, the BSF soldiers on duty inspected Shefali's and her cousin's voter identity cards and informed them that holders with addresses not in that particular village required further documentation. Shefali's face fell and she started shaking visibly from disappointment and the fear of an argument with the guards. Hopes dashed, the two cousins consulted in whispers, and decided that the cousin would go through and bring the gathered family right up to the fence at a point between the BSF patrols and Shefali would see them and talk with them through the fence for as long as possible.

Shefali swallowed back her tears as we marched down the metalled 'border road'. It felt like a defiant act because the BSF strictly control civilian use of this road, which although built by the Public Works Department, is monopolised for border security, for the guarding of the fence and movement of security force personnel and their vehicles. We had walked only a few minutes when an elderly woman in a white sari could be seen running towards the fence through the bare harvested fields. We waited, facing Bangladesh, breathing onto the concertina wire that filled up the space between the two rows of metal frames strung with rusting barbed wire. I turned away, keeping a watchful eye out for BSF soldiers who would come along patrolling the road on their bicycles. Soon the larger group of sisters-in-law, nieces, nephews and neighbours joined up with Shefali's mother and a frantic and tearful exchange of news took place; 'Please go for another round for 5 minutes,' I requested the young BSF constable who cycled up and asked what was going on, clearly understanding what was going on. 'You people hurry up, if my superior comes around by chance and sees this, I will be in trouble,' he said nervously. The cross-fence voices, put on pause, resumed as he cycled away slowly. 'Look after our girl,' said one of her sisters-in-law to me. 'We know there are a lot of rights and laws for women in India but we don't want any of that. We just want her to be happy, to feel she has her rightful place. And she should be able to come to visit.' The constable was spotted cycling back again, and so the emotional meeting ended abruptly with both parties turning away from the barbed wire to walk back into India and Bangladesh.

In her discussion of post-colonial intimacies, feminist and queer theorist Sara Ahmed urges to move beyond theories of intimacy based on temporal and geographical proximity, and to engage with intimacies 'as archives of cultural and historical complexity and of the messiness that histories of mobilities inject into spaces where bodies meet' (Ahmed 2013: 119–20). Ahmed's approach helps critique the naturalisation of spatial concepts of distance and scale used by nation-state projects of bordering and it reminds us of the historical traces that bodies and mobilities carry with them. Thus, Shefali's unsuccessful border crossing is not only an affective aspect of border securitisation but also an archive for a 'cultural and historical complexity'. What I call here 'relative intimacy' indexes both how she maintains relations through the changing security across the barbed wire border fence, as well as how she challenges the security state that disables the ongoing production of the heteronormative family by recalling historical changes in security practices.

As Kapur and Cossman (1996) note, the tremendous discursive power of the 'familial ideology' is to naturalise it, make these roles of dutiful daughter and self-sacrificing mother inevitable. With Shahida Bibi and Shefali Barman, the ubiquity of these structural expectations of gendered life-cycle exchanges and performances provide a counter-narrative of value—albeit within the bounds of a normative patriarchal discourse—to the legal regime of India's unilateral border-control architecture, subtly critiquing its validity from such a moral standpoint. The assertive reference of Shefali's 'rightful place' in 'India' as a widowed daughter-in-law—in the comment made by her sister-in-law—fuses heteronormative kinship obligations with a legal national jurisdiction. It does so by way of acknowledging the unequal structural relations between India and Bangladesh in gendered terms. What they are marking is a kind of a backhanded compliment—India as progressive to have rights and protections for women yet not progressive enough to allow border crossings for the reproduction of families that exceed the geo-body of the nation. Transnational kinship practices in the borderlands thus daily register the frictions and effects of distance between national and regional hierarchies.

A mother visiting her son, a daughter visiting her mother: the moral power of these subject positions excluded them from the infamy of illegality in broader social eyes, even though Shefali, Shahida and Ashadul, each of them wrestled with concerns for social status being diminished through the association with the 'illegal' border economy and questioning by the Indian BSF. Their fears— as well as strategies employed—indicate that there is a hierarchy of exception for 'people like us', visibly marked through, for example, dress in terms of class status, whose compulsions to undertake such activities are sympathetically considered by the BSFs. This is remarkably different from the moral discourses within which women's mobility for work, unprotected by the shared ideology of the family, is framed, prohibitively (Kapur 2005). The Indian state's inability to provide a measure for these legitimate citizen's needs, to the contrary, harassing and belittling them for these needs, was perceived as a great failing and heartless, in contradistinction to the Bangladeshi state characterised as more humane in the form of the compassionate BGB.

The ambivalences of gendered family roles thus merged with the asymmetries of border control between their spatial locations. The 'friction of distance' is defined by David Harvey (2006) as the time or cost incurred to traverse a particular distance. In this case, we find that the changing spatial practices between transnational kin in the Bengal borderland index a friction of distance, experienced as a material and experiential quality of space. Physical distances appear to increase and contract between kin, say in Putimari and Boraibari, depending on the nature of the border, border control and spatial practice employed; there is a mirroring within the kin relation in terms of emotional intimacy and moral vigour. Distance no longer remains a flat numerical figure or a metaphorical measure of intimacy within relationships; it appears in terms of material, social and affective frictions and textures, and accentuates the structural imbalances of power along gendered and national lines.

TRANSNATIONAL SEPARATION, NATIONAL STEREOTYPES: LEARNING TO LIVE AS NEIGHBOURS

While certainly, 'what the map cuts up the story cuts across' (de Certeau 1984: 129), the existence of national borders, however they may be overcome or enforced, has its own material and affective effects. The Indian state's investment in an increasingly militarised border security apparatus, from numerically higher boots on the ground, durable fencing, floodlights, night vision equipment and arms, and surveillance cameras,[14] is in stark contrast to the Bangladeshi state's material presence on their side of border security (less troops, no surveillance equipment and no fence). New historiography on the Partition has shown us that post-colonial regimes of citizenship were produced through elaborate bureaucratic controls on mobility (Zamindar 2007) and the management of refugees (Datta 2012). If citizen-subjects do imagine their polities in contradistinction to proximate others through objects, such as the map (Ramaswamy 2002), for example, we must consider the material and affective effects of unequal sovereign powers thus displayed at their shared border. How do close kin come to live as national neighbours? In other words, to pose the question of difference a little differently, when there are numerous and deep continuities across the borders of national maps, how is difference learned and imagined?

Master narratives of nation and national character are woven into the weft and warp of transnational family life that bear out the bitter reality of unequal neighbourly relations. Separate and divergent reflections on a cross-border visit amongst one transnational family are instructive in this regard. Majidul Hoque, a pharmacist in Kathalbari, is quite a contrast to Shahida Bibi in his preferences for observing transnational kin obligations. His wife is from an erstwhile Bangladeshi enclave in central Coochbehar; her sister, Fatima, is married into an old tobacco-growing centre, Bibiganj, now a Bangladeshi border village. As the *dulha bhai*, brother-in-law, he has received numerous invitations from Fatima, his sister-in-law, and niece to simply cross the unfenced border and the BSF checkpoint and visit them, especially since in their perception, as an Indian citizen he may be able to do that more easily than them. In his little room in the Kathalbari bazaar (Ind), stacked with medicines, he confessed that he was uncomfortable with breaking the law that comes with such border crossings.

> It is very difficult; they always put pressure on me to visit whenever we talk on the phone.[15] As it is they [his niece and his sister-in-law] come *abaidya bhabe*, illegally. Bangladeshis have more courage than us Indians, they can be *desperate*. I am afraid to take them around on my *bike*, even though they have cards.

Fatima of Bibiganj (BD) has three children; her eldest, Jui, is a young college-going woman, who with her fake Indian voter identity card had crossed the border and the BSF checkpoints passing through as an Indian citizen to visit her *khala*, maternal aunt, several times in Kathalbari (Ind) and was keen to return. One evening, I was seated in the courtyard of their modest tin-walled house in

Bibiganj and being hosted with steaming cups of spiced black tea, plates of sliced apple, biscuits, fried noodles and sweets. An appreciative comment from me about the spread of snacks to accompany tea drew an indignant response from Jui on her experience of difference in hospitality between this side and that side.

> When someone comes to our house, whoever it may be, the very least we will do, however poor we might be is to put some tea on the hearth. Biskut [sic], fruit, chanachur, if we have made some nashta [snacks] at home, at least two or three types of things. But I have seen what they are like on that side [referring to her visits]—they will ask if you want tea, if you should say no then that's the end! You won't even get tea! Nobody bothers with anything else. People think too highly of themselves on that side.

While Majidul Hoque was quick to separate differences in attitudes towards border control by deploying stereotypes about national character as 'Indian' and 'Bangladeshi' among his own kin, his niece Jui too read the differences she noticed in the hospitality practices among her family in the light of larger national differences and inequalities in bilateral relations. Wielding a common joke contrasting the miserly West Bengalis with the generous East Bengalis, the placement of us and them along national lines was enabled by a 'cultural intimacy' (Herzfeld 1997) that came from intimate knowledge circulating in a family and affirmation of cultural difference among proximate others. Ashadul's assertion of his self-respecting and proud national identity was jostling against such prevailing stereotypes of a 'desperate', law-breaking Bangladeshi, widely articulated by the BSF personnel and residents in the Indian borderlands. At what point would one cease to be a *atmiya sajan* (familial relative), and appear as embodying these national types, was an unresolved source of tension in cross-border family networks; in whispers, jokes and declined invitations, they erupted in intimate relations.

As we saw with Shahida Bibi and Ashadul, neither mother nor son wished to relocate, devoted as they are to the national identities with which they characterise themselves and their worlds today.[16] The resentment they share is directed at the inequality in neighbourly relations, deeply felt among transnational kin. While Indian kin in Bangladesh are not stopped by the BGB (as Ashadul testified and Shefali does not fear in her calculations), Bangladeshi kin found it practically impossible to visit in the other direction.[17] The toll this takes within families is not negligible and puts a further strain on the inequalities of exchange and reciprocity that are integral to kinship. This is evident as what makes it dangerous for Ashadul as a young male Bangladeshi Muslim to cross the BSF[18] compared to Shahida Bibi as an elderly Indian Muslim woman to cross the BSF is elided, and instead the matter tersely settled, within the family, in terms of affective attachments thereby flattening the imbalances of risk and humiliations of being positioned as a 'desperate' Bangladeshi, a threat to Indian border security.

'WE HAVE BEEN HERE, THE BORDER HAPPENED'; OR, ACCIDENTALLY TRANSNATIONAL

Close attention to these tensions in transnational kinship offer insights into the fraught relationship between subjectivity, national affinities and grounded narratives of historical change. Nation-states, with their ordering of histories and regimes of power, have been central in controlling and rupturing processes of movement and settlement. They seek to effectively control the power of legitimacy of historical narratives itself. Thus, as Alexander, Chatterji and Jalais have recently argued, 'The movement of brides thus calls to be placed in the context of national borders and practices, not just in the regulation of who can enter and stay within a country's borders, but in the broader sense of who "belongs" and who does not' (2016: 149). Cross-border marriages, a particular aspect of transnational kinship, are still being brokered for entirely pragmatic purposes that take the violent lessons of history, of territorial state making and communal polarisation seriously.

To look no further than Shahida Bibi, her predicament is the product of a complicated life history, one in which the upheavals of wars, its displacements and survivals are explicit themes, although it is not an uncommon story in the borderlands. She was born in Kathalbari (Ind) and was a little girl when she moved to Madhupur, then in East Pakistan, with her family as her father (still remembered in Kathalbari bazaar) exchanged his house, shop and four acres of land with a Ray family of Madhupur in 1965 in the tense lead up to the India–Pakistan war. Then, less than a decade later, they all moved back to Kathalbari for nine months to wait out the bloody war of 1971, putting up at the house of her father's old friend. That is where her fate was sealed, as she sees it today. After the war, her father married her to the son of the family that had sheltered them during the war. It was a way of staying connected to his beloved Kathalbari, of infusing deeper meaning into the bonds that had kept them alive in that trying year of 1971.

Remarkable too are the silences about cross-border kin and keeping contact with them in the space of everyday life in India, whether through regular phone calls or irregular visits. In the course of my ethnographic research, I found that it would be months after knowing someone in the Indian borderlands that I would discover his or her family connections in Bangladesh. Unless you were someone who was also known to be in the same position, people on the heavily surveilled Indian side—mostly Muslim—did not feel they could trust you with these confidences, which had transformed from being commonplace facts to sensitive information. Relative intimacies were, in such contexts, archives of the complex politics of migration, holding and embodying histories even when they could not be narrated widely. It was the reverse case in Bangladesh, where my own Indian-Bengali identity attracted unsolicited accounts of familial connections from Muslim residents; the Hindu minority was less forthcoming in a similar fashion to their minority counterpart in India. The state is, as Carsten notes, 'heavily implicated in the transmission of kinship memories' (2007: 21). So it was by chance that I came upon the now transnational details of Afzal Hossain's family network. A talkative septuagenarian, I had been summoned for sessions at dawn, after he read his first prayers of the day, to record his life history. The Bengali post-colonial trinity of Netaji, Gandhi and Nehru hung on his wall alongside framed award certificates received for contribution to education. Afzal master was giving an account of the high politics of the nationalist movement through which 'Hindoostan-Pakistan happened'. His kindly wife had brought us tea and breakfast, a distraction I seized as a break from the school textbook history lecture. 'Where is your *baper bari* [natal home]?' I asked her, a standard question with which I began conversations with married women of different generations, alert for patterns among and across generations. A long silence fell upon us as the elderly couple looked at each other uncomfortably. 'It's not close by,' said Afzal master, grey brows furrowed.

> You won't report this will you? Her *baper bari* is in Bangladesh; it is my *mamar bari* [maternal uncle's family]. When we got married it had just become Hindoostan-Pakistan, you wouldn't think there was a border for many years, everything continued as usual. Even trains used to run across the bridge here as before. Then it was only around the 6 September war that everything stopped.[19] The train that went from Kathalbari was stopped in Pakistan and war broke out. Our *jawa-asha* stopped completely too. Pakistan kept *kora* [strict] vigil at the border; you could not get past the Khan-sena. I was in a *sarkari chakri* [government job], our children had grown up ... what if they called us Pakistani? ... Then came the *ekattorer juddho* [war of 1971], border-torder everything disappeared.[20] *Pil-pil kore*, [in huge crowds] people came here from Pakistan. My in-laws' family came and took shelter in this house—my brothers-in-law and their families. Indira Gandhi gave them all rations in the camps! They all went back after Bangladesh became independent but the border was open for many years. We never went that way of course, *abaidya bhabe* [illegally].

Clearly not trusting his 'unworldly' wife to narrate their family history, Afzal master presented one to me that was carefully constructed in reference to official national historical events. His narrative emphasis on the righteous observance of law—embodied in his family's giving up the upkeep of kin relations by not crossing to East Pakistan/Bangladesh—was integral to his public and self-image as a good citizen and, in these times, a good Muslim. Despite being a respected and well-known community elder, he feared being reported—for being married for over 50 years now to someone who may today be labelled 'Bangladeshi'.[21]

Bengal's borders remained largely porous after Partition and uneven attempts by the state to control them were thus unsuccessful (Chatterji 2009; van Schendel 2005). From mainstream media to governmental reports and scholarly analyses, this porosity has been the defining characteristic in descriptions of the India–Bangladesh border. This affective narration of history, before the 'what happened' has been entirely subsumed into the 'that which is said to have happened', to follow Trouillot's (1997: 113) important semantic distinction, bears strong resemblances to the responses of divided and displaced families in the long years after Partition. It demonstrates that, although resembling the affective and familial strategies with which people coped with the new borders that slashed through the subcontinent, the strategies that continued in the several decades after, rooted within the borderlands, were anchored in particular political economies. As Shefali is faced with a new patrol stationed along the route she had been employing, as Shahida and her sons imagine the permeability of the same border very differently in relation to their own bodies, we realise that the openness and closures of a border are neither fixed nor singular.

These family histories, spread over generations, mark a parallel biography: that of the border itself. Starting with its birth in 1947, the biography unfolds in terms of closures and openings, porosity and impermeability, belying the modernist narrative of linear temporal progression from open to porous to increasing control and now approaching closure that we are familiar with for this particular border, and for porous borders more generally. This contradiction works at multiple levels. One, people marked clear moments of openness and closure, permissibility and porosity; in fact, it was the absolute openness at the time of the 1971 war that came after the experience of strict enforcement and closure of the border on the Pakistani side in the years leading up to the war of 1965, which generated an understanding of border security as unstable and capable of radical change. A progression from porous to closed was not taken for granted, as closed to open had been seen to happen before, and so residents with several generations-old ties remain hopeful. Second, cross-border marriages reoccurred across generations despite the border, not unaware of it, but taking its openings and closures, its indeterminacies into account. In fact, we find, through glimpses in the accounts here, that there were dense accretions of investment in cross-border ties as safety nets in times of crisis. My research finds that through marriages, among other things, cross kinship was validated and strengthened in times of political violence and communal tension. Residents, even when thwarted in travel plans at a given moment and in a given place, believed that it could not be permanent; it had never been before. And, finally, the view from within these transnational kinship networks suggests that closure and a negotiated porosity exists simultaneously in single temporal periods, becoming visible in relation to one's perceptible social position, as marked by religion, gender and class and refracted through hierarchies of regional geopolitics.

It was six months after the conversation I recounted earlier that Afzal master announced to me that he had applied for a passport and had to travel to Kolkata for the appointment to deposit his biometric data. He revealed that one of their daughters was married across the border and lived at the Hatibandha subdivision of the Lalmonirhat district. Afzal master's life history, highly organised and full of precise details, was dotted with ellipses. It was only with the passport application that he could proudly share his plans to visit his daughter in Bangladesh, indeed even acknowledge his daughter and her family across the border. The silences and hesitations I recorded among Indian borderland residents regarding their kinship ties across the border are as illuminating as the emotional words and actions shared vocally by several others. As Trouillot reminds us, 'Mentions and silences are thus active, dialectical counterparts of which history is the synthesis' (1997, 48). To recover the messy character of history as process and attending to the narrative pulls of chronology, that is, 'the transformation of what happened into that which is said to have happened' (Trouillot 1995, 113), includes silences alongside speech.

CONCLUSION

As I drew old-fashioned kinship diagrams in notebooks for the presently transnational families of Shahida Bibi, Shefali Barman, Afzal Hoque and numerous others, moving up or down the generations (depending on whom I started with), I was noting the place-name where each spouse was from. For the Partition generation, Coochbehar, Alipurduar, Jalpaiguri, Moynaguri, Rangpur, Kaliganj, Phulbari, Nageswari, Bhurungamari, Dhubri and Gaibandha were the names which plotted out the contours of a kinship geography that stretched across united northern Bengal and lower Assam, through the length and breadth of the Coochbehar princely state and the greater Rangpur district. As several elderly residents put it, they have not started doing anything new or different by way of marriage practices or observance of kinship relations. It is the border that happened to them and turned their lives into transnational ones. Practices such as residence and giving birth in one's *baper bari* (natal home), routinely practiced without much interference in the form of border control roughly in the years between 1947 and 1965 and then again from 1971 up to the late 1980s, suddenly took on new significance. For those who had records of these births in the form of birth certificates in India, a documentary practice rarely seen before the 1980s, they formed the basis for the acquisition of other documents marking residence and eventually citizenship—ration cards, voter cards. For those born in Bangladesh, with childhoods spent in their *nana* (maternal grandfather) or *mamar bari* (house of maternal uncle), figured as places of generosity and care, these experiences provided a vantage point to speak of the neighbouring nation, its people and places, with intimate affective attachments.

These produced, without intentional design, as the lives of Afzal master's family testify, transnational ties and social spaces. This is markedly different from the transnational networks and social spaces between places geographically distant, generated by labour migrations, which have been the primary basis of theorisation of 'transnationalism from below' (Smith and Guarnizo 1998). I have shown that close attention to the spatial practices employed by borderland residents opens up a world of negotiation with multiple contingent factors: the ambivalent pressures inherent in kinship, an unequal pair of border control regimes that demands certain performances of citizenship especially of its religious minorities, the discourses of national stereotypes that seep into familial tensions. Spatial practices range from individuals who undertake border crossings and risk the indignity of encounters with BSFs, and worse still arrest, to those who in refusing to engage in such risky illegal travels, perform citizenship in towing the line of their sovereign states. These accounts have foregrounded that existing relations did not end; they were recast and renewed and called upon for new roles as people had to learn how to sustain not only kinship ties but broader livelihoods and sociopolitical pressures, especially as religious minorities in their respective new nation-states. Marriage and kinship obligations function as social insurances in times of displacement. Furthermore, when there are no formal mechanisms for dispute resolution in networks and transactions that spread across the border, being embedded in kin obligations provide social protections, as is evident time and again through the often communally charged violent displacements and wars of 1947, 1965, 1971, the tense years of the Assam agitation in India, and more recently in the years under the Bangladesh National Party in Bangladesh.

Bringing a transnational feminist lens to the study of borders shows us how borders are not only processual and dynamic—that a lot of humanistic and critical social science inquiry has been doing—but that they are materialised in people's everyday lives via classed, gendered and heteronormative logics. Using relative intimacies to enter this field, we see that the borderland family is one site in which gender and sexuality aligns in a particular way to give form to borders and mobilities. Thinking through relative intimacies gives us a way to locate and recognise the range of gendered mobilities that cross this border and also to trace its connections at each scale from that of the body to the national, the regional and the transnational. The permissibility of kin-related border crossings, tentatively accomplished in civil–military relations at the border rest on the power of kinship as a hetero-patriarchal moral force and on the contradistinction by which other bodies and mobilities are agreed upon as real threats to national security.

This chapter has resituated kinship, gender, family and intergenerational dynamics firmly in relation to the issues of movement, trade and livelihood that dominate borderland studies (including accounts of security forces and their excessive violence or unsympathetic demeanour). It has argued that the borderland transnational family transgresses the public-private divide by becoming a site of and for 'public' matters of legality and national difference. This foregrounds the politics of affective relations and moral thresholds between border villagers and the border security forces, marking a significant departure from literature on borders and migration that has largely studied women's labour migrations, and in the frames of trafficking and sexual exploitation at the border (Ghosh 2015). I have argued instead that female border crossers are protected from stigma as the moral discourses of the family ideology sanction their desires and mobility unlike other women who cross for work without the cover of this legitimising discourse of the family. Overall, the moral righteousness inherent in the task of the observance of kin relations firmly separates border crossings for familial reasons from border crossings for economic reasons beyond these gendered roles. Even though there are those who choose to abstain from illegal mobility, a desire for it leads them to seek out other means, leaving traces in stealthy phone calls and Afzal master's triumphant passport acquisition.

NOTES

* My deepest gratitude is to all the families in the Indian and Bangladeshi borderlands who welcomed me into the histories and rhythms of their transnational lives and to the many security force personnel whose critical reflections and sympathies exceed their duties. The fieldwork on which this chapter draws was funded by grants from the Wenner-Gren Foundation, the Social Science Research Council, Macmillan Centre, Yale University and the National Science Foundation.

1. All names have been changed to protect the identities of the individuals. Words in Bengali have been italicised and their translation provided alongside. English words that were used in Bengali sentences have been italicised to indicate original usage.

2. All names of villages, *gram panchayat*s and union parishads are fictitious although there may be villages of these names in the districts of Coochbehar and Lalmonirhat as I have tried to use common names.

3. The Rash Mela in Coochbehar is the second largest fair in West Bengal. It is a significant annual feature on the cultural calendar of north Bengal, an event dating back to the days of the Coochbehar princely state. As a religious minority in Bangladesh, the scale and number of various fairs organised by Hindus are drastically smaller, and while in the past there have been communal tensions around these events, the present Awami League government has been particularly mindful of protecting such minority religious celebrations.

4. Chatterji (2007) has demonstrated the demographic reconfiguration of border-lying *thana*s in West Bengal as Muslim majority through distinct processes of migration, displacement and resettlement in the communally tense decades after Partition.

5. The attitudes of the Border Security Force (BSF) on the Indian side and the Border Guards Bangladesh and police on the Bangladeshi side are completely different when it comes to more large-scale organised networks of cross-border activities such as dealing with cattle and drugs (ganja and Phensedyl).

6. See http://www.hcidhaka.gov.in/pages.php?id=36, accessed on 12 March 2016.

7. The India–Bangladesh passport was phased out in November 2013. In the Coochbehar district alone, this passport had been popular right until its closure—948 issued in 2010, 1,074 in 2011 and 1,290 in 2012.

8. In Bangladesh, it is possible to acquire a passport at the divisional level—for example, Rangpur for those living in Lalmonirhat and Kurigram districts—in a way that is bureaucratically analogous to the state level in India (that is, Kolkata for those living in the Coochbehar district). However, distances were comparably greater given the geographical expanse of India.

9. Notable exceptions are Alexander, Chatterji and Jalais (2016) and Ibrahim (2018).

10. I use quotation marks here to indicate that these proper names were used as such by Shahida Bibi in our conversation.

11. A point most persuasively argued by Ibrahim (2018) and Alexander, Chatterji and Jalais (2016).

12. 'Toba Tek Singh' is an iconic Urdu short story written by Sadaat Hasan Manto and published in 1955 on the violence and madness of the Partition of the Indian subcontinent.

13. See this for an overview of this exchange process that unfolded in 2014–15: Hosna Shewly, 'India and Bangladesh Swap Territory, Citizens in Landmark Enclave Exchange', http://www.migrationpolicy.org/article/india-and-bangladesh-swap-territory-citizens-landmark-enclave-exchange, accessed on 22 October 2019.

14. See http://mha.nic.in/hindi/sites/upload_files/mhahindi/files/pdf/BM_Fence(E).pdf, accessed on 12 March 2016.

15. Residents on the Bangladeshi side use Indian SIM cards within the range of Indian mobile networks whose coverage extends for some distance into the Bangladeshi borderlands and vice versa on the Indian side with Bangladeshi mobile networks. This enables residents to make calls at local rates rather than exorbitant international call rates.

16. Radhika Gupta (2014) has written about similar sentiments of longing in the Kargili borderlands and their unstable location with the confines of the geo-body of the nation.

17. Visiting Bangladeshi kin are not only stopped but also arrested by the BSF under the Foreigner's Act. According to the officer-in-charge at the Dinhata Correctional Home, several of his Bangladeshi under trials belonged to that unfortunate category—visiting kin. I write more extensively about this asymmetry in border control elsewhere (Ghosh 2019).

18. The cover story of *Outlook* magazine in September 2012 explicitly suggested that the Bangladeshi Muslim man was '[t]he new enemy' in a series of stories on the threat of illegal migration to national security. See http://www.outlookindia.com/magazine/issue/10897.

19. I consistently found that in oral accounts of political and regional history, the 1965 India–Pakistan war was referred to as 'chhoy Septemberer juddho', referring to the date on which hostilities formally broke out between the two countries.

20. It is noteworthy that he uses 'ekattorer juddho', the war of 1971, a term commonly used by the lettered Bengali elite instead of 'gondogol', as the peasant masses used to describe it. This same use of terms is noticed and remarked upon by Mookherjee (2015).

21. This has to be read in the context of ongoing political violence in neighbouring Assam over the indiscriminate branding and violent intimidation of Bengali-Muslims as 'Bangladeshi infiltrators'. For insights into the increasing religious polarisation between previously coexisting Hindu and Muslim communities in the Bengal borderlands, see Jalais (2013).

REFERENCES

Aggarwal, Ravina, and Mona Bhan. 2009. '"Disarming Violence": Development, Democracy, and Security on the Borders of India'. *The Journal of Asian Studies* 68 (2): 519–42.

Ahmed, Sara. 2013. 'Not without Ambivalence: An Interview with Sara Ahmed on Postcolonial Intimacies'. *Interventions: International Journal of Postcolonial Studies* 15 (1): 110–26.

Alexander, Claire, Joya Chatterji and Annu Jalais. 2014. *The Bengal Diaspora: Muslim Migrants in Britain, India and Bangladesh*. New York/London: Routledge.

Bal, Ellen. 2007. *They Ask If We Eat Frogs: Garo Ethnicity in Bangladesh*. Singapore: Institute of Southeast Asian Studies.

Banerjee, Paula. 2010. *Borders, Histories, Existences: Gender and Beyond*. New Delhi: Sage Publications.

Baruah, Sanjib. 1999. *India against Itself: Assam and the Politics of Nationality*. Philadelphia: University of Pennsylvania Press.

Bhasin, Ritu, and Kamala Menon. 2000. *Borders and Boundaries: Women in India's Partition*. 2nd edition. New Delhi: Kali for Women.

Butalia, Urvashi. 2000. *The Other Side of Silence: Voices from the Partition of India*. Durham: Duke University Press.

———. 2015. *Partition: The Long Shadow*. Delhi: Zubaan/Penguin-Viking.

Carsten, Janet. 1995. 'The Politics of Forgetting: Migration, Kinship and Memory on the Periphery of the Southeast Asian State'. *The Journal of the Royal Anthropological Institute* 1 (2): 317–35.

———, ed. 2007. *Ghosts of Memory*. Oxford: Blackwell Publishing.

Charsley, Katharine. 2005. 'Vulnerable Brides and Transnational Ghar Damads: Gender, Risk and "Adjustment" among Pakistani Marriage Migrants to Britain'. *Indian Journal of Gender Studies* 12: 381.

Chatterji, Joya. 2007. *The Spoils of Partition: Bengal and India, 1947–1967*. Cambridge: Cambridge University Press.

———. 2009. 'New Directions in Partition Studies'. *History Workshop Journal* 67: 213–20.

Cons, Jason. 2014. 'Impasse and Opportunity: Reframing Postcolonial Territory at the India-Bangladesh Border'. *South Asia Multidisciplinary Academic Journal* 10.

Cons, Jason, and Romola Sanyal. 2013. 'Geographies at the Margins: Borders in South Asia—an Introduction'. *Political Geography* 35: 5–13.

Das, Veena. 2007. *Life and Words: Violence and the Descent into the Ordinary*. San Francisco: University of California Press.

Datta, Antara. 2012. *Refugees and Borders in South Asia: The Great Exodus of 1971*. London: Routledge.

de Certeau, Michel. 2011. *The Practice of Everyday Life*. Translated by Steven F. Rendall. 3rd edition. Berkeley: University of California Press.

Gellner, David, ed. 2013. *Borderland Lives in Northern South Asia: Non-State Perspectives*. Durham: Duke University Press.

Ghosh, Sahana. 2015. 'Anti-trafficking and Its Discontents: Women's Migrations and Work in an Indian Borderland'. *Gender, Place & Culture* 22 (9): 1220–35.

———. 2019. '"Everything Must Match": Detection, Deception and Migrant Illegality in the India-Bangladesh borderlands'. *American Anthropologist* 121 (4): 870–83.

Gupta, Radhika. 2014. 'Poetics and Politics of Borderland Dwelling: Baltis in Kargil'. *South Asia Multidisciplinary Academic Journal* 10.

Harris, Tina. 2013. *Geographical Diversions: Tibetan Trade, Global Transactions*. Athens: University of Georgia Press.

Harvey, David. 2006. *Spaces of Global Capitalism*. New York: Verso Books.

Herzfeld, Michael. 1997. *Cultural Intimacy: Social Poetics in the Nation-State*. New York: Routledge.

Hussain, Delwar. 2013. *Boundaries Undermined: The Ruins of Progress on the Bangladesh-India Border*. London: Hurst.

Ibrahim, Farhana. 2009. *Settlers, Saints, and Sovereigns: An Ethnography of State Formation in Western India*. New Delhi: Routledge.

———. 2011. 'Re-Making a Region: Ritual Inversions & Border Transgressions in Kutch'. *South Asia: Journal of South Asian Studies* 34 (3): 439–59.

———. 2018. 'Cross-Border Intimacies: Marriage, Migration and Citizenship in Western India'. *Modern Asian Studies* 52 (5): 1664–91.

Jalais, Annu. 2013. 'Geographies and Identities: Subaltern Partition Stories along Bengal's Southern Frontier'. In *Borderland Lives in Northern South Asia*, edited by David Gellner, 245–65. Durham: Duke University Press.

Jones, Reece. 2011. 'Spaces of Refusal: Rethinking Sovereign Power and Resistance at the Border'. *Annals of the Association of American Geographers* 102 (3): 685–99.

Kapur, Ratna. 2005. 'Cross-Border Movements and the Law: Renegotiating the Boundaries of Difference'. In *Trafficking and Prostitution Reconsidered*, edited by K. Kempadoo, B. Pattanaik and J. Sanghera. London: Paradigm.

Kapur, Ratna, and B. Cossman. 1996. *Subversive Sites: Feminist Engagements with Law in India*. New Delhi: Sage Publications.

Kaul, Suvir, ed. 2011. *The Partitions of Memory: The Afterlife of the Division of India*. Ranikhet: Permanent Black.

Mookherjee, Nayanika. 2015. *The Spectral Wound: Sexual Violence, Public Memories, and the Bangladesh War of 1971*. Durham: Duke University Press.

Peletz, Michael G. 1995. 'Kinship Studies in Late Twentieth-Century Anthropology'. *Annual Review of Anthropology* 24 (1): 343–72.

Ramaswamy, Sumathi. 2002. 'Visualising India's Geo-Body Globes, Maps, Bodyscapes'. *Contributions to Indian Sociology* 36 (1–2): 151–89.

Shneiderman, Sara. 2013. 'Himalayan Border Citizens: Sovereignty and Mobility in the Nepal–Tibetan Autonomous Region (TAR) of China Border Zone'. *Political Geography* 35: 25–36.

Smith, Michael Peter, and Luis Eduardo Guarnizo. 1998. *Transnationalism from Below*. New Brunswick: Transaction Publishers.

Stoler, Ann. 2010. *Carnal Knowledge and Imperial Power*. San Francisco: University of California Press.

Sur, Malini. 2013. 'Through Metal Fences: Material Mobility and the Politics of Transnationality at Borders'. *Mobilities* 8 (1): 70–89.

Trouillot, Michel-Rolph. 1997. *Silencing the Past: Power and the Production of History*. Boston: Beacon Press.

van Schendel, Willem. 2005. *The Bengal Borderland: Beyond State and Nation in South Asia*. London: Anthem Press.

Wilson, Ara. 2012. 'Intimacy: A Useful Category of Analysis'. In *The Global and the Intimate: Feminism in our Time*, edited by Geraldine Pratt and Victoria Rosner, 31–56. New York: Columbia University Press.

Zamindar, Vazira Fazila-Yacoobali. 2007. *The Long Partition and the Making of Modern South Asia: Refugees, Boundaries, Histories*. New York: Columbia University Press.

6

Reading Parijat in Nepal

The Poetics of Radical Feminism Negotiating Self and Nation

MALLIKA SHAKYA

Following a wave of political and social movements centring around identity politics which David Gellner (2007) called 'ethnogenesis', Nepal continues its search for cultural and social identities as a post-conflict nation-state. Its search for identity draws from the constitution promulgated in 2015 which formally closed the chapter of its decade-long Maoist insurgency and set the country on the path towards reconciliation among various cultural and ideological communities. This constitution states prominently its resolve to build an egalitarian society recognising the 'multi-ethnic, multi-lingual, multi-religious, multi-cultural and diverse regional characteristics' (Government of Nepal 2015). Further, it should not be forgotten that Kathmandu-driven constitutional discourses on diversity took a whole new dimension when challenged by people who live on the borders and whose loyalty to national sovereignty were questioned every so often. That this constitution was promulgated as a show of solidarity among previously warring political constituencies within Nepal, countering a strong message sent by the state of India[1] to concede to the demands of the border population or the Madheshis, signals that identity politics is multidimensional in Nepal as elsewhere. Nepal's rejection of what it considered 'imperialist interference' irked the Indian state to such an extent that immediately after the promulgation of the constitution, it imposed a six-month long blockade on its border with Nepal which had been left historically open for non-commercial flow of people and goods, causing an acute shortage of fuel and essential supplies thus bringing everyday life in Kathmandu to a halt.

Border politics played a central role in setting the direction for Nepal's earlier constitutions in addition to the one that frames contemporary Nepali nationalism. The 1992 constitution, promulgated after ousting the Hindu king's one-party Panchayat regime, came to fruition following a border blockade that lasted for 13 months. The constitution before this, promulgated in 1951, also was made possible by a dramatic border crossing by King Tribhuvan Shah into India, thus stripping cultural legitimacy off the rule of the Rana family, known as the 'lesser kings' among Nepali people but deriving their deliberative power from the British. It is reasonable to suggest that the politics of border and border crossing have politically and symbolically steered how the Nepal–India relationship evolved in the past half a century. What does it mean to build a (post-conflict) 'new'[2] Nepal has a lot to do with complexities of maintaining an 'open-border' with its powerful neighbour, especially in an era of hyper-nationalism increasingly calling for border militarisation in South Asia. Going further, what does it mean to be a bona fide Nepali citizen is a question entangled in the entrenched politics of border crossing into India.

My suggestion is that border is not just a political construct representing geographic frontiers of a nation-state but it also often becomes a vehicle for cultural homogenisation within a nation (E. Gellner 1983). Nestled within the public psyche of distrust for those across the border, nationalist imagination often lets borders be presented as unbroken, even if in reality borders permit both discontinuous and overlapping spaces which allow corporeal and subjective crossings. The contact and transcendence of such crossings may lead to more deliberate and self-conscious forms of public and personal imaginations about national belonging, which span a vast range from gendered concerns for intimacy, care and kinship (Baldassar and Gabaccia 2011) to cosmopolitan consciousness about the self–other dichotomy and its transcendence (Macey 2012).

In this chapter, I try to understand borders and their manifestations in defining Nepaliness expressed in terms of proximity to the culture of the ruling elites or the Bahun–Chhetris[3] and distance from what is perceived as the cross-border 'Indian' way of living which is often viewed with suspicion or treated as a threat. Taking renowned poet Parijat's life and work as a case study, I explore what it may mean for a non-Hindu and non-Bahun–Chhetri poet born and brought up in India to embrace Nepal as her home country. I try to understand the multiple layers of complex identities sieved through the border-crossing trajectories which inform our reading of the poet Parijat and a large body of work which has remained unread so far in anthropology as well as global–regional literary studies outside Nepal.

Wanting to unpack a rather opaque identity that she is anointed with, as 'one of the greatest Nepali poets', I dig into a corpus of Parijat's poetry and fiction to discuss what it may have meant for her to become a 'Nepali' despite being born on the Indian side of the border and not having many affinities with the cultural elites who ruled and hegemonised Nepal during the Panchayat regime.[4] This project reflects on the ironies of Parijat emerging as a leading Nepali icon despite not having a Nepali passport, of her mastering Nepali (Khas belonging to Bahun–Chhetris) literary writing despite hailing from an ethnic community whose mother tongue does not come from the Sanskrit family of languages and of being accredited for introducing individualist-absurdist writing to Nepali literature despite repeatedly swearing by Marxist solidarity.

Parijat's life criss-crossed between the territories of Nepal and India on more than one level. This chaotic interweaving of border crossings might have triggered a new poetic discourse on how she saw herself in terms of social and national framings. She was always a feminist; her personality was too poised as an individual for her to be anything but a feminist. A left-leaning outlook and a stoic way of living was something she maintained from the very beginning, but it was only much later into her writing journey that she openly embraced Marxism as her ideological anchor. It is interesting to dichotomise, as most literary critics studying her work have done, how her early feminism spoke of concerns of individual privacy and intimacy and how later these concerns morphed into public activism protesting gender and social injustice. Is this dichotomy necessary or useful in understanding the poet Parijat and situating her literary contributions within Nepal's modern history? Is it not 'one-dimensional', borrowing an expression that Chimamanda Ngozi Adichie popularised, to call Parijat a feminist poet while turning a blind eye to her public embrace of Marxism? This paper is a critique of this one-dimensionality and it hopes to initiate a discussion around intersectionality in Nepali feminist discourse while probing what border crossing might have meant for Parijat in embracing a post-national Nepali identity.

I begin with Parijat's most famous novel, *Shirishko Phūl* (Blue Mimosa), which has been translated into English by Tanka Vilas Varya and Sondra Zeidenstein (Parijat 1972), and is said to be Parijat's penultimate literary success. The irony about the halo around *Shirishko Phūl* (and another, very similar, novel *Mahattaheen* (Insignificant)) is such that most people would not know that Parijat was a prolific writer and had much more under her belt than these two somewhat short novels.[5] While I do not mean to dismiss *Shirishko Phūl* and *Mahattaheen* or devalue their importance in Parijat's oeuvre, my concern in this chapter is that portraying Parijat simply as an absurdist-feminist novelist runs the risk of reducing her versatile literary disposition into one dimension. In dealing with this concern, I look into a large corpus of her poetry to elucidate Parijat's journey from an introvert young thinker to an engaged public intellectual, while juxtaposing this personal journey to a broader discussion about cross-border nationalism. This review brings forth a rather unique way Nepal and India have maintained an open border which allows the citizens of one country to live on the other side of the border without the kind of bureaucratic control and paperwork mandatory everywhere else in South Asia.

WOMEN WRITING CULTURE AND NATION IN SOUTH ASIA

Why is it useful—even necessary—to turn to creative writing to theorise border and border crossing? Ruth Behar and Deborah Gordon (1995) invoked an earlier anthology seeking alliance with feminist poets to discuss an invisible border keeping doors shut for non-white, female sensibilities and barring them from embracing anthropology in equal terms. More specifically, speaking about borders of nations, Gordon discusses the importance of the 'textual turn' in anthropology for explaining how Puerto Rican women in the United States could never be represented 'ethnographically' by women who do not share their life circumstance where their poetic sensibilities are rooted. Reflecting on what it means to live as a Mizrahi Jewish woman on the Israel–Palestinian border, Lavie (1995) argues that the best anthropological theory she found was a poem about 'Yemeni' blackness of palms and voices tainting the white Jewishness of the state of Israel. Here, the 'tainting' being discussed is not only for the white supremacists but also liberals conveniently shedding their white burden through charity for outsiders while distancing themselves from the symbolic other within. Israel's othering of the Mizrahi (or black) Jewish population is then woven into a broader discourse of alienation: Behar and Gordon's radical opposition of white appropriation of non-white poetry and tales was born of a 'double crisis', of theorism and feminism, and it sought to strike a conversation between (white and male) puritanical anthropology and a (theoretically marginal) community of Chicana lesbian poet-critics. Invoking an earlier anthology *This Bridge Called My Back* (Moraga and Anzaldua 1983), which had by then consolidated itself as an anthem of non-white feminist writers reflecting sentiments of the racial, ethnic and geographic border zones of the United States of America, Behar and Gordon call for white feminist rage against the hegemonic anthropology of 'writing culture' to be humble, and reconsider the mainstream interpretations of belonging vis-à-vis borders of nation, race and class. Elsewhere, feminist interpretations of borders have called for porousness to allow flow of intimacy and care especially in times of humanitarian crises (Saldivar-Hull 2000; Mohanty 2003).

Closer to home in South Asia, I build on the tradition set by Gayatri Spivak (1990) and Ashis Nandy of reading poetry and fiction with fluidity which may question a rigid reading of theoretical reasoning. Nandy (2013) reminds us how the uncompromising versions of border and nation have 'piggybacked' on colonial oppression to pollute post-colonial sensibilities about multiculturality. Gayatri Spivak's decision to literally translate Mahasweta Devi's ethnographically rich novels on the tribal people in and around the Bengal region—as opposed to mining ethnographic data from novels to pursue non-subaltern theorising—speaks volumes about the centrality of poetics in subaltern reading. In altering social science categories by embracing literary imaginations, I take the view—as Shiv Visvanathan (2003) did—that the social sciences can and should borrow from creative literature to enrich its vocabulary on the violence and suffering that are presented as necessary evil for maintaining the seeming sanity of the nation-state. The caveat about social sciences seems especially true for Nepali dilemma about whether and how to join the club of subaltern studies (Des Chene 2007). Let me further clarify this through another piece Des Chene co-authored with Mahesh Maskey in 1999, arguing for Parijat's subaltern spirit being echoed by another Nepali poet Aahuti who has chosen to embrace a revolutionary life without letting 'wordsmithing' dilute into 'sloganing'. Here, Aahuti's poetry is not reduced to ethnography having to speak through highbrow anthropological theorising but represented in full poetic verses and treated as an alternative social science in its own right. In differentiating poetry-as-ethnography from poetry-as-theory, I have of course benefitted from a large corpus of the ethnographic engagements with literature within South Asia (Ali 2012; Langah 2012; Gupta 2014).

There is a rich body of Nepali literature on border and divide crossings, ranging from minstrel *gaine* (minstrel) songs and personal love letters which circulate in and around remote villages, at one end, to published fiction and poetry penned by intellectual writers which circulate in urban literary circles, at the other. Juxtaposed against these, there lies an emerging body of work ethnographising poetry and performance (Stirr 2017; Mottin 2018; Kunreuther 2014; Ahern 2001). Collectively, as Michael Hutt (2012) points out in his comprehensive review of Nepali fiction and poetry on emigration, they speak of both the pride and woes of *lahure*s (mercenary soldiers) and *muglane*s (economic migrants), often criticising the poverty, political instability and exploitative social organisation at home, but also of the grudges of those who remained home towards their compatriots who chose to enlist in foreign armies or take jobs outside the homeland.

Hutt (2012) has attributed Nepali poets' and fiction writers' laments about their compatriots' border crossing to their Marxist inclinations. He also pointed to the class, ethnic and other heuristic conditions of Nepali writers, making way for a kind of literary nationalism that considered emigration unpatriotic. On mercenary service, a renowned Marxist poet from Kathmandu, Bhupi Sherchan—a contemporary of Parijat who we will discuss later—compares Nepali *lahure*s with sacrificial buffaloes and puns *Gorkhali* (the warrior status of Nepali soldiers) with *goru khali* (mere oxen). He writes that the lovely decoration anointed by his military medals may 'emit sometimes the rising stench of the corpse of [the] kin' he killed (Sherchan 1984 [1969]: 63). The stench and taint constitute a regularly invoked trope of pollution when depicting *lahure*s. Mohan Himanshu Thapa (2030/1973: 28) says a returning mercenary soldier is carrying 'a speck of poison in the food [he] is bringing, some noxious gas in the cool breaths [he] breaths'. Another poet from Darjeeling in India, Agam Singh Giri, too urges the *lahure*s to shed their memories of war before entering homes, for they are bloody and polluted (Subedi 1978: 39). Although this may reflect a pacifist belief that border conflict is in itself polluting, or that a war fought for someone else's cause is tainted, the idea of pollution may hark back to the eighteenth-century rituals of 'cleansing' imposed by the Nepali state on Newa traders returning home from across the Tibetan border.[6]

Oscillating between the ethnography of border crossing and the advocacy of patriotic love for the nation, I carve out a space for a distinctive literary genre that looked into the psychology of border crossing beyond its corporeal and social manifestations. The query into the human psyche of reasoning or emoting about border crossing may be more about solitary reflection than social ethnography. A good example is Lainsigh Bangdel's *Muluk Bahira* (Outside the Country) (2008) which begins with a Nepali emigrant in Darjeeling reflecting on his violent outbursts that overpower him from time to time—signifying the violence and self-harm involved in the very act of emigration and border crossing. The story culminates by exposing the unfathomable darkness inside his heart—he runs away and eventually commits suicide in remorse after he murders his beloved wife in a fit of momentary rage. His rage and remorse are about the boundaries of personal hope and despair even as he has already crossed the boundary of nations. Alongside the border of materiality is the border of emotions, addressing a lived space of inner doubts and convictions being reworked into a complex self as a result of having crossed not only political and cultural frontiers but also ethical and emotional (Thapa 2015). These may snuff out the life of a human but he or she may also transcend such borders to embrace a trans-border way of being. This is where I wish to situate Parijat's life and work.

PARIJAT: SELF AND NATION

Parijat was born on the Lingiya tea estate of Darjeeling in April 1937, the daughter of the estate's medical doctor who later quit his job after his relationship with the British colonial owners soured. He introduced his young children to the philosophies of Marx, Engels and Gandhi—a privilege sometimes lacking in those brought up in self-isolated Nepal under the Rana regime which exercised an iron fist to suppress both political and intellectual consciousness.[7] Despite preaching liberalism, however, her father maintained an elitist way of life as, for instance, distancing the children from their working-class surrounding. Parijat lost her mother at an early age and suffered from chronic illness most of her life. She then migrated to Kathmandu as a teenager although she returned to India several times, initially to campaign for a revolutionary leftist cultural movement, Rālphā, and later for medical treatment. It is common for Darjeeling Nepalis to visit, work and even live in Nepal. Such trans-border life seems to have generated for Parijat a trans-border sensibility: her early literary writings reflect on the border as a private–public dichotomy rather than a national construct. Her later writings build on this sensibility to carve out a universalist, activist position on social justice. Contrary to Euro-American, feminist notions emphasising self-domain over class consciousness, Parijat's feminist focus is on intersectionality of class, class and ethnicity.

Parijat is associated with the Rālphā movement in the 1960s and 1970s which sought to generate political consciousness expressed through popular and folk culture.[8] A group of young singers, musicians and poets, Rālphālis travelled throughout the Himalayan foothills, criss-crossing its political borders between Nepal and India. They sang, wrote and debated social injustice invoking neo-Marxian views, at times travelling with no financial support other than spontaneous sponsorship of bus tickets, home meals and guest beds (Manjul 1988). For a self-styled Marxist group, Rālphā embraced creative anarchism in calling for public engagement on social justice. It is on this point that Rālphā needs to be differentiated from several other leftist cultural movements that Nepal saw during the Maoist movement several decades later. Even if the Left-leaning writers in general emphasised Marxist class resistance above all other forms of intersectionality, Rālphālis (Chapagain 2067/2010), including Manjul and Parijat, were inspired by a certain creative energy rebelling against the broader and eclectic social norms of sexuality, rationality and morality. Especially for Parijat, it may even be said that her boundaries were as much about emotive self-ostracisation as they were about social and economic class—let alone the borders of nationality.

> I demand more freedom, and I despair.... The philosophy that my life is mine alone and nobody else's shall claim any rights in it is something that has taken very, very deep roots in my heart.... (Quoted in Bhandari 2051/1994: 33–4)

Parijat's masterpiece *Shirishko Phūl* was her first novel published in 1965, clearly in the phase before she publicly embraced Marxism. It is an *visangatāvādi* (absurdist) expression[9] of deep anguish, expressed in terms of an unconquerable border demarcating the self from the surroundings. The plot of this novel revolves around a retired mercenary soldier traumatised by his violent experiences in the Second World War who develops an attraction for a young but un-femininely strong-minded woman. The trauma of war has transformed Suyog Bir Singh's life into a meaningless void that has alienated him from society while Sakambari has a chronic illness and she lives a life fiercely guarded against everything and everyone. One fateful evening, Suyog Bir impulsively kisses Sakambari just once on the mouth while she is enjoying the blue mimosas on the threshold of her home. The kiss shocks her and she walks away. They never meet again. In the following days, weeks and months, Suyog Bir hears first that Sakambari is sick; then that she is worse and eventually that she has died. The novel ends with a wasting Suyog Bir lamenting over Sakambari:

> Within the glass I see two deep dark eyes. I see a shorn head. I drink and I quench my thirst. My own fingers have become yellow with nicotine. I often look at them and I console myself. (Sakam)Bari does not exist and I recall that here, love does not exist either. I am living in an absurd world and, I always acknowledge, I am living in a great void. (Parijat 1972: 99)

Suyog Bir suffers inconsolably. He cannot overcome the boundary he has set for himself, as if the void he has inherited from the faraway war zone is a contagious one which he cannot help but transmit. This void is neither about hatred nor apathy. Hatred stirs action and may eventually lead to an outlet while apathy keeps Suyog Bir immune to the consequences of his inaction (Stovling 2051/1994).

It is the lack of love and one's inability to confess love that finally kills everyone including the killer. In Parijat's universe, borders are deeply subjective, populated not with pragmatic concerns—let alone considerations of political, cultural or geographic constructs—but with the core of the self.

The threshold of a home is the central material representation of border here. Sakambari's house is a homey one, populated by three unmarried sisters and a seemingly spouseless maid. The house is full of feminine manifestations of different kinds: the youngest who seeks the pleasures of love and elopes, and the eldest whose renunciation of sexual pleasures has turned her into a soft-hearted, conventional woman of contemporary Nepali society; it is the middle one, Sakambari, who defies all female stereotypes, who is sharp-mouthed, smokes endlessly and, using imagery of mimosa and bees, demands protection—self-destructive as it may be—from all external influences. She speaks of her borders in a language of fatality:

> one buds for oneself, blossoms for oneself. If one must fall, why jostle
> with a bee? If one must fall, why tolerate the assault of a bee? One falls
> within, with one's own will. (Parijat 2022/1965: 12, translated by author)

It is in the company of these three-four women that their bachelor brother basks in love, to the extent that Suyog Bir the homeless, loveless old soldier confesses, 'I am jealous of a man for the first time in my life' (Parijat 2022/1965: 29). Suyog Bir's fateful kiss on the threshold under the mimosa blossom is one fleeting moment when the border between Sakambari's self and the world collapses. The intensity of the transcendent moment does not last, and 'the magic vanishes' (Parijat 2022/1965: 52, translated by author). As Suyog Bir later reflects, his intense attraction to Sakambari had triggered memories of his violent wartime past as he served the British during the Second World War—the rape of a headhunter's proud daughter in the jungles of Assam and the betrayal of a Burmese tribal woman's love. These are brutalities to others but also to oneself, as he once told a woman he was about to rape, 'Why construct this wall of ideology with the dying lot like us? Come, let me rob you, you rob me too' (Parijat 2022/1965: 35). What separates Sakambari's threshold, thus, is not the street adjacent, nor the village, nor the nation; instead, the demarcation is between a Tagorean home and the world, love and waste, and construct of a border that denies a nation opportunities to explore its courses fluidly.

After an intense saga of introspection, Suyog Bir does approach Sakambari's threshold one more time, gathering all his courage to confess his love for her.

But it is too late and death has built its own border and asserted its power to transcend all other borders. There is no discussion of rituals commemorating death and hence no ethnography to draw on per se, but even so, it invokes the life–death analogy of border juxtaposed into the imageries it brings out so beautifully about Suyog Bir's soul being crushed by the weight of aggressive, Westphalian nationalism which culminated in the Second World War. Surviving the war, Suyog Bir has turned apathetic and nearly zombie-like—seeing from distance what love may be but unable to live it anymore. In this sense, his border is himself and the only thing he can offer to those who cross his way is violence, even in a kiss. Walls of violent apathy are being built one after another as he goes about his everyday chores, of drinking, thinking, loitering. This is not too different from what Ravina Aggarwal (2001) described in her ethnography of a faraway border village on the India–Pakistan border in the Himalayas where the national-religious feud ends up dividing the young from the old in the way they go about celebrating their centuries-old rituals of death and mourning.

LIBERATING PARIJAT FROM *SHIRISHKO PHŪL*

Quite a debate has brewed since Parijat died in 1993[10] about the ebbs and flows of her literary journey even though her contributions to social justice and affiliations with left politics have remained uncontested. A much-cited quote of hers is from some time in 1973, when she had allegedly made a public declaration, 'I have now crossed the road ... I now write as a Marxist' (cited in Chaitanya 2051/1994: 11). Even before this definitive statement came out, Parijat's writing had begun to shift from isolationism to radical public engagement. Dividing Parijat's writings into three specific phases, Chaitanya (2051/1994) states them to be: (*a*) Existentialist (until 1969), (*b*) neo-anarchist (from 1970 to 1972) and (*c*) Marxist-Progressive (1973 onwards). *Shirishko Phūl* referred to as her first significant writing and which catapulted her as Nepal's leading literary icon is part of her first phase and is credited to have introduced Freudian existentialism into Nepali literature. A well-known literary critic Shankar Lamichhane (2022/1965: ix) argued for the void following the emotional turmoil of Suyog Bir's kiss imposed on Sakambari to be read through Buddhist philosophy of *shunyata* (emptiness). But a closer look at her other (shorter) writings written around the same time, depicting the woes of the working class, express [neo-anarchist] rebellion rather than renunciation.[11]

These two early phases seamlessly segue into her third—Marxist-progressive—phase which saw publication of at least seven novels.[12] None of these could make the literary mark that *Shirishko Phūl* did among the Kathmandu-based and international literary circles, and they were at times dismissed as descriptive and *naravadi* (sloganistic) for lacking the depth of individual characters. Ishwar Baral (2056/1994: 153–6) has written that the Marxist Parijat must not be made the base in relation to the Parijat of *Shirishko Phūl*. When she tried to defend her latter novels, many literary critics seemed to have blamed her of literary dilution and even a lapse of judgement. Reflecting on this, renowned novelist Narayan Dhakal (2074/2017) lamented that the Left, however powerful its political activism might have been, remains under liberal hegemony when it comes to art and aesthetics, and hence there lacks an independent yardstick through which to differentiate a 'deep' Marxist novel from 'bajari' (cheap and sellable) page-turners. He attributes this less to Nepali critics' ability to judge or writers' ability to write, and more to the novel's historical association with European capitalism and European nation (Dhakal 2074/2017). Ashis Nandy (1994) echoed similar sentiments dismissing Robert Lukac's scathing critique of Tagore's *Gora* and *Ghare Baire* (The Home and the World). Timothy Brennan (1989: 4) has showcased lucidly that the genre of the novel historically came with the rise of nations in capitalistic/democratic Europe post–Second World War, pedagogically aiding the project of literary nation building through writing of the 'heteroglossia' of national life and offering tools to dialogically represent a nation.

FROM FICTION TO POETRY: FROM PRIVATE ESCAPISM TO PUBLIC ENGAGEMENT

Turning now to Parijat's poetry, there seems to be a much more seamless progress from existentialism to activist progressivism amid her 80 poems published in three anthologies,[13] which is quite a contrast from an abrupt switch critics have argued about between her novels. Parijat's early poems were about borders of intimacy and struggles of escapism echoing her early novels. They spoke about, for example, mute, unexpressed but endless cries (*mook, avyakta tara ashesh aartanaad*) and craving for tremors (*mero swar ma kampan bhari de*) within oneself. Her early poems are short and somewhat sketchy as if their voices have been muffled by the weight of expression; her style of writing comes across as experimental and at times her verses are written in structured stanzas which rhyme only partially. As in her early novels, her early poems also privilege individual pursuit of privacy and solitude: In 'Mahabhinishkramana' (Buddha's Great Departure Seeking Truth), part of her 1957 anthology *Akansha*, she validates Siddhartha's decision to renounce his family and community which is a sharp contrast to another poem 'Lahure Lai Ek Rogi Premika Ko Prem Patra' (An Ill Beloved's Love Letter for a Mercenary Soldier), published in her second anthology three decades later, where she takes issue with a mercenary soldier's one-sided abandonment of his lover for the sake of protecting the borders of the nation. But in this phase, she is also seen reasoning with a contemporary revolutionary poet Gopal Prasad Rimal about the definitions of the social duties of reproduction.[14] Then comes the third anthology which has clearly made a decisive departure from individual existentialism into Marxist solidarity, and her writings exhibit a renewed public engagement for social change. In the following paragraphs, I will individually discuss some of the poems from this last phase.

First is the poem 'Andolan' (Uprising) which declares that liberation is not an un-germinated seed in unsuitable soil or an aimlessly kicked ball but a retaliative energy that may twist life out of powerless hearts, and that a true liberation may even redden the horizons of Lumbini—the birthplace of Buddha and a geography of historical pride for Nepal. Two other poems in this collection form a gender binary. In 'Manushi' (Female Person), she asks,

> Has a woman ever raped you?
> Has a woman ever robbed you of your honour?
> Has a woman ever sold you anywhere?
>
> …
>
> I hold your hands firmly
> You may walk me to the place where you have reached
> That pinnacle, where
> I had already walked you at the very origin of [your] civilization.
>
> (Parijat 2073/2017: 127, translated into English by Mallika Shakya)

Followed by a call for public uprising, 'Timi Manchheka Jat Hau' (You Are the Caste of a Human),

> As a snake has his poison and a man his ego
> Against those who paint themselves stealing the colours of your body
> Do you not have an ago against them, my child?
> You are the caste of a human
> You ought to have an ego
> Because you are very much the caste of a human.
>
> (Parijat 2073/2017: 130, translated into English by Mallika Shakya)

There are six more poems in this anthology echoing Parijat's new feminist voice which is no longer isolationist but has now embraced public activism and speaks of the gendered intersectionalities of caste and ethnicity against a central trope of class. In 'Euti Swasnimanchheko Antarvarta' (Interview of a Woman), she writes,

> Yes, sir,
> I only know that I have worked
> I only know the sufferings I have lived
> I only know my wearing of torn-tops and hand-me-downs
> Oh, youth it is, that you are asking about?
> Excellency, I do not know youth's coming or going.
> The wise beings may say
> My youth has already flourished well in Lord Jimwal's wheat fields!
> Full blossomed in the marigolds of his garden yards!
> How bizarre
> My youth wouldn't bloom in my own eyes and lips
> But in someone else's properties?!
> Excuse me? Did you say I have the grace?
> Yes, excellency, that is what I also thought
> When I looked at the water in the pond
> But how could one rely on it?
> Mere reflection on the water.
> I swear on my flesh, I'm not lying
> Oh Dear God!
> I caught a glimpse of my husband only at our wedding platform
> A poinsettia tucked in his cap
> Two-three glitters glued on his forehead
> Wearing a hint of rose powder on his cheeks
> Had come my middle-aged groom
> Dark as the blacksmith's iron
> Rough as a hoe
> Oh, you are laughing, my dear excellency!
>
> ...
>
> Yes, sir,
> Now I have come to cherish love for this good old blacksmith
> What other choices does one have in life other than poverty?
> Even I have become ghostly and frightful
> With dandruff and wrinkles   —
> Do I look like a woman anymore?
> Oh, you are laughing again, my dear excellency!
> The meaning of life, is that what you ask?
> No, excellency, I have not understood a thing
> My blacksmith's colour and my iron's colour is the same, excellency.
> My worn skin's colour is also the same as the dust in the road.
> I have also become filthy, mucky, sooty

My blacksmith never weeps
But his toil's colour
Is the same as my tears'.
Excellency, excellency, it is only now that I am beginning to demand
That those who work
Ought to have the means
To eat.

(Parijat 2073/2017: 146, translated into English by Mallika Shakya)

Two other poems speak the voice of a Dalit woman: In 'Juthi Daminiko Abhivyakti' (Expressions of Juthi Damini), a woman is robbed of her love and dignity by the feudal lord.

I was like that poinsettia, Excellency
What beauty to be bestowed on a mere untouchable
That old feudal Bishtas would be greedy for me

…

This land of mine has remained far too infertile
Like that hillock infested with crop-eating creepers
Kindly intervene on my behalf if you can, plough it for me
Grace, Excellency…
Kindly help me moist this soil for the seeding.

(Parijat 2073/2017: 159, translated into English by Mallika Shakya)

In 'Gadhteerko Dhungama Aamako Samjhana' (Memories of Mother on the Stone on the Gadhteer, or River Banks), Parijat writes of a Dalit woman forcibly married off against her will so that her high-caste lover is not polluted by her love.

I call the sun as my witness, the sky as my witness
Who does not fall in love in life?

…

The way the Mukhiya made the village shiver
How can I ever forget that, mother?
You the corpse-eating caste.
Marry away your daughter immediately
Or else, I will shave her head
Strip her off and parade naked around the village.
That's how the Mukhiya had roared!

…

My mother!
How am I to have one soul live in my heart

And spend life with another?
One visits me in my dreams
How am I to call the other by his name once I am awake?
(Parijat 2073/2017: 170, translated into English by Mallika Shakya)

It is not only when speaking in the voice of others that Parijat seeks public engagement for radical change; even her autobiographical poem 'Mrityu' (Death) has shed escapist solitude to engage a collective activism with a distinct cause. It is striking to note that, within a short poem, a private death referred to as a single noun in the first set of verses is suddenly but seamlessly pluralised into 'deaths' marching among the crowds and turning into bayonets aimed at class enemies:

I had once the wish to write poetry,
That death is a curse
Death is contradiction
Death is the end of life.
At that time, I loyally embraced
The interpretations of death
From religious canons
Yet I live within me raw pain it brings,
Once, threatened by mounting sorrows of life
I tried to hide my face
In the veil of death
Even so, I do have some vivid stories of death within me.

...

Today, again, I feel like writing one other poem
That death is not a contradiction,
I want to say death is not the end of life
Death is a martyr
Well protected under its red flag
Deaths march among the crowds
Sacrifice is the other name of death
Deaths live on I now see
In the memories of those who live behind

...

Deaths become solidarities
And weave into the spirits of embrace
Get inscribed on slogans on the wall
Distributed as pamphlets
No, deaths do not die.

...

Deaths become bayonets
Getting aimed at class enemies
And blast as gun shots.

   (Parijat 2073/2017: 162, translated into English by Mallika Shakya)

PARIJAT AND THE IDEOLOGICAL BORDERS OF NATION AND BEING

In the first, existentialist phase, Parijat's poetic voice was that of a solitary individual with private concerns reflected in characters like Sakambari struggling to beat physical-psychiatric illness and Suyog Bir searching for the soul in the macabre remnants of the Second World War. As a well-known radical, Marxist Mohan Bikram Singh (2051/1994: 165–8) once put it, Parijat lived a private life until the fame of *Shirishko Phūl* turned her into a public icon. The initial followership she had earned was among the left-leaning intellectuals who later nudged her into Marxist inclinations—something she had nurtured from her early upbringing in India (see the section 'Parijat: Self and Nation'). Ironically, however, as Parijat's friend and literary critic Britta Stovling (2051/1994) reminds us, Nepal's Communist Party had initially dismissed *Shirishko Phūl*, considering that 'it treats only private matters and so it is politically incorrect'. Stovling went on to share that a Swedish publisher who turned down the English translation of *Shirishko Phūl* had considered the manuscript to be 'too private and lack[ed] local colour ... the plot could be enacted anywhere'. To this Stovling (2051/1994: 166–7) adds, 'Ah, yes, I cannot recall much local colour or common fates in the great antique Greek tragedies.'[15] The observation remains true that both the protagonists in *Shirishko Phūl* show almost no affiliation with national or cultural groupings, thus making the border which is at the heart of the novel to be about a personal (even intimate) quest calling for cosmopolitan and spiritual pacifism. They certainly lack, deliberately almost, any defining trait on ethnicity, religion, class and nation.

   While class, caste, gender and nation emerged as an entwined theme in her later writing, especially poetry, she seems to search for a fine balance between expressing her Janajati ethnicity and her class-ideological position while seeking to be identified as a Nepali. A collection of her letters to her sister and doppelganger Sukanya give away very little Janajati-ness in her everyday affiliations, of the times she split between public hospital beds in Delhi and a private bed at home in Kathmandu (Waiba 2075/2019). Even so, the Nepali she writes in these letters are decisively Janajati-Nepali leaning on the *anukaranatmak pras* (imitative melody), as opposed to Bahun–Chhetri Nepali policed with Sanskrit rules of grammatical correctness. What reverberates letter after letter is Parijat's grave medical concerns, worrying if and when she will ever be physically mobile again and her pressing anxiety about how to foot medical bills of bare survival, but clearly above it all, a deep sensibility about her belonging to the nation of Nepal and alienation from the culture of the Gangetic plains of India despite possibly still holding an Indian passport.

Every single letter Parijat wrote to Sukanya had a spontaneous expression or two about how she saw herself to be a Nepali national and were penned in expressions that may be called Tamang-Nepali; yet when a (Nepali) interviewer asked her bluntly, if unfairly, 'You are apparently somewhat communal, is it true?', her answer was:

> Not sure Teertha jee! This is a strange thing I am hearing. I come from the backward caste of Tamangs. But around here, when I meet some Tamangs and I tell them I too am a Tamang, they do not at all believe this. It seems, I am going to have to be caught in distrust of both sides!
>
> (Interview by Teertha Koirala for *Matribhoomi* magazine, 10 January 1989)

Choosing a national identity over ethnic is something the Janajati characters in Parijat's novel do routinely, and like the poet, the characters she created in her poetry and later novels are also clearly more expressive of their class positions than their ethnic ones. What I mean by this is that their progressive inclinations are expressed in indigenous wording but resonating a Listian or Szporlukian nation-state.[16] For example, in the novel *Salgi ko Balatkrit Aansu* (Salgi's Raped Tears), Salgi is a Tamang girl from the central hill district of Nepal who gets tricked and trafficked into an Indian brothel by a fellow villager of her own ethnicity. Weeping in agony, she cursed the fellow villager who had sold her into prostitution but her rage falls squarely on the 'Indian' men who quench their sexual thirst with her 'Nepali' body. Gorimaya of *Anindo Pahad Saigai* (With the Unsleeping Mountain) is a woman of few words who eventually amasses courage to rebel against oppressive patriarchy and annul her marriage to a lunatic. Later, she heads to the city on her own, eventually forging kinship into a household of inter-caste marriage caught in a political struggle against the oppressive national regime. The character who complements Gorimaya's submissive-supportive role in the country's transition from oppression to pseudo-democracy is a Janajati police officer Ale who had married a defenceless Chhetri woman and assumed guardianship of her young son. At the end of the story, the Janajati father and Chhetri son die untimely deaths, fighting in a political turmoil—one on behalf of the state and the other the rebels. What remains is the feminine solidarity between the Chhetri boss and the Tamang (Janajati) maid, who help each other get over this trauma and go on living the everyday nation-state that is full of turmoil, sabotage and fraud.

None of these Janajati characters that I discuss earlier live their Janajati spirit in the way Sakambari and Suyog Bir fully embody their absurdist consciousness. Commenting on her de-ethnicised public persona and the way she penned her characters, initially as absurdist individuals and later as class and gender activists but never quite as full ethnic beings, her friend Mahesh Maskey reflects that this may indicate social self-censoring of those days. A Janajati himself but from outside the Newa stronghold of Kathmandu, Maskey recalled that many progressive intellectuals chose to punctuate expressions of their ethnicity because it was considered communal both by the standards of Panchayat mono-nationalism as well as Left progressive-cosmopolitanism. Especially those with passion for Nepali (Khas belonging to Bahun–Chhetris) literature who engaged as readers and writers struggled somehow to find a position which dialogised their ethnic being with their Nepali literal sensibilities. Within Nepal, this may point to Panchayati cultural appropriation of ethnic identities into a hegemonic nationalism that privileged the Hindu high caste. But on the other side of the border where Parijat was brought up, the construction of a 'Nepali' micro-nationality (against hegemonic Indian) had long hoisted Nepali language as a lingua franca of the subaltern Janajati population fighting for linguistic, cultural and political autonomy from the state of north Bengal (Onta 1996).[17]

BORDERS TALKING BACK

Having uprooted herself from Darjeeling to settle down in Kathmandu, Parijat soon found herself returning to the Indian side of the border, this time to the hospitals in Delhi rather than the Himalayan foothills of Darjeeling where she grew up. This kind of border criss-crossing—as opposed to a one-time border crossing depicted in migration literature—is common for several Indian writers, singers, musicians, artists, intellectuals and workers of Nepali-Janajati origins who relocated to Kathmandu from the Himalayan foothills in north Bengal and became Nepali nationals. At the heart of this spaghetti bowl of border criss-crossing lies two subaltern literary movements from the mid-twentieth century that is worth taking note of: First is what Chalmers (2003) called 'a quest for *ekrupata*' (uniformity) among the community of ethnically divided Janajati-Nepalis living in north Bengal and northeast India. They chose for their lingua franca Nepali (Khas belonging to Bahun–Chhetris) as their subaltern voice for mobilisation against Hindi and Bangla hegemonies. Second is the literary grouping of Janajati poets within Kathmandu who learned and wrote in Nepali and found ways of registering their protest against the Panchayati oppression. Bhupi Sherchan and Bairagi Kaila of Parijat's generation built a strong legacy of Janajatised Nepali (Khas belonging to Bahun–Chhetris) language which later inspired the next generation of rebel poets writing in Nepali in India condemning Indian state's oppressive stance in troubled places like Kashmir (Puniani and Bogati 2016).

Michael Hutt (2012) has invoked Shamsher (1998) to state that cross-border poetics of political resistance in Nepal is caught in the dichotomy of 'slogans of poetry' (*kavitama nara*) and 'poetic sloganism' (*naravadi kavita*), dating back several decades (Sangraula 2027/1970; Vikal 2040/1983). Through this stream emerged Rālphā, discussed earlier in this chapter, a movement that championed sociopolitical consciousness through individual anarchism. Manjul, one of the Rālphālis, went on to write an exceptionally expressive anarchic poetry on a sloganist poet from the Janajati ilk, Siddhicharan Shrestha, which goes, 'Siddhicharan becomes Siddhicharans, and takes out a procession' (Manjul 2055/1998: 53), and the weight of this anomaly tires him so much that '[he] eventually picks up both his legs and rests them on his shoulders even as he keeps walking' (Manjul 2055/1998: 25). That Rālphā and Parijat later became the icons inspiring young activists in north Bengal protesting oppressive nationalism with a Left-progressive spirit perhaps what closes the loop on literary border-crisscrossing between the two countries.

In disentangling the literary conundrum through an anthropological reading of Parijat's poetry and fiction, my proposal in this chapter has been that the poetics of resistance may inform border studies as poignantly as ethnographies and survey data, but it is also important to call on field poetics to be accepted within mainstream social sciences, especially anthropology. I began this chapter with the internal battle faced by non-white anthropologies within their disciplinary homes in the 1980s. Almost four decades later, if we are to have any chance of course correction within the social sciences about hegemonic discourses on nationalism being mainstreamed, we must create space for alternative field voices to be heard. My use of creative writing is to explore the possibilities of it being one such device. In incorporating literary expressions within anthropology, we must— as Faye Harrison (1995) so poignantly put during the 'women writing culture' project—'offset the persistent pattern of relegating the work of [the ignored] to anthropology's periphery'. Prioritising form and discipline over diversity of outlook and expression runs the danger of bordering out interlocutors like Parijat, and their voices dismissed as ethnographic accessories while hegemonic anthropology continues its course uninterrupted.

NOTES

1. Landing in Kathmandu just two days before the set date for promulgation of its constitution, the Indian Foreign Secretary S. Jaishankar conveyed to the Nepalese president and the prime minister that the constitution should not be finalised until the grievance of the Madheshi people in Nepal's southern plains had been addressed. The Nepali side went ahead with the promulgation anyway, mustering a strong parliamentarian majority in its support.

2. The expression 'new Nepal' was earlier used vernacularly during the first democratisation of Nepal in 1951 following the end of the Rana regime that had ruled Nepal crypto-colonially in alliance with the British Raj in the rest of the region. The regime change of 1991, which also resulted in writing and promulgation of a new constitution, used variants such as 'democratic Nepal' or 'liberal Nepal', keeping its focus primarily on deliberative politics rather than sociocultural nation-building. In contrast, the post-conflict state-building actively referred to the writing of the new constitution and the implementation of federal governance, as well as identity-based affirmation action programmes as building of 'new Nepal' (Joshi and Rose 1966; Shakya 2016).

3. See Lawoti (2008) for a discussion on how the Hindu high-caste groups who he refers to as 'caste hill Hindu elites' or CHHE have hijacked Nepal's democratisation process since the 1990s.

4. The one-party Panchayat regime which ruled Nepal between 1961 and 1990 under the Hindu King pursued a hegemonic rhetoric that 'every Nepali is a Pancha and every Pancha is a Nepali' thus denying space for ideological and cultural diversity within the country.

5. It is true that many of Parijat's work have not been made easily available until recently, but although commercial book stalls do not have those, most public libraries do have them, and the Parijat Foundation set up and managed by her sister Sukanya has long provided access to serious collectors.

6. Upon unification (or conquest) of the Nepali kingdom, for example, King Prithvi Narayan Shah imposed such stringent conditions of cleansing on the Newars of Kathmandu Valley that the traders returning from Tibet, almost all of them

Buddhist, had to spend months with a Hindu priest undergoing *patia* (cleansing) of their—alleged—consumption of yak meat (the yak was held to be of sufficiently close kinship with the Hindu-revered cows that purification rituals were considered necessary) (Shakya 2013: 61). The ritual was even stricter earlier for Newar traders who returned from the southern districts under the Mughal realms, who supposedly had to 'undergo purifications by bathing for 40 days in cow's urine, drinking it, and eating cow dung occasionally', according to records kept by Father Ippolito Desideri in the early eighteenth century (Burghart 1984: 104).

7. The point about literary suppression in Nepal can be understood better from the realities that the Rana regime had made even functional literary classes legally punishable and the only school to exist in Nepal before 1950, the Durbar High School, accepted students only from the few elite (and certainly high caste) families.

8. Parijat never held a formal position in any of the communist parties, let alone taking up any public jobs or titles.

9. See Luintel's (2069/2012) argument that while Indra Bahadur Rai introduced absurdism in Nepali literature through his novel *Āja Ramitā Chha* (There Is a Spectacle Today), but Parijat perfected it in her novel *Shirishko Phūl*.

10. Parijat had succumbed to paralysis since the age of 26 and she had become incapacitated in her mid-30s.

11. I specifically mention three short stories penned in her early phase almost coinciding with the writing of *Shirishko Phūl*, namely, 'Workshop Bhitra' (Inside a Workshop), 'City Hall ko Budho Jyami Sanga' (With an Old Builder in the City Hall) and 'Sadak ra Pratibha' (The Street and the Talent).

12. Seven novels categorised to belong to her second phase of writing are: *Parkhal Bhitra ra Bahira* (Outside and Inside of the Wall), *Tori Bari, Bata ra Sapanaharu* (Mustard Fields, Paths and Dreams), *Antarmukhi* (Introspective), *Usle Rojeko Bato* (The Way She Chose), *Anindo Pahad Sangai* (With the Unsleeping Mountain), *Boni, Paribhashit Aankhaaharu* (Eyes Defined) and two short-story collections, *Salgi ko Balatkrit Aansu* (Salgi's Raped Tears) and *Badhshala Aaunda Janda* (Walking to and Back from the Slaughterhouse).

13. The first of these anthologies, *Akansha* (Aspiration), was published in 1957, *Parijat ka Kavitaharu* (Parijat's Poems) was published in 1987 and *Baisalu Bartaman* (Youthful Present) was published in 1996.

14. In a poetic conversation carried out in her second anthology in a poem 'Gopal Prasad Rimal Prati' (For Gopal Prasad Rimal), Parijat questions a fellow progressive poet Gopal Prasad Rimal's call for social duties to emerge from intimate concerns of love and affection, that 'a Buddha should be born, a Lenin should be born' out

of true love. Paijat pens, following her Nissaratavadi sensibility, that she prefers love to continue concerns for 'unclear and abstract ideals' (*ashpashta aadarsha*) when life is just a struggle of stray dogs fighting to eat rotten rice: *kuheko bhaata ka laagi bhusiya kukur sanga ladai* (Parijat 2073/2017: 45–6, 56–8). Further, see Shakya (2017: 143–4) for additional poetic engagement with the work of Parijat and Gopal Prasad Rimal on fatherhood in absentia.

15. It is only ironic that it was a Nepali publisher who did publish the English translation of *Shirishko Phūl* and that publication gave Parijat an international recognition as the leading novelist from Nepal.

16. See Ernest Gellner (1995) for a discussion on Roman Szporluk's thesis that Marx offered class affiliation as an alternative to national affiliation but that he was aware that a proletariat revolution was impossible without a necessary national categorisation, distinguishing but connecting various nation-states throughout various stages of development. In this scheme, the nation is not about imagined communities as Benedict Anderson (1983) describes it, but an affiliation to a nation-state with a promise for activism towards class liberation.

17. Pratyoush Onta has written how Bhanubhakta Acharya was cultivated as a Nepali-language icon initially in Darjeeling as part of the post-colonial struggle for Nepali-Gorkha identity within India and how this narrative was later embraced by the ruling Bahun–Chhetris within the state of Nepal to construct a monocultural nation-state under the Panchayati autocracy.

REFERENCES

Aggarwal, Ravina. 2001. 'At the Margins of Death: Ritual Space and the Politics of Location in an Indo-Himalayan Border Village'. *American Ethnologist* 28 (3): 549–73.

Ahern, Laura. 2001. *Invitations to Love: Literacy, Love Letters, and Social Change in Nepali*. United States of America: The University of Michigan Press.

Ali, Nosheen. 2012. 'Poetry, Power, Protest: Reimagining Muslim Nationhood in Northern Pakistan'. *Comparative Studies of South Asia, Africa and the Middle East* 32 (1): 13–24.

Anderson, Benedict. 1983. *Imagined Communities: Reflections on the Origin and Spread of Nationalism*. London and New York: Verso.

Baldassar, Loretta, and Donna R. Gabaccia, ed. 2011. *Intimacy and Italian Migration: Gender and Domestic Lives in a Mobile World*. New York: Fordham University Press.

Bangdel, Lainsingh. 2008. *Muluk Bāhira* (Outside the Country). Kathmandu: Ratna Pustak Bhandar.

Baral, Ishwar. 2056/1994. 'Parijat ka Kavita: Sankatgrasta Ahan ko Aalekh' (The Poems of Parijat: Writings of Crisis-Ridden Ego). In *Chhariyeka Sameeksha* (Scattered Appraisals), edited and collected by Sharad Chandra Sharma Bhattarai, 135–58. Kathmandu: Sajha Prakashan.

Behar, Ruth, and Deborah Gordon, eds. 1995. *Women Writing Culture*. Berkeley: University of California Press.

Bhandari, Jagadish Chandra. 2051/1994. 'Parijat: Āfnai Ātmakathamā' (Parijat in Her Own Autobiography). In *Parijat Smriti Grantha* (Parijat Memorial Book), edited by Ninu Chapagain and Khagendra Sangraula, 27–43. Kathmandu: Parijat Smriti Kendra.

Brennan, Timothy. 1989. *Salman Rushdie and the Third World: Myths of the Nation*. London: Palgrave Macmillan.

Burghart, Richard. 1984. 'The Formation of the Concept of Nation State in Nepal'. *The Journal of Asian Studies* 44 (1): 101–25.

Chaitanya. 2051/1994. 'Parijat: Saundarya Chintanko Vikās Prikriyā' (Parijat: The Development of Aesthetic Conscience). In *Parijat Smriti Grantha* (Parijat Memorial Book), edited by Ninu Chapagain and Khagendra Sangraula, 1–18. Kathmandu: Parijat Smriti Kendra.

Chalmers, Rhoderick. 2003. 'The Quest for Ekrupata: Unity, Uniformity and the Delineation of the Nepali Community in Darjeeling.' In *The Nepalis in North East India: A Community in Search of Indian Identity*, edited by A. C. Sinha and T. B. Subba, 339–59. New Delhi: Indus Publishing Company.

Chapagain, Ninu, ed. 2067/2010. *Mārxvādi Samalo Chanā-Paddati* (Marxist Critical Appreciation Process). Kathmandu: Bhrikuti Academic Publications.

Des Chene, Mary. 2007. 'Is Nepal in South Asia? The Condition of Non-Postcoloniality'. *Studies in Nepali History and Society* 12 (2): 207–23.

Dhakal, Narayan. 2074/2017. 'Kina Kamjor Chha Nepali Upanyas?' (Why Is Nepali Novel Weak?). *Annapurna Post Daily*, 20 Jestha 2074/3 June 2017. http://annapurnapost.com/news/72318, accessed on 5 June 2018.

Gellner, David. 2007. 'Caste, Ethnicity and Inequality in Nepal'. *Economic and Political Weekly* 42 (20): 1823–8.

Gellner, Ernest. 1983. *Nations and Nationalism*. London: Blackwell Publishing.

———. 1995. *Encounters with Nationalism*. Oxford and California: Blackwell Publishing.

Government of Nepal. 2015. *Constitution of Nepal.* Kathmandu: Kanun Kitab Bebastha Samittee.

Gupta, Radhika. 2014. 'Poetics and Politics of Borderland Dwelling: Baltis in Kargil'. *South Asia Multidisciplinary Academic Journal* 10: 1–18.

Harrison, Faye. 1995. 'Writing against the Grain: Cultural Politics of Difference in the Work of Alice Walker'. In *Women Writing Culture,* edited by Ruth Behar and Deborah Gordon, 233–48. Berkeley: University of California Press.

Hutt, Michael. 2012. *Eloquent Hills: Essays on Nepali Literature.* Kathmandu: Martin Chautari.

Joshi, Bhuwan Lal, and Leo E. Rose. 1966. *Democratic Innovations in Nepal: A Case Study of Political Acculturation.* Berkeley/Cambridge: University of California Press.

Kunreuther, Laura. 2014. *Voicing Subjects: Public Intimacy and Mediation in Kathmandu (South Asia across the Disciplines).* Berkeley: University of California Press.

Lamichhane, Shankar. 2022/1965. 'Bhoomika' (Foreword). In *Shirisko Phūl* (The Blue Mimosa), edited by Parijat. Kathmandu: Self-published.

Langah, Nukhbah Tai. 2012. *Poetry as Resistance: Islam and Ethnicity in Postcolonial Pakistan.* Oxford: Routledge, Taylor and Francis Group.

Lavie, Smadar. 1995. 'Border Poets: Translating by Dialogues'. In *Women Writing Culture,* edited by Ruth Behar and Deborah Gordon, 412–28. Berkeley: University of California Press.

Lawoti, Mahendra. 2008. 'Exclusionary Democratization in Nepal, 1990–2002'. *Democranisation* 15 (2): 363–85.

Luintel, Khagendra Prasad. 2069/2012. *Nepali Upanyāsko Itihās* (History of Nepali Novels). Kathmandu: Nepal Pragya Pratishthan.

Macey, David. 2012. *Franz Fanon: A Biography.* London and New York: Verso.

Manjul. 1988. *Samjhanākā Pāilāhāru* (The Footsteps of Memory). Varanasi: Nath Printers.

———. 2055/1998. *Siddhicharanharu* (The Siddhicharans). Kathmandu: Yugakavi Siddhacharan Pratishthan.

Moraga, Cherrie, and Gloria Anzaldua, ed. 1983. *This Bridge Called My Back.* New York: Kitchen Table Women of Colour Press.

Mottin, Monica. 2018. *Rehearsing for Life: Theatre for Social Change in Nepal.* Cambridge: Cambridge University Press.

Nandy, Ashis. 1994. *The Illegitimacy of Nationalism: Rabindranath Tagore and the Politics of Self.* Delhi: Oxford University Press.

————. 2013. *Regimes of Narcissism, Regimes of Despair*. Delhi: Oxford University Press.

Onta, Pratyoush. 1996. 'The Career of Bhanubhakta as a History of Nepali National Culture 1940–1999'. *Studies in Nepal History and Society* 4 (1): 65–136.

Parijat. 1972. *Shirisko Phūl* (Blue Mimosa). Translated by Tanka Vilas Varya. Kathmandu: Orchid Books.

————. 2033/1976. *Toribāri, Bātā ra Sapanāharu* (Mustard Fields, Paths and Dreams). Kathmandu: Nepal Rashtriya Pragya Pratishthan.

————. 2039/1982. *Anindo Pahadsangai* (With the Insomniac Hills). Varanasi: Nath Publishing House.

————. 2073/2017. *Parijat ka Sankalit Rachanaharu – 5* (The Parijat Omnibus, vol. 5). Kathmandu: Times Creation.

Puniani, Raja, and Manoj Bogati, eds. 2016. *Hastaxep*. Darjeeling: Hastaxep Prakashan.

Saldivar-Hull, Sonia. 2000. *Feminism on the Border*. Berkeley: California University Press.

Sangraula, Khagendra. 2027/1970. *Chetanāko Pahilo Dāk* (First Call of Conscience). Kathmandu: Bhanu Prakashan.

Shakya, Mallika. 2013. 'Nepali Economic History through the Ethnic Lens: Changing Stata Alliances with Business Elites'. In *Nationalism and Ethnic Conflict in Nepal: Identities and Mobilization after 1990*, edited by Mahendra Lawoti and Susan Hangen, 58–82. New York: Routledge.

————. 2016. 'Labour Militancy in Neoliberal Times: A Preliminary Comparison of Nepal with South Africa'. In *World Anthropologies in Practice: Situated Perspectives, Global Knowledge*, edited by John Gledhill, 41–58. London/New York: Bloomsbury.

————. 2017. 'Babu ko Thegan Nabhayekhar Prati' (To Those Who Do Not Know Where Their Fathers Are). *La.Lit. A Literary Magazine* 8 (1): 143–4. Translated by Muna Gurung.

Shamsher, Jagadish. 1998. 'Preface'. In *Siddharanharu* (The Siddhicharans), i–xxiii. Kathmandu: Dabali Press.

Sherchan, Bhupi. 1984 (1969). *Ghumne Mecmāthi Andho Mānche*. Kathmandu: Sajha Prakashan.

Singh, Mohan Bikram. 2051/1994. 'Parijat: Kehi Sansmaran, Kehi Mulyankan' (Parijat: Part Memoir, Part Appraisal). In *Parijat Smriti Grantha*, edited and collected by Ninu Chapagain and Khagendra Sangraula, 165–8. Kathmandu: Parijat Smriti Kendra.

Spivak, Gayatri. 1990. 'Women in Difference: Mahasweta Devi's "Douloti the Bountiful'". *Cultural Critique* no. 14: 105–28.

Stirr, Anna. 2017. *Singing across Divides: Music and Intimate Politics in Nepali*. Oxford: Oxford University Press.

Stovling, Brita. 2051/1994. 'Heart in Flames'. In *Parijat Smriti Grantha* (Parijat Memorial Book), edited by Ninu Chapagain and Khagendra Sangraula, 166–7. Kathmandu: Parijat Smriti Kendra.

Subedi, Abhi. 1978. *Nepali Literature: Background and History*. Kathmandu: Ratna Pustak Bhandar.

———. 2003. *Ghar aur Bāhar* (The Home and The World). Hindi Translation by Pradeep Pandit. Delhi: Diamond Pocket Books.

Talpade Mohanty, Chandra. 2003. *Feminism without Borders: Decolonizing Theory, Practising Solidarity*. Durham and London: Duke University Press.

Thapa, Manjushree. 2015. 'Women Have No Nationality'. *The Record*, 21 September. https://www.recordnepal.com/perspective/women-have-no-nationality/, accessed on 23 September 2015.

Thapa, Mohan Himanshu. 2030/1973. *Khukurimāthi Ek Chauta Bādal* (A Slice of Cloud on a Sword). Kathmandu: Yugantar Prakashan.

Vikal, Ramesh. 2040/1983. *Aviral Bagdachha Indāavati* (Indrāvati Flows Undisrupted). Kathmandu: Sajha Prakashan.

Visvanathan, Shiv. 2003. 'Interrogating the Nation'. *Economic and Political Weekly* 38 (23): 2295–302.

Waiba, Sukanya. 2075/2019. *Aparajita: Parijat ka Chitthiharu* (Aparajita: Letters of Parijat). Kathmandu: Book Hill.

7

Commodity Journeys and Market Circuits

Making Borders 'Natural' in Colonial Western Himalayas

ANIKET ALAM

One important reason that the British were attracted to the western Himalayas was the prospect of trade. From the eighteenth century onwards, there were regular attempts to find out the extent of the trade that was carried out through the mountains, the countries it was carried out with and the value of this trade. Whether it was the 'missions' of Moorcroft and Trebeck, or of the various other explorers and merchants who were either financed by the East India Company or were helped and encouraged in their personal voyages, the question of trade dominated the agenda. Until well into the nineteenth century, the British in India assumed that the control of the Himalayas and the Hindu Kush mountains would open trade routes to them into China and Russia, respectively.[1]

It was only in the mid-nineteenth century that it started becoming clear to the officials of the East India Company and the British government in London that the volume and value of trade, particularly through the Himalayan passes, was not worth the amount of military and financial commitment that was required to sustain it. It was only from this time that it is possible to discern a new discourse emerging in British accounts—both official as well as personal: that the Himalayas were a natural border of their Indian Empire.

Once the British realised that the scope for trade was limited over the Himalayas, much of their efforts in the nineteenth century were spent to find the 'natural' land borders of their Indian Empire which they could defend, most notably from the Russian Empire. Over the course of the nineteenth and twentieth centuries, these borders have been accepted as the geo-civilisational borders of India in much of popular imagination. Scholarly work too has implicitly accepted these 'natural' borders of British India, even if there is a recognition that the post-Partition, post-independence borders are clearly man-made; particularly in the last two decades or so with the emergence of focussed scholarship on this theme.[2]

There has been a fair amount of work by scholars, a large number of them anthropologists, about the role of trade in sustaining Himalayan communities. Many of these works have studied in detail the nature of trade crossing borders and frontiers, the people involved and the complex networks of circulation and affect these have created. Trade has not been seen as crucial in the making, defining or working of borders, particularly the Himalayan border. The study of trade in and through the Himalayas has been parallel to the study of borders, with the latter being acknowledged only as an external factor in the working of trade. Borders have not been seen as constitutive of trade relations.[3]

This study argues that trade was crucial to the formation of borders and boundaries in the Himalayas in the pre-colonial and colonial periods. If we only look at the military and political factors in the making of borders, we miss out on the role of trade in defining, forming and firming up borders.

This chapter will study two markets: The Lavi fair at Rampur-Bushahr, and the market which grew in the colonial town of Shimla. The Lavi fair was a market where traders from far-off regions in the Himalayas came to exchange goods with those from the plains. It was held in early November on the banks of the Sutlej at a location just after the river emerges from the Great Himalayan mountain range; the valley of the river providing relatively easy access to those who came here from both the trans-Himalayan regions as well as from the plains.

The market in Shimla grew to cater to the requirements of the British colonial elite who made this town their summer retreat. From a small town of a few dozen British establishments in the 1820s, it grew to become the summer capital of the Indian Empire in 1865, pulling in traders, labourers, money and commodities in ever-increasing numbers.

This chapter will look at how these two markets depended on two very different definitions of borders, how their trade routes and circulation of goods helped define borders and regions in the Himalayas as well as how the institution of borders changed them.

This chapter concludes by suggesting that Benedict Anderson's underutilised idea of 'journey' and 'circuits', which entrench arbitrarily drawn nation-state borders, may help us understand the role of trade and the circulation of commodities in the making of borders, and how and why borders (and the political communities they ensconce) come to have such salience. Anderson argues that the circuits formed by the journeys of administrators and soldiers of the new nation-states are circumscribed by their borders and bring together disparate people into one common bureaucratic pilgrimage which has a common 'Vatican' or centre (Anderson 2006). This creates a new hermeneutic geography which entrenches the nation-state's cartography within the materiality of its citizen's existence.

This chapter builds on this insight of Anderson to extend his argument about circuits and the consequences of these journeys within them to commodities and their circulation. It argues that just like the circulation of bureaucratic cadets of the nation-state, the circulation of commodities also builds 'meaning creating journeys' which feed into the making of national territories. As new borders get formed and new political and economic nodes emerge within the territories enclosed by these borders, they create new pathways for the circulation of commodities. Trade changes its routes, and commodities find new markets. A successful shift of the circulation of commodities from older routes to the newer ones helps build the 'naturalness' of these new borders. This chapter looks at trade and markets in the western Himalayas to explore whether, and how, this Andersonian argument can be extended from the circulation of people to the circulation of commodities, and whether this extension helps us understand the geopolitics of border making.

TRADE AND THE BRITISH IN THE WESTERN HIMALAYAS

Over the centuries, for people living in the plains who viewed the mountains, the Himalayas looked almost insurmountable and impenetrable. Few states based out of the river valleys in these plains could ever reach the Himalayas, given the geography and climate ecology of these mountains. There are many oral histories and historical texts which recount the migration of people from the plains to the mountains, whether these were remnants of ruling families of states in the plains who had lost battles for the control of their state or castes and communities which had migrated over time.[4] Social arrangements were markedly different, economic relations remained far less monetised than in the plains and political structures resisted the centralisation of authority in the Himalayas.[5] Thus, it can be argued that 'the border [in the Himalayas] lay in the separation from the plains rather than between each other [Indian and Chinese Himalayas]', as a contemporary historian has put it so pithily (Vasan 2006: 42).

This dialectic between the plains and the mountains, at least its political aspects, has been very well described by Scott. While he bases his arguments on South East Asia, it is quite possible to see parallels in the Himalayas, including its western part (Gellner 2014; Shneiderman 2010).

However, when we look at trade in and through the Himalayas, Scott's thesis of the mountains as a refuge from the state (of the rice-growing, settled agriculture plains) seems to explain less and less. There is overwhelming historical evidence that major trade routes passed through the Himalayas linking the river-valley economies in China with those in India, and both of them with the economies and states of agro-pastoral kingdoms in Central Asia. Iran, Turkey and the world beyond, too, were linked to these (Lattimore 1951).

More importantly, it is also not the case that the Himalayas were barren territories merely hosting trade routes. The Himalayas and its related ranges and plateaux hosted markets, and different groups of traders lived and traversed its ridges, valleys and passes. The Himalayas had states and polities of varying size and complexity which nurtured and survived on this trade as well as provided it with many commodities which were crucial to its sustenance.[6] As Lucien Febvre argued, using the example of Tibet, we need to make a distinction between the 'political soil' and the 'economic soil' on which states and societies are historically formed, and also mark the manner in which these two interact with each other to sustain their political entities (Febvre 1996: 88–9). Changes in the political economy change the nature of these two 'soils' and the nature of their interactions. It is thus that 'a people and region acted and reacted on one another. Between the men and the country which they held to be their own there was so much reciprocal adaptation....' (Febvre 1996: 87). This chapter focuses on the nature of trade—what can be termed the circulation of commodities—in the Himalayas and its adjoining mountain regions to understand how people adapted to the new political soil of colonial borders.

Between 1774 and 1811, the British sent nine official and one unofficial missions to identify and report on the trade which went from the plains of Hindustan through the Himalayas to Tibet and beyond (Vasan 2006: 44). The first accounts of Himalayan trade (both through and within it) were provided by Moorcroft and Trebeck, spread out over their reports and notes on their travels.[7] J. D. Herbert (1829: 227–58), Water Hamilton (1820), James Baillie Fraser (1820) and Alexander Gerard (1842) too have given detailed accounts of trade through the (western) Himalayas in the early years of the nineteenth century. According to these accounts, this trade spread out from Lhasa in the east to Yarkand (present-day Kashgar) and Urumqi in the north. Commodities and traders moved across the Tibetan plateau, the mountains and steppes of Xinjiang, present-day Tajikistan, Gilgit-Baltistan, Ladakh and the Kashmir valley. Traders and commodities also travelled up from Punjab through the valleys of Jhelum and Sutlej and from Delhi, Rohilkhand, Awadh and Nepal. Traders from the Indian plains met and exchanged commodities with traders who came from the river valleys of China in the markets of Lhasa and Yarkand.

Much of the trade that was carried out was of commodities which were either produced in the plains of India (and, to a lesser extent, in China) or were produced in the Himalayas and the related highlands and exported to the plains. These were mainly *pushum* (a fine quality goat wool used to make expensive clothes) and regular wool, borax (a mineral which is used in metallurgy, medicine and household work) and *churrus* (a form of cannabis).[8] Other commodities like precious stones, horses and silk were also traded over the Himalayas but the predominant commodity of trade was *pushum* which accounted for more than half the trade in terms of value. The value of the traded *pushum* rose through the early decades of British rule in the Indian subcontinent as is evident from Table 7.1.[9]

As an important aside, it needs to be remembered that the market at Lavi was one of the most important nodes of the trade network in the western Himalayas, but was complemented by, and in competition with, a range of other markets differing in scope and size. These competing and complementing markets stretched from Ladakh, Lahaul, Spiti and Gartok in the west and north,[10] to Garhwal and Kumaon in the east. The commodities traded were similar but most of these markets focussed on one or two products. There were specific markets for animals and animal products, for salt and borax, and so on.

Table 7.1 Tibet's Export Trade to Rampur (Lavi Fair), 1837 to 1841

		1837	1838	1839	1840	1841
1	**White Pushum**					
1a	Quantity katcha maund; 16 seers pucca	1,185	1,481	1,463	1,400	200
1b	Rate (Rupees per 2 pucca seers)	3 & 1/2	4-1	6-1	8-1	10 & 1/2
1c	Value in Rupees	33,180	47,392	70,224	89,600	16,800

		1837	1838	1839	1840	1841
2	**Black Pushum**					
2a	Quantity katcha maund; 16 seers pucca	175	190	119	151	23
2b	Rate (Rupees per 2 pucca seers)	1-12	2-1	3-1	4-1	5 & 1/4
2c	Value in Rupees	2,425	3,040	2,856	4,832	966
3	**Wool**					
3a	Quantity katcha maund; 16 seers pucca	1,092	784	787	1,570	58
3b	Rate (seers/Rupee)	8	8	8	7	6
3c	Value in Rupees	5,460	3,920	3,935	8,971	387
4	**Borax**					
4a	Quantity katcha maund; 16 seers pucca	394	566	678	505	22
4b	Rate (seers/Rupee)	13 & 1/4	16	15	13	13
4c	Value in Rupees	1,189	1,415	818	621	66
5	**Churrus**					
5a	Quantity katcha maund; 16 seers pucca	215	236	241	57	16
5b	Rate (seers/Rupee)	6 & 1/4	4 & 1/2	5 & 1/4	5 & 1/4	7 & 1/2
5c	Value in Rupees	10,750	8,496	10,122	2,394	960
6	**Miscellaneous Items**					
	Estimated value in Rupees	2,500	2,500	2,500	2,500	500
7	**Total Value in Rupees**	55,529	66,763	94,445	109,307	19,679

Source: Cunningham (1844).

Note: Rupee values in Re-anna-paise, 1/2 is 8 annas, 1/4 is 4 annas. Total values have been copied from the official document without independent computing.

These trade relations go back a few centuries at the least (Moran 2007: 148–9), with records of a trade pact between Rampur-Bushahr state and the Tibetan authorities from the 1600s (Vasan 2006: 42). This trade pact seems to have been made to keep the Sutlej valley the main trade route in the western Himalayas by removing all tolls and duties and providing armed protection to traders from 'bandits' who would often raid their caravans.[11]

With the consolidation of British rule, there was encouragement to this trans-Himalayan trade and after the initial years of instability, trade started to pick up on the back of political and fiscal incentives from the new European rulers. As Table 7.2 shows, the total value and volume of goods traded at Lavi rose in the decades after Punjab was conquered.

Table 7.2 Growth in Trans-Himalayan Trade

Merchandise at Rampur, Lavi Fair (Indian Rupees) Recorded on 10 November 1867	
From Kunawur, Yarkund, Cheen, and Ladakh	139,953
From Plains (Umballa, Jagadree, Mundee, Sookit)	116,441
From Kooloo	11,359
From Bussahir	4,251
Total	272,005

Source: Figures taken from Records of the Financial Commission, Government of India, No. 14, 1868, 'Rampoor Fair', Oriental and India Office Collections, British Library, 60–4.

The Lavi fair was the most important market in the Sutlej valley trade route. It was often the deepest point in the Himalayas that traders in the plains would be willing to come up to and it was also the farthest place where Tibetan and Yarkandi traders would come 'down'. There was a complementary market in Gartok in Tibet (also called Garoo in some British records). This market, which used to be a seasonal settlement coming up only in the summer, seems to rival the Lavi market in terms of traders attending it. Alexander Gerard writes: 'Garoo is the most famous mart for wool in Chinese Tartary, and there is a fair of 10,000 to 20,000 people in July, well attended by merchants from Yarkand. Wool, borax and salt are the principal exports, and these products are exchanged for produce of the plains of India' (Gerard 1993 [1841]: 144–5, quoted in Vasan 2006: 43).

Apart from the products which were traded between the plains of Hindustan and Tibet and Yarkand, there was also trade among people living in the Himalayas itself. However, a look at the figures for Lavi fair show that this was an insignificant amount even within the total trade here. Much of that is included within the category 'miscellaneous items' coming to just about 2 per cent to 4 per cent of the total value traded. Another estimation suggests that the amount of goods that came from Bushahr and Kulu to Lavi fair's market in 1868 did not exceed 5 per cent in terms of value (Alam 2008: 55–6). The items traded by the local communities were mostly agricultural produce, blankets, animals and herbs.

The point to remember about the local participants in this trade is that they came from a social formation which was largely without any cash and had very low levels of exchange.[12]

HIMALAYAN TRADE IN CONTEXT

It was this trans-Himalayan trade which tempted the British to expand their political-military control into the mountains. Until then, the rise of the mountains had been the 'natural border' for all states in the plains of the Indus and Ganges River valleys. The early travellers and other information led the colonialists in Calcutta and London to conclude that across the Himalayas lay the networks of the fabled 'Silk Route' waiting for the British to capture, control and profit from. There was also the assumption that a land route to China could be found through the Himalayas which could help the British open another route (military front?) to the Chinese court. There was also the pressing need to keep the expanding Russian Empire as far as possible from their possessions in Hindustan, as well as from the trade of the Silk Route.[13]

Soon enough, the British realised that the sheer topographical challenge posed by the Himalayas made them impracticable as military routes.[14] The British did not give up hope of profiting from Himalayan trade until the end of the nineteenth century. However, it became fairly evident that the value of trade did not lend itself to significant investments of political capital, nor could this trade rival or equal the value of trade in the markets of the plains, far from being comparable to the revenue from land. Even more significant was that over the nineteenth century, Himalayan timber emerged as an important commodity, both in terms of economic value as well as in its importance in the construction of the railways which had both political and military significance.

It would be instructive to compare the value of Himalayan trade with that of Himalayan timber in the late nineteenth century. In 1879–80, the total value of trade reported in Gartok stood at Rs 368,026. By the beginning of the twentieth century, it had declined to Rs 192,398 (see Table 7.3). At the same time, the small hill state of Jubbal, a part of the 24 hill states which formed the Shimla Hill States group, had an annual income of Rs 100,000 from the sale of wood from its forests.[15] This amount needs to be compared to the total annual land revenue assessment of Jubbal state at this time which stood at Rs 35,828.[16]

Table 7.3 Decline of Trans-Himalayan Trade

IMPORT/EXPORT AT GARTOK, TIBET (Indian Rupees)			
Year	Imports	Exports	Total
1879–80	345,894	22,132	368,026
1902–3	177,102	15,296	192,398
Decline	**168,792**	**6,836**	**175,628**

Source: Figures for 1879–80 taken from *Simla District Gazetteer* (1888–9: 75), and figures for 1902–3 taken from Vasan (2006: 44).

To appreciate the change this indicates, it needs to be remembered that forests were without any market value in the period before the British came to the Himalayas. Fraser is quoted as saying: 'What a seeming waste of noble timber! And how uselessly do these grand trees appear to flourish and decay' (Fraser 1820: 139). The first timber merchants went to Rampur-Bushahr in the 1830s and got a lease to working an entire forest range along the banks of the Sutlej (from where they would float the logs down to the plains) for as little as Rs 30 for the season.

This brings us back to the point made earlier about the very low levels of monetisation in the local Himalayan political economy. The absence of money is stark in all records and oral histories. Much of the exchange between village communities was based on barter. Similarly, much of the surplus collected by the states and other polities in the western Himalayas was in kind or in labour (through Begar and Beth).[17] Early British travellers in the western Himalayas speak of the trouble in getting food or labour even for payments four times those in the Ambala region in the plains just below as the Himalayan peasants had no idea of money or exchange value.

The timber from the Himalayan forests was one of the first items to be commoditised with the coming of the British. The other was labour.[18] The traditional forms of forced labour—Begar and Beth—were given 'free' to either the state or to the community. With the coming of the British these were marked to payment, and even if the labour remained forced (in the sense of involuntary) and the payments were more often than not withheld. Increasingly, the practice was to pay for it (Alam 2008: 136–9). This was followed by the commodification of agricultural produce. All this led to the infusion of money in the local economy and a growing market of commodities within the western Himalayas. This allowed land revenue collection to start getting monetised.

In the late 1850s, the old system of revenue collection in the state of Rampur-Bushahr (which was among the largest of the region) gives a sense of the lack of money in the local economy.

> [The old system of revenue collection] was composed of Rs 5,372 in cash collections and 18 different karhads, or collections in kind, which included everything from agricultural produce, pastoral goods, produce collected from the forests and articles manufactured at home. There was no value put on the karhads since no market measure was available. (Alam 2008: 136)

This near total absence of money and commodification within the western Himalayas provides one context to place Himalayan trade. The values traded and the volume traded were far larger than the local economy, including that of the hill states. The trans-Himalayan trade described above dwarfed the political economy of the local social formation.

There was, however, another context in which this trans-Himalayan trade needs to be viewed. This is the context of the colonial economy of the Indian Empire of Britain. The economy of just colonial north India dwarfed this trans-Himalayan trade in terms of both value and volume. Revenue from this, whether as tax or as profits for British enterprises or merchants, was soon overshadowed by just the value that Himalayan forests provided, as has been seen above. For the Himalayan peasant, the emergence of Shimla as a market (along with other European hill stations), the commodification and monetisation of their labour as well as their land and its produce overshadowed the importance of the trans-Himalayan trade and markets. The next section will discuss the emergence and growth of Shimla as a market and also describe the levels and manner in which peasant political economies were commodified and monetised.

SHIMLA AS A MARKET

Shimla is used in this chapter as a representative of the new markets which were introduced by the British Raj into the western Himalayas. It was the biggest in the region and there is a fair amount of information and economic data available for this growing town and the surrounding regions. The first European settlement came up just after the 1815 Anglo-Gorkha war and by the early 1830s it was already a well-known 'hill station' of north India.

The Governor General William Bentinck's trip to Shimla in 1832 required the conscription of 3,800 Begaris, each doing three trips from the plains for which they were paid 1 rupee and 8 annas each per trip. This appears to be a rate higher than what was prevailing and it is doubtful if this was actually paid. Even as late as 1904, the wage rate for skilled labourers in Shimla was recorded at '6 annas to 8 a day and for unskilled 4 annas'.[19]

At the time of Bentinck's visit, Shimla had a summer population less than 10,000 people of whom only a few hundred were Europeans; by 1881, Shimla's summer population of Europeans was recorded at over 3,000.[20] This illustration gives a relative sense of how much money was being pushed into the local Himalayan economy just through the payments for labour with the emergence and growth of the town of Shimla. 'Hill porters' were needed not just to carry the luggage from the plains to Shimla but also for transporting food items and other needs for the Shimla market; they were needed to fetch water from the springs and streams in the valley below Shimla; they were needed for almost everything as most of the labourers from the plains found the climate and topography difficult.

The conscription of local peasants as Begar labour was not without protests.[21] However, any attempt to reduce these was also met with strong protests[22] from the growing number of Europeans who were moving to Shimla for about seven to eight months every 'summer'. Here we are not so much concerned about the ethics or politics of the conscription of labour but rather with the objective trend of rising labour conscriptions, paralleled with the increasing payments for it. While these amounts were small, often not paid or paid in part, their importance relative to the local peasant economy as well as to the local markets needs to be acknowledged.

When the western Himalayas were first integrated with the British Indian Empire in the early 1800s, most of the local economy—labour, land, forests, pastoral products and manufactures—was non-monetised. The rapidity with which this changed was unprecedented. There was a major rebellion in Rampur-Bushahr in 1857–8 over the introduction of a new land settlement which calculated the revenue in money and not in kind, even if it kept most of the collections in kind. The local peasantry, it appears from British sources themselves, were unable to understand calculations of revenues and imposts in monetary terms.[23] It appears that the new revenue settlement was based almost entirely on the traditional system, with little change in the amounts levied or collected. From the accounts given, it seems the main objection was to the calculations being done in rupees and annas—money values—rather than in the traditional form of giving labour as well as different goods and products to the state.

However, by 1874 there was a new land settlement which retained only five of the original 19 *karhad*s (collections in kind), the rest being commuted to cash. The cash component of the revenue assessed (and collected) went up to Rs 13,640 out of a total land revenue assessment of Rs 28,649. The rest of the amount, Rs 15,009, was the cash value of the *karhad*s which was still to be collected in kind but, crucially, was now calculated in cash—without any objections.

What is interesting is that the amounts, in absolute terms, were very small compared to the larger economy of British India. However, these represented a historic change in the region—the introduction of money.

By the end of the nineteenth century, there was a regular market in land, the produce of the land, in animals and animal products, in the forests and in labour.[24] All land revenue was being paid in cash. Poppy, hemp, turmeric, ginger and potato were being cultivated in the regions around Shimla town and were principally exported to the plains.[25] The *Simla District Gazetteer* of 1904 also lists various vegetables like pumpkins, radishes, tomatoes, brinjal, beans, red peppers, carrots, different types of gourds, melons, cabbages, and so on, which were grown primarily to be sold in Shimla.[26] Rice, wheat and maize are also reported to being sold here. Prices for all agricultural commodities rose over the second half of the nineteenth century. The *Simla District Gazetteer* reports that between the 1850s and 1880s, prices of most agricultural commodities doubled and tripled.[27] Between that period and the publishing of the *Gazetteer* in 1904, prices seem to have doubled again.

Along with this rise in the prices of agricultural commodities, land too developed a value and saw rapid increases in it. Tenancies, which were largely based on traditional ties, and the collections in kind were now almost always calculated in cash and often paid in it too.[28] Similar was the rise in the value of plough bullock, cows and sheep. All these products first found a money value sometime in the middle of the nineteenth century and then over the next half a century or so established their presence as commodities in the market in Shimla, doubling and tripling their price. Some of the commodities, such as vegetables, fruits, milk and ghee, and labour and mules for hire, were meant mainly for consumption by the large, and growing, population of Europeans and Indians from the plains, who lived in Shimla each year between April and November. Others, such as spices and cannabis, rice and borax, wood and women,[29] were mostly for export to the plains.

It is difficult to tabulate the total turnover of the market in Shimla or even disaggregate it according to commodities, sectors or 'export' and 'import'. However, the information we have suggests that in size and range it soon became much larger than the Lavi or Gartok markets, both in terms of the value and volume of commodities traded as well as the number of people associated with it. The shift in economic weight is clearly visible even at the turn of the 20th century, even though Tibet trade still remained important (*Simla District Gazetteer* 1904: 83–8). Given the importance of Shimla as a 'European' town and the relatively high consumption patterns of its residents, the demand for commodities was also much higher than similar-sized towns elsewhere.

What is even more important is that while the trans-Himalayan trade had only a tangential connection with the political economy of the local peasant communities and hill states, the market in Shimla developed deep linkages with the latter and gave it an impetus which transformed not just its economy but also had major political, social and cultural implications on the local peasant communities and hill states. The trans-Himalayan trade was important to the finances and political power of some of the Himalayan states through which the trade routes passed. Some of the local peasantry also made some money by providing labour and pack animals to the traders. However, given the lack of commodification within the peasant economies of the western Himalayas, and the near absence of money, this trans-Himalayan trade remained peripheral to the local political economy. As we have seen above, the contribution of local manufactures and goods in this trade remained negligible. In contrast, by involving the local hill state, by commoditising the produce and labour of the Himalayan peasantry and providing a ready market with ever-growing demand for these commodities, Shimla (and such other British outposts) became integral to the political economy of the western Himalayas.

Interestingly, Shimla also became an all-season market for some of the commodities—horses, precious stones, borax, *pushum* and wool—which were earlier traded exclusively in the Lavi and Gartok markets.[30] Further, despite the growing commodification of agricultural produce and labour in the regions near Shimla and the increasing supply of these to its market, the local supply of goods and labour could never meet even half the demand. This demand was met by the exports from the plains, which were much costlier given the labour costs of transport. Of the 111,478 *maund*s of wheat and rice needed in Shimla in 1878, only about 33,678 *maund*s were supplied by the Himalayan agriculturalists.[31] Given the prevailing prices, this would suggest that a total of about Rs 25,000 of wheat and rice were sold in the Shimla market in the early 1880s by the Himalayan peasants.[32]

The *Simla District Gazetteer* of 1904 notes the relative decline of the trans-Himalayan trade. As early as 1881, there was a report which stated, 'There is a considerable falling off in the value of exports and imports from Chinese Tibet and Yarkand during the year under report', and then proceeded to give a list of probable causes such as the unrest in Tibet and Kashgar, the famine in Kashmir, and so on. But it then continued to say, '... there is no question that for other reasons trade is declining and is in a less flourishing condition than some years ago.'[33] The long-term reason given was the 'dishonesty' of the traders who have not repaid the advances from 'down country' buyers and it went on to give the illustration of the mother of the Raja of Bushahr who is said to have outstanding advances of Rs 40,000 which have yet to be repaid. This may or may not suggest dishonesty on the part of the traders, but it surely does suggest a crisis in the trade and a severe problem with recovering the costs of goods traded.

Until this point, this chapter has tried to show that prior to the coming of the British in the early nineteenth century, trans-Himalayan trade was a thriving robust network of goods, money and people being transported over long distances and linking up the non-mountainous river valley polities and economies of China, India, Central Asia and even beyond. The area under focus here—the western Himalayas—was an integral part of this trade network and hosted at least two major markets of the Lavi and Gartok trade fairs. With the coming of British rule in the western Himalayas, there was a rival market that developed which commoditised local produce, integrated the local peasant communities into this market and also diverted significant amounts from these traditional markets to the new British-established ones.

The chapter will now conclude by trying to explore how this historical process can help us understand the formation of borders in the Himalayas, particularly in the western part.

NETWORKS OF CIRCULATION

One of the most persuasive theories about the relation between the highlands and the plains has been that of James Scott where he argues that the former was a refuge for those who were escaping the state effect of the plains' polities. He makes a stronger claim that this was a deliberate political act of those who thus escaped and that they worked out strategies to keep state formation at bay among themselves (Scott 2009). Other scholars have argued that this idea could also be used productively to study and explain mountain societies in the central and western Himalayas.[34] Scott's proposition is very persuasive to explain the historical development of the local peasant communities and 'hill states' of the western Himalayas. It does not, however, help us understand the existence and support for the trans-Himalayan trade.

It is interesting that more than half a century before Scott argued his case for an anarchist history of the mountains, Owen Lattimore had a very different explanation for the relations between China's plains' empire and the pastoral trading communities on its eastern and northern mountainous and steppes neighbours (Lattimore 1951). Lattimore argued that the trans-Himalayan trade, also known as the Silk Route, was the result of active, and successful, Chinese imperial efforts to incorporate the nomadic traders of the Tibetan, Mongolian highlands and further of the Central Asian Steppes into the political economy of the imperial state. The trans-Himalayan trade was a way to grow strong economic and political interests within these nomadic tribal communities which would be dependent on the Chinese imperial political economy. In Lattimore's words,

> Trade must have been originally a result rather than the cause of this kind of imperial policy; though naturally trade interests that prospered and grew strong could later become a secondary influence favoring the continuance of the original policy. I suggest, therefore, that trade arose in the course of an adjustment of the activities of the Chinese to an environment akin to that of China in some respects but different in other important respects. The maintenance of Chinese imperial policy was expensive. The cost could not be met simply by imposing a grain levy, the major source of revenue in China proper. The cost of transporting grain back to China was prohibitive. Grain revenue could be used for the maintenance of local garrisons, it was true; but at the same time it was not practical simply to subjugate the oases and extract wealth from them. Revolt was too easy. The oases had to be encouraged to look toward Chinese overlords instead of toward steppe overlords.
>
> Forms of trade that would bring profit to the oases as well as to the Chinese must therefore have evolved both spontaneously and as the result of policy.
>
> ... trade of this kind had very little to do with the subject peoples of the oases. It was an affair of their rulers and the overlords of their rulers, but it suited Chinese imperial policy because it gave the native rulers of the oases an interest in political affiliation to China. (Lattimore 1951: 174–5)

This understanding of the relations between the populations of the mountains and the states of the plains helps us better understand and explain the existence of the trans-Himalayan trade, a glimpse of which we saw in the trade fairs of Lavi and Gartok. Yet it does not help us explain the thriving and resilient peasant and nomadic societies of the mountains, which kept the state at bay and which Scott explains so well. We are left with an uneasy coexistence of people, economies and historiographical theories.

It is here that I suggest that a relatively underutilised idea in Benedict Anderson's *Imagined Communities* could help us understand and explain how trade played a crucial role in the building of a 'natural' border in the Himalayas.

Anderson uses the concept of journey', as developed by the anthropologist Victor Turner, 'as a meaning creating experience' (Anderson 2006: 53). To explain the rise of nationalism among the 'creole pioneers' of Spain's American colonies, he says the modal journey is the 'pilgrimage'. He suggests that the sacred geography of ancient religious communities was 'experienced and "realized" (in the stagecraft sense) by the constant flow of pilgrims moving towards them....' He goes on to argue that in the pre-print age, a community was formed, or people felt connected in a singular purpose, through moving along long-established and accepted routes which linked the periphery to the centre(s). It was the travel for a common purpose, with common aims and experiences, which built the medieval religious community (Anderson 2006: 54). He goes on to suggest that the modern secular counterpart of this religious pilgrimage was the constant movement—journey—of the functionaries of the new states in concentric circles from the periphery to the centre. This difference between the medieval and modern 'journey' or 'pilgrimage' does not concern us here.

What is interesting is that regular journeys that people made, people who were not known to each other personally but who immediately recognised each other as part of the same journey in the same geography which was now their own through the very meanings that these journeys provided them, brought them together as a community or at least a group connected to each other through the practice of the journey. In the Spanish colonies in America, this meant that young men travelled on 'journeys' circumscribed by the boundaries of each colony, came to know each other as 'fellow travellers' connected by the same 'fate' of common birth, common boundaries and journeys. Anderson argues, most persuasively, that this formed an important material foundation for the emergence and solidification of nationalism (Anderson 2006: 54–9).

Anderson was primarily concerned about the development of nationalism. However, the idea of journey and circulation along well-developed routes which both circumscribed as well as brought together diverse people into a common purpose can perhaps be used productively for the matter at hand here. The journey of thousands of traders, their mule handlers and goods over the long-travelled roads brought together people from distant parts of the Asian highland massif—stretching from Central Asia to north India to the south of Siberia to the east and south of China—into one massive network of circulation; a circulation of men, money and commodities. Each part of this network had its own rhythm and social, economic and political bases. This network included people who would never meet and commodities which would never be exchanged with each other and yet which would have 'meaning' only as part of this larger unified circulatory network called the trans-Himalayan trade or the Silk Route. Together these, Anderson can perhaps be paraphrased to argue, experienced and realized the stage of their actions—the Asian highlands, of which the Himalayas are the part we are concerned with here.

With the coming of the British, there was no deliberate disruption of this trade. In fact, it can be shown that the British were pulled to the Himalayas to profit from the trans-Himalayan trade and made many efforts to encourage it (even if on their terms). Yet this Himalayan trade declined over the nineteenth century. A new circuit of 'journeys' for commodities, people and money was created with the coming of the British, of which towns like Shimla and their markets were the central nodes. The older journeys, or pilgrimages, were overshadowed by the new ones both in terms of value and volume; value both as money as well as a moral economy and a political capital.

CONCLUSION

It may be productive to draw again on Febvre here, as we can see that these novel journeys of commodities and markets created a new 'economic soil' in the western Himalayas. This new 'economic soil' cut the trans-Himalayan, Tibetan regions off from the Punjab hill states and Kangra district and created a new complementary 'political soil'. The latter is the very region which went on to become Himachal Pradesh after independence.

Anderson uses the term 'meaning creation' by these 'journeys' in not just an ideological or cultural sense but also as signifying political and economic qualities. The borders of British political authority emerged as 'natural' boundaries[35] of the successor nation-states over a century and a half of these new journeys competing with, overwhelming and finally supplanting the traditional journeys of the trans-Himalayan trade. By bringing the local peasant communities into this 'journey' or 'pilgrimage' of money, commodity and people centred on the new towns of British creation and circumscribed by the borders of their political authority, these new journeys created powerful 'interests' which identified far more closely with, and found far more 'meaning' in, the new administrative units than they did in their traditional 'journeys' and 'pilgrimages'. The new borders were not imposed, rather they perhaps helped create but were, eventually, created and established as 'natural' (as in accepted widely without dispute) by the circuits of 'pilgrimage' they helped establish; and these pilgrimages were, at least in the region under study, as much commercial and economic as political.

This is not to argue that other factors were not important in getting wide acceptance of the border within the local communities. The burden of this chapter's argument is that the role of markets and trade was not an external input to the political process of border making but an intrinsic part of the process. Anderson's idea of journey and pilgrimage helps us merge our insights of trade networks—the circulation of goods and money—with an understanding of the military and political acts of border making. It perhaps can help us establish the argument that border making cannot be viewed only as a political act but it is more productive to view it as a part of the emerging political economy of colonialism in the Himalayas. Viewed thus, it helps us to widen the understanding of how and why certain borders in the Himalayas came to be accepted as natural by the local population and why the same border in other parts of the Himalayas could never be 'naturalised'.

NOTES

1. Banerji (2011) and Alam (2008) discuss this in some length.
2. Among the most important and illustrative works are van Schendel (2002: 647–68; 2005) and Scott (2009). For example, Gellner (2014) and Shneiderman (2010: 289–312).
3. Recent works include Banerji (2011); Levi (2002); Radhu (2017) which give insights in the form of a memoir. Earlier works on this area include Chandola (1987); Fisher (1987); Rizvi (1999); van Spengen (2010); Singh (2003) and Singh (1997).
4. Hutchison and Vogel (1933) has detailed histories and genealogies of the ruling families in the various states and polities of the Punjab Himalayas. *Gazetteer of the Simla Hill States, 1910* (1992), the first volume of the three-volume Rose (1999 [1883]) and Emerson's anthropological study of Mandi and Bashahr have

many reports of oral history and texts on the manner in which migration of social groups from the plains into the Himalayas occurred over the centuries.

5. Apart from Rose (1999 [1883]) and Emerson's anthropological study, do also see Singh (1998) and Alam (2008) which give detailed descriptions of how Himalayan social, economic and political structures differed from those of the plains. There are quite a few anthropological (and sociological) studies too which give details of this point. See Majumdar (1962), Joshi (1984 [1925]) and Berreman (1997).

6. For more details of the trade in the western Himalayas, see Minhas (1998) and Vasan (2006: 41–55). See Moran (2007: 147–77) for a more focussed description of the trade that went through the state of Rampur-Bashahr in whose territory was located the Lavi fair which will be discussed later in this chapter, and how that trade both related to the state and its economy. Alam (2008: 53–7) too has information about the trade that passed through the Sutlej valley (Rampur-Bashahr state).

7. See Moorcroft and Trebeck (1844). These two volumes are an edited compilation of all their travel reports which are contained in over 50 boxes in the India and Oriental Office Archives of the British Library.

8. Intoxicant made from the resin of cannabis indica.

9. Also see Vasan (2006: 44) and Moran (2007: 152, 154–5). The figures for 1841 show a steep decline as trade was disrupted due to the military campaigns of Zorawar Singh, a military leader of the Sikh state of Punjab who was attempting to capture Tibet after having subdued Kashmir and Ladakh.

10. See Sherring (1906), especially chapters IX ('A Tibetan Trade Route'), XV ('Gartok and the Viceroys') and XVI ('The Market of Gyanema, the Sutlej valley, and the Kingdom of the Amazons'); Shuttleworth (1923: 552–8); Franke (n.d.), especially chapter XIV ('Account of the Trade Between the Kings of Ladakh and Kulu').

11. For a discussion of how and why the Sutlej valley provides a natural, all-weather route for travellers, see Singh (1998) and Alam (2008). One interesting point made in Alam (2008) is that Rampur-Bashahr was also perhaps a political liege of the Manchu Court in Peking. It quotes a report by Captain Cunningham from 1842 which claims that a caravan of mules was intercepted by him at Wangtoo where the trade route crossed the Sutlej River. This caravan was carrying 'tribute' to the court of Peking and was to be deposited in Gartok, from whence it would be taken to Lhasa and then finally to Peking (Beijing).

12. This point is made most persuasively by Singh (1998). See also Alam (2008).

13. The most detailed description of these impulses is given in Alam (2008: 104–6), and in some parts in Vasan (2006).

14. This happened as early as 1819 with Captain Herbert's (1829) report.

15. *Punjab States Gazetteer 1910,* Jubbal State (1912: 19, 25).

16. Ibid.

17. Alam (2008: 72–83) has the most detailed description of this. Singh (1998), Rathore (1987) and Negi (1995) are good sources for understanding the system of labour and how it linked with the political economy of the western Himalayas during the colonial period. Begar was the labour which was given by the peasant subjects to the deity and to the state. The Begar labour was a form of revenue, given in along with, and sometimes in lieu of, grains and cash. Beth was the free labour that landless and untouchable groups had to give to the peasants of the village.

18. The most exhaustive description of this is in Alam (2008: 133–46). Much of the following discussion draws on this.

19. *Gazetteer of the Simla District, 1904* (1997: 74).

20. Ibid.: 20.

21. There is a large body of work on this, for example, Pathak (1991: 261–79); Dutta (1997); Malhotra (1990); Negi (1995); Alam (2008), among others.

22. Edwards, 'Impressment of Coolies in Simla District', Political Department, Indian States, A-Proceedings, 5 December 1851, No. 163, National Archives of India, has details of how and how many 'coolies' were needed for the shift to Shimla and their wages and conditions. It also has an interesting account of a minor rebellion among the Europeans at Shimla when Edwards tried to reduce the number of these 'coolies', leading eventually to his removal from the post of the superintendent of the Shimla hill states.

23. Alam (2008: 150–62) has a detailed description of this rebellion and its 'pacification' by the British. He bases his account largely on G. C. Barnes, not dated, Memorandum on the District of Bussahir, and the Pacification of the Disaffected Portio of Its Inhabitants, Selections from the Records of the Punjab Government, vol. V, No. 4, Oriental and India Office Collections, British Library.

24. *Gazetteer of the Simla District, 1904* (1997) has lots of details of the new valuations of agricultural and animal produce, of labour and of forests. It also gives details of the working of the Simla market.

25. *Gazetteer of the Simla District, 1904* (1997: 64).

26. Ibid.: 68.

27. Ibid.: 73–4.

28. Ibid.: 72–3.

29. Along with the rise in prices of almost all commodities in the region, there was a sharp rise in bride price too. Most marriages were conducted through the payment of bride price which was traditionally given almost entirely in kind and

in labour; see Alam (2008: 88–95). However, this bride price started getting a cash component which kept increasing in size; it was reported at Rs 20 (along with a range of other goods) in the 1830s, which increased to Rs 100 (along with other goods) by the end of the century. In the first two decades of the twentieth century, this bride price went up by a few multiples. There were increasing cases of men from the plains 'buying' women using bride price and then trafficking the women to brothels in the plains; Alam (2008: 234–53).

30. *Gazetteer of the Simla District, 1904* (1997: 84).
31. Ibid.: 85.
32. Based on rough calculations from the prices given in ibid.: 73.
33. Major Nisbet's Report on trade with Tibet and Yarkand from 1881 is quoted in the *Gazetteer of the Simla District, 1904* (1997: 87).
34. See Shneiderman (2010). But also have a look at Singh (1998) and Alam (2008) who also seem to strengthen this argument with their explanation of the insularity of peasant communities and hill 'states' in the western Himalayas. Alam, in fact, gives substantial space to argue that most of what the British classified as a 'hill state' were actually non-state polities and that even where states had developed, like in Rampur-Bashahr, it was 'retarded' and held in check by strong 'tribal' polities.
35. For example, as described by Mathur (2014: 72–93).

REFERENCES

Alam, Aniket. 2008. *Becoming India: Western Himalayas under British Rule*. Delhi: Foundation Books.

Anderson, Benedict. 2006. *Imagined Communities: Reflections on the Origin and Spread of Nationalism*. Rev ed. London, New York: Verso.

Banerji, Arup. 2011. *Old Routes: North Indian Nomads and Bankers in Afghan, Uzbek and Russian Lands*. Delhi: Three Essays Collective.

Berreman, Gerald D. 1997. *Hindus of the Himalayas*. New Delhi: Oxford University Press.

Chandola, Khemanand. 1987. *Across the Himalayas through the Ages: A Study of Relations between Central Himalayas and Western Tibet*. Delhi: Patriot Publishers.

Cunningham, J. D. 1844. 'Notes on Moorcroft's Travels in Ladakh, and On Gerard's Account of Kunawar, Including a General Description of the Latter District'. *Journal of the Asiatic Society of Bengal* 13 (147): 210.

Dutta, C. L. 1997. *The Raj and the Simla Hill States: Socio-Economic Problems, Agrarian Disturbances and Paramountcy*. Jalandhar: ABS Publications.

Emerson, H. W. *Anthropological Study of Mandi and Bashahr*. Unpublished Typescript. H. W. Emerson Personal Papers, Oriental and India Office Collections, British Library.

Febvre, Lucien. 1996. *A Geographical Introduction to History*. New York: Routledge.

Fisher, James F. 1987. *Trans-Himalayan Traders: Economy, Society and Culture in Northwest Nepal*. Delhi: Motilal Banarasidass.

Franke, A. H. n.d. *Antiquities of Indian Tibet, Vol II, The Chronicles of Ladakh and Minor Chronicles*. Calcutta: Government of India Press.

Fraser, James Baillie. 1820. *Journal of a Tour through Part of the Snowy Range of the Himala Mountains and to the Sources of the Rivers Jumna and Ganges*. London: Rodwell & Martin.

Gazetteer of the Simla District, 1904. 1997. Lahore: Government of India Press. Vol. VIII-A. Reprinted New Delhi: Indus Publishing Company.

Gazetteer of the Simla Hill States, 1910. 1992. Lahore: Government of India Press. Reprinted New Delhi: Indus Publishing House.

Gellner, David N., ed. 2014. *Borderland Lives in Northern South Asia*. New Delhi: Orient Blackswan.

Gerard, Lieutenant Alexander. 1842. 'Narrative of a Journey from Soobathoo to Shipke, in Chinese Tartary'. *Journal of the Asiatic Society of Bengal* 11 (41): 363–91.

———. 1993 (1841). *Account of Koonawar in the Himalaya*. New Delhi: Indus Publishing House.

Hamilton, Water. 1820. *A Geographical, Statistical, and Historical Description of Hindostan and the Adjacent Countries*, 2 vols. London: John Murray.

Herbert, Captain J. D. 1829. 'An Account of a Tour Made to Lay Down the Course and Levels of the River Setlej or Satudra, as Far as Traceable within the Limits of British Authority, Performed in 1819'. *Asiatic Researches* 18 (1): 227–58.

Hutchison, J., and J. Ph Vogel. 1933. *History of the Punjab Hill States*, 2 vols. Lahore: Government of India Press.

Joshi, L. D. 1984 (1925). *Tribal People of the Himalayas: A Study of the Khasas*. Delhi: Mittal Publications.

Lattimore, Owen. 1951. *Inner Asian Frontiers of China*. Irvington-on-Hudson: Capitol Publishing Company and New York: American Geographical Society.

Levi, Scott C. 2002. *The Indian Diaspora in Central Asia and Its Trade*. Leiden: Brill.

Majumdar, D. N. 1962. *Himlayan Polyandry*. Bombay: Asia Publishing House.

Malhotra, Chaman Lal. 1990. *Himachal ka Krantikari Itihaas* (Hindi). Shimla: Jaishree Publishers.

Mathur, Nayanika. 2014. 'Naturalizing the Himalaya-as-Border in Uttarakhand'. In *Borderland Lives in Northern South Asia*, edited by David N. Gellner, 72–93. New Delhi: Orient Blackswan.

Minhas, Poonam. 1998. *Traditional Trade and Trading Centres in Himachal Pradesh*. New Delhi: Indus Publications.

Moorcroft, William, and George Trebeck. 1844. *Travels in the Himalayan Provinces of Hindustan and Panjab; in Ladakh and Kashmir; in Peshawur, Kabool, Kunduz and Bokhra; 1819 to 1925*. London: Murray.

Moran, Arik. 2007. 'From Mountain Trade to Jungle Politics: The Transformation of Kingship in Bashahr, 1815–1914'. *The Economic and Social History Review* 44 (2): 147–77.

Negi, Jai Deep. 1995. *Begar and Beth System in Himachal Pradesh*. Delhi: Reliance Publishing House.

Pathak, Shekhar. 1991. 'The Begar Abolition Movement in British Kumaun'. *The Indian Economic & Social History Review* 28 (3): 261–79.

Punjab States Gazetteer 1910, Jubbal State. 1912. Lahore: Government of Punjab Press.

Radhu, Abdul Wahid. 2017. *Tibetan Caravans: Journeys from Leh to Lhasa*. Delhi: Speaking Tiger.

Rathore, Mohan Singh. 1987. 'Nineteenth Century Cis-Sutlej Hill States'. PhD thesis, Himachal Pradesh University.

Rizvi, Janet. 1999. *Trans-Himalayan Caravans: Merchant Princes and Peasant Traders in Ladakh*. Delhi: Oxford University Press.

Rose, H. A. 1999 (1883). *Glossary of the Tribes and Castes of Punjab and the North West Frontier Province*. Delhi: Low Price Publications.

Scott, James C. 2009. *The Art of Not Being Governed: An Anarchist History of Upland Southeast Asia*. New Haven, CT: Yale University Press.

Sherring, Charles. 1906. *Western Tibet and the British Borderland*. London: Edward Arnold.

Shneiderman, Sara. 2010. 'Are the Central Himalayas in Zomia? Some Scholarly and Political Considerations across Time and Space'. *Journal of Global History* 5 (2): 289–312.

Shuttleworth, H. Lee. 1923. 'A Wool Mart on the Indo-Tibetan Borderland'. *Geographical Review* 13 (4): 552–8.

Singh, Chetan. 1997. 'A Strategy of Interdependence: Gaddi, Peasant and State in Himachal'. In *From Tribe to Caste*, edited by Dev Nathan, 374–86. Shimla: Indian Institute of Advanced Study.

————. 1998. *Natural Premises: Ecology and Peasant Life in the Western Himalaya, 1800–1950*. New Delhi: Oxford University Press.

————. 2003. 'Between Two Worlds: The Trader-Pastoralists of Kinnaur'. In *Mobile and Marginalised Peoples: Perspectives from the Past*, edited by Rudolph Heredia and Shereen Ratnagar, 35–64. New Delhi: Manohar.

van Schendel, Willem. 2002. 'Geographies of Knowing, Geographies of Ignorance: Jumping Scale in Southeast Asia'. *Environment and Planning D: Society and Space* 20 (6): 647–68.

————. 2005. *The Bengal Borderland: Beyond State and Nation in South Asia*. London: Anthem.

van Spengen, Wim. 2010. *Tibetan Border Worlds: A Geohistorical Analysis of Trade and Traders*. London and New York: Routledge.

Vasan, Sudha. 2006. 'Indo-Tibetan Border Trade in Himachal Pradesh'. *China Report* 42 (1): 42.

8

Frontiers, State and Banditry in the Thar Desert in the Nineteenth Century

TANUJA KOTHIYAL

This chapter explores British engagement with banditry on the frontiers of the Thar Desert in the mid-nineteenth century.[1] The extension of direct and indirect British rule over various parts of the Thar Desert made them encounter a range of groups engaged in banditry, highway robbery and plunder along the ill-defined frontiers of princely states and British territories. These encounters highlighted arguments about criminality, jurisdiction, legality, nomadism, settlement and governance in the Thar, which was viewed as a harsh and adversarial geography peopled by refractory nomadic groups. British records of early nineteenth and mid-nineteenth century view banditry through the lens of criminality, as a law-and-order problem that could be resolved through better administration, mapping, policing, as well as through a criminal justice system focused on retribution. However, in their encounters with 'criminality', British administrators were often faced with rather complex histories of 'bandits' and their complicated relationships with polity in the desert.

In contrast to the colonial view, recent approaches to banditry view it as a social and political response to exploitation. Banditry, as pointed out by Eric Hobsbawm in his classic *Bandits*, cannot be understood except as part of a history of political power (2000: 13). Stewart Gordon argues that a structured 'plunder ethic' centred around the accumulation of economic resources remained central to eighteenth-century state formation in Malwa (1999: 416–29). In her study of *dakaiti* in Bundelkhand, Malavika Kasturi views banditry as a 'multi-layered response by *biradari*s to the British attack on their territory, power, honour, means of subsistence, and military "masculine" culture' (2000: 203). Norbert Peabody's exploration of Rajput kingship in Kota views rebellion as a defining feature of Hindu kingship, which allowed Rajput *jagirdars* to assert their authority in the circle of kings which was the Rajput kingdom (1991: 29–56). Shail Mayaram's understanding of Meo banditry views it as resistance to state formation, one that forms a part of a dialectic between state and 'anti-state' (2004: 181). While being different representations of rebellion, what these examples do underline is a seamless intermingling of categories of the bandit and the rebel, and their locations on the margins of dominant state formations. Rather than being an act of criminality, banditry and plunder almost appear as part of a moral claim, whereby bandits locate themselves in hostile geographical and political frontiers and posit challenges to the state.

In attempting to understand the relationship between geography and 'moral claim' to resistance, I refer to the fourteenth-century Arab philosopher Ibn Khaldun, who points out that the basis of the dialectic of desert and city life was rooted in the harsh desert conditions, which engendered courage and fortitude in the Bedouins. The desert was the basis of all civilisation and the nomadic dwellers of the desert were prior to, and courageous and superior to, the sedentary people. Unlike the Bedouin, Khaldun writes, the sedentary people 'settle in fertile plains and amass luxuries and become accustomed to a life of abundance and refinement, their bravery decreases' (Dawood 2005 [1969]: 95–107). While the city, where the state was based, formulated the law, the desert people escaped further into the desert for fear of being meted out justice. In this sense, the Bedouin were always in a state of dissidence against the city dwellers, or the state. Ernest Gellner in his early work on the tribes of the Central High Atlas Mountains in Morocco, employs the idea of 'institutionalized dissidence' or 'siba' that existed in opposition to 'makhazen', which can be translated into the state. If 'bled el-makhazen' was the land of the pale, then 'bled el-siba' was the land beyond the pale, each constituting a menace to the other. The internal structures of the tribes that existed in the state of 'siba' or 'makhazen' being the same, there always existed a possibility of movement from the former into the latter. And yet a number of people chose to remain self-consciously dissident, beyond the pale in the state of 'siba' (Gellner 1969: 1–3). James Scott (2009: 30–1) takes the argument further in proposing that rather than being *ungoverned*, the people opting for the state of 'siba' were *self-governing* people (emphasis mine).

Through instances of banditry in the Thur-Parkar region of the Thar Desert in the mid-nineteenth century, this chapter attempts to explore the intersections between the categories of bandit, rebel and state. Could banditry in the arid Thar merely be understood through a criminal context, or was it located in a political context of power? Were the native rulers incapable of suppressing banditry or were their negotiations with bandits a part of a historical system of exchange? Did banditry, and the rebelliousness that it was inextricably located in, challenge the ideas about Rajputhood and warriorhood as they had emerged in the Rajput courts? Did banditry constitute dissidence, as a number of bandits were outlaws or *barwuttea*s,[2] exiles from their own states? Were the British, while understanding banditry through a criminal context, able to deal with it only as a question of lawlessness? These questions become important in the context of phrases like 'pacification' and 'tranquilization' of frontiers used in British reports, which suggest a state of constant turmoil. The efforts to induce 'tranquility, industry and order' in the frontiers by encouraging the settlement of agriculturalists were rooted in the premise that social hostility was ingrained in the adversarial geography of the region, and hence could be ordered.

I

The Thar Desert is a vast sandy plain located between the Aravali Mountains in the east, the eastern bank of Indus on the west, the Punjab basin on the north and the Rann of Kutch in the south, dotted with dry scrubland, grasslands, forts and urban and rural settlements. While being agriculturally deficient, the Thar provides excellent fodder and forage to pastoralists, as well as passage to mercantile caravans. In 1947, the Thar Desert was divided by the Radcliffe line, an international boundary between the new nation-states of India and Pakistan. Before Partition, the Thar Desert was part of several states that fringed it, like Sindh, Multan, Bikaner, Jaisalmer, Jodhpur, Umarkot, Kathiawar and Kutch. However, the arid Thar, while claimed by powerful chiefships was only nominally controlled by any of these. By the fifteenth century, emerging Rajput lineages had expanded their kingships through the extension of land grants in lieu of military service and established their fortress capitals like Jaisalmer, Bikaner, Jodhpur, and so on on the fringes of the desert, or in areas where water was available (Kothiyal 2016: 64–83). The political elitisation of ruling clans was accompanied by social elitisation, which resulted in the marginalisation of groups of warriors who either could not be accommodated or resisted being accommodated in the emerging aristocratic structures. This resulted in the pushing of older ruling groups into the heart of the desert, reducing them to being petty chiefs or *thikanadar*s.

These *thikana*s or chiefships like Pokhran, Chohtan, Barmer, Pugal, Nuggur, Veravow, Bhoyotra, Bakasir, and so on, while claimed by their powerful neighbours, paid nominal obeisance in the form of irregular tribute that often had to be extracted with the use of force. A number of these were located too far into the desert to ever be controlled either by Rajput kings or by the Mughal Empire into which they were theoretically assimilated. Their distant location, often on important trade routes, allowed them to exercise significant control on the movements on these routes, which they did by way of both pillage or levying of protection taxes, as the eighteenth-century records of Jodhpur state reveal.[3] These instances of banditry were not new to the region, but had been an integral part of medieval state formation in the region. *Munhata nainsi ri khyat*, a seventeenth-century comprehensive source to the histories of clans ruling in the Thar, mentions several instances where local chiefs engaged in brigandage and pillage, looting caravans, horses, camels, and so on that crossed the desert (Kothiyal 2016: 81). *Dhad*s or cattle raids had been an accepted form of warfare engaged in by most Rajput chiefs before their emergence as settled aristocracies. While medieval Rajput state formation fostered sedentarisation, in the arid infertile desert, control over routes determined access to power. This required Rajput states to enter into a range of formal and informal arrangements with *thikanadar*s and other warriors, terms of which could include warfare, extraction of tribute, payment of protection taxes as well as occasional overlooking of brigandage and pillage, in order to ensure safe passage of caravans through the desert. Most *thikanadar*s levied taxes like *bolawo* or *rukhwali ri bhachh* on commercial traffic, which unambiguously were protection taxes. A similar tax called *bolai* was levied by Bhil chiefs in Mewar (Jain 1993: 49). British officials also found these systems necessary even in the nineteenth century for 'affording a ready system of local protection to travelers, merchandise and property in the cause of ensuring safe transit to person through tracts where both stand in need of armed escort'.[4]

Following subsidiary alliances with the Rajput states between 1812 and 1818, and the conquest of Sindh in 1843, the entire Thar came under direct or indirect British control. With this began a long process of the settlement of Thar, with demarcation of boundaries that were to clearly define jurisdiction between British and native territories. This appeared to have been of particular necessity in the Thur-Parkar region, west and southwest of Marwar, where frontiers of a number of states like Sindh, Multan, Bikaner, Jaisalmer, Marwar, Umarkot, Kathiawar and Kutch met. This frontier region with shifting and contested boundaries came to be seen as a 'disturbed and disorganized' frontier, frequented by *barwuttea*s, roving bands of robbers, bandits and highway men. It was viewed as a 'den of thieves' where they found safe asylum and preyed upon neighbouring states.[5] Belonging to groups of locally powerful recalcitrant Rajput *thikanadar*s, Sindhi chiefs, 'criminal' tribes like Bhils, Mers and Minas or mercenary warrior groups like Khosas, Baluches, Sehraes, Larkhanis or Kuzzaks, these bands with their intimate knowledge of the difficult geography of the desert traversed across the desert with ease, preying upon travellers, merchants and herders alike. In one of the early descriptions of the region, James Tod highlights its solitude, desolation as well as its hostility through imageries of anxious toil of caravans that could come across 'lying in ambush, a band of Sehraes, the Bedouins of our desert, on the watch to despoil the caravan' (Tod, vol. II, 1997 [1829]: 236). This sense was further highlighted in the administrative report of the Mallani district (present-day Barmer), 1868, that underlined the absence of jurisdiction as the cause of lawlessness of the region, which was 'the common ground of plundering Scindees, Beloochees, and Rajputs. In these wilds they sought an easy refuge, and lived with their camels and herds, a nomad and predatory life; thence they sallied into Scinde, Marwar and Guzerat [*sic*], and were the pest of the country far and wide...'.[6]

British intervention in the affairs of Rajput states in the Thar often began with military action against recalcitrant chiefs or fugitives. For instance, in 1824, the Jodhpur Maharaja was forced to give away 21 villages in Kot-Kirana and Chang paraganas for the suppression of Khosas, a Baluch mercenary group operating in the Thar (Shah 1982: 19). In 1832, the Parkar Field Force, constituted to deal with banditry in the Thur-Parkar, carried out major offensives against Khosas and Rajput *barwuttea*s from Kutch.[7] Another region that required tranquilisation was Mallani, which was held by old families, descendants of Mallinath Rathor, who styled themselves Rawuls, and posed a threat to the authority of their Jodhpur clansmen. They were known to support freebooters of many kinds. With a view of establishing a 'strong centrical post in Balmeer', an offensive into Mallani was carried out in 1836.[8] Similarly, in the Shekhawati region that was the frontier between Jaipur, Jodhpur and Bikaner, an expedition was put together in 1834 to supress the Bidawat, Larkhani and Sulhedi chiefs (Shah 1982: 77). Similar operations were undertaken in Bharatpur and Kota states as well. These operations and expeditions invariably resulted in the disbanding of the kin-based military support that the Rajput chiefs had traditionally relied upon, as fugitive bandits often received shelter and support from the very chiefs who were expected to suppress them. A number of non-Rajput martial groups like Bhils and Mers, which themselves had at times been involved in banditry, were organised into irregular corps to deal with incidents of banditry on the frontiers of princely states. Efforts were made to include Khosas into the Parkar Field Force and Bidawats, Larkhanis and Sulhedis into the Shekhawati Brigade. The reasons for such inclusions were not merely the channelisation of the criminal tendencies of these groups, but very clearly the recognition of the fact of their intimate knowledge of the frontiers, besides being a tacit acceptance of their martiality. Besides, the ability to commit banditry and to control it were closely linked. British too were entering into agreements with the people who controlled the frontiers, except that they were far more powerful than the erstwhile Rajput rulers, and were able to impose terms. This, however, did not necessarily mean that 'pacified' bandits and outlaws always gave up their claims.

II

Bandits in the Thar belonged to no one particular group. They were Rajputs, Baluches, Minas and Bhils, who, either independently or in alliance with other groups, carried out plunder and pillage in the villages and on the highways, often accosting caravans. While grain, money, precious metals and arms were usually aimed at, camels and horses were also prized commodities. Camels laden with or without merchandise were waylaid and taken into a safe territory from where they could not be recovered without the use of force. Often the return of camels or merchandise was negotiated by paying ransoms.[9]

Early British campaigns against bandits and freebooters in the desert revealed the entangled networks of kinship ties and inter-state rivalries that allowed banditry to thrive. In the Thar Desert, people accused of banditry were usually local chieftains, *barwuttea*s or outlaws and mercenary warriors employed by the chieftains. Some of the early operations undertaken in the Thur-Parkar region from 1832 onwards by the Parkar Field Force, constituted to deal with lawlessness, were against the *barwuttea*s from Kutch and Kathiawar who had taken refuge in the Parkar region and had taken to banditry. The 'Parkur freebooters', as they were called, included Rajput *barwuttea*s from Kutch and Kathiawar, as well as Meena and Bagri *barwuttea*s.[10] In one instance, intelligence reports from Jaisalmer conveyed that about 100 men, accused of murder and robbery in Gujarat, had taken refuge in Chohtan and Mallani.[11] These fugitives, sheltered by Mallani chiefs, ventured into Jodhpur territory and engaged in banditry. After prolonged negotiations, the Parkar Field Force managed to secure aid from both Jaisalmer and Jodhpur states, as well as employ Khosas to carry out the operations.[12] However, more than being hampered by a lack of military aid, the operations became difficult because of internecine networks of kinship and loyalties. Most men who were supposed to be aiding the Parkar Field Force were found to be colluding with the *barwutteas*, having aided their entry into Mallani and even plotting their escape to Punjab. The level of collusion was such that Captain Cavafe of the Parkar Field Force reported that 'between the Khosas, Barwutteas and the authorities whoever is stationed near the Junnah kills a good number and that they secure a portion of the plunder from the marauders'.[13] A similar situation was reported from the frontiers Marwar and Bikaner in 1837 when an assembly of Kuzzak warriors, employed by the *thakur* of Mundea, was reported to be on the lookout for camels being taken to the Mundwa fair in Nagaur.[14] Similarly, subjects of Marwar, Mewar and Sirohi, who had carried out a spate of robberies in Palanpur, were found to have sought refuge in Sirohi.[15] Thus, the frontiers of Thar were ideal space for collusions between chieftains with old claims to authority, outlaws and mercenary warriors who formed parts of old supply lines of military labour in the region. These arrangements allowed for articulations of old claims to sovereignty on part of local chieftains subsumed by the Rajput state formation, as revealed by the following discussion on cases of banditry in Thur-Parkar in 1858.

In the year 1858, a series of cases of cattle theft and robberies were reported from the Jodhpur–Sindh frontier involving a Rajput *thikanadar* Khushaal Singh Chauhan of Bakasir, his brother Anar Singh and a Khosa bandit called Kapree Khan.[16] Of these banditries, most of them involved waylaying of cattle and camels that were often traced to the village of Khushaal Singh. In one of the cases, a camel contractor of the Commissariat Department was audaciously robbed of Rs 10,500.[17] Khushaal Singh's villages lay on the frontiers of Jodhpur, Mallani, Palanpur and Kutch, and after conducting raids in Sindh, he and his men often sought shelter in these territories where they were reported to have several kinsmen. Even when Khushaal Singh's men were captured, he managed to free them by the use of force. Not only did Khushaal Singh plunder neighbouring territories, he levied grazing taxes and imprisoned people who did not pay these taxes. It was reported that the property stolen from Sindh even when traced to villages of these *thakurs*, could not be recovered as they had forcibly removed the *thana*s of Jodhpur state in 1857 and refused to allow *thana*s to be set up in these villages.[18] These *thana*s had been set up in 1853, and the *thakur*s of Bakasir had repeatedly requested for the removal of these *thana*s that they saw as infringement.[19] In fact, Khushaal Singh was reported to have refused to allow Jodhpur durbar's authority to ever be exercised in his districts, in a sense declaring himself free of the authority of the Jodhpur state.[20]

In his predatory pursuits, Khushaal Singh allied with a Khosa bandit Kapree Khan, who belonged to a group of Baluch warriors, and had been discharged from the Thur-Parkar police force on charges of gross misconduct in 1852. The British interaction with Khosas, who traced their origins to Sira and Dera Ghazi Khan, began even before they conquered Sindh in February 1843. The Khosas had been the followers of the Kaloras, a religious sect that ruled Sindh until 1783. As the Talpur Wazirs ousted the Kaloras, the Khosas refused to serve the new rulers and escaped into the desert in the Nuggur-Parkar districts, seeking shelter with Rajput chiefs in Nuggur and Palanpur. They made a living out of plunder, highway robbery and extraction, besides lending their military services to petty Rajput chiefs of Mallani, which was viewed as a country with 'few scattered villages, which for ages had been a grazing ground for camels, kine goats and sheep', an anarchic region as it was totally devoid of cultivation and inhabited by the Khosas.[21] The Khosas often waylaid a large number of camels from the Sindh and Kutch frontiers, to the extent that Lumsden, the political agent in Kutch, reported that the entire frontier of Sindh was infested with the plundering Khosas.[22] They were said to 'locate themselves wherever it may best suit their convenience, with no other permission than that conferred by their swords, and upon the principle that might is right'.[23] Based on their ability of plunder and pillage, they collected protection taxes from the pastoralists, who visited the grazing grounds, cultivators as well as traders, who crossed the desert.

In September 1843, after the conquest of Sindh, Captain Jackson, the political agent of Mallani, had managed to negotiate the surrender of four Khosa chiefs, who, by their own admission, had led a life of plunder.[24] Among the terms of surrender were absorption of Khosa chiefs into the Jodhpur service, financial settlement and their organisation into some kind of an irregular corps dedicated to the eradication of banditry in the Thar. In the new emerging territorial arrangements after the conquest of Sindh, a new role was being envisaged for the Khosas which was to safeguard the British frontiers as part of the Parkar Field Force. This was in accordance with the settlement policies carried out with Bhils in Deccan and Khandesh, where they had been organised into irregular corps (Brown 2014: 72–5). The argument was that as a migratory and predatory group located on the frontiers of Sindh, Gujarat and Jodhpur, the Khosas with their knowledge of the desert could provide invaluable assistance in settling the region by being reinvented as militia for the protection of the frontier.[25] Captain Jackson viewed them as 'fierce and independent children of despotism' who 'have hitherto never dreamt of any law but that of their swords, and defied effectually the Rulers of

Sindhh, Joudpore and Jessulmere. From their cradles had been taught, that to yield their weapons without a strike, disgraced then forever amongst their brethren'.[26] However, the Jodhpur state was less than willing to employ Khosas who they did not trust, and strongly protested any move towards such accommodation.[27] Some Khosas were eventually included into the Parkar Field Force. Some of these such as Kapree Khan continued their plundering and eventually either deserted or were discharged for misconduct.

After being discharged from the Parkar Police Force, Kapree Khan joined forces with Khushaal Singh and continued to pillage. From the reports it is clear that after being joined by Kapree Khan, Khushaal Singh did not merely continue to venture beyond his villages, but managed to dispossess a camel contractor of the Commissariat Department of Rs 10,500, bringing him into direct conflict with the British.[28] On applying to the Jodhpur durbar, the British authorities were informed that the Bakasir *thakur*, Khushaal Singh, had been in a state of rebellion since 1857, and the Jodhpur durbar was in no state to provide any kind of assistance, as they no longer had *thanas* in Bakasir. In fact, British reports about the region suggest that the *thanadars* employed in the villages of Bakasir had themselves been in league with the robbers and demanded shares of the plunder.[29] In the face of the inability on the part of the Jodhpur durbar to prevent pillage by what were seen as its subjects, the British officials were left with little choice but to intervene into the Jodhpur frontier and help reinstate the *thanas* in Bakasir.[30]

Khushaal Singh's activities were seen to constitute a striking proof of growing disorder along the eastern frontier of Sindh, which by this time was a British territory. The deputy magistrate in Meerpur Khas, Sindh, reported that Khushaal Singh and his men kept the frontier between Jodhpur and Sindh 'in a perpetual state of excitement and disgust at the same time for their cattle are carried off into Bakasar or Boyotra districts [and] nothing can be done'.[31] He further reported that despite close linkages of marriage and commerce, the people of Thur-Parkar found it difficult to travel to Jodhpur on account of fear of plunder and pillage unleashed by Khushaal Singh.

The cases of Khushaal Singh and Kapree Khan, who are both recorded as notorious bandits, raise interesting questions about crime as assertion of sovereignty. Khushaal Singh belonged to an old Chauhan lineage, whose claims to his ancestral villages went further back than the Rathor clan that ruled over Jodhpur. However, he was not an important *thikanadar*, unlike the Pokhran *thakurs* who held important positions in the Jodhpur court. The *thikanadars* of Bakasir, in return for irregular tribute, had maintained their own control by way of levying grazing taxes, and so on. Banditry and highway robbery were obvious displays of control over the routes of movement. Until 1853, there was no evidence of Jodhpur *thana* in Bakasir. The *thana* which became the symbol of the extension of Jodhpur sovereignty in Bakasir was uprooted in 1857 and not allowed to be set up again until 1861. While marginal to Jodhpur politics, Bakasir's location at the frontiers of Jodhpur, Sindh, Kutch and Kathiawar made it an important point of access as well as escape. The histories of Rajput states have always been studied in the context of their contact with the Mughal Empire. However, for places like Bakasir, Nuggur-Parka and Veravow, greater associations existed with the western frontiers in Sindh rather than eastern Rajputana. These towns and villages also lay on the migratory routes connecting Sindh and Baluchistan to Kutch and Kathiawar, which is why they became the refuge of the Khosas after the decline of their patrons, the Kaloras, in 1783.

The collusion between Khushaal Singh and Kapree Khan was a continuation of old networks of military associations. British administrators had attempted to pacify and eradicate the Khosa plundering from 1840s onwards, as the flow of Baluch and Afghan military labour through Sindh and Thar threatened to extend the Afghan frontier to Sindh. Despite their depredations, Khosas were viewed though a lens of obvious martiality, which was at the same time fearsome as well as honourable.

However, for British administrators, the depredations such as those of Khushaal Singh and Kapree Khan also fed into the larger picture of lawlessness that they faced in the Thar. The frontiers of the Rajput states, Sindh and states in Kathiawar and Kutch were all ill-defined. Mobility across frontiers was easy, and so was escape. Often after committing robberies, bandits could escape into areas of rival jurisdiction. In such cases, it was impossible either to seek surrender or recover the loot. In this light, several military operations such as the one in Barmer, Mallani in 1836 were carried out. British administrators particularly saw Barmer as the 'key of the desert, a point which would give the most extended command and influence over the population of the surrounding region'.[32] Barmer was to become the point from where several military campaigns into Thur-Parkar, Sindh, Kutch and Kathiawar were undertaken. Khushaal Singh and Kapree Khan's banditry also provided the British officials grounds for intervention with or without the permission of the Jodhpur state. Frere, the commissioner of Sindh, proposed that 'if Joudpore Durbar objects to our interference, let it control its own subjects and afford us redress.... But if Joudpore Durbar is either unable or unwilling to keep its own subjects in order, I would solicit permission for our

Frontier Officers to deal with these petty plundering Thakoors without reference to Joudpore'.[33] By questioning the unwillingness and the inability of the Jodhpur state to intervene, the British clearly underlined the linkages between the bandits and Jodhpur state, as well as its failures at governance in the frontiers. In fact, Frere believed that the display of firmness on the part of the British had managed to placate a number of miscreants in Sindh, and even Khushaal Singh, on being threatened with armed action, had agreed to surrender his portion of the loot.[34] On examination, the claims of sovereignty made by Khushaal Singh were found to be incorrect, and the only way of keeping the British territories free of incursions from his depredations was by strengthening the Jodhpur position by reinstating the Jodhpur *thana*s. Paradoxically, it was also proposed to raise a force, on Jodhpur expenses, that could enter Bakasir at any point of time to investigate cases of robbery.[35] By 1861, depredations of Khushaal Singh and Kapree Khan had been brought under control, though there exist no records of their arrest.

III

Banditry thus raised several questions about borders, governance and jurisdiction. One of the most common problems faced in the region was the absence of mutually recognised boundaries, and therefore lack of clarity in matters of jurisdiction, which allowed people to move between the states with ease, particularly if they wished to escape jurisdiction for any particular reason. What was also interesting was not only the absence of clear boundaries, but the presence of zones where a third party, usually a powerful and often recalcitrant *thikanadar*, exercised influence. Pokhran at the borders of Jodhpur and Jaisalmer, Pugal at the borders of Bikaner and Jaisalmer, Thur-Parkar between Jodhpur, Jaisalmer, Sindh, Kathiawar and Kutch, Shekhawati located on the frontiers of Jodhpur, Bikaner and Jaipur and the forests of Aravalli between Jodhpur, Udaipur and Sirohi were all zones of contested jurisdiction, where refuge could be sought. These were also zones through which trade routes passed, and therefore making them zones not merely of refuge and escape, but ones where immense control could be exercised on circulation, particularly one that was commercial in nature.[36] While all states undertook measures to safeguard routes as well as the caravan traffic, there were often localities close to the routes where states did not exercise enough influence and had to negotiate either by overlooking illegal exactions and protection taxes, or negotiate ransom after thefts had been carried out. All examples mentioned above indicate that cattle-lifting and camel thefts were the most common forms of thievery. With the scale of theft, it is also clear that stolen cattle, horses and camels would have been diverted to markets through middlemen, or would have been returned after a ransom was received. In all such cases, the durbars were aware of their inability beyond a certain point, whereas the British officials not only insisted on defining boundaries and jurisdictions but also fixing responsibility for the loss of property, particularly if it was stolen from British territories. In keeping with the intent to suppress crime as well as to the tradition of granting asylum to criminals, by 1870 the British made the princely states sign extradition treaties that made it essential for people charged with crimes like dacoity, robbery, cattle theft, burglary, arson, and so on to be extradited. The princely states also agreed to refuse *sarna* or asylum which was seen as akin to abutting of offences (Aitchison 1909: 173).

Apart from military solutions, the British also encouraged agrarian settlements in areas like Mallani. This meant introducing Jat peasantry to supplement 'the roving class of graziers' and 'hamlets with their rain crops of millet and pulse spring up to relieve these deserts'.[37] Between 1865 and 1868, 70 villages had been founded in Mallani and the British appeared to compliment themselves on 'reclaiming people from their predatory pursuits and encouraging cultivation, trade and peaceful sources of income'.[38] However, new settlements brought new rivalries and therefore boundary settlements were undertaken to decide upon exact jurisdiction. However, mapping was necessary not only to settle disputes but also to know the region better in order to administer it. Though initial travellers like Captain Boileau, James Tod and Archibald Adams had all drawn geographical sketches as well as maps of the region, between 1870 and 1886, several topographical surveys of the western frontiers of the Jodhpur state along Barmer, Sindhree and Palanpur were undertaken and accurate maps drawn.

My engagement with banditry, robbery and theft in the Thar indicates that these were multiple representations of claims to authority often predicated upon control over mobility through the desert. In the dry arid Thar, the control over circulation of mobile wealth, like cattle or merchandise in transit, epitomised authority more than anything else. Located away from agro-centric polities of northern India, Rajput brotherhoods in the far-western desert, in association with other warrior groups, forced Rajput kingships to negotiate passage, and thus share authority. Such power-sharing arrangements, on the one hand, served the purpose of extending the authority of the states in areas that were practically out of bounds for them. On the other hand, for the bandits, who were often also local chieftains, these arrangements allowed the perpetuation of a bandit economy based on protection and extortion in the agriculturally deficient arid desert. Besides being claims to authority, by way of control over mobile wealth, banditry and plunder were also resistances emanating out of certain moral claims to true Rajputhood, one that thrived in difficult and hostile desert circumstances, as against the one located in the courts. While the citadel capitals or the durbars were located in fertile agrarian zones, the recalcitrant chiefs were all located in the desert, mountains or forests, spaces that were geographically hostile. A survey of the Rajput-ruling dynasties of the Thar such as the Rathors and the Bhatis indicates that their initial power struggles were located in the heart of the desert from where they moved and settled in fertile zones, building their citadel capitals (Kothiyal 2016).[39] The Thar Desert represented a geographical opposition to the agrarian zones where Rajput power centres were located. The claims of the recalcitrant *thikanadar*s in the frontiers were based on survival in harsh terrains that rendered them morally superior to the ruling clans. The Thar was a zone of interaction between core areas which represent the explicit sovereignty of the Rajput courts and the 'ambiguous, plural and shifting' sovereignty of the frontiers (Scott 2009: 61). For the durbars, the assertions of recalcitrant *thikanadar*s and *jagirdar*s were rooted in an older history of moral claims of entitlements, which were both acceded and contested. Often the claims of the recalcitrant chiefs went further back than the ruling families or at least were contiguous. Rajput brotherhoods, as well as other groups, with intimate knowledge of the desert, managed to enforce their terms on the Rajput courts by holding the key to safe passage across the desert. In this contract between the core and the frontier, banditry emerged as a system of exchange. Moreover, depredations carried out by the outlaw fugitive or *barwuttea* attracted a respectful acceptance and can be seen to represent a kind of 'institutionalised dissidence'. British administrators, finding it difficult to come to terms with this rather diffused model of flow of authority, focused on the centralisation of authority in the courts of princely states, while ascribing criminality to older power-sharing arrangements.

NOTES

1. A very early version of this chapter was presented at the annual conference of the Association of Asian Studies in Asia in Taipei in 2014. I thank my co-panelists Farhana Ibrahim and Aprana Kapadia, as well as the anonymous referee for the *Economic and Political Weekly* for their comments that helped me shape the chapter.

2. *Barwuttea*s were generally Rajput fugitives, but could also be Bhils, Minas or Mers. Outlawry was an institutionalised practice of dissidence by which a fugitive could be banished from the territory of a chieftain, or choose to become a *barwuttea* or an outlaw. In the past, this had often meant that warriors who became fugitives as a result of feuding went through a period of wandering or *vikhau*, in which they amassed resources or re-established themselves in some other territory. This system also entailed a provision shelter or *sarna* to *barwuttea*s or outlaws who carried out their raids outside of the territory of the host state or chief. A *barwuttea* could be provided shelter by a rival chieftain, but could well also choose to live a life of predation and banditry. British treaties with Rajput states invariably included clauses that required the Rajput states to not offer shelter to *barwuttea*s from other states.

3. For example, in 1766, the *thikanadar* of the village Chohtan, Barmer Sadul Bhimsi was reported to have waylaid camels travelling from Dhadhmala in Kutch. Ashadh Sudi 15, 'Jama Khrach ro Navo', Kotda, *Sanad Parwana Bahi*, No. 5, VS 1823/1766 CE. In 1773, the merchants travelling to Sindh through Bikampur requested the creation of a new route as they were harassed by the *thikanadar*s at Bikampur. Ashwin Sudi 14, Budhwar, Phalodi, *Sayer, Sanad Parwana Bahi*, No. 13, VS 1830/1773 CE. A charge of levying a new *bolawo* was made against the *thikanadar* of Pokhran by Sahu Roop Chand of Umarkot in 1783, when the merchant was already paying *rahadari* and *dan* (transit taxes) to the Jodhpur state. Miti Ashwin Sudi 6, Somvar, Jodhpur, *Sanad Parwana Bahi*, No. 29, VS 1840/1783 CE. Vikrami Samwat (VS) begins 57 years prior to the Common Era and was in usage in Jodhpur documents until 1868.

4. Foreign Political, 17 December 1838, 37–49, National Archives of India, Delhi. Henceforth, FP and NAI.

5. FP, 12 February 1830, 6–7, NAI, Delhi.

6. Administrative Report of the District of Mullani, 1868, 9, NAI, Delhi.

7. Military Operations against Parkur Freebooters, Jodhpur–Jaisalmer Military, Rajputana Agency, 1832, NAI, Delhi.

8. FP, 26 November 1832, 8, NAI, Delhi.

9. FP, 12 February 1830, 6–7, NAI, Delhi. David Gilmartin's work on colonial Punjab also indicates the presence of networks constituted of cattle lifters, village headmen and *rassagir*s who either disposed of the stolen cattle or negotiated their return for ransom; Gilmartin (2003: 33–56).

10. Lt Col. Litchfield of Parkar Field Force to Col. Lockett, Political Agent, 16 November 1832, Military Operations against Parkur Freebooters, Jodhpur–Jaisalmer Military, Rajputana Agency, 1832, f 45, NAI, Delhi.

11. Intelligence report of news writer in Jaisalmer, Military Operations against Parkar Freebooters, Rajputana Agency Political Branch File No. 4, Jodhpur 1832 II, f 36, NAI, Delhi.

12. Lt Col. Litchfield of Parkur Field Force to Col. Lockett, Political Agent, 16 November 1832, Military Operations against Parkur Freebooters, Jodhpur–Jaisalmer Military, Rajputana Agency, 1832, ff 37–8, NAI, Delhi.

13. Captain Cavafe to Henry Pottinger, 10 December 1838, Military Operations against Parkur Freebooters, Jodhpur–Jaisalmer Military, Rajputana Agency, fl 129, NAI, Delhi.

14. Copies of Arzees from Vakil Jeypore Durbar, 16 December 1837, Bikaner Vakil, 18 December, 1837 and Jhunhjunu Hakim, 24 December 1837, Disturbed State of Marwar on the Bikaner and Shekhawati Frontiers, Jodhpur, Jagirdars-Disturbances and Riots, 14-A—Jodhpur, Rajputana Agency, 1836–7, ff 54–9, NAI, Delhi.

15. FP, 8 September 1849, Nos 2–9, NAI, Delhi.

16. In the years 1857 and 1858, several instances of rebellions by *jagirdar*s were reported in Rajputana. A number of them were actually directed towards Rajput rulers rather than the British, in particular Takhat Singh of Jodhpur who had highly vexed relationships with his nobles.

17. H. B. E. Frere, Commissioner, Sindh, to AGG Rajputana, 15 January 1859, f 33, Disturbed State of Jodhpur Frontier Bordering on Sindh File 85, Jodhpur Old Vol. II, Rajputana Agency, NAI, Delhi.

18. H. B. E. Frere, Commissioner, Sindh, to Lord Elphinstone, Governor and President, Bombay, 1 May 1858, Letter 191 of 1858, ff 6–8, Disturbed State of Jodhpur Frontier Bordering on Sindh File 85, Jodhpur Old Vol. II, Rajputana Agency, NAI, Delhi.

19. Dy Magistrate Meerpur Khas and Thurr-Parkar to Political Agent, Jodhpur, 106 of 1858, dated 12 November 1858, ff 100–1, Disturbed State of Jodhpur Frontier Bordering on Sindh File 85, Jodhpur Old Vol. II, Rajputana Agency, NAI, Delhi.

20. Dy Collector Meerpur Khas and Parkar to Political Agent, Jodhpur, 513 of 1858, dated 25 October 1858, ff 97–8, Disturbed State of Jodhpur Frontier Bordering on Sindh File 85, Jodhpur Old Vol. II, Rajputana Agency, NAI, Delhi.

21. FP, October 1868, 69–80, NAI, Delhi.

22. I. G. Lumsden, Political Agent in Kutch to Maj. Lewis Brown, Political Agent Palanpur, No. 44 of 1843, dated 17 February 1843, ff, 32–3, Plundering Expeditions of Khosa Chiefs on the Borders of Cutch and Mallani, 32, Jodhpur, Boundary, Rajputana Agency.

23. Captain C. F. Jackson, Officiating Superintendent, Mullanee, to Col. J. Sutherland, AGG Rajputana, Balmeer, 20 May 1843, ff 96–7, Plundering Excursions of Khosa Chiefs on Lands of Cutch and Mullanee, 32, Jodhpur, Boundary, Rajputana Agency, NAI, Delhi.

24. Depositions of Ullah Buksh, son of Kamal Khan and Shobhdar, son of Shera Baloch taken at Jodhpur Political Agency on 5 August 1843, Surrender of Khosa Chiefs, 32, Jodhpur, Boundary, Rajputana Agency, ff 160–7, NAI, Delhi.

25. Political Commissioner for Gujarat and Resident at Baroda to Secretary to Government of Bombay, 28 April 1843, ff 84–5, Plundering Expeditions of Khosa Chiefs on the Borders of Cutch and Mallani, 32, Jodhpur, Boundary, Rajputana Agency, NAI, Delhi.

26. Report on the state of people and country on the frontier of Sindhh, Joudhpore and Jessulmere, File 32, Jodhpur, Boundary, Rajputana Agency Office, 1843, 102, NAI, Delhi.

27. Translation of a note addressed by the Jodhpur Vakeel on the 28 September 1843 to the Political Agent, Jodhpur, ff 160–2, Plundering Expeditions of Khosa Chiefs on the Borders of Cutch and Mallani, 32, Jodhpur, Boundary, Rajputana Agency, NAI, Delhi.

28. Telegram dated 4 January 1859, Disturbed State of Jodhpur Frontier Bordering on Sindh, File 85, Jodhpur Old Vol. II, Rajputana Agency, NAI, Delhi.

29. Captain J. B. Brooke, Officiating Political Agent, Joudhpoor to Captain G. B. Tyrwhitt, Deputy Magistrate of Meerpoor and Thurr-Parkur, No. 359 of 1858, 28 November 1858, ff 104–05, Disturbed State of Jodhpur Frontier Bordering on Sindh, File 85, Jodhpur Old Vol. II, Rajputana Agency, NAI, Delhi.

30. H. B. E. Frere, Commissioner, Sindh to Lord Elphinstone, Governor and President in Council, Bombay, 8 February 1859, Disturbed State of Joudpore Frontier along Sindh, 85-Jodhpur old, Boundary, Jodhpur, Rajputana Agency, ff 85–9, NAI, Delhi.

31. From the Deputy Magistrate of Meerpoor Khas Thurr-Parkur to the Magistrate of Hyderabad, No. 105 of 1858, dated 12 November 1858, ff 18–38, Disturbed State of Jodhpur Frontier Bordering on Sindh File 85, Jodhpur Old Vol. II, Rajputana Agency, NAI, Delhi.

32. FP, 7 October, 1843, 199–200, NAI, Delhi. Mallani was transferred to the Bombay government in 1836, and later to AGG, Rajputana, in 1839, and to political agent in 1843. It was restored to Marwar in 1898. However, Barmer remained a British military post.

33. Frere to Elphinstone, 8 February 1859, Disturbed State of Joudpore Frontier, f 85, NAI, Delhi.

34. Ibid., 86.
35. Deputy Collector and Magistrate, Meerpur Khas to Frere, Commissioner of Sindh, No. 113 of 26 January 1859, Disturbed State of Joudpore Frontier, ff 94–6, NAI, Delhi.
36. A quantum of opium transferred from Malwa to Karachi bunder, travelled on desert routes through Kathiawar, Jaisalmer and Sindh. Amar Farooqui suggests that in opium producing and trading zones of western India, several 'gangs' of 'banditti' mushroomed that included Pindarris, Bhils, Gonds, Ramoshis, Kolis and Minas, who had been previously employed by the Marathas. These gangs could not have operated without the support of local chieftains Farooqui (2005: 187).
37. FP, October 1868, 69–80, NAI, Delhi.
38. Ibid.
39. Rathors were initially located in the dry Mahewa belt before moving to Mondor in 1395 CE, around present-day Barmer. Bhatis had a long migratory history through the desert, with Tanot and Lodrovo being older power centres.

REFERENCES

Primary Sources

Sanad Parwana Bahis. No. 5/1766, No. 13/1773, No. 29/1783.

Foreign Political. 1830, 32, 38, 43, 49, 68, 69.

Rajputana Agency. Various files: Boundary, Riots, Military, Jagirdars, 1832–86.

Aitchison, C. U. 1909. *A Collection of Treaties, Engagements and Sanads Relating to India and Neighbouring Countries Vol III (The Treaties Etc. Relating to States in Rajputana)*. Calcutta: Government Printing Press.

Secondary Sources

Brown, Mark. 2014. *Penal Power and Colonial Rule*. United Kingdom: Routledge.

Dawood, N. J. 2005 (1969). *Ibn Khaldun: The Muqaddimah An Introduction to History: The Classic Islamic History of the World*. Edited, translated and introduced by Franz Rosenthal. New Jersey: Princeton University Press.

Farooqui, Amar. 2005. *Smuggling as Subversion: Colonialism, Indian Merchants, and the Politics of Opium, 1790–1843*. London: Lexington Books.

Gellner, Ernest. 1969. *Saints of the Atlas*. London: ACLS History e-Book.

Gilmartin, David. 2003. 'Cattle, Crime and Colonialism: Property as Negotiation in North India'. *IESHR* 40 (1): 33–56.

Gordon, S. 1969. 'Scarf and Sword: Thugs, Marauders and State Formation in Eighteenth Century Malwa'. *IESHR* 6 (4): 416–29.

Hobsbawm, Eric. 2000. *Bandits*. London: Abacus.

Jain, M. S. 1993. *Concise History of Modern Rajasthan*. New Delhi: Vishwa Prakashan.

Kasturi, Malavika. 2002. *Embattled Identities: Rajput Lineages and the Colonial State in Nineteenth-Century North India*. New Delhi: Oxford University Press.

Kothiyal, Tanuja. 2016. *Nomadic Narratives: A History of Mobility and Identity in the Great Indian Desert*. New Delhi: Cambridge University Press.

Mayaram, Shail. 2004. *Against History, against State: Counterperspectives from the Margins*. Delhi: Permanent Black.

Peabody, Norbert. 1991. 'Kota Mahajagat or the Great Universe of Kota: Sovereignty and Territory in 18th Century Rajasthan'. *CIS* 25 (1): 29–56.

Scott, James. 2009. *The Art of Not Being Governed: An Anarchist History of Upland South East Asia*. New Haven: Yale University Press.

Shah, P. R. 1982. *Raj Marwar During Paramountcy: A Study in Problems and Policies up to 1923*. Jodhpur: Sharda Publishing House.

Tod, James. 1997 (1829). *Annals and Antiquities of Rajas'than or, the Central and Western Rajpoot States of India*, 2 vols. Edited by Douglas Sladen. New Delhi: Rupa and Co.

9

Bureaucracy and Border Control

Ethnographic Perspectives on Crime, Police Reform
and 'National Security' in Kutch, 1948–52

FARHANA IBRAHIM

Studies on militarisation and borders in South Asia have often remained focused on zones of spectacular conflict such as Kashmir or Punjab during the Partition. This chapter tracks the production of a discourse on borders by those charged with border security such as the police and other senior bureaucracy in the decades following the Partition. It suggests that the 'border question' evolved gradually out of a series of everyday concerns over local criminality that finally coalesced into the more abstract category of 'national security'. While we know that the moment of Partition was experienced non-homogenously in different regions, this chapter argues that this is true not only for border residents but also for the bureaucratic and security apparatus that did not always work as a singular entity. The chapter examines bureaucratic debates on police reorganisation in Kutch between 1948 and 1952 to suggest that contemporary discourses on nation and borders were arrived at through intra-bureaucratic negotiations with the far less abstract categories of village, locality and region.

Anthropologists have written extensively on nationalism (Handler 1988; Munasinghe 2002; Verdery 1991; Williams 1989) as they have sought to theorise the state in an ethnographic mode (Trouillot 2001; Das and Poole 2004; Ferguson and Gupta 2002; Mathur 2016; Reeves 2014). Borderlands may be regarded as those conceptual sites where the relationship between the state and the nation can been productively interrogated and historicised (Bhan 2008; Cons 2016; R. Gupta 2013; Ibrahim 2009; van Schendel 2004). I contend here that anthropological literature on borderlands must also take seriously the 'mundane' and 'banal' ways in which a bureaucratic discourse on borders is produced. I argue that this discourse often precedes—but is also influenced by—the collective imagination of the national community and its attendant rules for sanctioning 'legitimate' claims on citizenship, identity and belonging, even as it delegitimises other ways of being as 'anti' or not properly 'national'. Due to constraints of access to contemporary official paperwork pertaining to aspects of national security that are deemed—though not always consistently—'sensitive', the ethnography of bureaucracy with regard to borderlands must necessarily turn towards an earlier period where, through cracks in officially constituted archives, some sort of narrative may be crafted.[1] Thus in this chapter, I take an ethnographic excursion into the first few years after Partition, a period that provides a fascinating sense of how freshly drawn up territorial borders were acculturated and translated into everyday practice at the level of the administration. Bureaucratic letter-writing between New Delhi and Kutch provides interesting insights into the following kinds of questions: What did the new border mean to law enforcement agents and to borderland residents? How were village disputes, thefts of cattle and sacred idols and cross-border incursions reported? How were transgressions of the border viewed? What were some of the concerns around reorganising police and paramilitary forces in the region? Far from being self-evident, I argue here that the new border had to be produced on a continuous basis, through letters, paperwork and administrative action. As the substance of the chapter will demonstrate, neither the border as a physical entity nor the territorial anxiety that typically marks the post-colonial borders of South Asia were necessarily uniformly or ubiquitously manifested.

An ethnographic reading of bureaucratic writing during the late 1940s suggests that the newly established post-colonial state did not have a clear or unambiguous understanding of the how the border was to be managed. Muslims, constituting a majority of border-resident citizens, both exacerbate the post-colonial state's position on national belonging—where the self-professed 'Muslim' states of Pakistan and Bangladesh are countered by ideas of a predominantly 'Hindu' India—even as they become poster children for India's so-called policy of 'tolerance' towards its minorities, allowing the state to craft a nationalist narrative in contradistinction to its immediate neighbours. The controversial Citizenship Amendment Act (CAA) passed in 2019 makes this position quite explicit. It states that persecuted minorities from the 'neighbouring' states of Afghanistan, Pakistan and Bangladesh are free to migrate into India and claim Indian citizenship.

However, by excluding Muslims from this clause, the Act legitimises citizenship as a 'natural' attribute for Hindus, regardless of the fact that many Muslim minorities may also be persecuted in the neighbourhood (for example, Ahmaddiyas, Shi'as, Rohingyas).[2] Given what we know to be the communally divisive atmosphere during Partition, as well as contemporary nationalist discourses that seek to craft a predominantly Hindu nationalist narrative over citizenship claims, I suggest that it is possible to trace the roots of present-day practices of exclusionary citizenship back to the early post-colonial years. As Niraja Gopal Jayal (2013) argues in *Citizenship and Its Discontents*, current debates on citizenship in India that seek to exclude the Muslim immigrant from claims to nationality are informed by early constituent assembly debates on the subject, thereby retaining the shadow of the Partition. I have suggested elsewhere that these debates can be traced even beyond the Partition, so that the Partition of 1947 is not seen as a singular ideological rupture in the constitution of debates around citizenship and belonging (Ibrahim 2018). However, the material addressed in this chapter suggests that even during the political upheavals of 1947 and its immediate aftermath, neither the state machinery nor the borderland residents acted in any predictable or pre-ordained manner.

Tracking the bureaucratic production of border management practices along India's western border, specifically the borderlands that divided Kutch—now a district in the western Indian state of Gujarat and at the time a state directly administered by New Delhi—and Pakistan's southern province of Sindh, I will suggest first, that subsequent to the announcement of a formal partition, functionaries of the state did not uniformly grasp the border in abstract nationalist terms of national security. Second, and related to the first point, the question of belonging was discussed in terms of village and region instead of the nation at large. Border security was often posited in local terms—the safety of village property and persons—rather than in terms of the nation. Third, the material examined here challenges the assumption that it is the state which espouses the narrative of 'national interest', which is resisted or challenged by subaltern narratives of resistance by those on its territorial margins. It will become evident that rather than being constituted by the state's discourse, which was uneven, contradictory and often mired in the language of locality, it was the so-called subaltern citizens on its borderlands who often articulated 'nationalist' concerns with clarity and prescience; thus it was the 'local' borderland residents, mostly Muslim pastoralists, who ended up speaking in the abstract language of the 'state' and the 'nation', while its administrators remained in the discourse of the 'local'.

Until 1965, when the first cross-border armed conflict took place on the India–Pakistan border, a border management regime emerged gradually but not always in a clearly defined direction. Key questions included: How was the Kutch–Sindh border to be policed? Should it be subject to a specially crafted security regime now that it was a national boundary or was it sufficient to continue with pre-existing arrangements? What was to be the policy governing the movements of those who lived in border villages, most of whom were Muslim pastoralists who had family on the other side? Far from being taken for granted at the time of the Partition in 1947, border management was actively produced through a series of written exchanges that shuttled back and forth between the administrative headquarters of Kutch at Bhuj and the Government of India in New Delhi. A close reading of the correspondence over law enforcement and police reorganisation in Kutch before 1965 allows one to trace a gradual—but by no means linear—crystallisation of a regime of citizenship and nationality over the border question. In the following sections, I will examine administrative debates on police reorganisation in Kutch between 1948—when the former princely state acceded to the Indian Union—and 1952, to show that contemporary concerns around national security in border regions were eventually arrived at through moments of non-linear negotiation with the far less abstract categories of village, locality and region. Letters and bureaucratic memoranda also provide a glimpse into the construction of the 'nation' via various 'publics' that were seen as the rationale for firm border-management practices. The initial threat of an unprotected border was posed as a problem to a secular and a far more locally grounded 'public'—for example, rich regional merchants who suffered losses of property at the hands of bandits and thieves. Over a period of time, by the 1950s, this threat was couched in a more specific and abstract vein—the nation was threatened both by an unprotected border as well as potentially treacherous Muslims who reside *within* the border. Finally, the role played by borderland people in the production of this bureaucratic discourse will be seen to be neither passive nor one of predetermined opposition or resistance. Through a dialogic engagement with the bureaucracy, they are far more central to the processes of state formation and the formulation of discourses around 'national security' than is usually assumed for the subaltern citizen.

This chapter is also an ethnographic illustration of the documentary practices of the newly post-colonial state, which belie the coherence of an ideal-typical, Weberian style rational bureaucratic regime. Taking on the observation that archival work often remains 'extractive' rather than 'ethnographic' (Stoler 2002), it looks not just at the content of bureaucratic documents located in archives or government offices but also urges attention to the conditions of their production (Tarlo 2001). Bureaucrats in service of the newly minted nation-state were not necessarily rationalist automatons executing their tasks in favour of a pre-defined nationalist goal. Not only were these goalposts not always very clearly defined but they also exercised their own judgement as the bearers of specific structures of feeling (Stoler 2002: 101–2). Veena Das' (2007) observation that bureaucratic modes of inscription are not only amenable to mimetic reproduction by others but are also malleable in their interpretation by state functionaries becomes crucial for this chapter, as will become evident in subsequent sections. Equally fluid are the subjectivities of those who are charged with the production of bureaucratic orders. By remaining attentive to the production of a bureaucratic discourse around borders, the chapter also contributes to ethnographic studies of the state, bureaucracy and administration where paperwork is a core ethnographic object (A. Gupta 2012; Mathur 2016, Navaro-Yashin 2012, Hull 2012). Rather than examining the effects of bureaucratic paperwork on the people who encounter it or are sought to be constituted through it (for example, Navaro-Yashin 2012), I maintain that paperwork constitutes a dialogic encounter between the state and the citizen. Between the movement of administrative files and secret memoranda within the bureaucracy, and the circulation of petitions submitted by citizens to the state, we get a glimpse into the constitution of the border as a particular kind of jurisdictional space inhabited by both the state and the citizen.

PARTITION AND BUREAUCRACY: MAKING NEW BORDERS

There is an abundance of existing and emergent scholarship on the Partition that discusses how each new border was experienced through various temporalities in different regions. Recent studies have focused on how Partition's borders affected migration, citizenship and refugee status, for instance, in Kashmir (Robinson 2012), Kargil (R. Gupta 2013), Bengal in 1947 (Chatterji 2007) and 1971 (Kabir 2013; Alexander, Chatterji and Jalais 2016) and Sindh (Kothari 2007). Each of them adds new ways of thinking about partitions in South Asia. The emergent relationship between religion, region and state along these distinct but also quite malleable borders was far from stable, challenging not only the notion of a clear-cut territorial or emotional boundary but also of 1947 as 'the' moment of Partition. An important body of work has highlighted the political and bureaucratic machinations that unravel the notion either of a spontaneous 'surge' of people across the border, fuelled by a 'desire' to relocate to the 'right' side or even of a 'surgical' partition of territories and people (Chatterji 1999; Das 1995; Zamindar 2007).

Vazira Zamindar presents a compelling case for the bureaucratic stakes at play during the Partition, and it is well worth recalling her arguments in the context of the CAA and the popular protests against it. In *The Long Partition and the Making of Modern South Asia* (2007), Zamindar writes of how a Hindu 'rehabilitation' in India could only be realised on the heels of a Muslim 'evacuation' to Pakistan. The so-called Muslim exodus from Delhi in the immediate aftermaths of 1947 was not only a flight from a state that was increasingly unwilling to protect Muslims who wanted to stay on in India (see also Kidwai 2011), it was also actively engineered by a bureaucratic discourse that used the relatively subjective evaluation of 'intention to migrate' rather than a 'desire to return' as key determinants of Indian citizenship for Muslims (Zamindar 2007: 84). As early as 1948, a significant tide of Muslim 'evacuees' chose to return to their Indian homes, but the Indian state would not accept them, creating, in effect, the 'introduction of citizenship provisions ahead of the constitution itself' (Zamindar 2007: 79; Jayal 2013: Chapter 2). In contrast to this were those Hindu women whom the Indian state classified as 'abducted' by Muslims and then sought to 'recover' regardless of their own desires (Das 1995). In the east, on the other hand, the movement of refugees in 1947 was not treated with the same finality as it was in Punjab; evacuee property was not taken over by the state, the assumption being that refugees headed eastward might return to take possession of their homes (Chatterji 2007). Similar assumptions configured the refugee regime in the princely state of Jammu and Kashmir where the people displaced were not considered to be 'Partition refugees' at all (Robinson 2012). Moreover, at the first Inter-Dominion Conference held in Calcutta between India and Pakistan in April 1948, it was agreed by both states to take steps necessary to *prevent* a large-scale population exodus along the scale of what had occurred in Punjab (Chatterji 2013). While the Punjab and Bengal Partitions are sometimes contrasted to represent two types of partition experience with regard to state policy and migration patterns, I suggest in this chapter that state policy regarding borders is the result of complex and uneven debates at various levels of administration even within a single borderland. This follows the acknowledgement of bureaucracies as sites of affect and personalisation which are somewhat removed from the Weberian ideal of the so-called bureaucratic rationality. While there is no doubt that bureaucratic documents produce affect among citizens (Navaro-Yashin 2012), they are also written by people who have particular views on the subject matter under discussion. Zamindar (2007: 90–1) draws attention to marginal notes in official files which demonstrate that state policy was often directly influenced by ideas and prejudices of the individuals whose notations appeared on files. Similarly, Chatterji (2013) has demonstrated in her work that when the political elites of India and Pakistan met at the Calcutta Conference of 1948, they cooperated with each other to produce a secular language to deal with the disorder and chaos that had ensued from the Partition. She suggests that even within an overall atmosphere of communal violence, administrators on either side were able to secure peace in terms that were based on a shared class habitus of the governing elite that was concerned more with the containment of 'disorder' from the lower ranks, 'the idea that it was lowly functionaries at the bottom of the food chain who spread the "contagion" of communalism, while their enlightened superiors looked on in horror' (Chatterji 2013: 46). This produced an 'overlapping consensus' (Chatterji 2013: 47) between the two otherwise hostile states over the management of the social mayhem in the wake of Partition. Chatterji suggests that this language eventually permeated the discourse of crime and border management in the west, where there was a corresponding shift in the reporting of cross-border raids and incursions away from terms that were 'unequivocally communal' and 'increasingly as secular crimes against persons and property' (Chatterji 2013: 47–8).

In Kutch, class conflict, rural disaffection and other 'non-communal' motives were attributed to crime and cross-border incursions, but these reports also coexisted with a far more broadly understood communal discourse that attributed to Muslim criminals a more specifically 'anti national' intent. While the latter view was more prevalent among the Kutch police department, senior bureaucrats—especially in their missives to New Delhi—were more likely to read crime and the border question in the more 'secular' categories of law enforcement and maintenance of local public order. The making of a political discourse around borders is therefore a far cry from a homogenous or linear process; key differences in perception between the local and national administration belie notions of a singular discourse on nation and borders. The bureaucracy is itself the site of multiple discursive strands, which contest and compete with one another in the production of official policy. Attention to the *intra-bureaucratic domain* becomes a crucial step in moving away from 'the tendency in academic work to reify state institutions into overtly purposeful, unitary, and motivated actors' (A. Gupta 2012: 187).

Police Reorganisation and Cross-Border Crime in Kutch, 1948–52

In 1948, S. R. Chaudhri, the inspector general of police (Delhi and Ajmer-Merwara), toured Kutch prior to submitting his recommendations on police reorganisation for the region. He was quite categorical in his recommendations, noting that there was no need for the commission of a separate border police force in the region. In his report on the reorganisation of the Kutch Police dated 2 February 1949, he wrote:

> As Kutch touches the boundary of Pakistan, the question of providing police for the border was carefully considered. The physical features of the country are, fortunately, helpful that way. There is a waste land (Ran) to the depth of between forty to sixty miles, all along the border where there is no population or habitation. That is sufficient determent for any raider from Pakistan area to visit any of the villages in Kutch State near the border *for purposes of loot only*. I was also told that the people on both sides of the border are *interrelated and are mostly Muslims*; so there can be *very little communal motive* behind a raid. There have been a few incidents near the border, but they related mostly to *the satisfaction of private grudges* against each other by the men from the other side. There have been no border raids of the type that is the case on the borders of Amritsar, Gurdaspur and Ferozepur districts in the East Punjab. It would not, therefore, be necessary to have a special police force for the purpose of protecting the border only.[3] (Emphases added)

Chaudhri proposed that existing police stations at border outposts were sufficient to tackle smuggling activities through known routes. Muslims on either side of the border were not perceived to be a threat to the Indian nation per se; in this view, cross-border raids from Pakistan could only have a local and not a communal, or even anti-national, motive. In his reckoning, cross-border ties of kinship did not threaten the stability of the nation; in fact, they created a joint local community that was invested in maintaining peace in the neighbourhood because of local, familial ties. Chaudhri's views differed sharply, however, from suggestions on police reorganisation given by the local commissioner of police in Kutch, H. R. Thakkar. Some months earlier, in a letter dated 10 November 1948, Thakkar had written to the chief commissioner who was the highest administrative officer in Kutch,[4] broaching the subject of police reorganisation.[5] Describing his inspection of the Bhuj Police headquarters and City police station, Thakkar expressed deep shock. He wrote that the constables were shabbily turned out; they 'hardly appeared to have any rudimentary knowledge of drill'. Such 'deplorable' conditions were 'never seen or heard of even in the most backward units of Kathiawar or any backward native state'. The predominantly Muslim composition of the force was also a cause for concern. He observed, '[A] majority of the men are illiterate and Muslims' and urged a firm overhaul in the standards of recruitment. 'Kutch,' he added, 'is more vulnerable to Pakistan activities, and therefore a strong, well-trained armed strength and intelligent L.I.B. [Local Intelligence Bureau] are fundamentally needed.' A month later, he wrote again to the chief commissioner underscoring the need for a strong police force, well trained in intelligence gathering, to check 'the ingress into the Province from Pakistan side [sic] or on the suspected smuggling activities'.[6] This letter contained a detailed proposal for the reconstitution of Kutch's police force, touching on almost all aspects of organisation—dress, recruitment, training, housing, salary, mounted constabulary, intelligence and the institution of the village police. Since police stations on the northern border were 'facing Pakistan and were inaccessible during the monsoons', he recommended the installation of a 'wireless transmitting station at each of these police stations'. In contrast to the visiting inspector general of police's assessment, the police commissioner in Kutch was of the firm view that the border required specific attention from the security point of view. He wrote, '[T]he Northern Boundary of Kutch faces Pakistan and intensified police patrolling is essential on this border.' Acknowledging the increased vulnerability of Kutch to 'Pakistan activities', he felt that 'a strong mounted patrol on the border line is all the more necessary for security purposes'.

Based on these firm and unequivocal recommendations, Chief Commissioner C.K. Desai forwarded a scheme for police reorganisation to the Ministry of States (MoS), Government of India (GoI), New Delhi on 11 December 1948. In April of the following year, he had still not received a reply from the MoS, by which time Chaudhri had already circulated his note dismissing the need for special border security. On 15 April 1949, on being prodded yet again by an impatient police commissioner, Chief Commissioner Desai followed up with a gentle reminder to the MoS stating that he was still awaiting a final order on police reorganisation from the ministry.[7] It is worth noting that this letter carried no reference to the undefended frontiers of Kutch, nor to the vulnerabilities of the Kutch frontier to 'Pakistan activity', so deeply underscored in the letters he had received from the police commissioner who had urged him to forward his case to the MoS. In his communication with New Delhi, Desai chose instead to highlight the threat to public order from 'the recent increase in dacoities' that caused nuisance to the 'local public mind'.

Only a couple of days back a serious dacoity[8] [*sic*] took place at the village Dumara where property worth Rs. 70,000 was looted. The *famine conditions* also have led to *discontented people* committing crimes. Most of the *rich Kutchees live in Bombay and have fairly large estates in the villages in Kutch*. Naturally when there are dacoities in the villages, these rich merchants in Bombay get nervous and the accounts of dacoities are published in the newspapers, owned or sponsored by them, in glowing colours. This in turn leads to an amount of insecurity and agitation in the *local public mind*. I therefore consider that it is absolutely necessary that the police reorganization scheme is sanctioned at an early date, as otherwise it is not possible to recruit suitable men in the Police Department. I hope you will give this matter your personal attention, and have the orders issued at an early date.[9] (Emphases added)

In this argument submitted to the MoS in New Delhi, the chief commissioner did not imply that the increase in criminal activity in Kutch had anything to do either with its proximity to the border or to the fact that the perpetrators may have come from Pakistan. On the contrary, he makes a clear and unambiguous connection between famine and economic discontent that led to criminal activity in the countryside. The 'local public mind' is a secular, classed category comprised of the rich and politically influential merchants who are worried about thefts on their 'large estates' and who live in the metropolis. The religion of these miscreants or their provenance is not included in the memorandum. The threat to public order comes from 'discontented people' who are of the lower classes and who threaten the social and economic stability of the mercantile elite, which in Kutch are both Hindu and Muslim. We have no specific information in this communication about the 'suitable men' that the Kutch Police want to recruit urgently even though in another letter addressed to the chief commissioner, the police chief urged his senior officer to remind New Delhi to 'expedite the required sanction without which I experience great difficulty in working out the police administration efficiently'. Here he also sheds more light on 'suitable' recruits:

Since late the well known decoit [*sic*] Silu has again *appeared in Kutch limits* and started his depredations, he committed two robberies one at Khanay and the other at Dumra, and as we are short of hands *with majority of Muslim strength* I get *no reliable officers* and men in reserve to put them after the gang. The *whole frontier of Kutch Province is open* which sometimes require [*sic*] to be guarded efficiently to prevent such criminals coming in.[10] (Emphases added)

It is clear that the police commissioner's reading of crime in Kutch is not couched in the relatively secular terms of class and rural discontent that his superior officer chose to underline when he wrote to the MoS. Thakkar assumes that the known criminal Silu has 'appeared in Kutch limits' from the outside, presumably from across a frontier that needs to be efficiently policed. Unlike his earlier letters, Pakistan is not mentioned directly, but he does comment on the communal composition of the police force. Muslims within the force do not make for reliable police, as indicated in this letter. It would appear then that such criminals were best fought off by non-Muslims, either because the criminals were Muslim or because they came from Pakistan, which amounted to much the same thing. The 'local public mind' in this rendition seems to exclude the Muslim (for example, Zamindar 2007) unlike the letter written by Desai to the MoS, which argued in favour of its class-based exclusivity.

Muslims in Kutch were presumed locally to be less reliable in securing the border, therefore of limited use in the police forces. This certainty is absent—or at least not the basis of argument—in the higher administrative echelons of the chief commissioner and the inspector general of police from Delhi who chose not to read cross-border criminality in terms that were anything other than locally driven, that is, for economic gain, and even when from Pakistan, driven by a desire for 'loot' rather than communal or anti-national intent. By 1952, the new Chief Commissioner S. A. Ghatge accounted for criminality and cross-border activity in terms that were not that far off the mark from his predecessors' descriptions to the extent of accounting for theft of village property, except that Pakistan (instead of the Muslim) is now much more clearly identified as the instigator of these raids against persons and property in Kutch. On the subject of 'dacoities in Kutch', Ghatge wrote to a joint secretary in the MoS, New Delhi, on 7 December 1952:

> The month of November 1952 was in a way very depressing for the State of Kutch. In this month two serious dacoities took place, having been committed by *Pakistani Kutchis* taking shelter in the southern part of Sind. The first dacoity took place in a village which may be regarded as a bordering one but the second one was much in the interior. The first dacoity took place on the 1st Nov 1952 at 6:30 pm at a village called Ratadia in the Lakhpat taluka. Four dacoits *dressed like Sindhis and talking Kutchi and Sindhi*—all between 25 to 30 years of age—entered Kutch through the Rann. Three of them had guns and one had a stick and an axe. They belaboured some of the Kanbis of the place, fired gun shots in the air, entered houses and looted property valued at Rs. 3,750. They took away a camel also from the village. They left

the same evening back for Pakistan through the Rann ... The next dacoity took place on the 17th November at about 5:30 pm at a village called Tumbdi in the Mundra taluka. Here too the dacoits numbering 7 entered the village, fired gun shots and took away property reported to be worth about Rs. 25,000. The dacoits also took away ornaments of an idol in a Jain temple. Here the dacoity was indeed very bold, since Tumbdi is in the southern side of Kutch. As the facts have been ascertained now, five dacoits came from Pakistan. Two joined them from Kutch.[11] (Emphases added)

If a 'secularisation' of the discourse of peacemaking in the immediate aftermath of the Partition meant that crimes were less often attributed to members of religious communities and more to their citizenship, for example, a religiously neutral 'Pakistani' intruder rather than a specifically 'Muslim' one (Chatterji 2013: 48), it is also true that the signifier 'Pakistani' increasingly implied the 'Muslim', even one who was Indian. Zamindar (2007) describes how an entire network of passes, permits and passports were devised to control the identity and mobility of people in the aftermaths of the Partition. At times, Muslims were deemed to be 'Pakistani' even if they had not moved out of India, in application of the rather vaguely defined 'intention to migrate' clause. In the letter cited above, Chief Commissioner Ghatge identified the criminals as 'Pakistani Kutchis', a remarkable phrase which manages to convey the impression of their being Muslim without quite saying so in 'communal' terms.[12] Finally, while this letter implies an association between criminality and Pakistan and/or Muslims, it also indicates crime with local economic intent. Criminals from across the border had accomplices in Kutch, their activities oriented towards loot alone. According to Ghatge, it became clear that the upshot of these two audacious raids was that 'the Pakistan government has been harbouring dacoits wanted by Kutch' who are also 'able to get arms and ammunition in Pakistan' and 'are even able to move out openly in Pakistan and are not arrested there in spite of the fact that intimation about such dacoits is communicated to the Police officers in Pakistan'. Implying some complicity in Kutch, he admitted, 'I feel that some persons in our bordering villages do come to know about their movements but our Police Department has failed to create that trust and confidence in them required for securing timely information'.[13]

While Ghatge, like his predecessor, treated these crimes as disruptions to public life and property, receiving applications from Jains in Bombay, Kutch and other places urging him to take action against the temple looters, he was also burdened with the prospect of how to secure the border with Pakistan, to prevent future recurrence of such crimes. Pakistan was identified as the instigator of criminal activity against villages in Kutch, even those that lay some distance away from the border, compounding their audacity, according to Ghatge. Unlike previous occasions when such crimes were read purely as a result of social and economic discontent *within* Kutch, Ghatge was aware of the fact that security on the borders of Kutch also meant building confidence among Muslims that lived on the border.

In the next section, I show that even as the dominant bureaucratic discourse of the time, couched in the 'secularised' language of economic crime, loot and 'dacoity', prevented Ghatge from referring to the perpetrators of crime using communal categories, Muslim residents of the border had no such compunctions and used their religious identity as 'Muslims' (homogenising a vast set of differences between the various Muslim groups that live along the Sindh border in Kutch) when addressing the state. Even as the state was engaged in writing about the border, its residents also chose to engage with the state using the same medium. While the state's overt bureaucratic memos display restraint in communal matters, its citizens take a far more pragmatic and direct view of the matter. It is around this time that it is possible to identify a gradual shift in the official perception of border-dwelling Muslims as potentially 'anti-national' elements, with the putative interests of the nation becoming more closely aligned with the Hindu majority, even among the more elite bureaucratic class. How closely are borderland Muslims aligned to the nation is now open to debate, the question of belonging no longer tied to the immediate locality, that is, of the Kutch–Sindh borderlands. However, the administrative discussions around this are still tentative and only conducted through the marginalia of secret memos and communiqués in the corridors of power in New Delhi, as the following section reveals.

NATIONALISM AND CITIZENSHIP ON THE BORDER: VOICES FROM THE 'MARGINS'

Even as letters and memoranda on the question of border security flew back and forth between Bhuj and New Delhi without generating any broad consensus on the subject, citizens on the border had their own interests in the matter. Tucked away inside some of these bureaucratic missives is evidence of Muslims living on the border, who tackled the question of identity, citizenship and security quite directly, leading to further debate in the administration. In 1951, a group of Muslims from the border areas of Banni and Khawda presented Chief Commissioner Ghatge with a resolution.[14] Writing to the MoS in New Delhi, he reported that while on a tour of these regions, he met with some leading Muslims of the area who formally gave him a resolution they had passed, written in the Gujarati script.[15] Referring to 'false propaganda … carried on by and in Pakistan' regarding the harassment of Muslims in India, this delegation wished to go on record to state that their 'sentiments are hurt by such propaganda as it is false'. This was followed by a firm declaration of loyalty, 'We declare that we are loyal to the Government of India, and if *Pakistan government attacks the Indian government* [*sic*] we will sacrifice our lives for the security of India, as did our forefathers in the past' (emphasis added).

The declaration begins, interestingly, with the statement, 'We, the Muslims of Banni and Khawda, the northern part of Kutch resolve as under.' The northern border of Kutch is populated by Muslims, primarily pastoralists of various subgroups and denominations, but also by other communities, locally referred to as Harijans and Adivasis. The latter two groups were well outside the Hindu fold, at least until relatively recent attempts were made to 'Hinduise' them. For the most part, these border communities have shared cultural traits such as dress, marriage practices, consumption of meat and mortuary practices that render it difficult to distinguish Harijans and Adivasis from their Muslim neighbours. The declaration purports to represent a collective 'Muslim' sentiment rather than a representation of borderland residents alone. Already by 1951 then, there appears to be a semblance of the suspicion that would begin to accrue more firmly to Muslims on the Indian side of the border after the armed conflicts with Pakistan. There is no doubt about the fact that this is a staunchly political deputation. The other noteworthy point about the declaration is its language which we have access to only in translation, presumably by the chief commissioner's office in Bhuj. In this translation, the Muslim delegation underscores its loyalty to the state as 'government'. If *Pakistan* were to attack *India* (note, not an attack on Kutch from across the border as the letter-writing bureaucrats tended to affirm), they assert that they are willing to lay down their lives for the nation, as they have always done 'in the past'.[16] This memorandum is couched within the terms of national security that we are more familiar with in the context of contemporary international relations; whether this is more accurately a reflection of the concerns of its authors or translators, it is difficult to say. This is likely a concern of the Muslims on the border too, for we hear from Ghatge's letter to the MoS that the Khawda delegation 'which consisted of more experienced people'[17] handed him three copies of this note with the request that one copy each be forwarded to the prime ministers of India and Pakistan respectively, and that one be retained by him. Even as senior officials were debating the contours of border security and the need for maintenance of public order, border-dwelling Muslims seem to have had a far more prescient understanding of 'the security of India', the institutional apparatus and parameters within which it was maintained, and how they would need to position themselves within it. While there are certainly valid questions to be posed regarding how widely representative this 'declaration of loyalty' was, the language it espoused was unequivocal about what it meant to be living along this border and an equally clear understanding of the need to perform loyalty to the nation using the universalist terms of state and nation rather than their immediate identity as borderland Muslims.[18]

Ghatge's correspondence with the ministry consequent to this declaration is also noteworthy, indicating the lack of a clear and well-defined policy on the social contours of border management at this stage. In the same letter where he reports on this memorandum of loyalty, Ghatge oscillates between dismissing it outright even as he hints at it being a disingenuous ploy by Muslims to divert attention from what he felt were their possibly illegal activities. On the one hand, he argued that such a declaration was superfluous, there being no cause to cast doubt upon certified citizens of the country: '[T]his is their home and they have a right to live [sic]. No such fresh allegiance is required.' This indicates that their presence in India (as opposed to their flight to Pakistan) constitutes their allegiance. He continues, 'I cannot see why it should be sent to the Prime Minister of Pakistan, out of all. As I look at it, we are not going to prove to Pakistan that we have been treating our people well. They owe nothing to Pakistan. The idea itself is mischievous.' On the other hand, he also implies that the declaration has 'no meaning', merely being 'the work of some ingenious brain following the usual façade of shouting one's loyalty'. He concluded, 'I would not believe a word of it. What I will be looking to will be their conduct.' As a consequence of the mixed conclusions drawn by him—secular nationalist in overt principle but unwilling to rule out surveillance on border-dwelling Muslims either—Ghatge concludes that he does not believe any action is needed and if the Government of India were to agree, he should 'kindly be informed so that I will tell the people so in my own way'.[19]

The response to Ghatge's letter arrived in the form of a secret memo issued by the MoS[20] indicating that there was nothing remarkable or objectionable about Muslims 're-affirming loyalty to the Government of India'. Stating that 'similar resolutions have been passed elsewhere in India', the memo suggested that the chief commissioner was 'free not to attach much importance to the resolution and to keep any suspicious persons under watch for *anti-national* activities' (emphasis added). It also expressed no discomfort with allowing the group to directly forward a copy of their resolution to the prime ministers of the two countries, if they so desired. It is in the marginal handwritten notes on this memo, made by three officials of the ministry in advancing order of seniority that we get a sense of the range of opinions between them. While the undersecretary advocated complete agreement with the chief commissioner, the joint secretary's note indicated that he should tell the delegation that their resolution has been forwarded to the Government of India but also that 'he must of course watch the behaviour of all sections'. The secretary on the other hand notes, 'I think the CC [chief commissioner] is unnecessarily suspicious in this case. The Muslims have tried to help us in counteracting Pak [*sic*] propaganda and for this they have to be commended rather than censured.'

In his classic study of the French borderlands in the eighteenth and nineteenth centuries, Peter Sahlins (1988) noted that discourses of nationality were often enunciated with greater clarity on the margins than at the political centres of state authority. Arguing against the view that borderlands had to be enfolded into a nationalist discourse that flowed outward from the centre, he suggested not only that ideas of the nation coexist with a local sense of identity but also that in some cases 'the nation appeared on the periphery before it was built by the center' (Sahlins 1988: 237). He also provided evidence of how local communities in the borderlands of France and Spain petitioned their states about village disputes in the eighteenth and nineteenth centuries, increasingly using the emergent language of the nation. As the 'memorandum of loyalty' passed by Muslims of Banni and Khawda reveals, residents of these border villages were all too conscious of their precarious position between two rival states. Their choice of language and format of engagement with the state—through a written resolution—mimics the state's own documentary practices even as it pushes the state to clarify its own stand on the matter which as we can see was far from univocal.

CONCLUSION

Intra-bureaucratic debates on police reorganisation in Kutch between 1948 and 1952 enable two important insights: First, that what we deem as contemporary concerns around border security, which are posited in the universalist terms of the nation and national security, were enabled through moments of non-linear negotiation with the far less abstract categories of village, locality and region, and second, that bureaucratic letter-writing reveals a number of ways in which the so-called unitary discourse of the state, even on sensitive issues such as national security, are filled with internal debates, inconsistencies and assumptions that are far from agreed upon. This chapter has argued that in the early discussions on police reorganisation there were two views on the subject of borderland Muslims. In one view, the fact that people on either side of the border were related to one another ruled out cross-border criminality directed at the 'nation' at large, remaining confined to the level of family disputes or personal grudges. The border in this sense was an acknowledgement of separate jurisdictions but did not yet bear the stamp of an overtly nationalist rhetoric. At the same time, however, the police department in Bhuj took a far more communally driven view of police reorganisation. This chapter has attempted to trace the early emergence of a discourse around borders and border Muslims in Kutch to argue that in the borderlands of Kutch and Sindh, an understanding of the border in abstract terms of religion or nation was not pre-given in the moment of the Partition but was the product of administrative debate and arrived at over a period of time. Furthermore, residents of the border had key stakes in this debate in which they were active participants rather than mere bystanders.

NOTES

1. Out of 104 file requisition slips pertaining to this period submitted to the National Archives of India (NAI) in New Delhi during spells of research in 2003 and 2004, the number returned with the following notations were 48 'NT' (Not Transferred), 6 'Closed', 3 'Secret', 6 'Under Search' and 3 'Sent for Microfilming'. On the production of 'sensitivity' on a borderland, see, for example, Cons (2016: 34–6).

2. Afghanistan is not, strictly speaking, a country with which India shares a land border. By including it and excluding, for example, Nepal, the Act makes it clear that it is referring to migration from what it deems as 'Muslim majority nations', even though this is not stated explicitly.

3. Report of I. G. Police (Delhi and Ajmer-Merwara) on the Reorganisation of Kutch Police, National Archives of India (NAI)/Ministry of States (MoS)/31 (15)—E, 1948.

4. Kutch State was administered by the central government through a chief commissioner during the period 1948 to 1956 when it was merged into the bilingual Bombay Province. In 1960, it became the largest district in the newly constituted state of Gujarat.

5. Commissioner of Police (CP) H. R. Thakkar to Chief Commissioner (CC), Kutch, dated 10 November 1948, NAI/MoS/31(15)—E, 1948.

6. CP to CC, Kutch, dated 3 December 1948, NAI/MoS/31(15)—E, 1948.

7. CC, Kutch to Joint Secretary (JS), MoS, dated 15 April 1949, NAI/MoS/31(15)—E, 1948.

8. Crime, from the Hindi term *dakaiti* with perpetrators referred to as *daku* (dacoit).

9. CC, Kutch to JS, MoS, dated 15 April 1949, NAI/MoS/31(15)—E, 1948.

10. CP to CC, Kutch, dated 16 April 1949, NAI/MoS/31(15)—E, 1948.

11. CC, Kutch to JS, MoS, dated 7 December 1952, NAI/MoS/22(157)—PA/52, 1952.

12. Kutch and Sindh have always been entirely distinct regions and the former has never been a part of Pakistan.

13. CC, Kutch to JS, MoS, dated 7 December 1952, NAI/MoS/22(157)—PA/52, 1952.

14. NAI/MoS/19(12)—PA/51, 1951.

15. CC, Kutch to MoS, dated 25 September 1951, NAI/MoS/19(12)—PA/51, 1951.

16. Interestingly, this theme has been reiterated in late 2019 and 2020 with the massive nationwide protests against the CAA. Muslim students and women—at the forefront of the over three-months long sit-in in New Delhi's Shaheen Bagh neighbourhood—emphasise that they have always stood by the Indian constitution and their forefathers have laid their lives down for the nation and they do not appreciate their loyalty being suspect now.

17. CC, Kutch to MoS, dated 25 September 1951, NAI/MoS/19(12)—PA/51, 1951.

18. When asked by a reporter why they did not protest when Muslims were being lynched in a series of incidents across the country, a Muslim woman responded by saying that if they protested when fellow Muslims were being attacked, their protests would be dismissed as being in the name of 'religion' alone. Instead, she emphasised, they were out on the streets now because they felt India's constitutional values and its secular principles were under attack. See https://www.youtube.com/watch?v=TQm7nBa49WQ, accessed on 23 January 2020.

19. CC, Kutch to MoS, dated 25 September 1951, NAI/MoS/19(12)—PA/51, 1951.

20. No. 4979—PA/51, dated 5 October 1951, NAI/MoS/19(12)—PA/51, 1951.

REFERENCES

Alexander, Claire, Joya Chatterji and Annu Jalais. 2016. *The Bengal Diaspora: Rethinking Muslim Migration.* London and New York: Routledge.

Bhan, Mona. 2008. 'Border Practices: Labour and Nationalism among Brogpas of Ladakh'. *Contemporary South Asia* 16 (2): 139–57.

Chatterji, Joya. 1999. 'The Fashioning of a Frontier: The Radcliffe Line and Bengal's Border Landscape, 1947–52'. *Modern Asian Studies* 33 (1): 185–242.

———. 2007. *The Spoils of Partition: Bengal and India, 1947–1967*. Cambridge: Cambridge University Press.

———. 2013. 'Secularisation and Partition Emergencies: Deep Diplomacy in South Asia'. *Economic and Political Weekly* 58 (50): 42–50.

Cons, Jason. 2016. *Sensitive Space: Fragmented Territory at the India-Bangladesh Border*. Seattle: University of Washington Press.

Das, Veena. 1995. 'National Honour and Practical Kinship: Of Unwanted Women and Children'. In *Critical Events*, edited by Veena Das, 55–83. Delhi: Oxford University Press.

———. 2007. 'The Signature of the State: The Paradox of Illegibility'. In *Life and Words: Violence and the Descent into the Ordinary*, edited by Veena Das, 162–83. New Delhi: Oxford University Press.

Das, Veena, and Deborah Poole. 2004. *Anthropology in the Margins of the State*. New Delhi: Oxford University Press.

Ferguson, James, and Akhil Gupta. 2002. 'Spatializing States: Toward an Ethnography of Neoliberal Governmentality'. *American Ethnologist* 29 (4): 981–1002.

Gupta, Akhil. 2012. *Red Tape: Bureaucracy, Structural Violence, and Poverty in India*. New Delhi: Permanent Black.

Gupta, Radhika. 2013. 'Allegiance and Alienation: Border Dynamics in Kargil'. In *Borderland Lives in Northern South Asia*, edited by David Gellner, 47–71. Durham: Duke University Press.

Handler, Richard. 1988. *Nationalism and the Politics of Culture in Quebec*. Madison: University of Wisconsin Press.

Hull, Matthew S. 2012. *Government of Paper: The Materiality of Bureaucracy in Urban Pakistan*. Berkeley: University of California Press.

Ibrahim, Farhana. 2009. *Settlers, Saints, and Sovereigns: An Ethnography of State Formation in Western India*. New Delhi: Routledge.

——— . 2018. 'Cross-Border Intimacies: Marriage, Migration and Citizenship in Western India'. *Modern Asian Studies* 52 (5): 1664–91.

Jayal, Niraja Gopal. 2013. *Citizenship and Its Discontents*. New Delhi: Permanent Black.

Kabir, Ananya Jahanara. 2013. *Partition's Post-Amnesias: 1947, 1971 and Modern South Asia*. New Delhi: Women Unlimited.

Kidwai, Anis. 2011. *In Freedom's Shade*. Translated by Ayesha Kidwai. New Delhi: Penguin.

Kothari, Rita. 2007. *The Burden of Refuge: The Sindhi Hindus of Gujarat*. Hyderabad: Orient Longman.

Mathur, Nayanika. 2016. *Paper Tiger: Law, Bureaucracy and the Developmental State in Himalayan India*. New Delhi: Cambridge University Press.

Reeves, Madeleine. 2014. *Border Work: Spatial Lives of the State in Rural Central Asia*. Ithaca: Cornell University Press.

Tarlo, Emma. 2001. 'Paper Truths: The Emergency and Slum Clearance through Forgotten Files'. In *The Everyday State and Society in Modern India*, edited by Chris Fuller and Veronique Benei, 68–90. London: Hurst and Company.

Trouillot, Michel Rolph. 2001. 'The Anthropology of the State in the Age of Globalization: Close Encounters of the Deceptive Kind'. *Current Anthropology* 42 (1): 125–38.

Munasinghe, Viranjini. 2002. 'Nationalism in Hybrid Spaces: The Production of Impurity Out of Purity'. *American Ethnologist* 29 (3): 663–92.

Navaro-Yashin, Yael. 2012. *The Make-Believe Space: Affective Geography in a Postwar Polity*. Durham: Duke University Press.

Robinson, Cabeiri de Bergh. 2012. 'Too Much Nationality: Kashmiri Refugees, the South Asian Refugee Regime, and a Refugee State, 1947–1974'. *Journal of Refugee Studies* 25 (3): 344–65.

Sahlins, Peter. 1988. 'The Nation in the Village: State-Building and Communal Struggles in the Catalan Borderland during the Eighteenth and Nineteenth Centuries'. *The Journal of Modern History* 60 (2): 234–63.

Stoler, Ann Laura. 2002. 'Colonial Archives and the Arts of Governance'. *Archival Science* 2 (1–2): 87–109.

van Schendel, Willem. 2004. *The Bengal Borderland: Beyond State and Nation in South Asia*. London: Anthem Press.

Verdery, Katherine. 1991. *National Ideology under Socialism: Identity and Cultural Politics in Ceausescu's Romania*. Berkeley: University of California Press.

Williams, Brackette. 1989. 'A Class Act: Anthropology and the Race to Nation across Ethnic Terrain'. *Annual Review of Anthropology* 18: 401–44.

Zamindar, Vazira Yacoobali. 2007. *The Long Partition and the Making of Modern South Asia: Refugees, Boundaries, Histories*. New York: Columbia University Press.

10

Frontier as Resource

Law, Crime and Sovereignty on the Margins of Empire*

ERIC LEWIS BEVERLEY

In March 1887, the Ahmednagar District Superintendent of Police, R. H. Vincent, requested sanction to offer a special reward to capture a bandit, 'the notorious Bhil dacoit Daji walad Malhari', who was wreaking havoc in his district. Daji had escaped from police in his native Hyderabad State the previous May after being extradited from the British-ruled Bombay Presidency. He had already absconded from the Nizam's or the British Raj's police thrice previously. According to the commissioner of the Criminal Department, Daji's activities threatened to undo colonial progress in remaking agrarian society in the frontier district:

> The outlaw had actually recommenced his depredations in the [Ahmed] Nagar District. The Bhils on the British frontier, as he lately found have fairly settled down as labourers and cultivators, but the presence of a reckless leader will soon unsettle them, and Government may have endless trouble in the monsoon if the man is not caught speedily by the offer of a substantial reward.[1]

Dacoit activity was constructed as a direct affront to British colonial policies of peasantisation and sedentarisation. As such, Bombay sought to induce Hyderabad to imprison figures such as Daji, a subject of the Nizam over whom the Raj had no jurisdiction. Daji, to whom we shall return, continued for the next several years to dog the colonial police with his border-hopping antics. His case underscores the indeterminate character of colonial legal sovereignty in frontier regions and the fragmented nature of sovereignty in an imperial era.

***

The liminal spaces of modern empires were many. They represented major challenges to officials and provided invaluable resources for people subjected to imperialism. The turn of the nineteenth century is often associated with the culmination of imperial consolidation in Asia and Africa but, in fact, empires remained heterogeneous entities unsettled by contested external frontiers and subordinated by sovereign polities within their domains. The fragmenting of sovereignty and the proliferation of jurisdictions produced possibilities for marginal people across imperial space.[2] Extraterritorial judicial initiatives of colonial empires were limited by subordinated states' attempts to safeguard their legal sovereignty. The legal history of the frontier between sub-imperial Hyderabad and British Bombay Presidency illuminates the productivity of fissures within imperial space during the height of European global political dominance. The productivity of the frontier depended on the incompleteness of the states' control over space. Contestations over jurisdiction between the Nizam of Hyderabad and the British Raj, and the Nizam's assertion of legal sovereignty over his subjects, rendered the frontier zone a critical social and political resource for officials of both the Raj and the Nizam and, crucially, for populations in the frontier zone. People in the region availed themselves of the possibilities produced by the proximity of borders to pursue livelihoods despite imperial pressure. Although I draw examples primarily from the last two decades of the nineteenth century, a period characterised by extensive extraterritorial colonial policing, the historical scope of these developments was considerably longer. Jurisdictional tensions between British India, Hyderabad and other imperial territories or sub-imperial states spanned the nineteenth century and continued well into the twentieth.[3]

The formulation 'frontier zone' serves as both an empirical description and an analytical concept that indicates the ambivalent and productive character of particular spaces. Empirically, frontier means a borderline separating two countries (Hyderabad and British India).[4] It also signifies a limitation or edge, marking what is beyond the purview of the dominant (in this case, colonial) state, and this second meaning is often connected to the frontier as a source of creativity and power (Turner 1920 [1894]: 1–38). In prominent historical accounts of places from North America to eastern Asia, however, the productivity of frontier zones disappears by a particular time, owing to successful political consolidation and other factors.[5]

Against prevailing models that emphasise closure of frontiers, I contend that the Hyderabad–Bombay frontier both remained open and retained its productive capacity well into the twentieth century, and indeed, the frontier zone's differential character endured throughout the high colonial period and beyond. While it had some characteristics of areas which scholars have described and theorised as 'borderlands', such as enabling negotiations and framing cross-border mobility, the frontier zone was not centred on an impregnable border.[6] In normative legal and institutional terms, the frontier represented a clearly demarcated edge rather than a space of fluidity, but in social and political practice the proximity of multiple, often conflicting, judicial authorities made the frontier a 'zone': a particular space differentiated from nearby areas in terms of the rules that applied or were suspended there. The Hyderabad–Bombay frontier resembles the 'zones of anomaly' that K. Sivaramakrishnan described as 'blank spots in the cultivated vistas of British sovereignty' (Sivaramakrashnan 1999: 38). In the context examined here, and in many other places in a world where expansive imperial geographic visions masked configurations of fragmented sovereignty, jurisdictional complexity made the frontier zone a vital resource for marginal people. Key here were sovereign states, and peoples' ability to play them against one another; in other words, the frontier zone was neither a 'zomia' outside state authority nor a patch of 'lumpiness' hierarchically integrated within a dominant, unitary colonial state sovereignty.[7]

Shifting legal arrangements between Nizam and Raj shaped the social and political world of the frontier. This empirical setting provides a lens through which we can examine meanings of sovereignty in colonial South Asia, not only for competing states but also, crucially, for people living on the frontier. I begin by sketching the complicated relationship between the two governments over policing and legal jurisdictions. I develop the picture by examining cases involving people who used the frontier as a resource to pursue livelihoods. Finally, engaging with scholarship on the question of 'social banditry', I reflect on the implications of lawlessness for states and subjects along the frontier. Existing scholarship on the relationship between legal consolidation and the making of modern states on the global scale is useful for framing some of these concerns.

CRIME, LAW AND STATE SOVEREIGNTY

In a comparative history of law in the colonial world, Lauren Benton described a global trajectory in which consolidating empires levelled early modern legal flexibility over the nineteenth century, and 'formally plural legal orders were transformed into state-dominated legal orders' (Benton 2002: 209).[8] At the core of Benton's argument is the notion—cast as irony—that colonised individuals seeking to advance their own agendas in court contributed to the liquidation of legal pluralism and imperial consolidation. In a key example, litigants at East India Company courts in early colonial Bengal 'helped to create a space for the colonial state'. Reifying the notion of colonisers' 'special relationship to truth' by participating in these forums, subjects unwittingly precipitated colonial legal hegemony, culminating in increasingly aggressive British claims to paramountcy during the nineteenth century (Benton 2002: 129, 131).

For Benton, the ascent of state-ordered legal regimes elaborates the meteoric rise of consolidated sovereignty during the long nineteenth century. What was visible in late eighteenth-century British India was manifest in Africa, Australia and the Americas by the twentieth. In late nineteenth-century Uruguay, she argues, Brazilian and imperial European claims to extraterritorial jurisdiction gave rise to the formalisation and aggressive assertion of state law over alternative forums. 'Constructing sovereignty' and asserting control over national territory, as in colonial settings, meant establishing and upholding state law against other authorities: 'The challenge to the state was not so much repressing "lawlessness" as controlling "other" law—the legal authority of caudillos [local strongmen], other states' claims to extraterritoriality, and litigants' recourse to legal strategies that placed them outside state control' (Benton 2002: 210, 216).

Benton's history describes similar processes constitutive of imperial consolidation and nation-state development. In both cases the state, viewed through the lens of the legal institution, became the sole sovereign entity in any given place. The victory of the centralised state with its consolidated and hierarchical legal order meant the loss of multiple forums that subjects could employ. As this chapter will show, Benton's tidy trajectory, in which legal regimes are consolidated worldwide by 1900, is questionable if the scenario is viewed from any of a number of frontier cases, such as the one considered here. One of her central methodological insights, however, is useful in pushing further the analysis here.

The relationship between sovereignty and law in imperial contexts, as Benton points out, is often clearest when viewed in terms of the experience of subordinated people: 'This process [transformation of "formally plural" into "state-dominated" legal orders] involved everywhere an extended historical moment in which the question of the legal standing of the most marginal people in the colonial order became symbolically central to the developing legal culture and the broader realignment of the political order' (Benton 2002: 209). Corresponding to this dynamic, the regulation of marginal populations was a primary concern of the Raj throughout the nineteenth century. Colonial officials suggested that endemic banditry had a deleterious effect on settled peasants, and in doing so, they presumed a fundamental difference between criminals and an ostensibly normative, law-abiding peasantry. This presumed relationship was invoked to justify cross-border policing in Hyderabad and other non-colonised regions of the subcontinent from the early part of the century. Bombay Presidency and Hyderabad State archives bear ample evidence of colonial attempts to encourage co-operation. In spite of, and partly due to, the multiplication of legal authorities in the area, resourceful subjects managed to manipulate the legal scenario on both sides of the Hyderabad–Bombay frontier.

The political context of the frontier zone was a product of the complex historical process of early modern state building in South Asia and the steady but geographically uneven expansion of the British colonial state circa 1750–1850. Starting in the early eighteenth century with the political dissolution of the centralising Mughal Empire, the subcontinent began an era of decentralisation in which smaller, regional states proliferated. Wide-ranging social ties were central to the articulation of political authority (Dirks 1993 [1987]; Peabody 2003). Establishing the loyalty and security of subject populations, wielding authority over agrarian and commercial revenues, and patronage of specific sites of symbolic power and material accumulation were all constitutive elements of state building and governance. These characteristics of South Asian state practice made borders between states fluid. The spread of British power entailed a distinctly territorialised geography of sovereignty, as reflected in the centrality of surveying and mapping projects to colonial governance (Edney 1997). British Raj officials demarcated precise boundaries around their territories and sought to pacify fluid frontier zones.

Colonial political consolidation was undermined by the recognition, and post-1857 reaffirmation, of sub-imperial states such as Hyderabad as formal sovereign entities. Distinctions between conceptions of political sovereignty in South Asia were dramatised by the means and limits of colonial political expansion. The broader, subcontinental (and empire-wide) condition of fragmented sovereignty during the colonial period provided the stage for a productive engagement between a British project and conception of territorialised sovereignty and other notions of state practice.[9] The cases I present later from Hyderabad are suggestive of this encounter. Decentralised and patrimonial features of Hyderabad governance—official intransigence with respect to colonial frontier policy, the enduring political importance of bonds of personal loyalty, insistence on the responsibility of the state to safeguard the livelihoods of the subject population—frame and underscore the story below of frontier-dwellers' use of the resources of the frontier zone.

POLICING IMPERIAL BORDERS

Colonial officials employed ideas of civilisational hierarchy to justify extra-legal cross-border interventions. The Raj, functioning largely by coercion in directly ruled areas, was circumscribed by the formal sovereignty of sub-imperial states. In this context, Hyderabad officials presented themselves as responsive to the same concerns as a colonial state increasingly vigilant about maintaining 'law and order'. An early twentieth-century Urdu narrative celebrated the advanced character of the Nizam's police force:

> The treasurer of Mysore [a large sub-imperial state near Hyderabad], Sev Rāo ... committed a great embezzlement and hastily fled ... but for a great while he evaded capture. Since this man had great riches and was under the protection of influential people, his capture was widely considered impossible. However, it was completely impossible to evade ... Nawāb Akbar Jang Bahādur [the *kotwāl*, or police chief, of Hyderabad].... One day in 1886 after Sev Rao took on a new disguise, he was captured ... [Prime Minister] Sālār Jang pronounced a *farmān* [declaration]: 'For the part he played in the detection, capture and pacification of the famous dacoit, I am honoring Nawab Akbar Jang with this sword and seals of honor, given as a reward by my own hand.' The sovereign's reassurance planted seeds of courage and manliness in Akbar Jang Bahādur's heart. He ... brought the importance of the office of the *kotwal* and responsibility to its precepts onto par with British India. Akbar Jang Bahadur's courage and reassurance grew owing to the sovereign's esteem of his work and heartfelt liberality.[10]

This section from a Hyderabad police chief's biography emphasises the great prestige to be gained by assisting the British Raj in combating dacoity. As the text put it, such work by officials put Hyderabad 'onto par with British India' in terms of policing.[11] It is somewhat incongruous, however, that the treasurer of nearby Mysore would be referred to as a dacoit. Indeed, colonial officials invoked the designation 'dacoit', like 'thug', an earlier term for alleged hereditary criminals, to describe putatively lawless, economically marginal mobile groups (Beverley 2015: Chapter 5). Moreover, the celebration of Nawab Akbar Jang Bahadur's capture of 'a famous dacoit' belied the fact that dacoity policing was a major bone of contention between the Raj and the Nizam around the turn of the twentieth century. Nevertheless, this incident was situated alongside accounts of the late *kotwal*'s life of accomplishments in Hyderabad and overseas.[12] Contributions to law and order on behalf of the Nizam and the empire were interwoven in the policeman's biography, implying that the methods and goals of both polities were broadly in confluence. However, extant evidence contradicts this portrayal of extraterritorial policing, and reveals instead much friction between the state apparatuses of Hyderabad and British India.

Frontier political relations were characterised by moments of limited collaboration amidst protracted Nizam–Raj disagreements. The legal scene was fragmented and pluralist around the frontier, splintered between different forums within Hyderabad, and between the Nizam's and the Raj's territory. This legal indeterminacy was in large part engendered by Hyderabad's strategic 'failure' to consolidate state sovereignty, often through the tactic of interminable delays in following up on Raj requests. While the ambivalence of the frontier zone was also a resource for the Nizam's officials at the central and local levels, the fragmentary character of the Nizam's disciplinary institutions served to justify colonial cross-border interventions. Beneath the story of states and their claims to sovereignty, frontier conditions served as a vital political and social resource for people who ran afoul of the colonial legal regime, such as 'hereditary criminals', fugitives, sex workers, bootleggers and carrying traders. Their lives were bound up with contestations between the two governments and ongoing institutional unevenness. A tangled configuration of fragmented sovereignties framed the frontier, but states and their policies did not completely circumscribe developments there.

'VERY DIFFICULT TO OBTAIN ANY CLUE': THE LIMITS OF COLLABORATION

Exchanges between Bombay and Hyderabad testify to colonial expectations of collaboration in frontier policing. The Raj often found Hyderabad a reluctant partner in this endeavour, and the initiative for policing the frontier zone came largely from Bombay, whose police captured Hyderabad subjects under suspicion and provided Hyderabad with information on fugitives in Bombay. The Nizam's officials tended to respond only after long delays, and they rarely pursued colonial initiatives and requests, citing alleged lack of evidence or problems identifying fugitives. Frequently, suspects apprehended by Bombay and extradited to Hyderabad were released upon arrival.

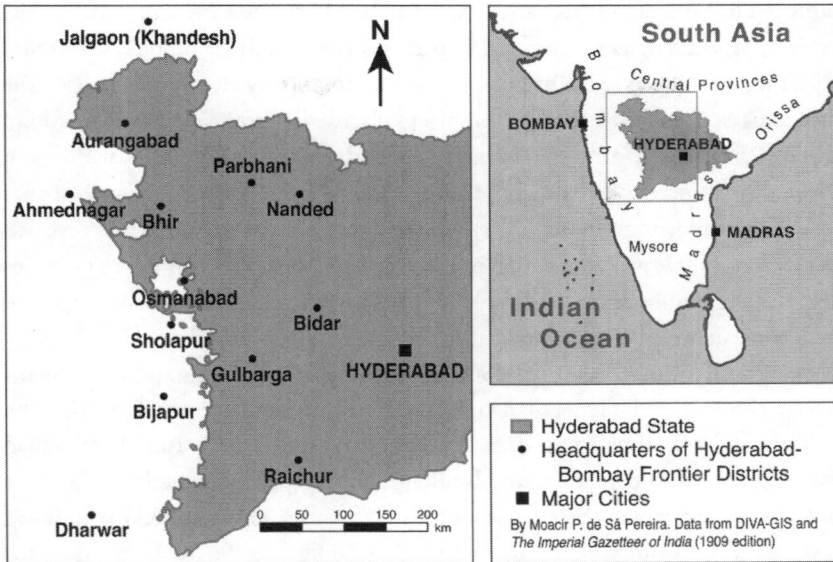

Figure 10.1 Hyderabad State–Bombay Presidency Frontier Zone, c. 1900
Source: By Moacir P. de Sá Pereira. Data from DIVA-GIS and *The Imperial Gazetteer of India* (1909 edition).

In 1887, some unnamed subjects of the Nizam were captured and tried for dacoity in Ahmednagar (Bombay).[13] However, since the crime in question was committed in Hyderabad territory, they were acquitted 'because the Court has no jurisdiction over Foreign subjects for an offense committed in Foreign territory'.[14] In another case, colonial authorities demanded the rapid extradition of 10 accused persons, witnesses and stolen property from a theft committed in the frontier district of Sholapur.[15] Hyderabad complied with the demand after great delay, ostensibly because the suspects resided within the jurisdiction of a noble's estate that was under indirect Hyderabadi administration. The Nizam's criminal jurisdiction over state subjects, and delays related to internal legal pluralism, impeded the efficient exercise of colonial justice.

Bombay authorities were generally vigilant in capturing and extraditing Hyderabadi subjects on the British side of the frontier, ranging from jail-breakers to petty thieves to dacoits.[16] Often in such instances, Hyderabad was neither grateful for assistance nor prompt in responding. In 1900, the district magistrate of Sholapur offered to extradite Bali *walad* (son of) Gangu Mahar, for a theft committed in Lohara in Hyderabad's Osmanabad District.[17] Hyderabad's Judicial Secretary, M. Aziz Mirza, requested further information, since it appeared to him 'very difficult, in the absence of fuller details, to obtain any clue in the case'.[18] The district magistrate replied the next month to clarify that 'some clothes were found which he (the accused) admitted to have obtained by theft at Lakdeshwar Borgaon [in Lohara]. These clothes, he said, belonged to a chati (cloth merchant) of that place'.[19] The following January, Mirza replied that an investigation had revealed that 'no case of theft was committed in Boregaon in Lohara'.[20] Numerous case files record similar communications from the British, with reminders to Hyderabad of extradition offers and, almost invariably, complaints regarding delays.

Tukaram Jiwaji's case of 1900 illustrates the coordination problems between colonial and Hyderabad officials. Jiwaji, a Kunbi (low-caste Maratha agriculturalist), was arrested at Khandesh (Bombay) for cattle theft in Aurangabad (Hyderabad).[21] Two complainants, Budhan and Gaupat, informed the Bombay police that he had stolen their cattle and fled across the border to sell them. Jiwaji was captured by Bombay officials and held pending transfer to Hyderabad for trial. During the six months before Hyderabad replied, Tukaram Jiwaji managed to escape and fled 'to his native place in His Highness' [the Nizam's] territory'.[22] There, as in other places, irrespective of actual jurisdiction, Bombay did most of the frontier policing. Despite colonial expectations of rapid extradition or prosecution of suspects, cases frequently broke down after being passed to Hyderabad. From Bombay's perspective, the Nizam's claim to legal authority over his subjects and territories was an impediment to the smooth and efficient operation of colonial justice. In Jiwaji's case, this caused a delay of several months, but in others, such as that of Bali referred to earlier, trials never occurred at all.

The proximity of multiple sovereign territories to one another, and the ease of crossing borders to flee the long arm of the law (or to bring rustled cattle to market), created leeway for subjects of either state whose livelihoods involved crime. If Tukaram Jiwaji could cross the border to delay his imprisonment, established figures in the rural scene, such as the cattle-owners Budhan and Gaupat, could direct complaints to multiple police forces and increase chances of regaining property and punishing offenders. Frontier legal pluralism provided structures that enabled some subjects to outwit the law and others to call it into play. Hyderabad–Bombay collaboration was hindered by both the flexibility of the legal situation and impediments such as Hyderabadi delays or refusals to prosecute. This institutional situation enabled a high capacity for lawlessness, which Hyderabad's staunch claims to legal sovereignty exacerbated.

INTERESTS OF JUSTICE VERSUS THE PROTECTION OF SOVEREIGNTY

In May 1869, three Banjara women, all Hyderabad subjects, were taken into custody in British Bombay on a charge of stealing cattle. They were held for eight months, and British officials neither brought them to trial nor addressed the Nizam's government, to whose jurisdiction they belonged.[23] When one woman became 'very ill and in a dying state' the others managed to get a petition to Hyderabad requesting that action be taken. The incident precipitated a lengthy correspondence between the two governments in which Hyderabad railed against lengthy imprisonment without trial of subjects 'arrested at the instances of Authorities in the British Government':[24] 'British Authorities in many instances cause the apprehensions of persons and take no notice of them afterwards for lengthened periods, and the cost of their subsistence falls upon His Highness' Government while these unfortunate wretches after suffering prolonged imprisonment, in some instances die.'[25] Hyderabad insisted that detaining prisoners on suspicion cease immediately, and that if state subjects were imprisoned, 'the requisite evidence of criminality from the British Authorities' be immediately forwarded to the Nizam's minister.[26] While they objected to state funds being spent on prisoners languishing in British Indian jails, Hyderabad officials underscored colonial mistreatment of the Nizam's subjects as a significant problem. Hyderabad's concern to protect their legal sovereignty provided the context for such exchanges and was decisive in the making of the frontier scene.

In Benton's account, extraterritoriality in Uruguay and elsewhere was seen 'as an attack on state sovereignty', and such jurisdictions were opposed. In Uruguay, 'exclusive control of the administration of justice in the country was a condition of sovereignty' (Benton 2002: 245, 251 and 240). For the Nizam the stakes were high, and he continually reasserted his legal sovereignty against colonial encroachment. Frontier problems were an empire-wide concern for the British, who dealt with intra-imperial flight from jurisdiction across the Indian Ocean region and beyond. The protection of state sovereignty was a key factor that shaped the legal landscape, and in turn the social world, on the frontier and across imperial space. The high politics of law in the late British Empire demonstrate the ongoing fragmentation of sovereignty and colonial attempts to address it.

In Benton's formulation, the end of the nineteenth century signalled the victory of state sovereignty in empires (British, French, Ottoman) and fledgling nation-states (Uruguay). The evidence from South Asia suggests, however, that colonial and formally sovereign polities possessed different degrees of influence and autonomy.[27] Subordinated states such as Hyderabad, despite British paramountcy, exercised legal authority and discretion. As one exchange over the constitution of the Thagi and Dakaiti Department (henceforth T&DD) in Hyderabad State suggested, the Nizam's jurisdiction could be overstepped in certain instances by negotiation: 'It may be assumed that the British authorities would apply for extradition [of Hyderabadi dacoits captured in British territory], and the Hyderabad Government, though undoubtedly chary of surrendering Hyderabad subjects, have agreed to surrender them if *the interests of justice* so require' (emphasis mine).[28]

Notwithstanding colonial expectations, the Nizam retained sovereignty over Hyderabadi subjects, even if colonial persuasion or coercion could occasionally wrest it away. Nonetheless, the power to mete out justice was jealously guarded and remained a primary condition of sovereignty in Hyderabad well into the twentieth century. The complex legal architecture of South Asia during the height of British colonial dominance suggests a more heterogeneous scene than Benton's picture of victorious colonial state sovereignty and legal consolidation.[29] Although imperial hierarchies sought to subjugate alternative law forums, subordinated yet sovereign states fragmented the political terrain of greater British India. Such cases were not merely exceptions but rather served to unsettle the entire imagined edifice of imperial 'law and order'. Colonial attempts to force the hand of sub-imperial states and other polities on extradition policy continued into the twentieth century, with only limited success. We cannot take the end of the nineteenth century as the moment when imperial or national entities eclipsed all other legal forms in their ascent to state sovereignty.

C. H. Alexandrowicz's depiction of an earlier period is useful for framing the multifarious character of high colonial sovereignty. In pre-1800 international law, the 'Family of Nations' was not the European and Christian configuration it was to become—Ceylon, Burma, Siam and the Marathas stood 'to a considerable extent on a footing of equality' with Portugal, the Netherlands and England (Alexandrowicz 1967: 1).[30] Alexandrowicz concluded his study of the foundations of international law with the eighteenth century, since the beginning of the nineteenth brought the contraction of the law of nations: 'European egocentricity left the Sovereigns of the East Indies, which had largely contributed to the prosperity of the European economy, outside the confines of "civilization" and international law shrank to regional dimensions though it still carried the label of universality' (Alexandrowicz 1967: 2). Had Alexandrowicz extended his time frame, he might have noted the continuing tension between recognition of formal sovereignty of non-European states and the fact of brute colonial power. This fragmentary global framework produced frontier zones that allowed people at many levels of society to wield power within, across and between, and not necessarily contained by, state sovereignties. On frontiers that were never fully consolidated, multiple legalities and temporalities jostled one another. Ensembles of overlapping institutions provided access to state power for those able to navigate complex legal terrain.

YELLAMMA'S FLIGHT: FRONTIER AS FIELD OF POSSIBILITY

If the frontier was a transitional space cross-cut by multiple jurisdictions, it was also a destination for flight from patriarchal legal and social structures in the Bombay Presidency. This is not to say that patriarchal institutions were absent in Hyderabad territory,[31] but rather that the jurisdictional externality, and physical distancing, to be achieved by border crossing opened up a field of possibility for women marginalised within the domestic world of the Bombay Deccan.

This was particularly so for women marginalised within the domestic world of the Bombay Deccan. In one 1886 case, which I will consider in detail, colonial authorities demanded the arrest and extradition of a woman accused of kidnapping a child bride in Bombay and absconding with her to Hyderabad territory. Nagapa, a resident of Sholapur, petitioned the Bombay police, demanding action to recover his wife and her possessions and punish her abductor. The district magistrate communicated the situation to the Hyderabad Resident:

> In about January last a woman named Narsa Saji, who was living near
> Nagapa's house at Sholapur, enticed away his wife by name of Yelama
> [Yellamma] about 11 years old out of the keeping of her lawful guardian
> [Nagapa] and carried her with property consisting of ornaments of the
> values of Rs 33-8-0 to a village Kongale [Kodangal] in the Gulbarga
> District in H. H. the Nizam's territory and thereby committed the
> offences of theft and kidnapping punishable under Sections 379 and
> 366 of the Indian Penal Code.

Whether her departure was voluntary or not, Yellamma figured in the case as her ornaments did: as property. The district magistrate went on to suggest that they had a sound prima facie case against Narsa Saji, a British subject, and prevailed upon the Resident to put the wheels of justice in motion in Hyderabad so that Saji might be apprehended and sent to Sholapur for trial.[32]

Throughout the nineteenth century, in colonial and metropolitan locations, the role of the law in enforcing wives' obligations to their husbands was hotly debated. This was particularly controversial in South Asia in the decades leading up to the incident in question. The 1884 Rukhmabai case in Bombay two years before, which reified the role of wives as property of their husbands, would have served as an important legal precedent here (Chandra 1998: 15–41). Yellamma's young age would have made the case also relevant to another, contemporaneous, controversy in Bombay: the region's conservative upper-caste elites staunchly opposed attempts to raise the marriage age for females in British India, culminating in widespread opposition to the 1891 Age of Consent Act (Nair 1996: 73–5; Kumar 1993: 24–7). In Yellamma's case, Bombay officials, under pressure to defend patriarchal prerogatives, acted at the behest of her husband, Nagapa, to see that she was returned and that Narsa Saji felt the full force of the law.[33] The colonial legal system was stacked against Narsa from the start, but other elements of the case made her position still more difficult.

The abstract of evidence consisted of a number of brief testimonies from various parties, some of whom had significant stakes in the case:

> Sayana wd. Sayana of Pacha peith Sholapur states: I know the complainant; his house is near mine; I know Narsa who lived in Timana's house. She was a public woman; about 3 1/2 months ago I and Chinaya saw Narsa with Yelama go out in the evening; Yelama had ornaments on her person.... Yelama had been living with her husband since her marriage up to the time she was taken away. Narsa was in the habit of frequently visiting the house of the complainant and had a great intimacy with Yelama. 2. Chinaya wd. Sayana, a neighbor of the complainant, states as above. 3. Sayana wd. Timana, also a neighbor of the complainant, states to the same effect. 4. Basaya wd. Bapaya who lives in the same peth [urban locality] in which the complainant resides, states the same as above. 5 and 6. Narsapa wd. Yelapa and Jaglapa wd. Yelapa, brothers of Yelama, of Maugalya peith, state: Narsa had been living in the house of Sayana and was a public woman. Narsa enticed away our Sister Yelama, who has been living with her husband.[34]

The testimony reveals the social and physical proximity of each of the testifying males—the first four resided in the same locality, including a father (Sayana) and his two sons (Sayana Jr. and Chinaya), and the latter two were brothers of the missing child-wife. More striking still is that all of the statements, many of which were identical, referred to Narsa as a 'public woman'. This would have been the Victorian English equivalent of 'whore' (*raṇḍī*) or 'courtesan' (*bā'ijī*, *tawā'if*) in the vernacular depositions (not preserved in the record). While the deposed did not attach a clear stigma to Narsa's profession—indeed, she resided in the house of the first four—clearly all of them thought it highly relevant. I shall consider the potential meanings of Narsa Saji's occupation later.

Raj officials sent a request for co-operation and an abstract of evidence, and six months later Hyderabad replied that arrests had been made. The Nizam's judiciary, however, released the detainees, based on 'difficulty in identifying the accused, who, it is said, seems to have no connection with the information furnished by you, and has, therefore, been released on bail'.[35] As in other cases, communication and policing across borders were hindered by delays and requests for additional information from Hyderabad. A subsequent communication by the district magistrate of Sholapur, who had sent a police constable on Narsa's trail, clarified the situation:

> Narsa Saji was arrested by the Tahsildar of Kalinjal [Kodangal, Gulbarga District, Hyderabad]; she had with her the wife of the complainant who has been kidnapped; both these persons were identified by the complainant and a Police Constable who has visited the place on purpose. Narsa Saji was then released on bail by the said Tahsildar. It will thus be seen that there is no difficulty in identifying the accused. I therefore request that you will be good enough to issue order for her surrender together with the girl kidnapped and the property stolen.[36]

Despite being identified in Hyderabad by the husband, Nagapa, and the British Indian police, Narsa Saji and her 'captive', Yellamma, remained at large in Hyderabad State, sheltered from the long arm of the Raj's law.

The women remained at large owing in part to the obstinacy of the Hyderabad police and judiciary. Evidently, the word of a Bombay constable was insufficient to convince the Nizam's officials to extradite Narsa Saji and repatriate Yellamma and her property. The case file ends with a note from colonial official M. S. Wadia consisting of a timeline of what he called 'a really bad case'. Wadia noted with clear frustration, 'More than 14 months delay has therefore taken place in the case which seems very simple and in which only one accused person is concerned.'[37] Records of the case do not reveal whether Yellamma was ever returned to her husband, or what became of the kidnapper, with whom she shared 'great intimacy'.[38]

The subjectivity of a figure such as Yellamma, whose voice is absent in these materials, is impossible to definitively reconstruct. She is mentioned only after her passage into Hyderabad occasioned official communication across borders and legal systems. The archive speaks clearly in the voice of the colonial state, certain segments of Sholapur society and more indirectly the machinery of state in Hyderabad. What this archival fragment does indicate are the alternative social worlds made possible by the proximity of the frontier, which divided the Raj's judicial regime from the externality of Hyderabad. The intervening space of the frontier zone presented a field of possibility for Narsa Saji and Yellamma, and the remainder of this section will elaborate on what this may have meant.

Sholapur Maratha and British colonial moral and legal codes defined Yellamma's liberation as state-initiated return (as property) to her socially mandated position as child bride of Nagapa. There are other discourses of liberation that Yellamma's flight, and possible initiation as sex worker under the tutelage of Narsa Saji, could be seen to enact. What it meant to be a 'public woman' in South Asia changed considerably during the colonial period. The erudite social value ascribed to the *tawa'if* (courtesan) in South Asian Islamicate culture was at loggerheads with the view implied by paradigms of regulation and prohibition of 'immoral activity'.[39] There was no evident initiative by Hyderabad officials to safeguard the livelihoods of prostitutes, but the productivity of the frontier zone provided conditions for Narsa Saji's successful 'abduction' of Yellamma. If one of Yellamma's possible social worlds was as a child bride, beholden to her husband and invested in the patriarchal social expectations that characterised much of South Asia, another would have been the life of a 'public woman'.[40]

Veena Talwar Oldenburg has argued that for many women taking up the occupation of a *tawa'if* was a path to liberation from oppressive social structures: 'It would be no exaggeration to say that their "life-style" *is resistance to rather than a perpetuation of patriarchal values*' (Oldenburg 1990: 259–87, original emphasis).[41] She further claimed that stories about women entering the profession via abduction were largely fabrications traceable to the stigmatisation of prostitution in British Indian and Urdu literature, discourse and social practice. Oldenburg contends that sex work in South Asia signified a novel form of womanhood offering liberation from the oppressions of community, gender roles and class.

Other factors suggest that the spectre of sex work in the depositions masked what may have seemed an even greater threat to Bombay Deccan patriarchal structures: Narsa Saji and Yellamma's possible status as *devadāsīs*. Referred to in colonial sources as 'dancing girls' or temple prostitutes, *devadasi*s are females dedicated to a temple and its deity, who forsake human marriage. The *devadasi* status of the characters in this case is implied by the name of the abducted child wife, since Yellamma is the name of the patron deity at whose temple *devadasi*s are dedicated and also a common name for initiates.[42]

Distinctive features of the institution made *devadasi*s a prime target of colonial and Brahminical reform movements.[43] Legislation placed increasing pressure on the institution in British India, starting with the 1860 de-recognition of *devadasi* social institutions, and continuing with the criminalisation of the community from 1880 onwards (Parker 1998: 589, 607). According to the British Indian courts' codified version of Hindu law, *devadasi*s, unlike most women in patriarchal caste Hindu society, had the right to adopt children, own property and inherit matrilineally (Jordan 2005; Nair 1994; Parker 1998).[44] The common mode of initiation—adoption of girls—provided continuity to women without female offspring, but also made *devadasi*s particularly susceptible to colonial legislation. A clause in the 1861 Indian Penal Code banning 'procurement' of minors for prostitution was frequently used to persecute *devadasi*s who adopted females (Kannabiran 1995: WS59). In applying this law, officials invoked the rhetoric of 'enticement into prostitution' to describe *devadasi* adoptions, and this appears in testimonies about Narsa Saji and Yellamma.[45] The language of the 1861 law allowed judges to apply criminal penalties in ambiguous situations, and strengthened the tools patriarchal society and the state used against *devadasi*s (Jordan 2005: 328).

The legal and social offensive in British India against *devadasi*s put women who sought to maintain control of property and adopt female heirs in a difficult situation. To carry out adoptions, they often crossed borders beyond Raj jurisdiction into sub-imperial states and other non-British territories such as French Pondicherry.[46] This, along with the fact that the anti-*devadasi* movement in Hyderabad remained relatively weak into the twentieth century, suggests that flight to the Nizam's territory would have provided refuge to Narsa Saji and her young protégée if they chose to live as *devadasi*s.[47]

As scholars of colonialism and nationalism have pointed out, South Asian women tended to be cast as instrumental objects rather than active subjects of liberation and improvement (Mani 1989: 88–126). The history of *devadasi* legislation proves no exception: a confluence of interests between colonial officials and upper-caste patriarchies, and a tendency to value textual precept over practice, helped normalise regimes of sexuality and marriage, patrilineal inheritance and male property ownership (Kannabiran 1995; Nair 1996; Parker 1998).[48] In the process, *devadasi*s were stripped of property rights and 'reduced to the status of proletarianised sex workers' (Nair 1994: 3165). In a process spanning much of the nineteenth century, *devadasi*s were disempowered and pushed to the margins of British Indian society, the latter quite literally since they fled to frontier zones and utilised them as resources to continue their livelihoods. Available sources provide little sense of the perspectives of either long-time *devadasi*s or recent inductees.

In British India, 'there was no instance of a court examining whether a minor had acted as a "free agent" in consenting to dedication as a temple dancing girl' (Parker 1998: 625). The case at hand bears out this point; both the depositions and the initial case description by the district magistrate, quoted above, describe Narsa's 'enticement' of her intimate friend Yellamma rather than specifying coercion. The word choice would have been deliberate, and the depositions were probably pruned in the process of translation and compilation to assure an effective prosecution.

While scholarship on *devadasi*s and courtesans suggests that these practices could provide women relief from patriarchal structures in British India, I do not mean to imply that Yellamma's departure to Gulbarga with Narsa necessarily represented freedom from the bondage of domesticity. We have no clear evidence detailing their experiences after crossing the frontier. Patriarchal colonial and upper-caste Hindu discourses constructed Yellamma's necessary return to her husband as liberation. Her potential participation in sex work or *devadasi* initiation could just as well be cast as liberation from other, perhaps more profound, forms of oppression.[49] Throughout all of this, young Yellamma—whether figured as bride (property), prostitute (criminal) or *devadasi* (victim)—is rendered instrumental by colonial officials seeking to uphold justice, her kinfolk attempting to recover her and perhaps by Narsa Saji seeking to induct her into a different livelihood.

The case does, however, bring into view the field of possibilities that the proximity of colonial and Hyderabad territory offered British subjects such as Narsa and Yellamma. The nascent state system Raj officials sought to consolidate ordered social worlds just as it produced pressures for flight and geographies of alterity. In the frontier zone, the reach and applicability of various canons of law and modes of social practice were indeterminate. This flexibility was a potential resource for those who could cross the frontier, perhaps to participate in alternative regimes of labour and sexuality.[50] If legal ambivalence allowed some, such as Yellamma and Narsa, to avoid colonial law, the proximity of jurisdictions also provided opportunities for rural people to invoke state power for their own purposes.

BEYOND STATE SOVEREIGNTY: INFORMERS AND THIEVES IN RURAL SOCIETY

The year 1888 saw a proliferation of requests for the remission of sentences from Hyderabad subjects imprisoned for dacoity in the notorious British Indian prison of Yerawada in Pune, nearly 100 miles from the Hyderabad frontier. These materials—English translations of vernacular letters addressed to Bombay

officials—reveal extensive extraterritorial T&DD activity in late nineteenth-
century Hyderabad. Colonial policing was based on a treaty that required the
Nizam to surrender suspects in 'the interests of justice'.[51] The petitions document
contestations within marginal Hyderabadi social groups and state tactics that
employed denizens of the frontier zone.

The 1887 remission request of Bhika Jamal and Sultan Dewa illuminates the
workings of the Hyderabad T&DD. The petitioners' claims can be summarised as
follows:

> The actions of the Resident were unjust. They were innocent of the
> charges. Two *gurundas* ['approvers' or informants], Rupchand and
> Balram, fabricated evidence. The gurundas were members of the
> same [Multani] caste as the petitioners, and themselves convicted of
> dacoity and sentenced to transportation for life and/or imprisonment.
> In exchange for their freedom, the gurundas turned witness for the
> T&DD, and caused the wrongful conviction of their fellow community
> members.[52]

Jamal and Dewa concluded their indictment of the corrupt system with what
was an important structural element in remission requests—appeal to superior
British justice:

> Our belief is that no oppression is exercised under British rule in
> connection with the administration of justice. We do not know,
> however, whether any special laws besides those in force in British
> India are made for the use of the Hyderabad Residency. We pray that
> your Excellency-in-Council will be pleased to call for all the papers
> in our case, to ascertain whether there was any other evidence against
> us besides the statement of the Gurundas and whether any stolen
> property was found with us, and to remit the sentence which we,
> innocent persons, have been unjustly undergoing.

These petitioners overestimated Bombay's willingness to regulate extraterritorial
Raj jurisdiction in Hyderabad, and officials declined to intervene in their case, but
the source nonetheless documents savvy frontier-dwellers navigating a plural legal
terrain.[53]

Another petition from the same era provides further detail on the social
conditions marginal people negotiated. In April 1888, three Hyderabadis in
Yerawada Central Jail (Sekh Gutki, Sekh Lal and Sekh Chand) requested the
remission of their sentences. The petitioners implied corruption on the part of
the Residency and the approvers who had offered evidence, caustically inquiring
as to whether the colonial government had ordered the Thagi Department at

Hyderabad 'to act independently of the law and purely on the statements of Gurundas irrespective of any other evidence'. They described their circumstances as follows:

> We are Multanis by caste. We used to support ourselves by traveling from place to place and dealing in wood. Rupchand and Balram [the same informants named in Jamal and Dewa's petition], two men belonging to our caste had been convicted and sentenced for some offence committed by them. To benefit themselves they accepted places of Gurundas. They falsely mention the names of poor people in connection with any dacoities that may have been committed, admitting at the same time that they were their own accomplices in those dacoities.[54]

These *gurunda*s, the same pair involved in the previous case, were apparently quite busy incriminating members of their caste. As itinerants, Multanis neatly fitted colonial sociology's profile of dacoits by dint of their mobility and lack of integration into the settled agrarian economy.[55] The machineries of colonial justice criminalised these marginal populations, and the imprisonment of members of any given community tended, through the institution of the *gurunda*, to produce cycles of incrimination.[56] The T&DD penetrated deep into Hyderabad rural society, and its victims employed a variety of tactics to gain the upper hand.[57] Another 1888 petition, from Kamiya *walad* Tuliya, says that he served the Nizam's government as a watchman, and had been convicted based on *gurunda* testimony despite the intervention of the village *kulkarnī* (rural accounting officer).[58] Even low-level state employees were not exempted from dacoity persecution. Kamiya claimed he did not know his accuser, but other dacoity cases reveal *gurunda*s taking revenge on rivals. Ravya *walad* Balya Mang claimed he was imprisoned in Nanded District with his fellow villagers Chinya, Pochu and Garibya (all Kaikadis), and subsequently,

> A quarrel took place between these persons and myself in connection with our work, and they bore a grudge against me for this. On [Pochu's] going to Hyderabad he became gurunda (approver) and at a time when there were only ten months wanting to complete the period of my sentence, he to take revenge upon me came to the jail and on the expiry of the period of my sentence arrested me and took me to Hyderabad.[59]

The position of *gurunda* was an important resource for criminalised members of frontier society. Not only could they exchange information for commutation of sentences but they could also settle grudges with fellow villagers by initiating dacoity persecutions. Ravya, a Mang, and Pochu, a Kaikadi, were members of castes on the margins of Hyderabadi rural society.[60] It was Ravya's misfortune that his offer 'to produce [criminal] evidence of my fellow villagers' came only after Pochu had fingered him as a dacoit.[61]

Like Rupchand and Balram Multani, Pochu Kaikadi was prolific in his informant work. According to another petition, Chandu *walad* Arjuna Kaikadi was arrested by Pochu, tried over the course of a year, found innocent and released. Sometime later, he was arrested again by Pochu for the same crime, found guilty after a two-year trial and sentenced to 10 years' rigorous imprisonment at Yerawada.[62] Chandu questioned the veracity of the *gurunda's* testimony and the legality of trying him on the same charge twice, since double jeopardy was illegal in British Indian law. Operating as a parallel legal order, the T&DD in Hyderabad functioned by providing institutional shelter for state illegality. This means of splintering colonial sovereignty subjected marginal frontier figures to arbitrary and corrupt colonial judicial practices. But it also allowed members of rural society, as *gurundas*, to enact the colonial state's extraterritorial sovereignty. They did so by manipulating the very instruments of governmentality that criminalised them in the first place: social identification of depressed or mobile castes and tribes.[63] However, the power that approvers possessed to carry out vendettas by informing on their enemies was not without its costs.

Frontier society in Hyderabad responded to *gurunda* activity by drawing lines between good and bad neighbours. Pilu *walad* Raghu Mahar described his case in a petition:

> The Resident at Hyderabad passed upon me a sentence of five years on a charge of robbery. I pray that the sentence may be remitted for the following reasons. I did not commit the offence with which I was charged. No stolen property etc was found in my possession. Sidu Dhangar, one of the Gurundas (approvers), has a quarrel with me under the following circumstances: The Dhangar [shepherd caste] Gurunda had once come to our village for drinking *Shindi* liquor. Knowing him to be a Gurunda, myself and some others told him not to come any more to our village. For our having said this to him, the Gurunda some days afterwards arrested and took me [to Hyderabad] and caused the sentence to be passed upon me.[64]

If turning *gurunda* allowed the accused to empower themselves using the frontier's political resources, this act came at a certain social price: as Sidu Dhangar found, his status as a colonial informer rendered him unwelcome in Hyderabadi rural society. It is unclear from the record whether his banishment from the village and access to its liquor ceased after he incriminated Pilu, but it is likely that the *gurunda* stigma remained. As the earlier examples demonstrate, *gurunda*s used their powers to imprison marginal rural people (often of their own castes), agriculturalists and even state employees.[65] Those who became representatives of extraterritorial colonial sovereignty were in response ostracised in the rural social world of Hyderabad. For all parties—from petitioners in Yerawada who cast aspersions on informers and the T&DD to *gurunda*s themselves—and for frontier society at large, the legal pluralism of the borderlands was a vital resource for negotiating the circumstances in which they found themselves.

BANDITRY, SOCIETY AND STATECRAFT

The Hyderabad–Bombay frontier's jurisdictional complexity reveals the lasting incompleteness of colonial attempts to consolidate legal sovereignty. Frontier developments elaborate the productive relationship between political authority and crime and lawlessness in modern South Asia. Following Eric Hobsbawm's work on 'social banditry', historians have attempted to understand how putative criminals fit into rural societies. Hobsbawm's argument ran as follows:

> Social bandits ... are peasant outlaws whom the lord and state regard as criminals, but who remain within peasant society, and are considered by their people as heroes, as champions, avengers, fighters for justice, perhaps even leaders of liberation, and in any case as men to be admired, helped and supported. This relation between the ordinary peasant and the rebel, outlaw and robber is what makes social banditry interesting and significant. It also distinguishes it from two other kinds of rural crime: from the activities and gangs drawn from the professional 'underworld' or from mere freebooters ('common robbers'), and from communities for whom raiding is part of the normal way of life. (Hobsbawm 1969: 13–14)

He further specified that these brigands and the visions of liberation they gave to peasants embodied the last gasp of a pre-capitalist agrarian world in which extant modes of social ordering (kinship, tribal loyalties) were rapidly disintegrating. Social bandits—or 'primitive rebels', as he called them elsewhere—belonged to the realm of the pre-political and were nostalgic figures upon whom peasants projected their political desires.[66]

    In contesting the teleological language that framed Hobsbawm's presentation, critics have questioned the liberatory implications he ascribed to social banditry. Anton Blok argued that brigandage in peasant societies advanced agendas of nobles and officials by keeping peasants docile (Blok 1972: 495–503; Hobsbawm 1972: 503–5). Assessing banditry in nineteenth-century Egypt, Nathan Brown argued, 'The *idea* of a crisis of banditry was a powerful tool, though not one that peasants could use.' Rather, 'Banditry as a national problem was invented as a political weapon by Egypt's rulers as a part of the process of creating a stronger, centralized state apparatus and as an effort to keep that apparatus out of British hands' (Brown 1990: 259–60).[67] Contrary to the Egyptian state's intentions in making banditry policing an autonomous institutional domain outside the purview of the encroaching British, the perceived epidemic of brigandage precipitated colonial conquest. For Brown, banditry in this context was not a practice supported by the rural masses, but rather part of the tripartite plague visited upon the Egyptian peasantry of 'bandits, rulers, and occupiers' (Brown 1990: 279–80).

All of these accounts share the presumption that banditry, or criminality in general, was a domain related to, but analytically distinct from, stable categories of peasantry, nobility and state. Hobsbawm, Blok and Brown strove to clarify the relationship between the idea and practice of lawlessness and other discrete domains.[68] Evidence from the Hyderabad–Bombay frontier suggests, however, that criminality—whether figured as dacoity, simple theft, kidnapping or otherwise—was deeply intertwined with frontier peasant society. Rather than categorically distinguishing bandits from peasants, evidence here suggests that lawlessness was a constituent feature of rural society. What the Raj treated as criminality was, in fact, coterminous with the everyday life and livelihoods of many marginal people in the frontier zone.

Lawlessness was not only an integral aspect of peasant society but also bore a close relationship with political sovereignty. The connection between, first, raiding, crime and what appeared as anti-state insurgency and, second, the process of state building, has been elaborated in scholarship on politics in early modern South Asia. Stewart Gordon's work on eighteenth-century Malwa argued that the raiding that later colonial commentators criminalised as 'thugee' was an effective strategy to mobilise the popular support and resources necessary to establish political authority. In his estimation, banditry and state formation occupied the same continuum (Gordon 1994: Chapter 1).

If raiding was a path to political authority in South Asia, particularly in the Deccan and central India, just before the rise of the British Raj, then an imperative of the expansive colonial state was to shut down these avenues to power. This was an essential stage in the British move to liquidate competition and seize political authority. The early stages of the T&DD campaign during the first half of the nineteenth century can be seen in this light (Singha 1993, 1998: Chapter 5). In the second half of the nineteenth century, the Raj began to represent the consolidation of its authority by framing British paramountcy within a doctrine of suzerainty, an integrative political language that carved out domains of power for sub-imperial states within a hierarchy of sovereign polities. This image both masked and fed jurisdictional tensions. Colonial state sovereignty was consistently undercut by alternative legalities of sub-imperial states such as Hyderabad, amidst territories that comprised of British India. Lauren Benton's argument suggests an untrammelled rise of unitary state sovereignty through the global consolidation of legal regimes by the end of the nineteenth century. In South Asia, however, contradictions posed by sub-imperial states and other sovereign polities, or anomalous zones, reveal a contingent trajectory in which flexible and multifarious legal arrangements were incorporated into high-colonial political geography.

FRAGMENTED SOVEREIGNTIES, UNRULY STATES

C. H. Alexandrowicz and Lauren Benton both detailed legal arrangements prior to the nineteenth century where legal authority was not yet concentrated in European hands. Benton describes the simultaneous presence of multiple legalities in any given place, before the rise of state sovereignties linked to clearly demarcated territories by 1900.[69] Alexandrowicz's complementary argument emphasises the multifarious character of political sovereignty before the nineteenth century (Alexandrowicz 1967). Both histories end with the consolidation of European colonialism and the consequent end of legal and political sovereignty for non-European states and subjects. The scenario I have described here is difficult to fit into such a teleology.

In a world of splintered and often functionally overlapping sovereignties such as that of South Asia in the colonial period (and much of the world circa 1900), the putatively early modern, global legal order, with all of the resources it offered to subjects, was never completely liquidated. Bombay territory may have been under a cohesive colonial legal regime, while the Raj penetrated Hyderabad through extraterritorial illegalities. But the frontier provided access to jurisdictional difference and spatial distance from the colonial state's disciplinary apparatuses. As Yellamma's alternative roles as child bride, sex worker or *devadasi* suggest, these political and social resources were not necessarily liberating. Nevertheless, the frontier zone was productive of possibilities, different in degree if not in kind from those available in spaces firmly within British Indian terrain.[70]

The legal environment of the Hyderabad–Bombay frontier was distinct from the early modern scenario in two decisive ways. First, early modern legal pluralism often occurred in the same places at the same time. In the modern context, multiple legal orders were in close proximity with some overlap, but jurisdictional maps theoretically corresponded to clear territorial demarcations. Second, the modern period witnessed increasingly systemic attempts by dominant states, such as the Raj, to regulate social worlds by means of disciplinary apparatuses such as policing and surveillance. This point is borne out by colonial forays into Hyderabad—a foreign territory—in the form of cross-border policing, often relying on local informers, and extraterritorial jurisdictional arrangements such as the T&DD. Even as the Raj refined its techniques for transgressing frontiers, subjects practiced creative and effective tactics to manipulate the contradictions of colonial sovereignty and stay one step ahead of the law.

***

This chapter began with the late 1880s confrontation between Daji the notorious Bhil and the Bombay frontier police official R. H. Vincent. It is to Daji that I now return by way of conclusion. In a letter of April 1887, Vincent summarised Daji's history, starting with his rise to notoriety in 1883 and continuing with his flight across the border into Bombay and his apprehension the next year by colonial police in Ahmednagar (Bombay). Daji escaped, but was caught by a joint Raj–Nizam task force in Gangapur (Aurangabad District, Hyderabad). However,

> He again escaped from custody some months afterwards and ... several [Bombay] Detectives were deputed to search for him and one of them found him, *dressed in the uniform of the Nizam's Police*, near the village of Holkar [Rahuri Taluka, Ahmednagar District, Bombay Presidency]. The detective was unarmed and Daji Bhil perceiving this agreed to quietly accompany the Police officer but suddenly drew a sword, which he had hidden behind him, rushed at the Head Constable and made good his escape.[71] (Emphasis mine)

In addition to border-hopping, then, Daji masqueraded as a member of the Nizam's police to outwit the joint task force. This tactic not only endowed him with the cloak of officialdom but also provided him a ready excuse for carrying a weapon.

After escaping, Daji went on to commit more crimes in Ahmednagar, and was once more captured by British Indian police, who intended to pass him to the Nizam's authorities for trial. While still in Vincent's custody, he agreed to give evidence on previous crimes and implied a familiarity and allegiance with a Bombay Police Patil. The promised evidence was never provided, however, since without a guarantee of pardon, Daji 'would never come to the point'. Lacking a sound case to pass over to the Hyderabad police, a regretful Vincent was compelled to set Daji free. In classic outlaw fashion, the notorious Bhil assured the police officer that he would 'soon hear from him again'.[72] Bombay returned to Daji Malhari's case in 1889, and officials criticised Hyderabad for the 'inadequacy of [his] punishment'.[73] Apparently, after all of Bombay's efforts in apprehending Daji and the many crimes he allegedly committed, the Hyderabad judiciary sentenced him to a mere three months' imprisonment.[74] According to the police docket on the matter, the only possible solution was to press Hyderabad officials to mete out stricter punishment.[75] The docket also diagnosed the root problem: 'The position is quite clear! The Bhil is in league with the officials. He gets caught when a large reward is offered and he gets off to recommence his tricks.'[76] Jurisdiction over such figures—'now on this, now on that side of the frontier'—lay with the state of which they were subjects; in Daji's case, Hyderabad.[77] And if Daji and his ilk could continue their activities and avoid significant legal consequences, this was in part a result of their ability to forge allegiances with police officials in Bombay, and no doubt some in Hyderabad. This was not a simple matter of corruption— the multiple sovereignties clustered around the frontier splintered the reach and availability of state power.

***

As I have suggested, it was the proximity of multiple legal regimes that made possible the putatively illegal livelihoods of the 'notorious Bhil' Daji Malhari, the 'public woman' and kidnapper Narsa Saji, the cattle rustler Tukaram Jiwaji, various *gurunda*s and countless others. Near the frontier, British Raj officials (Bombay, Central Provinces, T&DD), the Nizam's police and internal Hyderabadi authorities all exercised jurisdictions over different subjects in different places. Cross-border policing and judicial collaboration functioned to a degree but were severely circumscribed by logistical matters. Moreover, the Nizam's claim to sovereignty over his own subjects made collaborations uneasy. All of these factors undermined the efficiency of colonial attempts to pacify the Hyderabad border.

In varied historical settings in South Asia and elsewhere, subjects manipulated the powerfully substantiated authority of colonial courts. In colonial Sri Lanka, as John Rogers has shown, British courts never functioned according to design, and through them subjects were able to summon state power to serve their needs. Indigenous legal cultures wherein subjects made instrumental use of putatively colonial institutions underscored courts' lack of popular moral authority (Rogers 1987). On the Hyderabad–Bombay frontier, as in much of Greater British India, the instrumental use of courts was supplemented by the resource of judicial difference across space. Both provided avenues for subjects within the enormous penumbra of empire to carry out livelihoods inimical to colonial visions. Hyderabad, and state officials such as Kotwal Nawab Akbar Jang Bahadur, clearly did not condone such livelihoods. Indeed, the Nizam's statist imperatives, together with colonial expectations, impelled Hyderabad to affect the appearance of emulating the British in identifying and stamping out 'crime'. However, persistent institutional underdevelopment in the frontier zone enabled the ways of life of Daji and others. Although conditions of lawlessness and sheltering of fugitives there were not a product of state design, Hyderabad's attempts to retain judicial and police sovereignty over subjects produced friction and played a major role in maintaining the situation. It is impossible to say with certainty how Daji the notorious Bhil obtained the Nizam's police uniform he wore on the day colonial officials tried to arrest him, but it is not inappropriate that he clad himself in a symbol of Hyderabadi sovereignty.[78]

NOTES

*   This is a slightly revised version of Chapter 6 in Beverley (2015).

1.   'Ahmednagar, Daji Walad Malhari. Offer of a reward of Rs 500 for the capture of the dacoit. Recapture of—by the Ahmednagar Police'. Bombay Judicial Department, 21 March 1887. Maharashtra State Archives, Mumbai (MSA), Hyderabad, 55/924. British colonial texts used the term 'dacoit' to cast certain South Asian groups as hereditary thieves. Acute colonial concerns and policies for addressing dacoity, and related modes of criminality known as thagi, were central to the early nineteenth-century colonial project. Whether hereditary criminality was an effect of the social and economic history of colonialism or an imaginative figure of colonial discourse is a matter of continuing scholarly debate, see Beverley (2015: 162–3, n. 46). On the colonial use of monetary rewards to capture criminals, and their limited effectiveness during the early nineteenth century, see van Woerkens and Tihanyi (2002: 51–2); Lloyd (2006: 2–3); Lloyd (2008: 208). Bhils were a non-settled community, primarily of central and western South Asia, which colonial sociology regarded as dacoits.

2. By 'marginal' I refer both to the geographical location and political irregularity of the frontier zone, as a margin between two states, and the social and economic statuses of the populations considered here.

3. On the ambivalence of sovereignty in international law, see Beverley (2015: Chapter 2).

4. This departs from a view of 'frontiers as borderless lands' or 'empty' terrain. See Adelman and Aron (1999: 816) and Baud and van Schendel (1997: 213–14).

5. On the United States, see Turner (1920 [1894], 1–38); Cronon (1991); White (1991). On Asia, Perdue (2005); Tagliacozzo (2005).

6. On the borderlands concept in historical scholarship, see Adelman and Aron (1999) and Baud and van Schendel (1997). For an application of the concept to South Asian 'princely states' as 'arenas of multi-tiered negotiations among a variety of actor', see Zutshi (2010: 597).

7. 'Zomia' refers to the areas of highland Southeast Asia defined by a lack of effective integration into states. For an elaboration of the concept, see van Schendel (2002: 647–68). For a detailed argument about 'zomia' as a result of deliberate avoidance of state power, see Scott (2009). On the 'peculiar and enduring lumpiness of imperial legal space' produced by 'the layering of overlapping, semi-sovereign authorities within empires', see Benton (2010: xiii, 290).

8. Benton's study attempts to describe thoroughgoing global changes in the working of legal regimes, not merely colonial contexts.

9. On comparable developments in Southeast Asia, see Winichakul (1994).

10. 'Ek mashhūr ḍākū kī giriftār a'lā-ḥaẓrat bandigān-'ālī kā aẓhār khūshnudī' (The Capture of a Famous Dacoit and the Visible Pleasure of the Sovereign), in Khān (1907: 57–8).

11. See Beverley (2015: Chapter 5) for a view of the making of the frontier from the perspectives of the two states, and a detailed consideration of state policies on thagi, dacoity and criminal tribes.

12. Khāṅ (1907): Chapter 4 (on his trip to Arabistan to procure horses), Chapter 5 (on his role in the suppression of the 1857 uprising), Chapters 6–8 (on his Abyssinia campaign), Chapters 15, 16, 21 (on his role in pacifying urban and rural gangs and local toughs) and Chapter 22 (on organizing public meetings).

13. MSA Political Department, Hyderabad, 55/633, 1887.

14. Secretary, Government of India to Chief Secretary, Government of Bombay, 22 March 1887, MSA Political Department, Hyderabad, 55/633, 1887.

15. 'Extradition. Delay in the extradition of certain persons accused of having committed theft in Sholapur'. MSA Political Department, Hyderabad, vol. III, 59/141, 1888.

16. For the Raichur jailbreak, see Telangana/Andhra Pradesh State Archives, Hyderabad (T/APSA), 71/31/1, 1886. Citations for other cases are below.

17. 'Bali wald Gangu Mahar (Theft)', Judicial, Political, and General Secretary (M. Aziz Mirza) to Private Secretary, 17 October 1900, T/APSA 71/32/34, 1901.

18. His Highness' Minister (Private Secretary) to Mr. Jardine (Resident's Office), 18 October 1900, T/APSA 71/32/34, 1901.

19. District Magistrate, Sholapur to Assistant Resident, Secunderabad, 15 November 1900, T/APSA 71/32/34, 1901.

20. Judicial Secretary M. Aziz Mirza to the Private Secretary of the Minister, 10 January 1901, T/APSA 71/32/34, 1901.

21. 'Tukaram Jiwaji Kunbi (Theft of Bullocks)', T/APSA 71/32/36, 1901.

22. District Magistrate, Khandesh to First Assistant Resident, 24 November 1900, Resident W. Haig to Vikarul Umara Bahadur, 18 April 1901, both in T/APSA 71/32/36, 1901.

23. 'Complaint of instances having occurred in which subjects of His Highness have been arrested and have been suffered to remain for indefinite periods in prison', MSA Political Department, Hyderabad, 26/277, 1870–1. On the unnamed Banjara women, see 'Purport of Roobakaree to the Talookdar NW Division at the 14th Ramzan, 1286 H', 18 December 1869, MSA Political Department, Hyderabad, 26/277, 1870–1.

24. First Assistant Resident to Chief Secretary, Government of Bombay, 4 February 1870, MSA Political Department, Hyderabad, 26/277, 1870–1.

25. 'Purport of Roobakaree to the Talookdar NW Division at the 14th Ramzan 1286 H', 18 December 1869, MSA Political Department, Hyderabad, 26/277, 1870–1.

26. Translation of letter from His Highness the Nizam's Minister to Resident, 17 February 1870, MSA Political Department, Hyderabad, 26/277, 1870–1. The last item in this file, an internal communication between Bombay officials, suggested that the case be subjected to inquiry, but it is unclear whether this took place. Political Department to Resident, 2 March 1870, MSA Political Department, Hyderabad, 26/277, 1870–1.

27. This scenario also worked in reverse. Britain assumed territorial control in the subcontinent based on agreements with established sovereigns, such as the Mughals. Colonial military cantonments in Hyderabad and elsewhere were granted on temporary leases, and remained under non-colonial sovereignty until the end of the empire.

28. Resident Trevor Chichele-Plowden, Esq., CSI to Secretary of Government of India, Foreign Department. Hyderabad Residency, 16 November 1897, 'Working

of the Rules in the Manual of the Thagi and Dakaiti Dept and Trial of Cases Prosecuted by the Dept in Hyderabad', Letters from India 1898, 153–423, India Office Records, British Library, London (IOR) L/P&S/7/381. Debates over the application of the 1881 Fugitive Offenders Act (FOA) in Greater British India, including Hyderabad, use identical language, invoking the need to safeguard 'the interests of justice', 'Memorandum explanatory of Agendum No. 6. Extension of the provisions for the Fugitive Offenders Act, 1881, to Indian States and Administered Areas', 1923, IOR L/P&S/13/523, 1924–1937. See discussion of FOA in Beverley (2015: Chapter 5).

29. Benton accounts for 'legal anomalies' in empires as part of a colonialist geographical logic of enclaves and corridors within a larger sovereign imperial terrain. Within her framework, the likes of 'princely states' and inaccessible mountainous regions under colonial rule are analogous: Benton (2010: Chapter 5).

30. On post-colonial implications of this alternative legal history, see Alexandrowicz (1969: 465–80).

31. On the official legal recognition, and in some cases regulation and sponsorship, of some varieties of sex work in nineteenth-century Hyderabad State, see Leonard (2013: 423–48).

32. J. F. Fleet, District Magistrate to First Assistant, Resident of Hyderabad, 16 June 1886, 'Complaint by the District Magistrate of Sholapur of delay in surrendering accused persons on the part of His Highness the Nizam's Govt', MSA Political Department, Hyderabad, 55/1676, 1887.

33. On collusion between the colonial state and established patriarchies, see Chowdhry (2004: 55–84).

34. Abstract of Evidence, enclosure in Fleet to Assistant to Resident, 2 July 1886, MSA Political Department, Hyderabad, 55/1676, 1887.

35. A. H. Martindale, First Assistant Resident to DistrictMagistrate, Sholapur, 11 February 1887, MSA Political Department, Hyderabad, 55/1676, 1887.

36. Fleet to First Assistant to Resident, 28 March 1887, MSA Political Department, Hyderabad, 55/1676, 1887.

37. Fleet to First Assistant to Resident, 28 March 1887, MSA Political Department, Hyderabad, 55/1676, 1887.

38. Abstract of Evidence, enclosure in Fleet to Assistant to Resident, 2 July 1886, MSA Political Department, Hyderabad, 55/1676, 1887.

39. On the demeaning of the courtesan figure in colonial law and Urdu literary imagination, see Waheed (2014: 986–1023).

40. On gender relations in Maratha country, see O'Hanlon (2000).

41. Oldenburg's data comes primarily from fieldwork carried out in the 1970s and 1980s, but encompasses both the colonial and post-colonial periods.

42. Ashwini Tambe suggested to me that the name Yellamma would imply a connection with the devadāsī institution (2009, personal communication). For a consideration of the empowerment of women dedicated to the goddess Yellamma within an alternative sexual order, see Ramberg (2009: 501–22). Ramberg notes in particular the prominence of the institution in the present states of Karnataka, Maharashtra and Telangana. The Hyderabad state comprised of adjacent portions of each of these regions.

43. On anti-devadāsī developments, see Jordan (2005: 325–45); Kannabiran (1995: 59–69); Nair (1994: 3157–67); Nair (2008: 208–26); Parker (1998: 559–633); Srinivasan (1985: 1869–76); Raj (1993: Chapter 6) and Vijaisri (2005: 387–411).

44. Raj (1993: 117) notes that in early nineteenth-century Madras 'education of females was only known among devadasis'.

45. On post-1861 legal references to 'enticement' or 'carrying away' of girls or women into prostitution, see Tambe (2009: 28). On the language of 'seduction' in 1819 statutes, see Singha (1998: 146–7).

46. Parker (1998: 627) notes that many were accused of taking minors outside colonial territory for initiation. On flight to 'native states' and European territories from Madras Presidency, see Raj (1993: 123).

47. On the anti-devadāsī movement in Hyderabad, see Vijaisri (2005: 406–8).

48 On the colonial law's strengthening of caste Hindu property claims in early twentieth-century Bombay Presidency, see Rao (2009: Chapter 2).

49. Work on the Partition of British India has suggested that the violence and rupture created by the abduction of women has been overemphasised, and that the state's acts to 'return' women to their previous communities fortified patriarchal structures. See Butalia (1998) and Das (1996).

50. Ramberg (2009: 518) describes 'Yellamma women', or devadāsīs, as being 'implicated in a different sexual order', and Oldenburg (1990: 271) suggests that courtesans taught community members a 'new meaning of being an aurat [woman]'.

51. Hyderabad Resident Trevor Chichele-Plowden to Secretary of Government of India, Foreign Department, 16 November 1897, 'Working of the rules in the Manual of the Thagi and Dakaiti Dept and trial of cases prosecuted by the Dept in Hyderabad', Letters from India 1898, 153–423, IOR L/P&S/7/381.

52. This summary paraphrases the following documents: 'Bhika Jamal and Sultan Dewa, prisoners in the Central Jail Yerrowda, Praying for the remission of the

sentence passed upon them on a charge of dacoity', 21 April 1888, Oriental Translation Department 'translation of the vernacular petition' submitted by appellants 6 April 1888 to Governor-General of India in Council, MSA Political Department, Hyderabad, vol. I, 57/214, 1888. The term gurunda (informant or approver) is most likely a variant of the Persian term goinda or goyanda (literally, 'one who talks') commonly used in the subcontinent. On the central Indian use of goranda for goyanda, see Russell and Lal (1916: 365). The social roles of these convicts-turned-informers in Hyderabad will be considered in detail presently. On goindas in the early nineteenth century, see Lloyd (2008: 208); Singha (1993: 83–146).

53. Assistant Secretary, Government of India to Resident, Hyderabad, 14 June 1888, MSA Political Department, Hyderabad, vol. I, 57/214, 1888.

54. 'Petition to the address of the Government of India. From Sekh Gutki walad Sekh Mahabub and two other convicts in the Central Jail at Yerrowda, praying for the remission of the sentence passed upon them by the Sessions Court at—on a charge of dacoity', 7 April 1888, from Oriental Translation Department, MSA Political Department, Hyderabad, vol. I, 57/1068, 1888.

55. A roughly contemporaneous colonial text glosses Multanis as Muslim Banjaras (also known as Kanjars) as 'professional dacoits, highway robbers, and cattle-lifters, but not burglars' who ranged from Rajputana and Gujarat to the northern reaches of Hyderabad State. The text describes two distinct groups of Multanis: the just-noted itinerant criminal tribe; and a settled non-criminal group that dealt in timber and firewood. The people considered here seem to combine elements of both groups. See Gunthorpe (1882: Chapter 7).

56. On the 'approver' figure in colonial law, see Amin (1987: 166–202).

57. 'Hyderabad. Petitions from Kamia walad Tuljia, Bijou Chandy walad Arjoon Bania Batia and Bhagia walad Bapu, convicts in the Yerrowda Central Jail praying for the remission of the sentences passed on them by Criminal Courts in—on charges of dacoity', Oriental Translator's Department, 26 June 1888, MSA Political Department, Hyderabad, vol. II, 58/1494, 1888.

58. 'Translation of a petition from Kamiya valad Tuliya [of] Bandhallir, Taluka Udgir, zilla Bedar in His Highness the Nizam's territory, to His Excellency the Viceroy and Governor-General of India-in-Council', dated 30 April 1888, received for translation 19 June 1888, MSA Political Department, Hyderabad, vol. II, 58/1494, 1888.

59. 'Translation of a petition from Ravya valad Balya Mang, inhabitant of Dongargaon, Taluka Halgaon, Zilla Nanded, in His Highness the Nizam's territory, to His

Excellency the Viceroy and Governor-General of India-in-Council', dated 30 April 1888, received for translation 19 June 1888, MSA Political Department, Hyderabad, vol. II, 58/1494, 1888.

60. Mangs are described as an unclean and superstitious caste with 'a tendency towards crime'; Hassan (1920, vol. II, 462). The Kaikadis are glossed as a 'wandering tribe' of 'notorious highway robbers', in Great Britain, India Office; Hunter et al. (1908: 149).

61. 'Translation of a petition from Ravya valad Balya Mang, inhabitant of Dongargaon, Taluka Halgaon, Zilla Nanded, in His Highness the Nizam's territory, to His Excellency the Viceroy and Governor-General of India-in-Council', dated 30 April 1888, received for translation 19 June 1888, MSA Political Department, Hyderabad, vol. II, 58/1494, 1888.

62. 'Translation of a petition from Chandu valad Arjuna Kaikadi at present a convict at the Yerrowda Central Jail, to His Excellency the Viceroy and Governor-General of India-in-Council', dated 30 April 1888, received for translation 19 June 1888, MSA Political Department, Hyderabad, vol. II, 58/1494, 1888.

63. On similar trends in British India, see Amin (1987); Nigam (1990a; 1990b).

64. 'Translation of a petition from Pilu valad Raghu Mhar, inhabitant of Hunasval, Taluka Dubalgandi, zilla Hyderabad (Deccan) and at present a convict in the Central Jail at Yerrowda, to His Excellency the Viceroy and Governor-General of India-in-Council', dated 30 August 1888, Oriental Translations Department, 3 October 1888, MSA Political Department, Hyderabad, vol. II, 58/1749, 1888.

65. For petitions from Koli agriculturalists accused by the gurunda Sidu Dhangar, see 'Petitions from Mansing walad Malhari Koli and Marpali, son of Saheboo, convicts in the C. J. at Yerrowda, praying for the remission of the sentences passed upon them by the Sessions Court at Hyderabad on a charge of dacoity', MSA Political Department, Hyderabad, vol. II, 58/1559, 1888.

66. For a critique of the concept of the 'pre-political' in Hobsbawm, see Guha (1983).

67. The parallel with Hyderabad is striking, where a similar panic over dacoity authorised British cross-border policing in the sub-imperial state.

68. On social banditry in modern South Asia, see Kasturi (2002: Chapter 6); Mayaram (2003: 315–38) and Wagner (2007: 353–76).

69. 'The familiar fluidity of legal orders in the early modern world provided institutional continuity that itself gave legal politics a certain similarity across widely disparate legal systems. The territories for which this condition of jurisdictional fluidity was true are so vast and diverse that they can be described as encompassing a global legal regime'; Benton (2002: 261).

70. Benton elaborates the key role of geography in producing anomalous legal spaces within the empire. For her consideration of South Asian 'princely states' within this framework, see Benton (2010: 236–64).
71. R. H. Vincent (DSOP [District Superintendent of Police], Ahmednagar) to A. T. Crawford (Commisioner, CD, Poona), 4 April 1887, MSA Political Department, Hyderabad, 55/924.
72. Vincent to Crawford, 4 April 1887, MSA Political Department, Hyderabad, 55/924.
73. J. G. Moore, Officiating Commissioner to the Secretary of Government, Poona, 15 January 1889, 'Hyderabad. Dacoit Daji walad Malhari Bhil trial and punishment by the authorities of His Highness the Nizam's Government of', MSA Political Department, Hyderabad, vol. II, 64/541, 1889.
74. E. A. Bulkey, Acting DSOP, Ahmednagar to Waddington, 8 November 1888, MSA Political Department, Hyderabad, vol. II, 64/541, 1889.
75. Docket entry for 26 January 1889, MSA Political Department, Hyderabad, vol. II, 64/541, 1889.
76. Docket entry for 28 January 1889, MSA Political Department, Hyderabad, vol. II, 64/541, 1889. See also Vincent's gloss: 'Daji Bhil has, I know, some very good friends among the Patils and Sowkars of this District and I strongly suspect that some of my own men are not over anxious either to catch him', 28 September 1888, MSA Political Department, Hyderabad, vol. II, 64/541, 1889.
77. See Vincent's description of Daji and his gang, in DSOP, Ahmednagar to G. Waddington, District Magistrate, Ahmednagar, 28 September 1888, MSA Political Department, Hyderabad, vol. II, 64/541, 1889. Frontier as resource 217.
78. For a discussion of the enduring resonance of Hyderabadi sovereignty and parallel forms in South Asia and beyond, see the conclusion in Beverley (2015: 286–308).

REFERENCES

Adelman, Jeremy, and Stephen Aron. 1999. 'From Borderlands to Borders: Empires, Nation-States, Institutions and the Peoples in between in North American History'. *American Historical Review* 104 (3): 814–41.
Alexandrowicz, Charles Henry. 1967. *An Introduction to the History of the Law of Nations in the East Indies: (16th, 17th and 18th Centuries)*. Oxford: Clarendon.
———. 1969. 'New and Original States: The Issue of Reversion to Sovereignty'. *International Affairs* 45 (3): 465–80.

Amin, Shahid. 1987. 'Approver's Testimony, Judicial Discourse: The Case of Chauri Chaura'. In *Subaltern Studies V: Writings on South Asian History and Society*, edited by Ranajit Guha, 166–202. New Delhi: Oxford University Press.

Baud, Michel, and Willem van Schendel. 1997. 'Towards a Comparative History of Borderlands'. *Journal of World History* 8 (2): 211–42.

Benton, Lauren A. 2002. *Law and Colonial Cultures: Legal Regimes in World History, 1400–1900*. Cambridge: Cambridge University Press.

————. 2010. *A Search for Sovereignty: Law and Geography in European Empires, 1400–1900*. Cambridge: Cambridge University Press.

Beverley, Eric Lewis. 2015. *Hyderabad, British India and the World: Muslim Networks and Minor Sovereignty, c. 1850–1950*. Cambridge, UK: Cambridge University Press.

Blok, Anton. 1972. 'The Peasant and the Brigand: Social Banditry Reconsidered'. *Comparative Studies in Society and History* 14 (4): 495–503.

Brown, Nathan. 1990. 'Brigands and State Building: The Invention of Banditry in Modern Egypt'. *Comparative Studies in Society and History* 32 (2): 258–81.

Butalia, Urvashi. 1998. *The Other Side of Silence: Voices from the Partition of India*. Delhi: Penguin.

Chandra, Sudhir. 1998. *Enslaved Women: Colonialism, Law and Women's Rights*. Delhi: Oxford University Press.

Chowdhry, Prem. 2004. 'Private Lives, State Intervention: Cases of Runaway Marriage in Rural North India'. *Modern Asian Studies* 38 (1): 55–84.

Cronon, William. 1991. *Nature's Metropolis: Chicago and the Great West*. New York: Norton.

Das, Veena. 1996. *Critical Events: An Anthropological Perspective on Contemporary India*. Delhi: Oxford University Press.

Dirks, Nicholas B. 1993 (1987). *The Hollow Crown: Ethnohistory of an Indian Kingdom*, 2nd edition. Ann Arbor: University of Michigan Press.

Edney, Matthew. 1997. *Mapping an Empire: The Geographical Construction of British India, 1765–1843*. Chicago: University of Chicago Press.

Gordon, Stewart. 1994. *Marathas, Marauders, and State Formation in Eighteenth-Century India*. Delhi: Oxford University Press.

Guha, Ranajit. 1983. *Elementary Aspects of Peasant Insurgency in Colonial India*. Delhi: Oxford University Press.

Gunthorpe, E. J. 1882. *Notes on Criminal Tribes Residing in or Frequenting the Bombay Presidency, Berar and the Central Provinces*. Bombay: Times of India.

Hassan, Syed Siraj ul. 1920. *Castes and Tribes of H.EH. Nizam's Dominions.* Vol. II. Bombay: Times of India Press.

Hobsbawm, Eric J. 1969. *Bandits.* New York: Delacorte.

———. 1972. 'Social Bandits: Reply'. *Comparative Studies in Society and History* 14 (4): 503–5.

Hunter, William Wilson, James Sutherland Cotton, Richard Burn and William Meyer. 1908. *Imperial Gazetteer of India.* Vol. VII. Oxford: Clarendon Press.

Jordan, Kay. 2005. 'Devadasi Reform: Driving the Priestess of the Prostitutes out of Hindu Temples?' In *Religion and Law in Independent India,* 2nd enlarged edition, edited by R. D. Baird, 325–45. Delhi: Manohar.

Kasturi, Malavika. 2002. *Embattled Identities: Rajput Lineages and the Colonial State in Nineteenth-Century North India.* New Delhi: Oxford University Press.

Kannabiran, Kalpana. 1995. 'Judiciary, Social Reform and Debate on "Religious Prostitution" in Colonial India'. *Economic and Political Weekly* 30 (43): WS59–69.

Khān, Muḥammad Aḥmadullāh. 1907. *Savāniḥ-yi 'umrī: Navvāb Akbar Jang Akbaruddaullah Akbarulmulk bahādur marḥūm Sī. Es. Ī. Sābiq kotvāl-i Ḥaidarābād Dakan, jismeṅ kotvāl sāḥib marḥūm ke ḥālāt-i zindagī ibtidā se intihā tak daraj ki'e gā'e haiṅ.* Agra: Maṭba'-yi Shamsī.

Kumar, Radha. 1993. *The History of Doing: An Illustrated Account of Movements for Women's Rights and Feminism in India, 1800–1990.* New Delhi: Zubaan.

Leonard, Karen. 2013. 'Political Players: Courtesans of Hyderabad'. *The Indian Economic & Social History Review* 50 (4): 423–48.

Lloyd, Tom. 2006. 'Acting in the "Theatre of Anarchy": The Anti-Thug Campaign and Elaborations of Colonial Rule in Early Nineteenth-Century India'. *Edinburgh Papers in South Asian Studies* 19: 1–50.

———. 2008. 'Thuggee, Marginality and the State Effect in Colonial India, circa 1770–1840'. *The Indian Economic & Social History Review* 45 (2): 201–37.

Mani, Lata. 1989. 'Contentious Traditions: The Debate on Sati in Colonial India'. In *Recasting Women: Chapters in Colonial History,* edited by K. Sangari and S. Vaid, 88–126. New Delhi: Kali for Women.

Mayaram, Shail. 2003. 'Kings versus Bandits: Anti-Colonialism in a Bandit Narrative'. *Journal of the Royal Asiatic Society of Great Britain and Ireland* 13 (3): 315–38.

Nair, Janaki. 1994. 'The Devadasi, Dharma and the State'. *Economic and Political Weekly* 29 (50): 3157–67.

———. 1996. *Women and Law in Colonial India: A Social History.* New Delhi: Kali for Women.

————. 2008. '"Imperial Reason," National Honour and New Patriarchal Compacts in Early Twentieth-Century India'. *History Workshop Journal* 66 (1): 208–26.

Nigam, Sanjay. 1990a. 'Disciplining and Policing the "Criminals by Birth", Part 1: The Making of a Colonial Stereotype—The Criminal Tribes and Castes of North India'. *The Indian Economic & Social History Review* 27 (2): 131–164.

————. 1990b. 'Disciplining and Policing the "Criminals by Birth", Part 2: The Development of a Disciplinary System, 1871–1900'. *The Indian Economic & Social History Review* 27 (3): 257–287.

O'Hanlon, Rosalind. 2000. *A Comparison between Women and Men: Tarabai Shinde and the Critique of Gender Relations in Colonial India*. Delhi: Oxford University Press.

Oldenburg, Veena Talwar. 1990. 'Lifestyle as Resistance: The Case of the Courtesans of Lucknow, India'. *Feminist Studies* 16 (2): 259–87.

Parker, Kunal M. 1998. '"A Corporation of Superior Prostitutes": Anglo-Indian Legal Conceptions of Temple Dancing Girls, 1800–1914'. *Modern Asian Studies* 32 (3): 559–633.

Peabody, Norbert. 2003. *Hindu Kingship and Polity in Precolonial India*. Cambridge: Cambridge University Press.

Perdue, Peter. 2005. *China Marches West: The Qing Conquest of Central Eurasia*. Cambridge, MA: Harvard University Press.

Raj, M. Sundara. 1993. *Prostitution in Madras: A Historical Perspective*. Delhi: Konark.

Ramberg, Lucinda. 2009. 'Magical Hair as Dirt: Ecstatic Bodies and Postcolonial Reform in South India'. *Culture, Medicine and Psychiatry* 33 (4): 501–22.

Rao, Anupama. 2009. *The Caste Question: Dalits and the Politics of Modern India*. Berkeley: University of California Press.

Rogers, John D. 1987. *Crime, Justice and Society in Colonial Sri Lanka*. London: Curzon.

Russell, Robert V., and Rai Bahadur Hira Lal. 1916. *The Tribes and Castes of the Central Provinces of India*. Vol. I. London: Macmillan.

Scott, James C. 2009. *The Art of Not Being Governed: An Anarchist History of Upland Southeast Asia*. New Haven: Yale University Press.

Singha, Radhika. 1993. 'Providential Circumstances: The Thuggee Campaign of the 1830s and Legal Innovation'. *Modern Asian Studies* 27 (1): 83–146.

————. 1998. *A Despotism of Law: Crime and Justice in Early Colonial India*. Delhi: Oxford University Press.

Sivaramakrashnan, K. 1999. *Modern Forests: Statemaking and Environmental Change in Colonial Eastern India*. Stanford: Stanford University Press.

Srinivasan, Amrit. 1985. 'Reform and Revival: The Devadasi and her Dance'. *Economic and Political Weekly* 20 (44): 1869–76.

Tagliacozzo, Eric. 2005. *Secret Trades, Porous Borders: Smuggling and States along a Southeast Asian Frontier, 1865–1915*. New Haven: Yale University Press.

Tambe, Ashwini. 2009. *Codes of Misconduct: Regulating Prostitution in Late Colonial Bombay*. Minneapolis: University of Minnesota Press.

Turner, Frederick Jackson. 1920 (1894). 'The Significance of the Frontier in American History'. In *The Frontier in American* History, 1–38. New York: Holt.

van Schendel, Willem. 2002. 'Geographies of Knowing, Geographies of Ignorance: Jumping Scale in Southeast Asia'. *Environment and Planning D: Society and Space* 20 (6): 647–68.

Vijaisri, Priyadarshini. 2005. 'Sacred Prostitution and Reform in Colonial South India'. *South Asia: Journal of South Asian Studies* 28 (3): 387–411.

Wagner, Kim A. 2007. 'Thuggee and Social Banditry Reconsidered'. *Historical Journal* 50 (2): 353–76.

Waheed, Sarah. 2014. 'Women of "Ill Repute": Ethics and Urdu Literature in Colonial India'. *Modern Asian Studies* 48 (4): 986–1023.

van Woerkens, Martine, and Catherine Tihanyi. 2002. *The Strangled Traveler: Colonial Imaginings and the Thugs of India*. Chicago: University of Chicago Press.

White, Richard. 1991. *The Middle Ground: Indians, Empires, and Republics in the Great Lakes Region, 1650–1815*. Cambridge, UK: Cambridge University Press.

Winichakul, Thongchai. 1994. *Siam Mapped: A History of the Geo-Body of a Nation*. Honolulu: University of Hawaii Press.

Zutshi, Chitralekha. 2010. 'Rethinking Kashmir's History from a Borderlands Perspective'. *History Compass* 8 (7): 594–608.

About the Contributors

Aniket Alam teaches history and digital humanities at the International Institute for Information Technology, Hyderabad. His book, *Becoming India: Western Himalayas under British Rule* (2008), explored the contours of colonialism in the western Himalayas. He was a journalist (*The Hindu*, 2001–5) and was executive editor of the *Economic and Political Weekly* until July 2016. He has also worked with international donor agencies and NGOs. At present, he is exploring ways in which computational tools like GIS, NLP and data analysis can help create and identify new archives, broaden understandings of our past and change historical methods. His areas of academic interest relate to histories of mountain societies, family history, emergence of the modern nation-state and evolving historical methods in the digital age. He is working on two books: one is an attempt to understand black money and corruption in India by historicising its structure, and the other is a reassessment of mountain histories in the Himalayas outside the narratives of nation-making in the twentieth century. He is also lead investigator for an ICSSR project on the social history of religion in the Spiti Valley.

Eric Lewis Beverley is associate professor of history at State University of New York, Stony Brook, USA. His research on modern and early modern South Asia and the Indian Ocean world examines topics ranging from sovereignty and the making of the global state system to law, crime and borderlands to transnational connections and urban change. His book, *Hyderabad, British India, and the World: Muslim Networks and Minor Sovereignty, c. 1850–1950*, published by Cambridge University Press (UK 2015; India 2016), sketches eclectic global intellectual circuits that informed political experimentation in areas of state ideology and diplomacy, frontier legal administration and urban development. The book redefines the nature of state sovereignty in the era of colonialism, and identifies the close relationship between Muslim rule and political modernity. His research examines borderlands in modern South Asia, cultural difference in early modern Indian Ocean cities, colonial era forms of sovereignty and their legacies, and the history of South Asian cities in the modern and contemporary periods. His current book project is a study of the urban history of twentieth-century Hyderabad City that views urban expansion and connections through the lens of urban property.

Sahana Ghosh is a postdoctoral fellow at the Harvard Academy for International and Area Studies, Harvard University. Her research focuses on borders, the mobility of people and goods, trans/national security assemblages, agrarian borderland economies, and gender and geo/politics in contemporary South Asia. She has written academic and other essays on these topics and is writing her first book on the devaluations wrought by the militarisation of the 'friendly' border between India and Bangladesh.

Swargajyoti Gohain is assistant professor of sociology and anthropology at Ashoka University, Haryana. She has a PhD in anthropology from Emory University, USA, and has held postdoctoral positions in the International Institute for Asian Studies, Leiden, Netherlands, and the Institute of Economic Growth, Delhi. Before joining Ashoka University, she was an assistant professor in the Department of Humanities and Social Sciences, IIT Kanpur. Swargajyoti Gohain has published several articles on the politics of language, development, state formation and identity politics among Tibetan Buddhist communities in Arunachal Pradesh, India. Her first book, *Imagined Geographies in the Indo-Tibetan Borderlands* (2020), is an ethnography of cultural politics in Monyul, a Tibetan Buddhist region in Arunachal Pradesh. She has been the recipient of Wenner-Gren Dissertation Fieldwork Grant, German Academic Exchange Service (DAAD), Charles Wallace India Trust award and others. Her research interests include borders and state, culture and politics, migration and diaspora, indigenous identities, development, infrastructure, education and Tibetan Buddhist communities, and she has fieldwork experience in Northeast India and the Himalayan region.

Farhana Ibrahim is professor in the Department of Humanities and Social Sciences at the Indian Institute of Technology, Delhi. Her research interests include the study of borders, policing, migration and ethnographic perspectives on the state. Her first book, *Settlers, Saints, and Sovereigns: An Ethnography of State Formation in Western India* (2009), was based on ethnographic research among Muslim pastoral communities in Gujarat along the Kutch–Sindh border. Her second book, *From Family to Police Force: Security and Belonging on a*

South Asian Border (2021) is an ethnography of policing, civil–military relations, kinship and surveillance on a South Asian borderland.

Tanuja Kothiyal is professor of history in the School of Liberal Studies at Ambedkar University, Delhi. She has been studying shifts in regional formations and questions of authority and sovereignty in the borderlands. Her monograph *Nomadic Narratives: A History of Mobility and Identity in the Great Indian Desert* (Cambridge University Press 2016) explored identity formation in relation to circulation of people, cattle, commodities, ideas and traditions in the Thar Desert between the sixteenth and the nineteenth centuries. As part of her research, Tanuja Kothiyal has been engaging with the oral archive in the form of oral narrative traditions in the Thar Desert. Through this engagement, she has been trying to map region formations along with the circulation of narratives and their performative structures. She is currently working on her second book, which engages with contours of history writing in late nineteenth and early twentieth century Rajputana, addressing questions of the constructions of historical consciousness and archives.

Anubhuti Maurya teaches history at the Shiv Nadar University, Dadri, Uttar Pradesh. She has taught in Bharati College, Delhi University, and has been visiting faculty at the Department of History, Columbia University, New York. Her areas of research are Kashmir in the sixteenth and seventeenth centuries, the Mughal Empire and early modern South Asia.

Townsend Middleton is associate professor of anthropology at the University of North Carolina at Chapel Hill. He is the author of the book *The Demands of Recognition: State Anthropology and Ethnopolitics in Darjeeling* (2015) and numerous essays on Indian political culture. He is also co-editor of *Darjeeling Reconsidered: History, Politics, Environments* (2018) and *Limn Ten: Chokepoints* (2018). His current research examines the history and afterlives of quinine in India.

Vasudha Pande taught history at Lady Shri Ram College, University of Delhi until her retirement in 2020. Her research focuses on the history of modern Kumaun and Far Western Nepal in the Central Himalayas, with special reference to Gorkha and British rule in the highlands. She also studies Pahari culture and folk traditions. She held the SEPHIS Fellowship from Rotterdam University and a Fellowship at the Nehru Memorial Museum and Library (NMML). She teaches environmental history and her current project is on writing an environmental history of the Central Himalayan region. She has recently published *Anthropogenic Landscapes of the Central Himalayas* (2018).

Mallika Shakya is a senior assistant professor in the Department of Sociology at South Asian University and served as the acting head of the department until recently. She works on two distinct themes: social embedding of industrialisation and poetics of nationalism (and pan-nationalism). Her book *Death of an Industry: The Cultural Politics of Garment Manufacturing during the Maoist Revolution in Nepal* was published by Cambridge University Press in 2018. She has translated *Twenty Love Songs and a Song of Despair* by Pablo Neruda into Nepali. Her writings have been published in the *Journal of Royal Anthropological Institute*, *Dialectical Anthropology*, *Journal of Modern Craft*, *Contributions to Indian Sociology*, *Economic and Political Weekly*, and so on. She periodically appears in mainstream visual and print media in Nepal and India.

In addition to her academic duties, she served as the Girls Hostel Warden at her university from 2016 to 2020 including during the Covid19 lockdown. Prior to joining academia, she worked for the World Bank and UNICEF for 14 years where she advised governments in Asia, Africa and Eastern Europe on their economic and social policies and programmes. She is interested in labour issues, nation and borders, and poetics of public narratives.

Index